Early Childhood Practicum Guide

Early Childhood Practicum Guide

A Sourcebook for Beginning Teachers of Young Children

Jeanne M. Machado
SAN JOSE CITY COLLEGE

Helen C. Meyer
CALIFORNIA STATE UNIVERSITY—HAYWARD

Contributor: Irene Sterling
Infant Center Site Director
Young Families Program
San Jose, California

Delmar Publishers Inc.

This book is dedicated to student teachers who have taught us, trusted us, and become a memorable part of our lives, and to our children, Cynthia, Karl, Richard, Thomas, Mary Katharine, Danielle, Katrina, Claire, and Hale, from whom we have learned so much as their mothers and practice teachers.

For information, address Delmar Publishers Inc.
2 Computer Drive West, Box 15-015
Albany, NY 12212

Printed in the United States of America
Published simultaneously in Canada
by Nelson Canada,
A Division of International Thomson Limited

10 9 8 7 6 5 4 3

Library of Congress Cataloging in Publication Data

Machado, Jeanne M.
  Early childhood practicum guide.

  Includes bibliographical references.
  1. Student teaching—Handbooks, manuals, etc. 2. Education, Pre-
school—Curricula. 3. Nursery schools. 4. Lesson planning. I. Meyer,
Helen C. II. Sterling, Irene. III. Title.
LB2157.A3M28   1984   370'.7'33   83-71047
  ISBN 0-8273-2080-9

Contents

SECTION 6 PARENTS

SECTION 7 KNOWING YOURSELF AND YOUR COMPETENCIES

SECTION 8 PROFESSIONAL CONCERNS

SECTION 9 INFANT/TODDLER PLACEMENTS

SECTION 10 EMPLOYMENT

Preface

Early Childhood Practicum Guide is designed for students who are assuming teacher responsibilities under guided supervision. Student teaching is a memorable, individual struggle to put theory into practice. It is a synthesizing experience from which each student emerges with a unique professional style. This text attempts to help each student reach that goal.

Early Childhood Practicum Guide covers every aspect of teaching that affects the student teacher, both now as a student and later as a professional. The topics are diverse, including, among others, teaching the "special" child, dealing with parents, principles of classroom management, interpersonal communication skills, observation and assessment (of both children and student teachers), values clarification, teacher advocacy, legal ramifications of teaching, and job-seeking skills. Each topic is discussed in detail, using case studies and applying theories.

All of the units offer learning objectives, unit-end summaries, suggested activities, review questions, and a list of resources. Numerous tables, charts, and illustrations reinforce the textual material. An Instructor's Guide includes answers to the review questions, additional student activities, a comprehensive evaluation which assesses the student teacher's growth in technique and knowledge at the end of the program, topics for discussion, and teaching aids that encourage class participation.

It is the authors' wish that this text guide student teachers in their studies and in the practical application of the knowledge acquired. *Early Childhood Practicum Guide* will serve as a useful reference tool for teaching tips and problem-solving techniques as the student enters the professional world.

Acknowledgments

The authors wish to express their appreciation to the following individuals and institutions for their contributions to this text.

Reviewers

Margaret Budz, Department Head, Early Childhood Education, Triton College, River Grove, Illinois

Linda Carson, Department Head, Child Development, Des Moines Area Community College, Ankeny, Iowa

Margot Kaplan-Sanoff, Assistant Professor, Wheelock College, Boston, Massachusetts

Illustrations and Photos

Nancy Martin

Jody Boyd

The parents of photographed children

Individual Assistance

Cia McClung, Roberta Immordino, Mary Sweeney, Sharon Antonelli, colleagues, and fellow instructors.

Achsah Davy, Cherie Van der Molen, Lu Kurani, Doris Fukumoto, Barbara Solorozano, and Kathy Blanton for their assistance with photographs.

Harriet Althouse and Susan Brackenbury for student-authored unit examples.

Lynn Grincewich, Ann Cambra, Katrina Elena Machado, and Mary Katharine Meyer who typed the manuscript. Katrina Elena Machado for her proofreading and text assistance.

Preschools and Centers

San Jose City College Child Development Center

Evergreen Valley College Child Development Center

Young Families Program, San Jose, CA

California State University Associated Students' Child Care Center

Pexioto Children's Center, Hayward, CA

Parent-Child Education Center, Hayward, CA

Festival Children's Center, Hayward, CA

We also wish to express our appreciation to We Care Day Treatment Center, Concord, CA, for permission to photograph their children for inclusion in Unit 14.

About the Authors

The authors of this text, Jeanne M. Machado and Helen C. Meyer, are actively involved in child care and teacher training programs. Jeanne received her M.A. degree from San Jose State University and a Vocational Life Credential from University of California, Berkeley. She is an early childhood education instructor and department chairperson at San Jose City College. In addition, Jeanne is the liaison for San Jose City College Child Development Center and Evergreen Valley College Child Development Center. As a past president of two professional associations — Northern California Association for the Education of Young Children (Peninsula Chapter) and California Community College Early Childhood Educators, Jeanne is deeply involved in early childhood teaching issues. Her text *Early Childhood Experiences in the Language Arts* is currently in its second edition.

Helen C. Meyer received her Ph.D. from the University of Alabama. She also received a Life Credential in Psychology. Currently, Helen is a professor of education in the Department of Teacher Education at California State University, Hayward. In addition, she serves as coordinator of the Early Childhood Education master's program. She is advisor to the campus Early Childhood Education Center and the Parent-Child Education Center of the Emergency Shelter Program of Southern Alameda County. Helen is an active member of two professional organizations: California Professors of Early Childhood Education and the California Association for the Education of Young Children.

Irene Sterling, guest author of Unit 27 (Student Teaching in an Infant/Toddler Center), currently instructs at the Young Families Program in the San Jose Unified School District. Her experience includes supervising cooperating teachers at Evergreen Valley College Infant-Toddler Program.

Section 1 Orientation to Student Teaching

Unit 1
Introduction to Student Teaching Practicum

OBJECTIVES

After studying this unit, the student will be able to:

- Identify some important goals of a student teaching experience.
- Describe the relationships and responsibilities of student teachers, cooperating teachers, and supervisors.
- List three professional conduct considerations for student teachers.

Student teaching is both a beginning and an end. It begins a training experience which offers the student a supervised laboratory in which to learn. New skills will develop, and the student will polish vocational skills already acquired. The student teachers' vocational "know-how," feelings, motivations, values and attitudes, uniqueness, abilities, talents, and possible limitations are examined through self-analysis, observation, and consultation with others. As the final step in a formal training program offering a certificate or degree, student teaching completes a period during which exposure to theory and practical application have occurred. It requires the synthesizing of all previous training, workshops, and background experience.

Congratulations! You have satisfied all the prerequisites for student teaching. Now you will assume teacher responsibilities and duties with young children, becoming a member of a professional teaching team.

INITIAL FEELINGS

Many students approach student teaching with mixed feelings of trepidation and exhilaration. The challenge presents risks and unknowns, as well as opportunities for growth, insights, and increased self-awareness. Starting a diary is a good idea. Record your initial feelings toward the student teaching experience. It will be memorable; one you will cherish and share with others as a "growing stage" of your development as a person and teacher. A diary can also be used as a communication device and shared with the person who is watching your progress. In addition, a datebook or daily appointment calendar is recommended since many important meetings, appointments, and deadlines will occur.

THE MECHANICS OF STUDENT TEACHING

Student teaching (sometimes called practicum or field experience) in an early childhood program involves three key people — the student teacher, the cooperating teacher who is responsible for a group of young children, and a supervisor who is a college instructor or teacher trainer. The cooperating teacher models preschool teaching techniques and practices, and the supervisor observes and analyzes the development of the student teacher's skills. Alex Perrodin defines the roles of the three key people as follows:

Student
  Teaching —   The period of guided teaching during which the student takes increasing responsibility for the work with a given group of learners over a period of consecutive weeks. (Other terms used: practice teaching, apprentice teaching, internship.)

Supervising
  Teacher —   One who teaches children or youth and who also supervises student teaching and/or other professional laboratory experiences. (Other terms used: cooperating teacher, laboratory school teacher, critic teacher, master teacher, directing teacher, resident teacher.)

College
  Supervisor —   The college representative who is responsible for supervising a student teacher or a group of student teachers. (Other terms used: off-campus supervisor, resident supervisor, clinical teacher.) (1966)

Some student teachers who are unable to leave employment are put in the awkward position of being both student teacher and cooperating teacher. Other arrangements for employed students can involve the use of other team teachers or directors employed at the same school. The consequences of this type of student teacher placement are as follows:

- The student teacher may not have the benefit of a growth-producing training model.
- Observation and feedback may be linked to job security, and become part of the school's employment performance records.

- Time spent in discussions may be minimal.
- It is difficult to learn from one's own past performance.

STUDENT TEACHER'S PROGRESS If the student completes student teaching duties and responsibilities successfully, the student receives recognition of teaching competency. Observation and analysis of the student's performance, followed by consultation with the teaching team, is an integral part of student teaching. There is a wide variety of methods of observation and analysis. Written observations, narratives, checklists, rating scales, and video tapes are common. Many supervisors focus upon child, group, and adult reaction to student teacher/child and student teacher/adult interactions.

A child care center is seen as a growing place for everyone, not only for the student teacher. Every human who enters the class can grow from each experience. It is presumed that all adults — even the cooperating teacher and supervisor — are unfinished products. Each participant is viewed as a combination of strengths and talents, with the possibility of expanding. A caring and supportive relationship between the student teacher, the cooperating teacher, and the supervisor is crucial to this growth process. Most supervisors and cooperating teachers respect the differences in the talents and backgrounds of student teachers. Although the training sessions and classes are the same, there are dissimilar, as well as similar, values, attitudes, and past experiences. Cooperating teachers are uniquely individual; the differences in their personalities and teaching techniques are readily apparent. Diversity is the one similarity to be expected among cooperating teachers.

Supervisors often assign student teachers to cooperating teachers' classrooms after orientation sessions. In some cases, it is necessary to assign the student teachers immediately, with little opportunity to match them with cooperating teachers. Since student teaching can take place both in a child facility or laboratory and in community programs, the first criterion to be considered may be the availability of transportation.

Ideally, students should analyze the type of program to which they prefer to be assigned if the supervisor requests it. Many situations do not permit the luxury of fulfilling the students' placement preferences for a number of reasons. All initial contacting of community programs is done by the supervisor whose responsibilities include finding appropriate training sites and cooperating teachers who are willing to accommodate the student teacher training requirements. Many students are eventually hired by training sites if they have demonstrated competent teaching methods.

ORIENTATION

Introductions, tours, oral and written guidelines, instructions and informational data, and completing forms are all part of student teaching orientation meetings. Remembering names and taking notes is advisable. First impressions are important, and "body language" will send many messages to others.

Introductions and tours enable the student teacher to become familiar with people and settings, and help reduce anxieties. Anxieties may increase when responsibilities and requirements are described. Supervisors and cooperating teachers may require the completion of various assignments. Keeping each in order may mean coding or keeping different folders or binders. As always, the newness, attention to details, and the amount of information to remember and read may produce stress temporarily. Creating a buddy system with other student teachers can be helpful, and every effort from the start will promote supportive understanding and a caring atmosphere for student teachers.

Various informational written materials provide helpful guidelines for orientations. They are categorized as follows:

Supervisor

- Supervisor's Course Guide Sheet
- Supervisor's student teacher placement responsibilities, figure 1-1
- Supervisor's tips, aids, figure 1-2
- Supervisor's assessment forms
- Supervisor's forms for cooperating teachers, figure 1-3

Education Center

- Parents' guide and policy statement
- Center guides for student teachers, volunteers, and adults, figure 1-4
- Center newsletter
- Policy for visitors and observers
- Children's records

Cooperating Teacher

- Student teacher assignments, responsibilities rating sheet, figure 1-5
- Children's daily schedule, figure 1-6
- Children's names (with pronunciation guides if necessary)
- Student teacher rating sheets
- Staff meeting dates and times (optional)
- Guidelines, figure 1-7

1. Be prompt and prepared.
2. If you are ill on your assigned days, call your supervisor and cooperating teacher as close to 8 a.m. as possible.
3. Remember, the cooperating teacher depends on your services as a fellow teacher.
4. Sign in and out if required.
5. Consult with your supervisor on lesson planning when help is needed.
6. Make an appointment with your supervisor to discuss class-related questions or problems.
7. Remember to avoid conversations which label children or deal with confidential information.
8. It is your responsibility to sign in the lesson plan book at least one week in advance if your cooperating teacher or supervisor requests it.
9. Complete assignments.
10. Complete your student teacher file, and take it to the director's office as soon as possible. (Included in this file are TB clearance, personal data sheet, rating sheets, mail back envelope.)
11. Please see and do what needs to be done without direction. Ask questions. Stretch yourself; assume as much teaching responsibility as you can handle.

Fig. 1-1 Sample of student teacher responsibilities

1. Get your TB clearance to your center's director as soon as possible.
2. Leave your belongings in place provided.
3. Sign in.
4. Enter children's room quietly, wearing your nametag.
5. Look for emergency room evacuation plans (posted on wall).
6. Consider child safety. Watch and listen for rules and expectations.
7. Actively involve yourself helping staff and children. See what needs to be done. Ask only what is necessary of staff after saying hello or introducing yourself. (Do not interrupt activity. Wait until cooperating teacher is free.)
8. Let staff handle child behaviors which are puzzling on first days.
9. Write down any questions concerning children, programs, and routines that baffle you, and discuss them with your supervisor.
10. If you are sick on your scheduled day, call both your supervisor and cooperating teacher.
11. Keep a brief diary of your activities, feelings, perceptions, etc. You may want to buy a small pocket-sized notebook.

Fig. 1-2 Sample of trainer's tips for student teachers' first days

1. Let your student take as much responsibility as possible.
2. Give feedback on progress if possible.
3. Written tips, hints, and suggestions on lesson plans are helpful.
4. Let your student teacher work out the "tight" spots when possible. You may want to set up a signal which indicates the student wishes you to step in and remedy the situation.
5. Gauge your student's ability. (Some student teachers may be able to handle a full morning's program from the beginning.) Each student needs the experience of handling the group.
6. Discuss and correct the student teacher's performance in confidence after the activity. Some suggestions while an activity is occurring may be necessary for child or equipment safety.
7. Your rating will not be shown to your student teacher by the supervisor. If you wish to discuss it with the student teacher before mailing, this can be beneficial.
8. Your student teacher may ask you for a letter of reference.
9. Peer evaluations have been assigned. This means perhaps another student teacher may observe and rate the student assigned to you. This may happen twice during the semester.
10. Please call the student's supervisor if a difficulty or question arises.
11. The student should be rated on the last week of participation. A rating sheet is part of your student teacher's folder. The student will remind you a week in advance to rate and mail the form.
12. The student teacher has been instructed to consult with you on lesson plan activities. If you want the activities to deal with particular curriculum areas or themes, this is your choice. The student has been told to abide by your wishes.
13. Your student's Personal Data Sheet has information concerning special interests and background, etc.
14. The student's supervisor will visit periodically to give the student feedback on competencies and possible growth areas.
15. Frequent conferences help the student obtain a clear picture of skill progress.

Thank you for taking on the extra work involved in having a student in your classroom.

Fig. 1-3 Sample of supervisor's tips to cooperating teachers

To Participating Student Teachers:

We at the Community Nursery School feel it is a privilege to have you in our school, and we hope that, in turn, you will feel privileged to be here. We want to make your teaching experience as meaningful as possible to you, as well as productive for ourselves. Therefore, we intend to treat you as professionals. We expect professional behavior in return. Please use the following guidelines:

1. **Sign-in Sheet**
   Please sign the ledger in the Director's office when you arrive each morning. We need an accurate record of your participation to determine your dependability, reliability, and sense of responsibility, as well as the state of your health. (Frequent absences might indicate that you should choose a less strenuous occupation.)

2. **Absences**
   We expect you to notify the school in advance of *all* cases of absence. Failure to do so is grounds for termination of placement with the Community Nursery School.

3. **Orientation**
   During your first nine hours at the school we will help you become familiar with the school handbooks, the classrooms, schedules, supplies, and the indoor and outdoor equipment. We will also hold group discussions on teaching techniques and professional conduct and will give you a chance to observe each classroom.

4. **Participation**
   You will be assigned to a classroom for a period of two to four weeks. Your duties will include supervising small groups, supervising an entire group for short periods, and planning for, implementing, and supervising an entire school day — including clean-up.

5. **Curriculum**
   You will have opportunities to develop your professional skills by working in a wide variety of curriculum areas with the children. These will include, but will not necessarily be limited to:

   - Storytelling and language experiences
   - Motor activities
   - Art experiences
   - Block play
   - Music and rhythmic activities
   - Dramatic play
   - Role playing
   - Cooking
   - Science
   - Mathematical concepts
   - Manipulative activities
   - Woodworking
   - Field trips
   - Routines — personal care, clothing, food, rest, toileting, etc.

6. **Staff Meetings**
   You will be expected to participate in at least one staff business meeting (and more if possible) and one staff in-service training meeting. These meetings are held at noon on Mondays, alternate weeks. Please make an appointment with the Director for the days you plan to attend. Discussions at these meetings are considered to be privileged information. (Professional integrity will be considered in our evaluation of your service to us.)

7. **Parent Conferences**
   You will be given an opportunity to sit in on a parent conference as an observer (with the permission of the parents involved, of course).

8. **Other Duties**
   You will also be expected to attend at least one parent-school function and to plan the bulletin board displays for a full week in one classroom.

Other Trainees and Observers

1. More recently, high school students from community outreach classes have been coming to observe.
2. We also train handicapped people from time to time, either as classroom assistants or office workers, depending on the individual's particular abilities and her particular handicap.
3. Teachers and administrators from other schools have an open invitation to observe our program at any time.

Fig. 1-4 Sample of child care center's guide for student teachers (From *Nursery School & Day Care Center Management Guide*, Revised Edition, by Clare Cherry, et al. Copyright © 1978 by Pitman Learning, Inc., Belmont, California.)

Name _____   Date _____

STUDENT TEACHER RESPONSIBILITIES AND EVALUATION FORM

Each activity will be evaluated on a rating scale of 1 to 3: 1 — very good; 2 — adequate; 3 — needs work.

	Preparation	Presentation	Control	Rapport
1. Observation in the center				
2. Bilingual or multicultural activity				
3. Number or math activity				
4. Problem-solving language activity or activity from a language kit				
5. Science activity				
6. Dramatic play situation or story dramatization, fingerplay, etc.				
7. Health/safety activity				
8. Music activity (teach 1 song, conduct movement or musical instrument activity)				
9. Large motor physical game or activity				
10. 2 group-savers and 1 poem				
11. Read a quality book				
12. Involve one parent in an activity				
13. Cooking experience				
14. Creative art activity				
15. Make one bulletin board display with children				
16. Set up and conduct the workjob room				
17. Animal activity/outside guest (optional)				
18. Extra credit work				
19. Plan a complete morning program for four sessions. (Keep in mind that a morning program will entail large and small groups with a complete theme for concept development.)				

Fig. 1-5 Sample of cooperating teacher assignment and rating sheet

VALLEY CHILD DEVELOPMENT CENTER PRESCHOOL SCHEDULE

8:00– 9:00	Health check Free play/workjobs Creative art Snack/cooking activity
9:00– 9:30	Large-group activities: opening, talk-time, music, stories, introduction of new concepts
9:30– 9:45	Group art (theme concept)
9:45–10:15	Outside
10:15–10:30	Large-group activities: dramatic play, poetry, storytelling, health, science, and/or multicultural activities
10:30–11:00	Small-group activities: language development, bilingual program, and perceptual motor
11:00–11:20	Outside
11:20–11:30	Clean up for lunch
11:30–12:00	Lunch
12:00–12:15	Brush teeth, get ready for rest
12:15– 1:45	Rest
1:45– 2:00	Snack
2:00– 2:30	Large-group activity
2:30– 3:00	Outside

INFANT/TODDLER SCHEDULE

8:00– 9:00	Free-choice time (health check)
9:00– 9:10	Cleaning room; washing for juice
9:10– 9:25	Juice
9:25–10:00	Group time for older toddlers/free choice for infants (story, some fingerplays)
10:00–10:30	Outside time
10:30–11:00	Inside time (includes art activity or theme art for interested children)
11:00–11:10	Clean up room, wash for lunch
11:10–11:40	Lunch
11:40–12:00	Wash after lunch, clean room, get ready for naptime
12:00– 2:00	Naptime
2:00– 2:30	Get up from nap, change, and dress
2:30– 3:00	Juice and outside time

Fig. 1-6 Sample of children's daily schedule

Adults should offer a minimum of interference in the Center. We are here to guide and supervise. However, in situations involving health and safety (i.e., block throwing, destruction of property or the work of another child), do not hesitate to redirect children in a positive way. When in doubt, ask.

Suggestions for guiding behavior:
1. Redirect negative behavior in a positive way whenever possible (i.e., feet belong on the floor, not on the table).
2. Do not give a choice when one does not exist.
3. Avoid shaming or ridiculing a child.
4. Give help only when it is needed; encourage the children to work independently whenever possible.
5. Do not be afraid to limit or channel destructive behavior.
6. Help the children understand what you are asking something of them by explaining.
7. Encourage children to use their words rather than their hands during peer disagreements. Offer them a verbal example (e.g., "John, you make me *so* angry when you take my blocks!").
8. Inform the children a few minutes ahead of the next activity to come. ("It's three minutes until clean-up/snack.")
9. Watch for situations that may be explosive, and step in before they blow up. Try to let the children settle problems themselves. If they cannot, redirect them.
10. Remember, an ounce of prevention is worth a pound of cure.

Inside:
1. Playdough stays in the creative activities room.
2. Parents have been asked not to send their children with toys, except on sharing days. Toys will stay in the children's cubbies.
3. Running is for outside; walking is for inside.
4. Encourage children to pour their own juice, milk, etc. from the pitchers provided. This will probably mean frequent spills so sponges should be available on all tables. Have children pass things to each other.

Outside:
1. Adults need to distribute themselves throughout the center and the playground, rather than grouping together. Your attention should be on the children, observing them so you can be ready to step in when guidance is needed. Never sit with your back to the children.
2. Children are to climb up the ladder and slide down on their bottoms when using the slide.
3. All sand play and sand toys must be in the designated area.
4. Remind the children that water from the fountain is for drinking. Sand and cornmeal should be kept away from the water fountain to avoid clogging.
5. Help children park wheeled toys along the fence before going in. Please keep the gate area clear.
6. All wheeled toys have a specific use and must be used properly.
7. Toddlers are allowed on climbing apparatus. *Don't panic!*

Fig. 1-7 Sample of child development center guidelines

The following forms are common to student teaching. Many must be on file before the student's first working day.

- Class schedule (location, rooms, and times of any additional courses)
- Student teacher sign-in sheets (to keep track of arrival, departure, volunteer, and assigned work hours)
- Tuberculin (TB) clearance (mandatory in many states)
- Staff information form, personnel record
- Personal background form, figure 1-8
- Physical examination, physician's report

PERSONAL DATA SHEET

NAME _____

ADDRESS _____ CITY _____

PHONE _____

CAR yes _____ no _____

FAMILY DATA (optional)

HEALTH _____

EXPERIENCES with children (past employment, volunteer, family, etc.)

_____

_____

_____

COLLEGE   year _____   major _____

COURSES in early childhood major not presently completed

_____

_____

Previous college work

_____

_____

Presently Employed _____   Where _____

Hours _____   Duties _____

_____

SPECIAL INTERESTS _____

_____

WHAT WOULD YOU LIKE YOUR COOPERATING TEACHER TO KNOW ABOUT YOU? _____

_____

HOBBIES AND SPECIAL TALENTS OR SKILLS _____

_____

Fig. 1-8 Sample of personal background form

PROFESSIONALISM

As a student teacher you represent a profession. As a professional, you are asked to abide by certain regulations, including a professional conduct code. Confidentiality is an integral part of this code as it protects children and families, and it should be maintained at all times. Staff meetings and individual conferences are conducted in a spirit of mutual interest and concern for the children's and adults' welfare and the center's high standards. At such conferences, student teachers are privy to personal information which should not be discussed elsewhere.

The student teacher's appearance, clothing, and grooming contribute to a professional image. Fortunately, comfortable, functional clothing which allows a student teacher to perform duties without worrying about mobility or messy activity supervision is relatively inexpensive. Many supervisors suggest a pocketed smock or apron and a change of shoes.

RESPONSIBILITIES A clear picture of the responsibilities of the student teacher, cooperating teacher, and supervisor will help students make decisions about handling specific incidences as professionals. As a general rule, it is better to ask for help than to proceed in any questionable situation that goes beyond one's responsibilities and duties (barring emergency situations which call for immediate action).

Student's Responsibilities

- Attendance and promptness
- Performance and completion of all assignments and duties
- Work with a minimum of direction
- Translate theory into performance

Supervisor's Responsibilities

- Clearly outline duties, responsibilities, and class assignments
- Conduct orientations
- Arrange and monitor placements
- Observe progress and confirm strengths and talents
- Provide feedback
- Help student develop individual plans for future growth

Fig. 1-9 Consultation with the cooperating teacher sets the stage for growth.

- Work as a liaison between cooperating teacher and student, consulting frequently as a team member
- Be aware of cooperating teacher's assigned tasks for student teacher
- Serve as a resource and model when possible
- Evaluate student's competencies

Cooperating Teacher's Responsibilities

- Orient student teacher to room environment, schedules, class rules, and children, figure 1-9
- Serve as a model of philosophy, teaching style, and teaching technique
- Clearly outline student teacher expectations, duties, and assigned work
- Answer questions
- Give feedback on observations when possible
- Provide ideas for child activities and materials
- Increase the student teacher's opportunity to gain and sharpen skills by giving increased responsibilities when appropriate

Responsibilities of All

- Maintain professional conduct
- Communicate ideas and concerns; seek aid when in doubt
- Gain new skills, and sharpen existing skills
- Work as a supportive, caring team member

STUDENT TEACHING GOALS

The most important goal of student teaching is to gain adequate (or better) teaching competence. The acquisition of good skills allows the completion of training and new or continued employment.

Specific objectives vary but they generally are concerned with understanding children, planning and providing quality programs for children and families, technical teaching skills, and personal and professional development. A list of common student teacher objectives follows:

- Awareness of child's and family's individuality
- Building rapport
- Understanding ethnicity, and neighborhood and individual group cultural values
- Identifying the child's needs
- Promoting child growth and development
- Identifying goals of instruction
- Acquiring an individual teaching style
- Offering child activities and opportunities
- Applying theory and past experiences to present situations
- Preparing interesting classroom environments which allow the children to grow
- Learning teacher's duties and responsibilities
- Learning school routines
- Developing self-confidence
- Evaluating effectiveness
- Personal and professional growth
- Acquiring good communication skills
- Experimenting and creating
- Using creative problem-solving techniques
- Guiding child behavior appropriately
- Establishing and maintaining working relationships
- Assessing strength and endurance
- Understanding supportive family services
- Developing personal philosophy of early childhood education

Individual goals reflect each student teacher's idea of professional conduct and skill, and how each feels about the kind of teacher and person they would like to become.

YOUR PERSONAL PHILOSOPHY From your readings on early childhood education, and your observations and interactions with preschool teachers and trainers, you have formed your own ideas regarding the "best" early childhood education, the "right" teaching techniques and methods, and the "proper" room environments. You have opinions on the why, what, where, when, who, and how of group programs for young children. As you student teach, you will revise your philosophy based upon new experiences with children, adults, and different programs.

Summary

The student teaching experience is the last step in a training sequence for early childhood teachers. Three key participants — the student teacher, the cooperating teacher, and the supervisor — form a team enabling the student teacher to gain new skills and sharpen previously acquired teaching techniques.

Student teaching involves the integration of all former training and experience. The cooperating teacher and supervisor guide, model, observe, and analyze the student teacher's progress in an assigned classroom as the student teacher assumes greater responsibilities with children and their families. Initial orientation meetings and written requirements and guidelines acquaint the student teacher with expectations and requirements. The student teaching experience is unique to each training institute, yet placement in a children's classroom with a supervisor's analysis of competency is common to all.

A caring, supportive atmosphere helps each student teacher attain the established goals, and helps develop the student teacher's personal style and philosophy.

Suggested Activities

A. Read all of the following student teacher goals. Place them in order of priority from 1 to 5, number 1 being the highest. Name two goals other than those listed which are important to you.

  Understanding children
  Learning teacher's duties
  Understanding minority groups
  Developing self-confidence
  Evaluating effectiveness
  Developing rapport with children
  Acquiring an individual teaching style
  Gaining experience
  Experimenting and creating
  Gaining guidance ability
  Applying theories and ideas to practice
  Clarifying individual philosophy
  Personal growth and development as a professional

B. Write about the goals that you wish to attain during your student teaching experience. In small groups discuss your goals.

C. Read the following essay by Patricia Pruden Mohr (from California Child Development Centers' Administrators Association Newsletter). Which ideas and/or phrases do you feel are important? Discuss with the class how this description relates to centers where you have observed or been employed.

Philosophy for a Children's Center

A philosophy statement for a children's center is a critical starting point. It presents the ideal toward which a staff and parents strive. It establishes a basic premise from which all activities of the center emanate. It's a returning point, a centering, in time of crisis.

Here then is a philosophy adhered to by one center, perhaps it will facilitate you in developing or reassessment of yours.

The Children's Center is designed to create an environment of trust where people can grow emotionally, intellectually, socially and physically. The people of the Center are those children and adults who participate in its program. Each person is a learner, each a teacher, each a valued individual.

What a young child experiences is what s/he will learn. There is that of the young child in all of us. The Center is a learning place, a place to experience oneself in relationship to others and to the environ-

ment. The Center is a place of feeling, a place where the individual and his or her feelings are accepted and valued. The Center is a place of wonder that provides the opportunity to question, to explore, to succeed, to celebrate. It is a sharing environment based on the premise that each of us has a unique gift to share — the gift of self. The Center is a pluralistic environment that has a commitment to support ethnic, economic, and social similarities and differences.

Each of us is here together to experience, to learn, to support one another in the experience that is life. Each person has a right to experience him/herself as a person of worth who participates in determining his/her own destiny as much as s/he is able without causing harm to self or others. Each person has the obligation to recognize, respect, and support the rights of others. Each person has the right to move at his or her own pace honoring his/her individual development rate. The Children's Center is designed to support the search for direction of children and adults who participate in the program and to permit each person to set the design of his/her own becoming.

D. In groups of three, each student will assume the role of student teacher, supervisor, or cooperating teacher. Discuss the duties and responsibilities of the position you chose. List any differences of opinion and discuss them with the class.

E. Cut a large gingerbread figure out of paper. With crayons, illustrate your feelings toward student teaching at this point of the experience — the first days. Pin the figure to your blouse or shirt, and silently walk around the room studying others' gingerbread figures. In groups of two, discuss your interpretations of each gingerbread figure. Discuss similarities and differences between your gingerbread figure and others. Briefly discuss your discoveries with the class. (Figures can be pasted to a large chart, then posted.)

F. Interview a practicing teacher. Discuss the teacher's experiences while student teaching.

G. Imagine there is a line (continuum) extending across the classroom. Stand on the line in a spot which best suits your feelings based on the following premises. Explore your reasons for choosing your spot with those around you.

A _____ Z

I'm in the wrong class.   No problem. I'll
Student teaching will   sail right through.
be difficult.

H. Identify five feelings which may be helpful in accomplishing student teaching duties and responsibilities. Identify five feelings which can be detrimental to one's display of abilities and competencies.

Review

A. Identify the individual (student teacher, cooperating teacher, or supervisor) whose duties are described.

1. Models teaching techniques and skills
2. Consults with parents about children's needs
3. Observes and evaluates student teacher competency
4. Performs tasks assigned by cooperating teacher
5. Completes assignments by due dates
6. Tries new planned activities with children after obtaining approval
7. Arranges classroom time schedules
8. Arranges community placements for student teachers
9. Identifies classroom rules on equipment use
10. Writes information notes to children's parents
11. Has ultimate authority for children's safety and welfare
12. Seeks advice when in doubt
13. Assumes increasing responsibilities as competency and confidence grow
14. Makes the student teacher feel needed and secure in the classroom
15. Serves as a resource in activity planning
16. Writes lesson plans for single activities
17. Directs volunteers or aides in classroom
18. Develops individual child growth plans
19. Conducts training sessions for adults
20. Records child attendance and releases child to parent at program's closing time

B. Choose the statements that describe what you feel are important goals of a student teaching experience.

1. The student teacher increases the quality of the children's daily program.
2. The student teacher evaluates the cooperating teacher's style.
3. The student teacher becomes aware of vocational skill strengths and weaknesses.
4. The student teacher develops unique capabilities.
5. The student teacher gains practical experience.
6. The three key members stimulate each other's growth through supportive, caring interactions.
7. The centers reduce costs by working with training programs.
8. The student teacher is another expert with whom parents can consult regarding their child's progress.
9. Communities benefit when early childhood teacher training produces well-trained, competent teachers.

C. Select the answer that best completes each statement.

1. Student teaching practices and procedures are
   a. very similar when one compares different teacher training programs.
   b. as different as pebbles in a creek.
   c. uniform and dictated by state law.
   d. different at training institutions and agencies but always involve five key individuals.
2. The individual who is supposed to gain the most new skills through student teaching is the
   a. student teacher, but the cooperating teacher's and supervisor's new skills may surpass the student's skills.
   b. child.
   c. supervisor, who has learned each student teacher's unique way of performing duties.
   d. reader of this text.
   e. Impossible to determine
3. Being observed and analyzed during student teaching means
   a. being watched and criticized.
   b. self-evaluation and evaluation of others will take place.
   c. others will try to pinpoint the areas where the student teacher needs to sharpen skills.

d. parents, directors, and all members of the adult team will evaluate student competency.

e. children's behavior will determine ratings of student teacher competency.

4. In most states, the record which must be filed before the student teacher works with children is the student teacher's
   a. health history.
   b. personal history.
   c. bonding agreement.
   d. insurance clearance.
   e. TB clearance.

5. Professional conduct can mean
   a. insisting that a child say please and thank you.

b. dressing appropriately with attention to personal hygiene.

c. speaking candidly to a parent about the limitations of a cooperating teacher's method.

d. None of these

Resources

Perrodin, Alex F. *The Student Teachers' Reader.* Chicago: Rand McNally & Co., 1966.

Unit 2
Placement — First Days on the Teaching Team

OBJECTIVES

After studying this unit, the student will be able to:

- Describe pre-placement activities and considerations.
- Identify valuable information which can be obtained on a student teacher's first day.
- Pinpoint three activities a student teacher can use as an introduction, to learn the children's names, or develop rapport with the children.
- Identify three valuable skills for staff meetings.

PREPARING FOR YOUR FIRST DAYS

Before your first day of student teaching, you have been given your cooperating teacher's name and the school's address, and you may have attended orientation meetings for student teaching and your placement site. Your first working day is near. You have either an "on campus" or "off campus" child center assignment.

A stroll through the neighborhood where the children live will help you discover something about them. Observe the community, its businesses, its recreation, its uniqueness. A close look will tell you much. What type of transportation brings the child to school? Where do the parents work? Try to think about family life in this community. Notice the people, their dress, and the kind of activities going on. As Riley and Robinson point out:

> Places, people, and the processes of a community can be thought of as a significant part of the environment that support learning. (1980, p. 9)

Soon you will be trying to understand the children from this neighborhood. Your visit will serve as an initial frame of reference. Do not overlook the opportunity to observe this community's resources for planning child activities. Perhaps a construction site is an interesting possibility for a field trip, or an orchard or park holds treasures to be discovered.

With an on campus laboratory school placement, you may have previously participated in the children's program and perhaps completed observation assignments. The center, its staff, and children may be familiar. You will now assume the role of student teacher. Take a new look at the campus and the resources of the campus community.

If you have been told to meet with the director of the preschool, call to make an appointment. Plan to have the meeting at least fifteen minutes before you are scheduled to be in the classroom.

It is time to dust off the resource idea files and books you have collected during your training since you will be using them to plan activities. Choose a short activity to offer on your first day, even if it has not been assigned. Brush up on fingerplays or short songs to be used as "fill-ins" or transitions. Put them on cards that slip into a pocket, if they are not memorized.

Some good ideas for first-day activities which have worked well for other student teachers are as follows:

- A nametag-making activity
- A puppet who tells a short story about his or her name, introduces the student teacher, and wants to know the children's names
- A favorite book or record to discuss
- A simple food preparation activity
- An art or craft activity which uses children's names
- A collage or chart that shows interesting things about a student teacher's life
- A collection of photographs which are important to the student teacher
- A game made by the student teacher that involves children's names and places in their community
- A bean bag activity that uses children's names
- A flannelboard story
- A new song or movement activity
- A "my favorite thing" chart on which the student teacher shows three favorite objects, and then writes the children's favorite things next to their names.

LAST-MINUTE PREPARATIONS   Activities which can be easily carried and quickly set up work best. Get necessary materials together the night before your class. If you received a set of classroom rules and a schedule of routines and planned activities, study it beforehand.

Think about clothing. Make sure they will be comfortable and appropriate. A smock with pockets, shirt, or apron will hold a small notebook, pen, Kleenex, etc. You should wear shoes which will protect your toes and help keep your balance and speed on the playground.

If you will be driving, plan to park a short distance from the center so as to avoid staff or parent parking spots or drop-off areas.

MEETING WITH THE ADMINISTRATOR

It is customary to meet with the administrator before going to the classroom. At that time, the student teacher's records will be added to the personnel file. The file usually includes a TB clearance, a physical examination form, an emergency form, a personal background form, cooperating teacher guidelines (hints), and rating sheets from the supervisor.

Some topics which you might discuss are the procedures for storing your coat and personal items, sign-in and sign-out requirements, and miscellaneous details. You might be introduced to the secretarial staff before you are directed to your classroom. Esther Gordon-Nourok (1979) mentions the following as possible subjects for this first meeting with the administrator.

- The general plan of classes under the administrator's domain
- The administrator's philosophy about what a school should be and how it should be run
- The staff and their special skills
- The children attending the school and their socioeconomic group
- The percentage of parent participation
- The center's community involvement
- The administrator's expectations of a student teacher

YOUR CLASSROOM

There will probably be time for a smile and a few quick words with your cooperating teacher. Your introduction to the children can wait until a planned group time. Introduce yourself briefly to other classroom adults when you are in close proximity. Your cooperating teacher may ask that you observe instead of participate. Otherwise, actively participate in supervising and interacting with the children. Pitch in with any tasks that need to be done.

Ask questions only when necessary; jot down others on a pad of paper which you should carry with you. Use your judgment as to where you are needed most. Do not worry about assuming too much responsibility; your cooperating teacher will let you know if you are overstepping your duties. New student teachers tend to hold back and wait to be directed. Put yourself in the teacher's place. Where would the teacher direct you to supervise or assist children when the teacher is busy with other work? Periodically scan the room to decide if you are needed elsewhere.

EMERGENCY AND IDENTIFICATION INFORMATION

(To be completed by parent or guardian and updated at recertification and as changes occur.)

I.   Family Information

Father's name _____

Mother's name _____

Child's name _____ Birth date _____

Child's address _____

Father's business address _____

Mother's business address _____

II. Names of Persons Authorized to Take Child from the Facility. (This child will not be allowed to leave with any other person without written authorization from parent or guardian.)

Name	Relationship

III. Additional Persons Who May Be Called in Emergency to Take Child from the Facility

Name	Address	Telephone	Relationship

IV. Physician to Be Called in Emergency

Name _____ Telephone _____

Address _____

If physician cannot be reached, what action should be taken? _____

_____

_____

V.   Medi-Cal Number _____ Medical Insurance _____

Insurance Number _____

VI. Allergies or Other Medical Limitations _____

_____

VII. Permission for Medical Treatment. Administrative procedures vary among medical personnel and medical facilities with regard to provision of medical care for a child in the absence of the parent. The exact procedure required by the physician or hospital to be used in emergencies should be verified in advance.

In case of an accident or an emergency, I authorize a staff member of the child development agency to take my child to the named physician or to the nearest emergency hospital for such emergency treatment and measures as are deemed necessary for the safety and protection of the child, at my expense.

Signature _____ Date _____
                    Parent or guardian

Fig. 2-1 Sample of emergency information form

MEDICAL STATEMENT FOR ADMISSION

Child's name _____ Date of examination _____

I do hereby give my permission for the attending physician to give to the authorized representative of _____
_____ School any medical information which would be helpful for the care of my child.

Parent's signature _____

Part I: History (May be completed by parent or medical staff) If the child had any of the following conditions, what year?

Measles (3-day)	_____	Epilepsy	_____	Diabetes	_____
(red)	_____	Heart disease	_____	Hernia	_____
Chicken pox	_____	Pneumonia	_____	Otitis media	_____
Whooping cough	_____	Mumps	_____	Convulsions	_____
Diphtheria	_____	Scarlet fever	_____	Mental retardation	_____
Rheumatic fever	_____	Poliomyelitis	_____		

Any physical handicaps _____

Allergies _____

Immunizations	First date	Revaccination		First date	Revaccination
Diphtheria	_____	_____	Smallpox	_____	_____
Tetanus	_____	_____	Typhus	_____	_____
Whooping cough	_____	_____	Influenza	_____	_____
Measles	_____	_____	Other	_____	_____
Poliomyelitis	_____	_____			

List in chronological order all surgical procedures performed on the child.

Date	Type of surgery	Results
_____	_____	_____
_____	_____	_____
_____	_____	_____

Summary of admissions to hospital _____

Is child currently under the care of a doctor? If so, for what reason? _____

Part II: (To be completed by physician) Results of examination of:

Scalp	_____	Weight	_____
Eyes and vision	_____	Heart	_____
Ears and hearing	_____	Pulse	_____
Nose	_____	Abdomen	_____
Teeth and mouth	_____	Genitalia	_____
Throat	_____	Extremities	_____
Neck	_____	Reflexes	_____
Lymph glands	_____	Rectum	_____
Spine	_____	Skin	_____
Lungs	_____	Thorax	_____
Height	_____		

Please indicate any condition which might affect this child's performance at school or any condition the staff should be aware of: _____
_____

Recommendations _____

The above named child has been given a routine medical examination and has been found free of infectious or contagious diseases.

Signature of physician _____

Fig. 2-2 Sample of health history form and record (From *Early Childhood Education: Planning and Administering Programs* by Annie L. Butler. Copyright © 1974 by Litton Educational Publishing, Inc. Reprinted by permission of Wadsworth Publishing Company, Belmont, California 94002.)

SUPPLIES Familiarize yourself with storage areas to minimize the need to ask questions about the location of equipment and supplies. Check with your cooperating teacher when he or she is not involved with children or parents. Make your inspection when you are free from room supervision. Become familiar with yard storage also. During team meetings, you should inquire about your use of supplies for planned activities.

CHILD RECORDS Some early childhood centers will allow student teachers to have access to child and family records. Knowing as much as possible about each child increases the quality of your interaction. Remember confidentiality should be maintained at all times if permission to review the records is granted. During this review, you may wish to make note of any allergies, specific interests, and special needs of each child. For example:

> Roberto — eats no milk, cheese, etc.
> Clorinda — needs pink nap blanket
> Jake — like horses
> Pierre — occasionally gets leg cramps
> Lei Thien — uses toothbrush with own special paste

Each child's file may contain the following:
* Emergency information, figure 2-1
* Health history and record, figure 2-2
* Physical examination form
* Application form and family or child history (see Appendix)
* Attendance data
* Anecdotal records, figure 2-3; timed observation records, figure 2-4; assessments; and conference notes.

EMERGENCY PROCEDURES Acquaint yourself with the location and use of first aid supplies. If your previous training did not include emergency first aid procedures, contact the American Red Cross or another agency that offers such courses. For emergencies such as fire, become familiar with evacuation plans showing exit routes. Most states require that these plans be posted. Enforce all health and safety rules. If you have any questions regarding health and safety, be sure to note them so they can be discussed later.

PITFALLS During the first days of work, it is not unusual for the student teacher to unconsciously acquire some bad habits. It helps to be aware of these pitfalls in advance.
* Having extended social conversations or small talk with other adults; seeking the company of other adults as a source of support. (Use your breaks for this purpose if necessary.)

Name: ____Sandy____	Age: ___4 years, 9 months___
Date: ___October 29, 1976___	Setting: ___Swings, outdoors___
Time of day: ___9:35 A.M.___	Observer: _____O.B._____

Observation:	Summary:
Jerry was swinging on the swings. Sandy was pushing him. Jerry was laughing as Sandy pushed him higher and higher. Jerry stopped laughing and said, "Sandy, you're pushing me too high, stop it." Sandy continued to push him. Jerry said, "Stop, stop, I want to get off." Sandy said, "Chicken, chicken, you're a little baby chicken." Jerry said, "Stop, stop" in a loud voice and started to cry. Sandy said, "Chicken, chicken, you're a chicken." Then some other children came and asked Sandy to play Batman. He left with the other children, still chanting, "Chicken, chicken, you're a little baby chicken." Jerry's swing slowed down and finally stopped. He sat on the swing and continued to cry for several minutes.	After reviewing several anecdotes on Sandy, I have found that he is still bullying children as evidenced by this incident. It would be useful to observe and learn the causes of such behavior.

Fig. 2-3 Sample of a completed anecdotal record (From *Teaching Young Children* by Joan M. Bergstrom and Rose K. Margosian. Columbus, OH: Charles E. Merrill Publishing Co., 1977.)

Name:	Susy	Age:	3 years, 11 months
Date:	March 23, 1976	Setting:	Playschool — manipulative materials area
Time of day:	10:20 –10:40 A.M.	Observer:	P.S.

Time:	Observation:
10:21 A.M.	Susy walks slowly by the shelves with the small manipulative materials on them. She walks from one end to the other, turns on her heels, and pauses at the color cubes. She picks up a red color cube between the thumb and forefinger of her right hand, turns it around with her fingers, and puts it in her left hand. She quickly replaces the color cube and continues to walk along the shelves.
10:23 A.M.	Susy stops in front of the puzzle rack, turns to face it, and runs her right forefinger down the edge of the seven to eight puzzles stored in the rack. She lifts her hand and starts running her finger down the rack. Her finger stops on the edge of a blue wooden puzzle. She quickly lifts the puzzle out of the rack with both hands.
10:26 A.M.	Suzy turns on her heels and walks quickly to a round table adjacent to the small manipulative materials. She puts the puzzle down on the table with both hands, then pulls the back of a chair out from under the table using both hands. She sits down quickly, places her hands on the sides of the seat, lifts the chair, and moves herself and the chair under the table.
10:28 A.M.	Susy flips the ten-piece puzzle over and dumps all of the pieces onto the table. She then turns the frame upside down so that the head of the figure is closest to her. She quickly turns each of the puzzle pieces right side up, using both hands.
10:30 A.M.	Ms. Jones approaches her and says, "Susy, why do you have the puzzle frame upside down?" Susy looks up slowly and says, "It's more fun to do it this way." Ms. Jones asks, "Have you done this puzzle before?" Susy answers, "Yep." Susy then places the head of the puzzle in the frame correctly without moving the piece around before placing it in the frame. Ms. Jones walks away.
10:33 A.M.	Susy has placed each of the pieces into the frame one by one. She picks up one of the arm pieces with both of her hands and begins to manipulate and examine it. She places the arm in the correct position. Suzy then picks up a foot piece, moves it around, and places the foot in right side up. (The puzzle frame is upside down.) She wrinkles her brow, rubs her upper lip with her left forefinger and then smiles. She turns the foot piece around and places it in the frame. She then picks up the last leg, looks at it for a moment, quickly turns it to the right position, and puts it in place. She pauses briefly and runs the tips of her fingers of her right hand over the completed puzzle. She puts her hands on the puzzle frame, one on either side, and shakes the puzzle gently.
10:40 A.M.	She pushes her chair out from under the table with her feet, picks up the puzzle with both hands, and looks at the puzzle as she walks slowly back to the puzzle rack. She puts the puzzle back on top of the puzzle rack and runs away.

Fig. 2-4 Sample of a completed timed running record (From *Teaching Young Children* by Joan M. Bergstrom and Rose K. Margosian. Columbus, OH: Charles E. Merrill Publishing Co., 1977.)

- Talking about children in their presence. (Avoid the tendency to label a child. Save questions for staff meetings. Keep your judgments and/ or evaluations to yourself.)

INTRODUCTIONS Group time is introduction time. Children are quiet and attentive. Your cooperating teacher may ask you to introduce yourself. You might start by saying, "My name is Miss Smith. I'm a teacher, and I'm going to be here every Tuesday and Thursday until December." Your face and body language should express acceptance and warmth. Alternatively, you might do a short "hello" activity that emphasizes your name.

   _____ says 'hello' with a finger. . .
   _____ says 'hello' with a hand. . .(Julius, 1978)

Continue the activity using your elbow, arm, etc. and finish by using your whole body to say hello. Then have the children repeat the entire activity with you.

If you have prepared an activity, briefly check with the cooperating teacher regarding the best time to do it. Briefly describe your planned activity.

BEGINNING DAYS

Your first few working days are going to be both exciting and exhausting. Many factors contribute to the situation.

The induction of the student into actual teaching is a delicate and critical process. Unfortunately, no procedure exists that would guarantee universal success because many uncontrollable factors must be considered. The attitude of the student, the classroom climate, the inclination of the cooperating teacher, and the time of year are but a few of the many factors. (Kraft and Casey, 1967)

Kraft and Casey list the following four guidelines for beginning days:

1. The student teacher should be gradually inducted into the responsibilities of actual teaching.
2. The plan of inducting the student teacher will be from the easy to the difficult, the simple to complex, from observation to participation, and to long-term teaching.
3. The student teacher is to be thought of as a distinct personality, capable of growth, sensitive to success and failure, and deserving of help and consideration.
4. The student-teaching activities should be conducted in as natural and typical a situation as possible. (Kraft and Casey, 1967, p. 200)

AFTER-SESSION CONFERENCING At the team meetings, after important issues are discussed, your cooperating teacher and other classroom adults will be interested in the questions and impressions you have developed after the first sessions. Be prepared to rely on your notes. They are useful in refreshing your memory.

This meeting is also an appropriate time to clarify your cooperating teacher's expectations during your next few work days. If a class calendar, figure 2-5, is available, it will aid your activity planning. Most schools have their own system of planning activities or lessons. You will often be asked to schedule your own activities at least one week in advance on a written plan.

Ask for suggestions on the theme of your next week's activities. The cooperating teacher may want you to stay within the planned subject areas or may give you a wide choice. Copies of a student teacher activity calendar sheet, figure 2-6, can be made and given weekly to the cooperating teacher. Its development is a joint effort. Ask when it is the best time to consult with your cooperating teacher.

JOINING THE TEAM

You are now a member of an important team of people in a group of young children's lives, figure 2-7. In addition to your own growth and development, one of your major goals as a team member is to add to the quality of young children's experience. This involves teamwork. Teamwork takes understanding, dedication, and skill. Your status and acceptance as a member of the team will be gained through your own efforts.

MAY						
SUNDAY	MONDAY	TUESDAY	WEDNESDAY	THURSDAY	FRIDAY	SATURDAY
						1 JAPANESE AM. WEEK ←
2	3	4 Megan's Birthday 🎂	5	6	7 LIBRARY ←→ WORLD HEALTH DAY County nurse visits	8
		← BIRDS (MOTHER'S GIFTS) →				
9	10	11	12	13	14 LIBRARY ←→	15
		← PLANTING SEEDS →				
16	17 Paul's Birthday 🎂	18	19	20	21 LIBRARY ←→	22
		← BUGS AND INSECTS →				
23	24	25	26	27 SECRETARIES DAY	28 LIBRARY ←→ ARBOR DAY ←→	29
		← ANIMALS OF THE WOODS →				

Fig. 2-5 Sample of a class calendar

Student Teacher _____ Week _____

Training Teacher _____ Conference Time with Training Teacher _____

STUDENT TEACHER RESPONSIBILITIES

Time	Monday	Tuesday	Wednesday	Thursday	Friday

Fig. 2-6 Sample of a student teacher activity calendar sheet

Fig. 2-7 Adding to the quality of a child's experience is one of your major goals as a student teacher.

For purposes of this field of study, teams are those people employed or connected with the daily operation of an early childhood center who work to achieve the goals of that center. They include paid and volunteer staff and parents. Understanding the duties and responsibilities of each team member will help you function in your role. First, let us identify team members.

- Teachers and aides
- Directors and assistants
- Clerical and secretarial staff
- Food service personnel
- Maintenance staff
- Community liaisons

- Health and/or nutrition staff
- Volunteers
- Parents
- Consultants and specialists

Each school's team is composed of unique individuals who interact and combine efforts. Observation will help you determine how each person contributes to the school's operation and realization of its goals. The special talents and duties of each team member will become apparent. A job description of each position, figure 2-8, and an organizational chart, figure 2-9, may be available from your center's director.

Title: Education Coordinator

Role: Serves as instructional leader of the daily program. Is responsible for program development, evaluation, and supervision of instructional teams.

Specific Responsibilities:

1. Works with instructional staff to devise a sound educational program to meet specific objectives. Facilitates the planning, implementation, and evaluation of the instructional program.
2. Supervises the instructional staff and assists head teachers in supervising assistant teachers and volunteers.
3. Develops, implements, and evaluates an ongoing staff development program.
4. Works as a member of the multidisciplinary supportive services team to assist in the delivery of comprehensive services to individual children. Coordinates work of team in early identification and remediation efforts.
5. Makes formal monthly report to the administrative director about the progress of the instructional program, its staffing, and budgetary expenditures to date.
6. Works with instructional team to identify the instructional resources needed to implement the program (i.e., equipment, supplies, volunteers, additional staff) and works to secure the needed resources.
7. Works with instructional team to identify the particular needs of individual children in the program.
8. Monitors the expenditures of the instructional program (i.e., equipment, supplies, auxiliary personnel) in terms of budgetary allocations.
9. Works with the instructional team to promote and maintain optimal parent involvement.
10. Works with the multidisciplinary team to utilize their expertise to meet staff training needs and the educational needs of children.

Qualifications:

1. A bachelor's degree in early childhood education, with advanced graduate work in early childhood education. Thorough knowledge of appropriate program procedures for young children.
2. A minimum of three years' teaching experience with young children.
3. Demonstrated leadership ability.
4. Ability to work collaboratively with multidisciplinary team and with parents and lay persons from a variety of ethnic, educational, and socioeconomic backgrounds.
5. Sound physical and mental health.
6. Experience in program development, program evaluation, and supervision of instructional personnel highly desirable.

Fig. 2-8 A sample job description [From Joseph H. Stevens, Jr. and Edith W. King, *Administering Early Childhood Education Programs*. Copyright © 1976 by Little, Brown and Company (Inc.). Reprinted by permission.]

TEAM GOALS Forming a team effectively balances and integrates the unique and diverse strengths which a group of people have to offer. The assimilation of such talent benefits children in their early years, and both the children and their families in later years. Some of the goals of teaming include:

- Breaking down barriers that inhibit honest communication between staff members of different positions.
- Making decisions and generating action based on the input from all team members.
- Forming a commitment to group responsibilities and tasks.
- Providing opportunities for each team member's fulfillment, need for affiliation, self-acceptance, and self-esteem.
- Encouraging Identification with the center's curriculum model.

Team interactions which promote "the team spirit" include joint planning, open communication, mutual problem solving, resolving of conflicts, resource identification, and use of positive feedback.

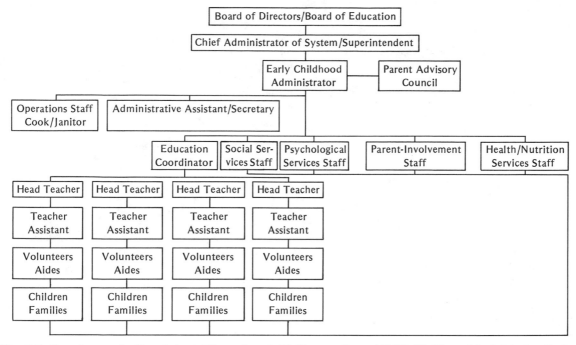

Fig. 2-9 Sample organizational chart [From Joseph H. Stevens, Jr. and Edith W. King, *Administering Early Childhood Education Programs*. Copyright © 1976 by Little, Brown and Company (Inc.). Reprinted by permission.]

GOALS OF THE TEAM AND PROGRAM

Knowing the goals of instruction helps you understand how your work contributes to the realization of the center's goals. You should read and review the center's program goals, if a copy is available. In your activity planning and preparation, you will have a chance to offer the children growth experiences, which is one of the prime goals of the center. Team meetings will help you realize how the planned activities relate to the center's goals. The feeling of team spirit is enhanced when your efforts reinforce or strengthen the efforts of other members.

TEAM MEETINGS   Team meetings often include only the staff members associated with child instruction. Since staff meetings are new to student teachers, they are full of learning opportunities. Attend staff meetings if your student teaching schedule permits. The extra time involved will be well spent. To make these meetings as successful as possible, and to make

them work for you, there are several things you can do before, during, and after the meeting.

During

- Mark the time, date, and place of the meeting on your calendar.
- Clarify your role. Are you a guest, an observer, or an active participant?
- Make sure you understand the purpose of the meeting.
- Bring your notes and notebook if necessary.
- Review your notes from the last meeting you attended.
- Arrive on time.
- Prepare to stay for the entire meeting.

During

- Listen attentively.
- Take notes, particularly when the discussion concerns student teachers.
- Participate and contribute when appropriate.
- Help staff members reach their objectives.

- aggression
- putting others down
- sarcastic humor
- crediting oneself with ideas of others
- being negative
- stubbornness
- blocking progress
- being irrelevant
- side conversations

- never contributing
- seeking recognition
- not attending
- interrupting
- monopolizing conversation
- constantly telling fears, troubles, insecurities
- pleading for special interests
- a "sky-is-falling" stance
- exhibiting false anger or emotion

These characteristics bog down teamwork and often create strained relationships which destroy team spirit.

Fig. 2-10 List of inhibiting behaviors during team meetings

After
- Mark the date of the next meeting.
- Complete your responsibilities.
- Prepare to report back at next meeting.

TEAM BEHAVIORS A number of behaviors may be exhibited during team interactions. Some of these can be evaluated as positive team behaviors because they move a team toward the completion of tasks and handling of responsibilities. The following is a summary of supportive and positive team behaviors.

- Giving or seeking information; asking for or providing factual or substantiated data.
- Contributing new ideas, solutions, or alternatives.
- Seeking or offering opinions to solve the task or problem.
- "Piggybacking," elaborating, or stretching another's idea or suggestion; combining ideas together.
- Coordinating team activities.
- Emphasizing or reminding the group of the task at hand.
- Evaluating by using professional standards.
- Motivating the team to reach decisions.
- Bringing meeting to a close and reviewing goals; making sure everyone understands the outcome.
- Recording group ideas and progress.

During team meetings, individual team members sometimes exhibit attitudes and sensitivities which soothe and mediate opposing points of view. Some examples are as follows:

- Encouraging, praising, respecting, and accepting diverse ideas or viewpoints.
- Reconciling disagreements and offering "a light touch" or humor to help relieve tension.
- Compromising.
- Establishing open lines of communication.
- Drawing input from silent members.
- Monitoring dominance of discussion.

Additional team behaviors can be viewed as inhibitors of team process. For a list of such behaviors, see figure 2-10.

WORKING RELATIONSHIPS

Your relationship with other staff members depends on your communication and respect for the contributions of each staff and team member, figure 2-11. Being friendly and taking the initiative in meeting each person will give you a real sense of belonging. You have much in common, and will often be combining efforts. Members of other staff may often be able to answer your questions, as well as provide valuable insight.

As a student teacher, you may have a clearer picture of the student teacher/cooperating teacher relationship than you do of the relationships between the assistant teacher, aide, parent, and student teacher. Usually student teachers, aides, and volunteers work under the cooperating teacher who makes the ultimate decisions regarding the workings of the classroom.   A student teacher is the closest to that

Fig. 2-11 Working together on a joint project strengthens a relationship. (Courtesy of Nancy Martin)

status, and assumes greater responsibility as time passes moving from assistant to co-teacher. Because of the changing role and increasing responsibilities clear communication is a necessity.

PARENT CONTACTS   Upon first meeting with parents, they may wonder who you are or immediately accept you as another classroom adult worker. Read their faces, and introduce yourself if they seem interested. Be friendly and open rather than talkative. Mention your student teacher status and your training program. Remember: In this meeting, as in all others, you are representing the early childhood teaching profession.

Direct any questions regarding children's evaluations, the school, or its curriculum to your cooperating teacher. Try to mentally match children with their parents. Most programs work on a first name basis with parents. Find out if this is true of your placement site. Knowing the location of each child's cubby and daily art or project will help you be of more service to the parents and the child. It will also save time, allowing more to be spent meeting other parents.

Summary

Before your first day of student teaching, it is a good idea to get an understanding of the children's environment by acquainting yourself with the school's neighborhood and community. Also, you may wish to plan an activity to introduce yourself on the first day.

Active classroom interaction, as well as asking questions, should typify your first days. You can obtain necessary information concerning your work from the cooperating teacher when both you and the cooperating teacher have no supervision responsibilities. If you feel you require additional background information on the children, find out whether their records can be made available to you.

It is helpful to become acquainted with other staff members. They can offer answers and insight which can aid your adjustment to the center. In time, you will develop smooth working relationships and earn team status and acceptance. This type of relationship will work well when it is time for you to participate in team meetings. Meetings are important vehicles for learning, and they will be a part of your future employment. You will be able to understand how each staff or team member contributes to the goals of a particular child center through observation, interaction, and a review of job descriptions.

Suggested Activities

A. Invite the director of your placement center to discuss particulars of past experiences with student teachers.

B. Make an appointment with your cooperating teacher to develop a calendar of student teaching activities. Pinpoint tentative dates and times for your part of the program.

C. In small groups discuss the positive and negative aspects of being able to review children's records.

D. Complete a placement observation form similar to figure 2-12. Prepare a daily teaching responsibilities list similar to figure 2-13.

E. Make a list of all individuals you feel are directly involved with the achievement of your school's goals.

1. Make a rough map of your classroom and yard. Include separate eating, sleeping, isolation, staff room, and any other important center areas.
2. Briefly describe the group. Identify children about whom you would like additional information.
3. List names of staff members.
4. Describe your relationship with your cooperating teacher during your first days.
5. Describe available materials and equipment. Do you feel they are adequate and satisfactory in all aspects?
6. What are some memorable experiences of your first days?

Fig. 2-12 Placement observation form

Three-year-olds — Morning program

8:00–8:30   Check to see that room is in order and materials are on proper shelves. Check snack supplies.

Check day's curriculum. Know what materials are needed.

8:30–8:45   **Arrival of Children**
- Greet each child and parent.
- Help children locate their lockers.
- Help children with nametags.
- Help children initiate an activity.

8:30–9:20   **Free-Play Time Inside** — Art, block play, dramatic play, manipulative materials, science, math, housekeeping area, language arts.
- Supervise assigned area. Proceed to another area if there is no child in your area. All children walk inside and use " inside voices."
- Interact with children if you can. Be careful not to interfere in their play.
- Encourage children to clean up after they finish playing with materials.
- Manipulative materials, including playdough and scissors, must stay on the table.
- Be on the child's level. Sit on the floor, on a chair, or kneel.
- Children wear smocks when using paint or chalk. Print children's names on their art work in upper left corner.
- Give five-minute warning before clean-up time.

9:20–9:30   **Transition Time** — Clean up, wash hands, use bathrooms. Praise the children for helping. Sing a clean-up song. Help with clean-up. Guide children to bathroom before coming to group. All children should use the bathroom to wash hands and be encouraged, but not forced, to use the toilet.
- Place soiled clothes/underpants in plastic baggies, and place them in their cubbies.
- Children flush the toilet.
- Let them wash hands, using soap.
- Bathroom accidents should be treated matter-of-factly.
- Use word "toilet."
- Help children with their clothes, but remember to encourage self-help skills.

9:30–9:45   **Large Group** — Assist restless children. Leave to set up snack if it is your responsibility. Put cups and napkins around table. Make sure there are sufficient chairs and snack places.
- Teacher of the week leads group time.
- Other teachers sit behind children, especially those that are restless.
- Show enthusiasm in participating with the activities.

9:45–10:00   **Snack**
- There should be one teacher at each table.
- Engage in pleasant conversation.

Fig. 2-13 Guide to daily teaching responsibilities

- Encourage self-help skills. Provide assistance if needed.
- Encourage children to taste or take a bite of food on their plates.
- Demonstrate good manners such as please and thank you.
- Help children observe table manners.
- Children should throw napkins in trash can.
- If spills occur, offer a sponge. Help only if necessary.
- Quickly sponge down tables.

10:00–10:45 **Outside Play** — Check children and cubbies to make sure children are wearing outside clothing if the weather is cold. If a child does not have sufficient clothing, check the school supply of extra clothing.

Outside Activities — Tricycles, sand toys, climbing equipment, balls, etc.
- Supervise all areas. Spread out. No two teachers should be in one spot except if all children are there.
- Help children share toys, take care of the equipment.
- Always be alert to the physical safety of the child.
- When necessary, remind them that sand is to be kept in the sandbox.
- Water faucet is operated only by adults or when there is adult supervision.
- Children may remove shoes during warm weather only.
- If raining, children must stay under the shelter.
- Teachers should refrain from having long conversations with each other. Attention should be to the children all the time.
- Bring tissue outside to wipe noses if needed.
- Give five-minute warning to clean up and go inside.
- Children must help return toys to the storage room.

10:45–11:00 **Clean up, Use Bathroom, Prepare for Small Group**
- Children go to assigned small groups.
- Each child sits on a carpet square.
- Extra teachers should sit behind children to quiet them when needed.

11:00–11:20 **Small Group** — Transitional activities include flannelboard stories, discussion with visual aids, games, filmstrip if applicable, songs, and fingerplays. Teacher puts children's rest mats out.

11:20–11:30 **Rest Time**
- Children lie on mats.
- Quiet music is played.
- Children do not have to be perfectly still as long as they do not bother other children. Whisper to restless children, and tell them it is a quiet time.
- Teacher tells the children to get up, and turns on lights. Children fold blankets, rugs, or mats and put them in their cubbies.

11:30 **Departure**
- Get children's art work to take home and put in their cubbies.
- Help children with coats, shoes, etc.
- See children off.

11:30–12:00 **End of Morning Session** — Help with clean-up. Double-check that all areas are clean and all materials are in their correct places. Share any observations with teachers, and solicit their observations and feelings during your team meeting.

NOTE: This daily guide is typical of guides used in morning laboratory school placements for student teachers. A similar guide can be developed for any placement site by a student teacher once room schedules are known.

Fig. 2-13 (continued)

F. Keep a separate folder to contain a summary of all meeting discussions which mention you as a student teacher and any aspect of your work.

G. In groups of four or five, develop a chart which pinpoints behaviors leading to smooth relationships between team members. Do the same for those behaviors which lead to awkward relationships.

H. In groups of five or six, take turns role playing the following situations. The rest of the class can serve as an audience to determine each role. Students can choose their roles from the list in figure 2-14.

Situation A: Part of a teaching team wants to give up the staff room and turn it into a dance studio for the children. Others see such renovation as a waste of valuable space.

Situation B: Some staff members wish to try fund raising to increase their salaries. Other staff members are not interested and think it is a poor idea.

Situation C: The janitor is doing a terrible job maintaining the building even though many requests have been made to improve conditions. The janitor happens to be the preschool owner's son. The owner never attends team meetings. The team members are baffled as to what step to take next.

Constant shoulder crying	Seeking information	Adding irrelevant ideas
Encouraging and praising	Offering new suggestions or solutions	Using sarcastic humor
Serving as an audience for ideas	Asking for opinions	Mediating opposing positions
Recording	Evaluating teamwork	Stubborn and resistant
Compromising	Calling on team to move toward decisions	Horseplay
Aggressively attacking	Making sure all understand outcome of team discussions	Interrupting often
Side conversationalist	Monopolizing discussion	Pleading for special interests

Fig. 2-14 Roles for suggested activity exercise

I.   Rate each of the following items according to the scale of 1 to 5. Discuss the results as a group.

1 strongly agree	2 mildly agree	3 cannot decide	4 mildly disagree	5 strongly disagree
Team status is not earned. There is always a pecking order.	Food service people are usually held in high regard by early childhood teachers.	Ethnic and cultural differences are the cause of most staff disagreements.	Children are affected by team spirit.	
One team member may be responsible for enthusiastic team meetings.	Giving dignity and respect to each job is the key to positive team relationships.	Maintenance staff and teaching staff have few interactions at most early childhood centers.	It would be a good idea for staff members to trade positions for one day.	
Team meetings should be evaluated.	Aides and assistants in the classroom regard student teachers as threatening.	Cooperating teachers do not see student teachers as co-teachers.	The student teacher is the only one who is observed and evaluated.	
It is easy to get along with team members.	Speaking up in staff or team meetings can be scary.	Most student teachers are used to participating in meetings and group efforts.	It would be a good idea to post a student teacher's photograph in the lobby of a preschool.	
There are some people who just will not talk at meetings.	A golden rule in staff relationships is to leave an area as orderly as you found it.	All team members should be on a first name basis.	Food and coffee can help break barriers at staff or team meetings.	
Close consideration of a meeting room should be given.	Everything that is said in a meeting is confidential.	The children's progress is the subject of most meetings.	Individuals should rate themselves on both the quantity and quality of their input at meetings.	

Review

A.   List four considerations in preparing for your first day as a student teacher.

B.   Describe two activities you might plan for your first day as a student teacher. List two reasons why you selected these activities.

C.   Rate each of the following student teacher actions with either a plus (+) or minus (−). A plus means a good idea or behavior; a minus means a questionable idea or behavior.

1.   Bring a small gift for the cooperating teacher.
2.   Bring a small gift for the director.
3.   Bring enough snacks for all the children.
4.   Permit children to call you teacher.
5.   Correct children who call you teacher, saying "I am a teacher named Estelle."
6.   Let your cooperating teacher know how nervous you are.
7.   Invite the cooperating teacher to dinner at your house.
8.   Stay two hours or so beyond your assigned time.
9.   Make sure you speak with each parent.
10.   Observe children from the sidelines your first day.
11.   Do light housekeeping activities.
12.   Peek in closets.
13.   Evaluate your cooperating teacher's techniques during conferencing.
14.   Use the telephone frequently or receive a number of calls.
15.   Ask questions about break times.
16.   Ask if you can rearrange the furniture in the classroom on your next workday.
17.   Spend some of your active periods in conversation with adults.

18. Watch children in the area near you, and let the cooperating teacher and other adults watch children in other areas.
19. Find a comfortable spot and remain seated when children are near.
20. Hold and touch each child at some time during the day.
21. Ask children about schedules or rules.
22. Introduce yourself as a teacher rather than a student teacher.
23. Know the location of emergency first aid supplies but follow the cooperating teacher's lead in their use.
24. Park in front of the center.
25. Ask for a key to the school.
26. Eat with the children at lunch and snack time if invited.
D. Read "How to Get the Most Out of Practice Teaching," figure 2-15. Write one piece of advice for yourself and other student teachers.

---

1. Be clear about your expectations. You are there to learn. Don't be shy about trying new techniques and making mistakes. Let your supervisor know through words and actions that you expect to be given responsibilities and feedback that will enable you to learn.
2. Ask questions. Don't be afraid of sounding ignorant. You are there to learn. When work schedules do not permit time for questions, you may need to arrange to arrive early, stay late, or write your questions and submit them to your supervisor.
3. Use your best judgment. When faced with uncertain situations, use your best judgment and ask for clarification of rules later.
4. Be professional. Arrive on time; be prepared to work. Let your supervisor know your schedule and the times you can be expected to be at school. Call if you are late or absent. Offer to make up the time.
5. Respect the teacher's need to give first priority to the children and parents. The teacher may not have time to take you on a guided tour. Use your time — observe, get to know the children, and study the environment. Familiarize yourself with locations of toilets and fire exits, and look to see where equipment is kept. Study the daily routine.
6. Look for a need and fill it. Make a mental note of the times a teacher might appreciate your assistance. Offer to redirect children, plan a project, hold a restless child on your lap, or simply step in to free the teacher for something else. Don't wait to be asked.
7. Make yourself a welcome addition to the staff. Schools are busy places. Don't wait for others to make you feel welcome. Learn the names of children, parents, and members of the staff. Smile; be friendly. Your job is to fit in quickly and be of help. Do your share — and more.
8. Contribute something positive to the school. Look for ways in which you can help improve the school: suggesting a new curriculum idea, repairing a piece of equipment, leaving something that will be appreciated.
9. Model yourself after effective teachers. Watch good teachers interact with parents and children. Listen to what they say and watch how they behave. Adapt their styles to your own.
10. Avoid socializing with other adults. Supervising teachers sometimes complain that students just "stand around and talk to each other" even when they have been assigned to specific areas to observe or supervise. Even when children are playing happily, stay alert for potential problems.
11. Avoid staff politics. Do not get involved in the problems of staff members. Taking sides may close off opportunities for you to learn.
12. Withhold judgment about the school and staff. Don't jump to conclusions about "good" or "bad" teaching. A few short visits can be misleading. Keep an open mind. The techniques you have learned in lab school or have read about in a book may not work in every situation.
13. Learn from your experiences. Replay in your mind the things you did that were effective. Ask for evaluations and suggestions for how you can improve.

Fig. 2-15 How to get the most out of practice teaching (From *Teachers of Young Children* by Robert D. Hess and Doreen J. Croft. Boston: Houghton Mifflin Co., 1981.)

E. Rate the following student teacher meeting skills in order of priority from 1 to 10, number 10 being the highest. You may give equal points to items if necessary.

- Speaking one's mind
- Listening
- Being prepared
- Following through
- Asking questions
- Staying the whole meeting
- Not interrupting
- Bringing notes
- Giving solutions
- Suggesting innovations
- Giving data
- Taking notes

F. List the team and staff members of preschool centers.

G. Describe why regularity of meetings is important to student teachers.

H. List student teacher behaviors which can contribute to smooth relationships with other staff and team members.

I. Identify some of your placement site's program goals in the following child development areas.

1. Academic — intellectual — cognitive
2. Social — emotional development and behaviors
3. Physical development and skill
4. Creative potential development
5. Language development
6. Multicultural understanding
7. Self-help skills

J. Make an organizational chart for your placement site

Resources

Gordon-Nourok, Esther. *You're a Student Teacher!* Sierra Madre, CA: SCAEYC, 1979.

Julius, Arlene Kahn. "Focus on Movement: Practice and Theory." *Young Children* (Nov. 1978), p. 19.

Kraft, Leonard, and Casey, John R. *Roles in Off-Campus Student Teaching.* Champaign, IL: Stipes Publishing Co., 1967.

Riley, Roberta D., and Robinson, Bryan E. "A Teaching Learning Center for Teacher Education." *Young Children*, 36 (Nov. 1980), p. 9.

Section 2
Programming

Unit 3
Review of Learning Theory

OBJECTIVES

After studying this unit, the student will be able to:

- Identify four major child development theories influencing early childhood education.
- Describe how children learn.
- List five ways in which the student teacher can help a child learn.

THEORIES ON LEARNING AND CHILD DEVELOPMENT

It has been said that a teacher training program is successful if its graduates know just one thing well — how children learn. Current learning theory is based upon views of human development which differ among experts. The concept that each child is a unique individual who learns in his or her own way further complicates the issue. How does a beginning teacher begin to understand how children learn?

There is a basic knowledge about children's learning that forms the base upon which theories have been built (Hendrick, 1980). Dr. Joanne Hendrick has identified the following:

- Children pass through a series of stages as they grow.
- Children learn things a step at a time.
- Children learn best through actual experiences.

- Children utilize play to translate experience into understanding.
- Parents are the most important influence in the development of the child.
- The teacher must present learning within a climate of caring. (1980, p. 5)

Stevens and King have compared four different views of learning and development, figure 3-1. Note that the program models differ based on the bias of each theory. According to the stimulus-response theory, education is a series of stimuli planned by the teacher to which the children respond. In programs such as DISTAR and DARCEE, the teacher gives signals to which the children are expected to make certain responses. The nature of the learning process is seen as observable changes in behavior. Stimulus-response theorists define learning as a more or less permanent change in behavior (Stevens and King, 1976).

Developmental Theory	Stimulus–Response (S–R)	Cognitive–Interactionist	Psychosexual: Interactionist	Maturationist
Theorists and researchers	Skinner Bushell Baer Resnick Englemann Karnes Miller & Camp	Piaget Kamii Weikart Lavatelli Nimnicht Hughes	Erikson Biber	Gesell Ilg Ames
Type of program exemplars	Preacademic/academic Behavior analysis DISTAR DARCEE Ameliorative	Cognitive-discovery Montessori Weikart cognitively oriented curriculum Nimnicht responsive Tuscon (TEEM) British primary/open models	Discovery Bank Street Educational Development Center	Discovery Traditional nursery schools Play schools
Nature of content	Preacademic/academic Skills/attitudes necessary for cultural competence	Development of logical thinking skills Development of internal cognitive structures, schemes, typical ways of thinking, acting on environment	Social-emotional development — of basic attitudes/ values and ways of interacting with others	Development of whole child
Expected outcomes	Child who is competent to perform specific operations that are culturally requisite	Child who confidently acts on environment and organizes experience; exhibits flexibility	Autonomous, mastery-oriented, powerful child	Child who has developed his unique abilities
Nature of learning process	An observable, measurable change in behavior directly transmitted through teaching	Learning through spontaneous active play Active construction of reality, internalization of external reality	Active, reflective resolution of problems and difficulties given social constraints through effective ego functioning	Nonoppressive, enriched environment that is supportive of natural development and learning

Fig. 3-1 Theoretical frameworks for early childhood education curriculum models [From Joseph H. Stevens, Jr. and Edith W. King, *Administering Early Childhood Education Programs*. Copyright © 1976 by Little, Brown and Company (Inc.). Reprinted by permission.]

Developmental Theory	Stimulus–Response (S–R)	Cognitive–Interactionist	Psychosexual: Interactionist	Maturationist
Sequence of content	Nonstage Simple→complex Concrete→abstract Logical analysis/task analysis Prerequisite skills Component skills Empirical validation	Developmental stages Sensorimotor Preoperational Concrete operations Formal operations	Erikson's developmental stages Trust Autonomy Initiative Industry	Following genetic givens
Resolution of Hunt's problem of the match	Match by teacher of each learning task to child's level of skill development	Match by child of skill to learning task within environmental structuring by teacher (At times match provided by teacher)	Match by child of skill to learning task within some structuring by teacher	Match by child alone of skill to learning task
Role of teacher	Assesses/diagnoses Prescribes objectives and task Structures favorable environment Teaches directly Reassesses Models Selectively reinforces	Observes Assesses child's interest and skill Structures environment in line with child's interest and skill Questions Extends Redirects	Observes Helps child to recognize problem situations Helps to resolve problems in socially appropriate ways Supports development of mastery and autonomy Structures environment	Observes Structures environment
Role of child	Respondent role — operates on environment in response to cues, discriminative stimuli	Active experimentation, exploration, selection	Active exploration and self-directed activity	Self-directed activity
Purpose of early schooling	Acceleration of child's development	Enhancing child's breadth and depth of total development	Assist child in resolving developmentally appropriate personal-social problems	Allow child to grow and develop at own rate
Scope of content	Basic skills Reading, Arithmetic, Science, etc. Attitudes Achievement motivation Persistence Delay of gratification	Physical knowledge Social knowledge Logical knowledge Development of symbolic function	Development of healthy attitudes and modes of interacting	Development of whole child Social, emotional, physical, intellectual development

Fig. 3-1 (continued)

In contrast, the traditional approach by maturationists emphasizes discovery by the child. This approach is the basis of learning at the traditional nursery school and play school. The approach of cognitive theorists, notably Piaget, has led to programs such as Montessori and the Weikart cognitively oriented curriculum. The studies of Erikson, a psychosexual interactionist, are less concerned with cognitive development and more concerned with social-emotional development. Emphasis is placed on social interaction and discovery (Stevens and King, 1976). In view of these different approaches to child development, it is obvious that no one theorist has the final word on how children learn.

HOW DO CHILDREN LEARN?

Learning occurs as a child interacts with the environment using the five senses: seeing, hearing, touching, tasting, and smelling. Some theorists say there is a sixth sense, the kinesthetic, or the sense of where the body is in relation to space (Ayers, 1973; deQuiros, 1979).

Look at a baby; offer a new toy. What does the baby do? The baby looks it over carefully, shakes it to see if it makes any noise, puts it in the mouth, and turns it over and over in the hands. It seems that the baby uses all of the senses to discover all there is to know about the toy. Look at a small child. Look at how the child is concentrating, figure 3-2; the child stares intently, and grasps the blocks carefully. We may assume the child is listening closely, with the mouth open and tongue pressed against the teeth to help concentration. All of these actions show us that the child is learning. A learning sequence may proceed as follows:

- The child attends and records.
- The child experiences and explores.
- The child imitates actions, sounds, words, etc.
- The child becomes aware of similarities and differences and/or matching events.
- The child responds appropriately to actions and words.
- The child talks about that which has been learned or discovered.
- The child remembers and uses knowledge.

When something is learned, the child may respond with appropriate nonverbal behavior. The child may point to, show, or do what has been discovered. In addition, the child may name or talk about what has been learned and may apply the knowledge.

Discussions of child learning usually include the following:

- If a child's action receives positive reinforcement immediately, there is a strong possibility that the act will recur.
- If a child's action receives negative feedback or is ignored, repetition of the act will be discouraged.
- Habit behavior is difficult to change.
- Periodic positive reinforcement is necessary to maintain the children's favorable actions.

Fig. 3-2 Nonverbal behavior tells us this child is concentrating and learning.

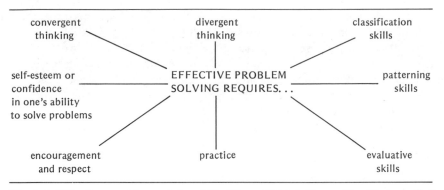

Fig. 3-3 Effective problem-solving skills (From "Think Power" by Victoria Felton and Joan Henry. Presentation at the NAEYC Conference, November 6, 1981.)

- The motivation level may increase persistence in learning tasks.
- All classroom experiences have a "feeling tone" for each child, ranging from pleasant to neutral to unpleasant.
- Motivation may contain a degree of tension, which may aid or inhibit success.
- There are two types of motivation: intrinsic and extrinsic motivation. Intrinsic motivation is acting a certain way because it feels good or right. Extrinsic motivation is acting a certain way because it is dictated by a particular situation.

PROBLEM SOLVING In a rapidly changing world, the ability to solve problems will become a survival skill. Dr. Victoria Felton and Joan Henry believe "problem solving is really a synthesis of convergent and divergent thinking skills, of classification, patterning and evaluation skills." (1981) In order to become a more effective problem solver, the child must:

1. have a general knowledge of the properties of objects
2. have the ability to notice incongruities or inconsistencies and define the problem (the "what is wrong here")
3. have the ability to think of new and unconventional functions for familiar objects
4. have the ability to generate many possible solutions
5. have the ability to evaluate various solutions

6. have the ability to implement a solution he/she thinks will best fulfill the requirements of solving the problem (1981, p. 3)

Early childhood student teachers need to analyze whether problem solving (figure 3-3) is a priority in their planning and daily interactions with young children.

TYPES OF LEARNERS Recent studies have tried to identify children who learn more efficiently through one sense rather than through others. A child who enjoys looking at books and notices your new clothes may be a visual learner as opposed to the child who listens intently during storytime and is the first to hear a bird chirping outside the window. The latter child may be an auditory learner, figure 3-4. The child who enjoys playing with materials of different textures, e.g., fingerpaint, clay, feelie-box games, may be a kinesthetic learner, one who learns best through touch and body motion, figure 3-5. Many children are visual learners, but most, especially preschoolers, use a combination of all the senses to gather impressions. A teacher can expect greater retention of knowledge if all senses are involved.

In addition to learning from the use of their senses, children also learn from the adults in their lives. Some children, however, demand more attention as they learn than others. The terms *field sensitive* and *field independent* can be used to describe certain types of children. Field-sensitive children like to work with others and ask for guidance from the teacher. They have difficulty completing an open-ended

Fig. 3-4 Children who enjoy listening activities may be auditory learners.

Fig. 3-5 Children who enjoy playing with materials of different textures may be kinesthetic learners.

FIELD-SENSITIVE OBSERVABLE BEHAVIORS

Instructions: Evaluate the child for each behavior listed below by placing a check in the appropriate column.

Child's Name   Grade   School   Date

Observer's Name

Situation (e.g., art, block play, etc.)

FIELD-SENSITIVE OBSERVABLE BEHAVIORS	FREQUENCY				
	Not True	Seldom True	Sometimes True	Often True	Almost Always True
RELATIONSHIP TO PEERS					
1. Likes to work with others to achieve a common goal					
2. Likes to assist others					
3. Is sensitive to feelings and opinions of others					
PERSONAL RELATIONSHIP TO TEACHER					
1. Openly expresses positive feelings for teacher					
2. Asks questions about teacher's tastes and personal experiences; seeks to become like teacher					
INSTRUCTIONAL RELATIONSHIP TO TEACHER					
1. Seeks guidance and demonstration from teacher					
2. Seeks rewards which strengthen relationship with teacher					
3. Is highly motivated when working individually with teacher					
CHARACTERISTICS OF CURRICULUM WHICH FACILITATE LEARNING					
1. Performance objectives and global aspects of curriculum are carefully explained					
2. Concepts are presented in story format					
3. Concepts are related to personal interests and experiences of children					

Fig. 3-6 Field-sensitive child rating form

FIELD-INDEPENDENT OBSERVABLE BEHAVIORS

Instruction: Evaluate the child for each behavior listed below by placing a check in the appropriate column.

Child's Name   Grade   School   Date

Observer's Name

Situation (e.g., free play, outdoor play, etc.)

FREQUENCY

FIELD-INDEPENDENT OBSERVABLE BEHAVIORS	Not True	Seldom True	Sometimes True	Often True	Almost Always True
RELATIONSHIP TO PEERS					
1. Prefers to work independently					
2. Likes to compete and gain individual recognition					
3. Task oriented; is inattentive to social environment when working					
PERSONAL RELATIONSHIP TO TEACHER					
1. Rarely seeks physical contact with teacher					
2. Formal; interactions with teacher are restricted to tasks at hand					
INSTRUCTIONAL RELATIONSHIP TO TEACHER					
1. Likes to try new tasks without teacher's help					
2. Impatient to begin tasks; likes to finish first					
3. Seeks nonsocial rewards					
CHARACTERISTICS OF CURRICULUM WHICH FACILITATE LEARNING					
1. Details of concepts are emphasized; parts have meaning of their own					
2. Deals with math and science concepts					
3. Based on discovery approach					

Fig. 3-7 Field-independent child rating form

assignment without a model to follow. The field-sensitive child waits until the other children begin an art lesson to see what they are doing, and then starts to paint. The field-independent child, in contrast, prefers to work alone, is task oriented, rarely seeks guidance from the teacher, and prefers open-ended projects. The field-independent child will try new activities without being urged to do so. In terms of learning, this child enjoys the discovery approach best. Study the rating forms, figures 3-6 and 3-7, for each type of child. Which children at your center are field sensitive or field independent?

Children also reveal different temperaments. These can determine how a child relates to the environment. Examine figure 3-8, which lists the characteristics of temperament. Where do you fit on the lines between the extremes? Are you more or less active? Are your body rhythms regular or irregular? Do you tend to be impulsive or cautious in making decisions? Do you see yourself as an adaptable person? Do you have a quick or slow temper? Are you generally an optimist or a pessimist? Are you easily distracted, or could the house burn down around you when you are reading a good book? Your answers to these questions describe your temperament.

Anne K. Soderman (1981) suggests that there are three general models of children: easy to handle children, hard to handle children, and those who are slow to warm up, depending upon where they fall on the nine characteristics. Children who are easy to handle have moderate activity levels and regular rhythmicity. They are moderate in decision making, adaptable, slow to anger (without being so slow that they do not assert themselves when appropriate), both quick and slow to respond depending upon the situation, and more optimistic than pessimistic. They tend to have low levels of distractibility and lengthy attention spans. These children may also be more field independent than field sensitive. The behavior of children who are difficult to handle goes to extremes. The children have fast activity levels and irregular rhythmicity. They are cautious, nonadaptable, quick to anger (temper tantrums), generally negative, and easily distracted. They have short attention spans. Children who are slow to warm up tend to be so cautious in making a decision that they will often wait for a decision to present itself before they move. They are slow to respond, have low adaptability levels, and are generally more pessimistic.

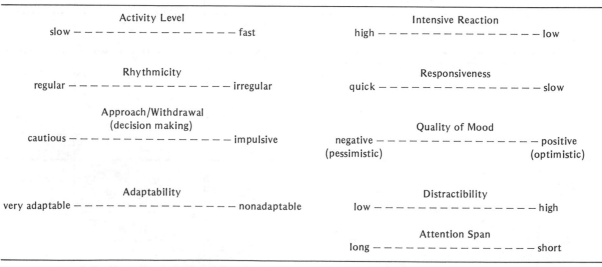

Fig. 3-8 Characteristics of temperament (Adapted from "Marching to a Different Drummer: A Look at Temperament in the Development of Personality" by Anne K. Soderman. Presentation at the NAEYC Conference, November 6, 1981. Updated from Thomas, A., Chess, S., and Birch, H.G. *Temperament and Behavior Disorders in Children.* New York: New York University Press, 1968.)

Fig. 3-9 Children's temperaments vary and must be responded to individually.

You should be aware that there are no good or bad temperaments; there are only different ones, figure 3-9. Take another look at where you fall on the line between the extremes. Generally, you will have difficulty relating to children at opposite extremes from you. For example, if your body rhythms are very regular, you may have less patience toilet training a child who does not have regular body rhythms. This can happen because you may not understand why the child is not regular like yourself. If you are a trusting, optimistic person, it may be difficult to relate to the suspicious, cautious child. The teacher with a lengthy attention span and low level of distractibility may have less patience with the child who is easily distracted and has a short attention span. In planning, the teacher may feel that an activity will take fifteen minutes only to discover that this child flits through it in three minutes.

What is the teacher's role in working with children of different temperaments? First, be careful not to label a child with a different temperament as good or bad. Second, take a cue from the characteristics, and plan the lessons accordingly. The child with a short attention span can learn to lengthen it. Give the child activities which can be completed quickly at first. Look to see what activities the child prefers. Then plan an activity which will take a little longer to finish and encourage the child to remain with it. Gradually, you can persuade the child to attend to the activity for a longer period of time.

All teachers soon realize that children do not accomplish the lesson or skill at the same speed, and they differ in the amount of time and attention they devote to activities. The number of repetitions needed for children to memorize or know varies. In general, the memory of an experience will become stronger each time it is encountered.

Frederick J. Moffett's poem "Thus A Child Learns" gives additional advice for dealing with the process of learning:

Thus a child learns; by wiggling skills through his fingers and toes into himself; by soaking up habits and attitudes of those around him, by pushing and pulling his own world.

Thus a child learns; more through trial than error, more through pleasure than pain, more through experience than suggestion, more through suggestion then direction.

Thus a child learns; through affection, through love, through patience, through understanding, through belonging, through doing, through being.

Day by day the child comes to know a little bit of what you know; to think a little bit of what you think; to understand your understanding. That which you dream and believe and are, in truth, becomes the child.

As you perceive dully or clearly; as you think fuzzily or sharply; as you believe foolishly or wisely; as you dream drably or goldenly; as you bear false witness or tell the truth — thus a child learns.

LEVELS OF REPRESENTATION   According to Piagetian theory, children represent the real world at four levels and progress from the lowest to highest levels in thinking abilities. Henry E. Draper and Mary W. Draper have reviewed these levels as follows:

1. Object Level — Learning about the real thing by interacting with the real object. For example, Janet learns about the telephone by touching it, dialing, listening to someone talk through it, listening to the ring, and seeing others actually use it.

2. Index Level — The second level is called the index of the real object. This level requires the use of one or more of the five senses. Either some part of the real thing or a sound, smell, or taste from it alerts the child to what the real object is. For example, the child hears the telephone ringing. The child who has had a lot of object experiences with the real telephone does not have to see it to know that the ring refers to the telephone.

3. Symbol Level — Only after the child has had ample experience at the object and index levels will that child use symbols. Only then will the child be able to represent the real object with a symbol such as a picture. The picture is not the real thing and there is no sound, smell or taste coming from it. But often after adequate experience at both the object and index levels, the child will recognize a picture. The child recognizes the picture of the telephone and knows that is represents the real thing. The adult world is full of symbols. It is easy to assume that children can use pictures and other symbols such as television and drawings to represent the real things. Observe children closely and you will see that they do not always see pictures as adults do. A hat may look like a cap to a child, or a bat may look like a stick. A drawing of a round face may look like a cookie. Only after we know children understand the object and index levels can we expect them to represent reality by the use of symbols.

4. Sign Level — This fourth level is the use of a sign such as a word to represent the real thing. The word telephone will mean little to a child who does not know how to read. Many children learn their own names — signs which refer to them. Even though they cannot read, many young children begin to recognize signs if they have lots of experience with them. Have you ever heard a mother say to the father in front of the young child, "We will have c-o-o-k-i-e-s (spells it aloud) after lunch." And the child says, "Mom, can I have a cookie now?" They have heard this sign used enough to know what it refers to even though they cannot see, touch, smell, or taste the cookies. (1977)

Summary

Four identified theories currently influence decisions and views about child learning. Individuality in learning is apparent; children learn at different rates and learn best from different techniques. The teacher's understanding of learning theory, and the idea of how children will learn best, should serve as the basis for the children's guidance and growth.

The senses gather information that is stored mentally and under continual revision as new situations are met. There is a definite sequence to the learning processes, and teachers need to be aware of individual styles of learning to make the experience easier for each child.

Suggested Activities

A. In groups of three or four, discuss the usual methods of motivating children to try new materials or experiences.

B. Rate the following situations as A (appropriate; justified by current learning theory) or I (inappropriate). If appropriate, cite the theory that supports the answer. Discuss your choices with four or five others in a class group meeting.

1. Marilee, a student teacher, encounters two children who want to learn to tie their shoes. Since she realizes shoe tying is a complex skill, she says, "When you're a little bigger, you'll be able to do it."

2. Thien, a student teacher, would like to tell a group of three-year-olds about the country of his birth, Vietnam. However, Thien realizes they probably would not be able to grasp the concept of a foreign country so he presents a simple Vietnamese song he learned as a child instead.

3. A cooperating teacher presents an activity in which she names and praises children who give correct answers.

4. Toni notices Mike and Eduardo are using the toy razors to shave their legs. She redirects their play, asking them to shave their faces like their fathers do.

5. Elena notices that Tilly, an independent child, always hides when inside time is announced. She decides to interest Tilly in an indoor activity before inside time is called to avoid having to find Tilly and coax her in.

6. Johnny refuses to attend any group activities. Laura suspects that he has had negative experiences at previous group times, and decides to make group time so attractive Johnny will want to join in. Laura has planned an activity with large balloons which children sit on and pop.

7. Lisa, Garrett, and Thad often gather at the reading corner and read new books. Stephanie Lynn, the student teacher, sees this as an example of intrinsic motivation.

8. Bud notices that his cooperating teacher always calls on each child by name in any conversation at circle or discussion times.

9. Carolyn, a student teacher, feels she needs only to set out activities for the children, and they will select the ones they need for their intellectual growth.

10. Gregorio, age three, has just poured water on the floor. The student teacher approaches, saying, "You need to tell me why you poured water on the floor."

11. Carlos says he hates carrots. Susan, the student teacher, tells him she likes them.

12. A child whines, "You know, so tell me!" Joanne, the student teacher, is reluctant to give a direct answer because she feels the child should explore the toy and find out for himself which puzzle piece fits. "Try turning the piece," she suggests.

13. Upon driving to her assigned preschool, Margo notices a street barricade. When the first parent arrives, she asks what is happening.

14. There is a new child in the classroom. This child has a tattoo which fascinates other children. The cooperating teacher feels it is best not to ask the child about it at group time since it might embarass the newcomer. When a child asks about it, she answers, "I can see you're really interested in the mark you see on our new friend's arm."

15. In Mrs. Clements' preschool, the children select activities, and they have the choice of attending group times or engaging in other quiet activities.

C. In groups of three, act out a teaching/learning situation (two children, one teacher) based on one of the four major theories discussed in this unit. Have other groups guess which theory you chose to role play.

D. Divide the class into four groups. Have each group write a description of the furnishings and arrangements found in the classroom which adhere to the four major theories previously discussed.

E. Read and discuss the following story. What are the implications for early childhood educators?

The Top of the Class

Once upon a time, the animals decided they must do something heroic to meet the problems of a "new world." So they organized a school. They adopted an activity curriculum which consisted of running, climbing, swimming, and flying. To make it easier to administer the curriculum, all the animals took all the subjects.

The duck was excellent in swimming. In fact, he was much better than the instructor. However, the duck received only a passing grade in flying. He was doing poorly in running also. Consequently, he had to stay after school to practice running. After a while, his webbed feet were so badly worn, he was only average in swimming. But average was acceptable in school, so nobody worried about it except the duck.

The rabbit started at the top of the class in running, but had a nervous breakdown because of so much make-up work in swimming.

The squirrel was excellent in climbing but was very frustrated in flying class when the teacher made her start from the ground up instead of from the treetop down. She also developed charley horses from over-exertion, and only earned a C in climbing and a D in running.

The eagle was a problem and had to be disciplined severely. In the climbing class, he beat all the others to the top of the tree but insisted on using his own method to get there.

At the end of the year, an abnormal eel that could swim very well and run, climb, and fly only a little had the highest average and was valedictorian.

The prairie dogs stayed out of school, and fought the tax levy because the administration would not add digging and burrowing to the curriculum. They apprenticed their child to a badger, and joined the groundhogs and gophers to start a private school.

Review

A. Choose the best answer to complete each statement.

1. Beginning teachers should
    a. have a clear idea of how children learn best because research has discovered the learning process.
    b. realize that there are a number of learning theories.
    c. expect children to learn in their own unique ways, making similarities between the children's learning patterns insignificant.
    d. look to their own experiences for clues on child learning.
    e. None of these

2. A theory is someone's attempt to
    a. gain fame.
    b. help instructors teach.
    c. make sense of a vast series of events.
    d. control others.
    e. make others think like the theorist.

3. It is generally accepted that children should
    a. be grouped according to ability.
    b. be grouped according to age.
    c. be asked to practice and recite learnings.
    d. play because it promotes learning.
    e. be exposed to planned group times that teach basic survival skills.

4. When one hears that children pass through stages in their development, it means that
    a. all the children pass through stages in an orderly, predictable way.
    b. children should tour buses and theaters.
    c. there seems to be phases in growth that teachers and parents can expect.
    d. most children will return to previous stages at times.
    e. All of these

5. The four major theories of child development and learning are
    a. useful in gaining ideas concerning how children learn best.
    b. only a few of the many theories which exist.
    c. generally accepted by early childhood educators as having merit.
    d. limited if one wants to plan a child's program for all aspects of a child's development.
    e. All of these

6. Montessori preschools are considered to be based upon the
    a. stimulus-response theory.
    b. psychosexual interactionist theory.
    c. maturationist theory.
    d. cognitive interactionist theory.
    e. humanist theory.

7. To help teachers gain additional insights into child learning, there is a need for
    a. space.
    b. time.
    c. money.
    d. new buildings.
    e. research.

8. If a child repeats behavior, it
   a. is probably intrinsically rewarding.
   b. indicates the child is not growing or learning.
   c. is easier to change the behavior using positive reinforcement.
   d. means the teacher does not need to reinforce it.
   e. None of these

9. The act of knowing (cognition) is
   a. a simple process of experiencing and sorting.
   b. a complicated experience unique to each individual.
   c. promoted and made more efficient by teachers.
   d. dependent on only a few factors.
   e. None of these

10. Being tied up in a test where you find you cannot remember things you know is an example of
    a. your intellectual limitation.
    b. too much motivational pressure.
    c. taking a test that is too hard for you.
    d. trying to recall information you have not learned.
    e. weak motivation.

B. Match the theorist and well-known program model to the theory. In some cases, the theory will match more than one program.

1. Stimulus-response
2. Cognitive interactionist
3. Psychosexual interactionist
4. Maturationist

   a. Erikson
   b. Gesell
   c. Skinner
   d. Englemann
   e. Piaget
   f. Montessori
   g. Traditional nursery school
   h. British open primary
   i. Discovery model
   j. DISTAR
   k. Play schools

C. List any accepted learning theories you feel were excluded from this unit. Cite your source (text, individual, etc.).

D. Define convergent thinking, divergent thinking, symbol level, and sign level.

Resources

Ayers, A. Jean. *Sensory Integration and Learning Disorders*. Los Angeles: Western Psychological Services, 1973.

Draper, Henry E., and Draper, Mary Wanda. *Studying Children*. Peoria, IL: Chas. A. Bennett Co., Inc., 1977.

Felton, Victoria, and Henry, Joan. "Think Power." Presentation at the NAEYC Conference, November 6, 1981.

Hendrick, Joanne. *Total Learning for the Whole Child*. St. Louis: C.V. Mosby Co., 1980.

deQuiros, Julio B., M.D., Ph.D. *Neuropsychological Fundamentals in Learning Disabilities*, rev. ed. Novato, CA: Academic Therapy Publications, 1979.

Soderman, Anne K. "Marching to a Different Drummer: A Look at Temperament in the Development of Personality." Presentation at the NAEYC Conference, November 6, 1981. Updated from Thomas, A., Chess, S., and Birch, H.G. *Temperament and Behavior Disorders in Children*. New York: New York University Press, 1968.

Stevens, Joseph H., Jr., and King, Edith W. *Administering Early Childhood Education Programs*. Boston: Little, Brown and Co., 1976.

Unit 4
Writing Activity Plans

OBJECTIVES

After studying this unit, the student will be able to:

- Complete a written activity plan form.
- Identify three ways of assessing child interest.
- List criteria for child activity planning.
- Describe the benefits of written activity plans.

IDENTIFYING CHILD INTERESTS

You will plan, prepare, and present classroom activities. The teaching day contains structured (teacher-planned) and unstructured (child-chosen) activities. The cooperating teacher's philosophy, the school's philosophy, the identified program goals, and classroom setting determine the balance between child-chosen activities and teacher-planned activities. In activity-centered classrooms, or those with a Piagetian view, student teachers arrange room centers to invite and promote child discovery and learning. "Every time we teach a child something, we keep him from reinventing it. On the other hand, every time a child discovers it himself, it remains with him for the rest of his life." (Piaget, in film "Patron: Piaget In New Perspective")

You will be searching for activity ideas that will interest and challenge the group of children to which you are assigned. Observing children's play choices and favorite activities will give you clues, figure 4-1. Children's conversations provide clues as to what has captured their attention. (You can make comments in your pocket notebook concerning individual and group curiosity and play selections.) Watch for excitement among the children. What were they eager to try? Was considerable time spent exploring

Fig. 4-1 Trying on hats is fun for children and is an interesting activity idea.

or concentrating on an experience? (See figure 4-2.) John Holt emphasizes that teachers need to be aware of children's interests.

We can begin by thinking of ourselves not as teachers, but as gardeners. A child's mind, like a flower, is a living thing. We can't make it grow by sticking things on it any more than we can make a flower grow by gluing on petals and leaves. All we can do is surround the growing mind with what it needs for growing and have faith that it will take what it needs and will grow. Our job as teachers is not to get the child to learn what we want but to help him learn what he wants. (1964)

Go back into your own experiences as a child and learn from them. Remember your enthusiasm for certain activities, and your discovery and avid participation in others.

ACTIVITY RESOURCES

Files, resource books, and activity ideas you collected during training will now come in handy. Research books that describe child activity ideas. You will have to discern whether the ideas fit your group.

Fig. 4-2 Discovering together is an enjoyable aspect of teaching. (Courtesy of Nancy Martin)

Teachers' and children's magazines often have timely seasonal and holiday activity planning ideas.

Draw upon your own creative abilities. All too often student teachers feel that tried and true ideas are superior to what they invent. The new and novel activities you create will add sparkle and uniqueness to your teaching. Do not be afraid to draw from and improve a good idea or change successful activities your children have already enjoyed. Some classroom activities are designed because of an overabundance of scrap or donated material. Take another look at materials in storage which are not receiving much attention or have been forgotten. Perhaps these can be reintroduced in a clever, new way.

CURRICULUM AREAS

Most preschool curriculums include: arts and crafts; music and movement; language; science; large and small motor skill development; cooking and nutrition activities; numbers and measurement; perceptual motor activities; health and safety activities; social learnings; multicultural awareness activities; and plant and animal study.

Newly evolving areas of study with different degrees of acceptance include: economics and consumer awareness; ecology and energy study; moral and ethical values; the study of changing sex role responsibilities; the study of changing family patterns; introduction to photography; introduction to computers; sex education; gardening and preserving activities; and structured games.

TYPES OF ACTIVITIES Planned activities can promote child growth through teacher discussion and interaction. Important factors which need consideration in the planning and preparation of any activity are:

- Child safety
- The goal or objective of the activity
- Appropriateness to children's ages, experiences, and skill levels
- Setting surroundings or its comfort, lighting, and sound level
- Number of children and adults
- Duration and time of day

- Materials, furnishings, objects to be used
- Expense
- Clean-up provisions
- Transition to next activity
- Nonsexist and nonracist language; appropriate values

It is generally agreed that activities for young children should:

- Capture and hold their attention
- Provide opportunities for active involvement with minimal time spent waiting
- Provide first-hand sensory experiences and explanations when necessary
- Allow for discovery and pursuit of interests
- Give children a sense of confidence in themselves and their learning competence
- Be connected to past experiences so they can bridge the gap between what they already know and the new experience. However, activities should not be too closely related so as to slow down the child's learning due to boredom. Also, activities should not stretch beyond the child's capacity for learning; this could result in feelings of frustration and a sense of boredom (Hunt, 1974).
- Add to the quality of their lives
- Be of a reasonable duration
- Fit into quiet and active periods, and be planned according to noisy or quiet locations
- Provide for individual differences
- Have clearly stated directions and expectations if necessary
- Be flexible enough to provide for unexpected child interests
- Be intellectually stimulating

WRITTEN ACTIVITY PLANS These are useful devices which encourage student teachers to thoroughly think through the different parts of their planned activities. They help beginning teachers foresee possible problems and find solutions. With adequate preparation through written planning, the student teacher can approach each planned activity with a degree of confidence and security. Cooperating teachers and supervisors often contribute ideas on the student's written plans or consult with the student,

Fig. 4-3 Monitoring children's interest in a planned activity is one of the teacher's tasks.

making plans a team effort. Written plans are a starting point from which actual activity flows, depending on the children's reception and feedback. Monitoring the children's interest is a teaching task, figure 4-3, and will often result in improvising and revising the activities to suit their needs.

A teacher needs to observe students during instruction to identify those who have the greatest difficulty becoming actively engaged. However, simply to identify them is not enough. The teacher must determine the reasons for their lack of participation and how to evoke more active participation. Students may be uninvolved for different reasons — boredom, anxiety, fatigue, personal problems, inability to understand the instruction, or involvement in matters unrelated to the classroom. Sometimes the teacher's interest in students and their needs or "private attention" can improve motivation and involvement. (Levin and Long, p. 12)

Figure 4-4 shows one classroom's weekly plan. This particular classroom was staffed with one full-time teacher, one part-time assistant, and three high school volunteers. Since the classroom was organized into

Area \ Day	Monday	Tuesday	Wednesday	Thursday	Friday
Math	Chart worms eaten by turtle.				
Science	(Steve)		(Steve) Tubes, corks, water and food coloring.		
Language Arts			(Sara) Write dictation.		
House Area	(Ted) Add materials for table.	(Ted) Applesauce — Sharon & Tom.	(Ted)	(Ted)	(Ted)
Blocks	Add transporta- toys.				
Art Table	Object painting.		Add new objects for printing.		
Music	Resonating bells.			(John)	
Story	(Jan) (Steve)	(Ted)	(Ted)	(Ted) (Susan)	(Ted) (Jan)
Group Time	(Jan)	(Jan)	(Jan)	(Jan)	(Jan)
Outdoor Play	Old tires for rolling down hill.		Visiting goat.		
Trips or Visitors					
Snack	Celery and peanut butter.	Applesauce.	Juice and graham crackers.	Tapioca pudding.	Juice and raisins.

Fig. 4-4 Sample of teachers' weekly plan sheet (From Schickedanz, et al., *Strategies for Teaching Young Children*, © 1977, p. 15. Reprinted by permission of Prentice-Hall, Inc., Englewood Cliffs, N.J.)

learning centers and a wide variety of basic materials was always available to the children, it notes only additions in materials or special projects to be started or continued (Schickedanz, et al., 1977). This plan indicates which adult is responsible for which room area or activity. Written lesson plans proceed one step farther and isolate a teacher's or student teacher's plan for what will happen during a specific time block and in a specific location.

The activity plan guide in figure 4-5 is one of many possible forms which can be used by student teachers. It is appropriate for most but not all planned activities. Storytimes, fingerplays, flannelboard stories, songs, and short-duration activities usually are not written in activity plan form. Activity plan titles are descriptive such as Sink and Float, Making Farmers' Cheese, or Tie Dyeing. They quickly clarify the subject of the planned experience.

Filling in the space for curriculum area sometimes leads to indecision. Many early childhood activities are hard to categorize. Subjects seem to fall into

1. Activity title _____

2. Curriculum area _____

3. Materials needed _____
    _____
    _____

4. Location and set-up of activity _____

5. Number of children and adults _____

6. Preparation _____
    _____
    _____
    _____

7. Specific behavioral objective _____
    _____
    _____
    _____
    _____

8. Developmental skills necessary for success _____
    _____

9. Getting started _____
    _____
    _____

10. Procedure _____
    _____
    _____

11. Discussion (key concepts, attitudes, facts, skills, vocabulary, etc.) _____
    _____
    _____
    _____
    _____
    _____

12. Apply _____
    _____

13. Clean-up _____

14. Terminating statement _____

15. Transition _____

16. Evaluation: activity, teacher, child _____
    _____
    _____
    _____
    _____
    _____
    _____
    _____
    _____
    _____
    _____

Fig. 4-5 Activity plan guide

more than one area. Use your own judgement and designation; it is your plan!

Identification of materials, supplies, and tools comes next. Some activities require visual aids and equipment for teachers as well as those materials used by children. Estimating exact amounts helps calculate expenses, and helps during preparation. You will simply count out the desired quantities. Student teachers generally know what classroom supplies are available to them and what they will have to supply themselves.

The location of a planned activity has much to do with its success. The following questions can help decide the best location.

- What amount of space will children need?
- What room or outdoor features, e.g., windows, water, flat floor, storage or drying areas, rug, lighting, grass, shade, are necessary?
- Will electrical outlets be necessary?
- Will noise or traffic from adjacent areas cause interference?
- Will one adult be able to supervise the location?

Self-help and child participation in clean-up, if necessary, need consideration. Activities which actively engage children and invite exploration suit young children's needs. Random set-ups can lead to confusion and conflict over work space and supply use. A good set-up helps a child work without help and promotes proper respect for classroom supplies and equipment and consideration for the work of others. Each set-up reflects a teacher's goals and philosophy of how children best learn.

Student teachers usually begin planning for small groups, and then tackle larger groups and the total room activity plans. A number of fascinating early childhood activities call for close adult supervision, and can happen safely or successfully with only a few children at a time. Instant replays or on-going activities may be necessary to accommodate all interested children. Waiting lists are useful in these cases, and children quickly realize they will be called when it is their turn, figure 4-6. The number of children on activity plan forms can read two groups of four children, etc.

Preparation sections on lesson plans alert the student teacher to tasks which must be completed

Fig. 4-6 These children have had to wait for their turn to touch the rabbit.

prior to actual presentation. This could include making a number of individual servings of paste, moving furniture, mixing paint, making a recipe chart, or a number of similar teacher activities. Preparation includes attention to features which minimize child waiting and decrease the need for help from the teacher.

BEHAVIORAL OBJECTIVES

Planned and unplanned activities and experiences have some type of outcome. Written student teaching plans include a section where outcomes are identified. This serves as the basis for planning and presentation and all other form sections. Some early childhood professionals have resisted a movement to pinpoint and measure the outcome of a planned curriculum.

The goals of early childhood education are measurable, although we have preferred to say they are not. In the last five years, researchers have shown us that we can collect evidence showing the extent to which our procedures are successful. It should be the supervisor's role to help the teacher make use of new knowledge in child development and early education by making explicit what is required to achieve the desired objectives. It is also the supervisor's responsibility to help teachers learn to state behavioral objectives and select appropriate strategies to achieve these objectives. (Litman, in Anderson's and Shane's *As the Twig is Bent,* 1971)

Studies on accountability and cost effectiveness have increased early childhood curriculums which have adopted specific behavioral objective identification measurements. Since attitudes, feelings, and degrees of creativity are difficult to observe in child behavior, some curriculum areas are excluded. Most early childhood professionals feel there are a number of important learnings and outcomes gained through preschool attendance which cannot be measured by behavioral means.

Specific behavioral objectives as defined by Robert F. Mager (1962) describe "terminal behavior" (what the learner will be doing), which includes three components:

1. identification and naming the overall behavior act;
2. definition of the important conditions under which the behavior is to occur; and
3. definition of the criterion of acceptable performance.

A specific behavioral objective, therefore, pinpoints exactly what is expected by giving the student teacher a clear idea of an activity's objective. The lesson plan creates strategies to reach this objective. Written specific behavioral objectives use verbs which clearly describe observable behavior, figure 4-7.

Cooperating teachers and supervisors differ in requiring activity plans with specific behavioral or instructional objectives. Instructional objectives are more general in nature and may defy measurement. Examples of specific behavioral objectives (SBO) and instructional objectives (IO) follow:

SBO: When given four cubes of different colors (red, blue, green, and purple), the child will point to each color correctly on the first try when asked.

IO: The child will know four colors — red, blue, green, and purple.

SBO: When given a cut potato, paper, and three small trays of paint, the child will make at least one mark on the paper using a printing motion.

IO: The child will explore a printing process.

SBO: After seeing the teacher demonstrate cutting on a penciled line and being helped to hold scissors with the thumb and index finger, the child will cut apart a two-inch strip of pencil-lined paper in two out of five attempts.

IO: The child will learn how to cut on a line.

It is best for beginning teachers to accomplish one objective per activity, doing it thoroughly and well, and keeping the activity short and lively. Student teachers tend to teach activities involving multiple concepts or skills. Usually, none of these skills are accomplished because of the amount and diversity of learning. Objectives of any kind may or may not always be realized. Evaluation sections analyze whether the student teacher achieved what was set out to do. Centers with clearly defined objectives, combining

ask	dry	mix	put hand on	sponge off
attempt to	explore	nail	remove	take
close	find	name	replace	tell
collect	finish	open	return	touch
color	hold	paint	say	turn
comment	jump	paste	select	use
complete	look at	pick	show	use two hands
contribute	make motions	point to	sing	wash
cut	mark	pour	solve	weigh

Fig. 4-7 Verbs used in writing specific behavioral objectives

their teaching team's efforts, have a greater chance of realizing their objectives.

DEVELOPMENTAL SKILLS

Each activity builds upon another. A child's skill and knowledge expands through increased opportunity and experience. Knowing the children's developmental skills makes student teachers aware of their capacities and levels. The ability to sit and focus for a period of minutes can be the requirements in a planned preschool activity, and having the ability to pick up small objects can be part of another. Planning beyond children's capacity occurs because of the student teacher's eagerness to enrich the children's lives and try out different ideas. A close look at the children's achievements and abilities will help the student plan activities which are successful for both the children and the student teacher. Levin and Long comment upon prerequisite skills in relation to new learning.

Each new learning task requires some cognitive prerequisites on the part of the student. These prerequisites help students relate new ideas, skills, or procedures to what they already know, and better understand the instruction. (Levin and Long, p. 6)

GETTING STARTED Planning a first statement which motivates children by creating a desire to know or do increases their attention. Motivational statements need to be studied for appropriateness. Statements which create competition ("The first one who. . .") or are threatening ("If you don't try it, then. . .") cause unnecessary tensions. Appropriate motivational statements strike a child's curiosity and often stimulate the child to action or exploration.

John bought a special pet from the pet shop. I think you'll want to see him.

There are some new items in the collage box for pasting today. Where have you seen a shiny paper like this?

Today you'll be cooking your own snack. Raise your hand if you've seen your mom or dad make pancakes.

Do you remember the sound our coffee can drums made yesterday? There's a bigger drum with a different sound here today. Let's listen.

Focusing activities such as fingerplays, body movement actions, or songs are often used as a "getting started" routine. If planned, this is written in the "getting started" section of the lesson plan. Many teachers find helpful the routine of pausing briefly for silence which signals that children are ready to find out what will happen next. The following types of statements are frequently used.

When I hear the clock ticking, I'll know you're listening. . .

If I see your eyes, I can tell you're ready to find out what we're going to do in the art center today. Martin is ready, Sherry is ready. . .

Lowering the volume of one's voice motivates children to change their behaviors so they can hear. This creates a hushed silence, which is successful for some teachers. Enthusiasm in a teacher's voice and manner is a great attention getter. Children are quick to notice the sparkle in the teacher's eyes or the excitement in the voice tone, stress, and/or pitch, figure 4-8.

Fig. 4-8 The teacher's enthusiasm is contagious. (Courtesy of Nancy Martin)

During an activity's first few minutes, expectations, safety precautions, and reminders concerning class or activity rules should be covered if necessary. Doing so will avoid potential activity problems.

PROCEDURE If an initial demonstration or specific instruction needs expressing, this can be noted and written briefly in a step-by-step fashion. Since involvement is such an important aspect for the young child's learning, active, rather than passive, participation is part of most planned activities.

This section of the plan outlines sequential happenings during the activity. Student teachers must identify important subcomponents chronologically. The student teacher mentally visualizes each step, its particular needs and actions.

DISCUSSION Although teacher discussion and questioning is appropriate for many child activities, it can be intrusive in others. When deeply involved, children do not usually benefit from a break in their concentration. Other activities lead to a vigorous give and take, question and feedback format which helps children's discovery and understanding.

The following questions clarify the written comments that may be included in this lesson plan section.
1. What key points, concepts, ideas, or words do you intend to cover during conversation?
2. What types of questions, inquiries, or voluntary comments might come from the children?
3. Are you going to relate new material to that which was learned previously?

APPLICATION Sometimes an activity leads to an immediate application of a new knowledge or skill. If the idea of a circle was introduced or discovered, finding circular images or objects in the classroom can immediately reinforce the learning. Repetition and practice are key instruments in learning.

EVALUATION Hindsight is a valuable teaching skill. One can evaluate many aspects of a planned and conducted activity. Goal realization, a close look at instructional techniques or methods, and student teacher actions usually come under scrutiny. The following questions can aid activity and self-evaluation:
1. Was the activity location and set-up appropriate?
2. Would you rate the activity as high, middle, or low in interest value and goal realization?
3. What could improve this plan?
4. Should a follow-up activity be planned?
5. Was enough attention given to small details?
6. Did the activity attempt to reach the instructional objectives?
7. Was the activity too long or too short?
8. If you planned to repeat the activity how would you change it?
9. Were you prepared?
10. Which teacher/child interactions went well? Which ones went poorly?
11. Was the size of the group appropriate?
12. Was the activity a success with the children?
13. Was the activity above, at, or below the group's developmental level?
14. What did you learn from the experience?

Evaluation and comments from others will add another dimension. Team meetings usually concentrate on a total day's happenings but may zero in on the student's supervised areas and planned activities.

OTHER ACTIVITY PLAN AREAS Many activity plans pay close attention to clean-up. Usually, both children and adults clean up their shared environment. Drying areas, house-cleaning equipment, and hand washing can be important features of a plan, figure 4-9.

Terminating statements summarize what has been discovered and enjoyed, and tie loose activity ends together, bringing activities to a satisfying group conclusion.

After watching Roddie, the hamster, eat today, Leticia noticed Roddie's two large teeth. Sam plans to bring some peanut butter on toast for Roddie tomorrow to see if he likes it. Ting wants to telephone the pet store to ask the storekeeper what hamsters eat. We decided to get a library book about hamsters to find out. Our list shows Roddie nibbled on celery and lettuce today.

Fig. 4-9 Clean-up time is an important step in activity planning.

TRANSITIONS Transitions are defined as statements that move children in an orderly fashion from one activity to the next.

> After you've placed your clay pot on the drying rack, you can choose to play in the block area or the yard.
>
> Raise your hand if you're wearing long pants that touch your shoes. If your hand is up, get your jacket and meet Carol near the door. Raise your hand if you're wearing a belt today.
>
> Suzette, I can see you're finished. If you look around the room, you'll see something else you want to do. Bill is in the loft reading to Petra and Alphonso.

USING COMMUNITY RESOURCES   The whole community is a learning resource for young children's activities. Each neighborhood has unique features and people with special talents and collections. Industries, businesses, and job sites may provide field trip opportunities, resource speakers, or activity material "give-aways." Cultural events and celebrations, ethnic holidays, parks and recreation areas, and buildings easily integrate into the school's activities and promote a "reality-based" children's program.

PITFALLS   The biggest pitfall for the student teacher is the tendency to stick to the plan when children's feedback during the activity does not warrant it. Teachers should take their cues from the children's interest and encourage its growth. Expanding the children's interest can mean spending additional time, providing additional opportunities and materials. In some cases, it can mean just talking about it if the children want to know and do more.

If children's interest cuts into other activities, some activities can be postponed. Others may be revised to fit into the schedule. The unforeseen is always happening. It sometimes captures and holds the children's attention. Getting the children to refocus on a planned activity may mean having to clear the children's minds of something more important to them.

Teachers usually try to relate unexpected occurrences to the planned activity. For example, "That was a loud booming noise. We can listen for another while we finish shaping our bread before it goes into the oven." If efforts to refocus fail, a teacher knows the written plan has been preempted.

A real teaching skill involves using unplanned events to promote identified specific curriculum objectives or objectives which were not even considered but are currently timely and important.

TEACHING TIPS   As mentioned before, your enthusiasm while presenting the lesson plan must be emphasized. When your eyes sparkle and your voice sounds excited about what you and the children are accomplishing, the children will probably remain interested and focused. Your level of enthusiasm needs to be genuine and appropriate.

You will be eager to start the activities you have designed. You will be anxious to see if you have captured the children's attention and stimulated their developmental growth. When you feel that the group joins in your excitement and discovery, no other reward is necessary.

Look for the unexpected to happen during your activities. Children will see things that you do not, ask unexpected questions, and make statements you will find a challenge to understand. Listen closely to the children's responses. If you cannot understand them, probe further. More often than not, you will understand the wisdom of their thoughts which are based on their unique past experience.

Do not panic when a child corrects you or you do not have an answer. Develop a "we'll find out together" attitude. A teacher who has all the answers often fails to notice the brilliance, charm, and honesty of children.

Summary

Planning, presenting, and evaluating activities is a part of student teaching. Written activity plans are usually required and encourage student teachers to examine closely all aspects of their curriculum. Guidelines and criteria for planning activities promote overall success. Consultation with teachers often aids in the development of written plans. Learning objectives can be written as instructional objectives or in measurable specific behavioral objective terms.

A number of lesson plan forms exist; this text provides one suggested form. Preparing a written plan allows greater student teacher confidence and less stress, and averts potential problems. A lesson plan is only a starting point, and has the flexibility to change or be discontinued during its presentation, depending on interest and need among the children.

Many planned activities do not need to be put into lesson plan form because of their simplicity or their focus on creative expression. Lesson plans are a beginning teacher's attempt to be thoroughly prepared.

Suggested Activities

A. Collect and compare lesson plan forms.

B. Invite practicing teachers to discuss the merits of written lesson plans.

C. In groups of two to four, identify which activity plan section needs greater attention by the student teacher in the following situations.

1. Danielle is presenting an activity with her collection of seashells. She has repeatedly requested that children look while she explains the details of the shells. Most of the children who started the activity are showing signs of disinterest.

2. Jerome introduced a boat-floating activity that has children excited to try it. The children start pushing, shoving, and crowding.

3. Frank prepared an activity with airplanes landing on a tabletop landing strip. Children are zooming loudly and running about the room, interfering with the work of others. The situation is getting out of hand.

4. Claire's activity involves making a greeting card. Many children are disappointed because Claire has run out of metallic paper which was used for her sample card. Others are requesting help because their fingers are sticky with glue.

5. Kate's activity making cinnamon toast works well until Joey burns his finger on the toaster oven.

6. Spencer has given a detailed verbal explanation of how the children should finish the weaving project he has introduced. However, the children seem to have lost interest already.

7. During Jackie Ann's project, paint gets on the door handles, and the children are unable to turn on the faucets because of slippery hands.

8. Chris and Katrina have combined efforts during an activity. They have spent ten minutes returning the area to usable condition for the next activity.

D. In groups of two to three, write up a plan using a form similar to figure 4-5. Fill in those lesson plan sections which seem to fit your idea. Give it to your instructor for comments.

E. Using the criteria in this unit, rate the following student teacher statements or actions as A (appropriate), U (unsure), or I (inappropriate). Briefly state why you judged any inappropriate actions as such.

1. Doug offers an activity which involves a demonstration by two local karate experts.

2. Children are assisted in making and frying donuts.

3. The children are making Mother's Day cards. Josh asks, "Can I make a Mother's Day card for my dad?" Tisha responds, "Father's Day is next month. We'll do it then, Josh."

4. "In just a minute you'll be able to shake our butter-making jar. Mick's turn is first, then Alfie, Christa, Dana, Martin, and Ali."

5. "Sure you can do it," Cantrell, the student teacher, says. The planned activity involves drawing and cutting a boat before pasting it on the class mural.

6. "Let me show you how this works," Rob says during his planned activity. "This handle goes up, then the lid opens. You reach in for the small box. It opens if you push down. Now I'll tell you how this one opens. It has a key. First, I'll put it here in the lock. Lucy, what did you say? Well, I wish you could try it, but these are very valuable boxes so today you can watch, and I'll show you."

7. "Here's the way pieces of wood are sanded to make them smooth. You'll have your own piece of wood and your own sandpaper to use. Feel your wood. How does it feel? Rough and scratchy? Does your hand slide across it easily? Feel this one now."

F. In groups of five or six, discuss why many activities are not prepared in written lesson plan form. Share key ideas with the total group.

Review

A. List two ways to identify children's interests.

B. Write three examples of motivational statements for activities you plan to present or could present.

C. Define:
Curriculum
Transition
Specific behavioral objective
Motivation

D. Write three examples of specific behavioral objectives.

E. Write three examples of transitional statements.

F. Match items in Column I with those in Column II.

I	II
1. curriculum area	a. ethnic dance group
2. specific behavioral objective	b. "Those with red socks can wash their hands for lunch."
3. transitional statement	c. four out of five times
4. motivational statement	d. "Snails have one foot which slides along on a slippery liquid which comes from the snail."
5. an activity plan criterion	e. nutrition
6. set-up	f. has three parts
7. community resource	g. "Have you ever touched a bird's feathers?"
8. performance criterion	h. too many concepts attempted
9. summary statement	i. paper left, then patterns, crayons, scissors at far right on table
10. pitfall in student teacher lesson planning	j. child safety

G. Write your feelings concerning written activity plans. How long do you feel they should be for activity planning and preparation?

Resources

Holt, John. *How Children Fail*. New York: Dell Publishing Co., 1964.

Hunt, Joseph McVicker. "Reflections on a Decade of Early Childhood Education." Urbana, IL: ERIC Clearinghouse in Early Childhood Education, 1974.

Levin, Tamar, and Long, Ruth. *Effective Instruction*. Alexandria, VA: The Association for Supervision and Curriculum Development, 1981.

Litman, Frances. "Supervision and the Involvement of Paraprofessionals in Early Childhood Education," from Anderson, Robert H., and Shane, Harold G., *As The Twig is Bent*. Boston: Houghton Mifflin Co., 1971.

Mager, Robert F., Ph.D. *Preparing Instructional Objectives*. Belmont, CA: Fearon-Pitman Pubs., Inc., 1962.

Piaget, Jean, from film "Patron: Piaget in New Perspective." New York: Parents Magazine Films, Inc.

Schickedanz, Judith A., York, Mary E., Stewart, Ida Santos, White, Doris. *Strategies for Teaching Young Children*. Englewood Cliffs, NJ: Prentice-Hall, Inc., 1977.

Unit 5
Instruction — Circle Times and Teaching Units

OBJECTIVES

After studying this unit, the student will be able to:

- Plan a circle time activity.
- Discuss factors which promote circle time success.
- Describe a teaching unit (theme) approach to early childhood instruction.
- Cite two possible benefits and limitations of theme-centered curriculums.
- Outline preparation steps in theme construction.

CIRCLE EXPERIENCES

Circle times can be a real concern for beginning teachers and student teachers. Circle times can run the extremes of falling flat, boring children, ending in complete chaos, or being an eagerly awaited highlight of the day.

Teachers know when the children are "with" them, figure 5-1. The children's questions can be abundant and rapid as they press to know and experience. A hushed silence may happen as children become awed and enthralled. There are times the children strain to hear, see, taste, smell, and touch whatever captures their interest. At these times student teachers feel competent and valuable.

DIFFERENT CIRCLE PROGRAMS   Circle times differ greatly between programs. They are alike

Fig. 5-1 Every child is focused on this planned activity.

because usually the whole group is present. Some schools, however, prefer to have instant replays or two concurrent circles to preserve the intimacy of a small group. Instructional intent is often dissimilar. Some circles are conducted mainly for roll call and announcing information about the day's special activities. Others may handle classroom problems, offer new learnings, language, literature, and music, or combine features. The student teacher can attempt to duplicate the cooperating teacher's circle or discuss and plan, with the cooperating teacher's approval, another type.

CIRCLE TIME PURPOSE

It pays to think about and analyze circle elements that promote success. Student teachers will tend to imitate their cooperating teachers' circles, and carry them into their own future classrooms.

Identifying the purpose of circle times precedes their planning. During these times, the children not only learn but draw conclusions about themselves as learners. The following goals for planned circles are considered to be most important:

- Preserving each child's feeling of personal competence as a learner.
- Strengthening each child's idea of self-worth and uniqueness.
- Promoting a sense of comfortableness with peers and the teaching team.
- Helping children gain group attendance skills such as listening to others, offering ideas, taking turns, etc.
- Helping children want to find out about the world, its creatures, and diversity; helping children preserve their sense of wonder and discovery.

CHILD CHARACTERISTICS AND CIRCLE TIMES

How can circle time become what you would like it to be? Go back in your memory to age and stage characteristics. Group times are based upon what a teacher knows about the children for whom activities are planned. The children's endurance, need for movement, need to touch, enjoyment of singing, chanting, ability to attend, etc. are all taken into consideration. The dynamics of the group setting and the children themselves can affect circle progress. Two children seated together could mean horsing around. Maybe some children have sight or hearing problems. Perhaps there is a child who talks on and on at circles. All situations of this nature should be given consideration.

PLANNING

Student teachers often plan their circle times with other adults. The following planning decisions are usually discussed:

- Which adults will lead? Which adults will be aides?
- When and where? How long? How will the children be seated?
- What will be the instructional topics, activities, and goals?
- How many adults and children will attend?
- Will there be one presentation or instant replays?
- What materials or audiovisuals will be needed?
- Who will prepare needed materials?
- How will children be gathered?
- In what order will events happen?
- Can the children actively participate?
- Will a vigorous activity be followed with a slow one?
- Will children share in leading?
- How will the results of circle time be reviewed or tied together if necessary?
- How will children leave at the conclusion?

There seem to be distinct stages of circle times. For example, there is the gathering of children and adults. This then leads to a focusing of the children's attention. There is a joint recognition of the persons present at circle time. At that point, someone begins to lead and present the activity. This is followed by the children participating and reacting. In the final stage of circle time, there can be a brief summary and then a disbanding.

BUILDING ATTENTION AND INTEREST

Teachers use various methods to gather the children and get their attention.

- A signal like a bell or clean-up song helps to build anticipation.

"When you hear the xylophone, you'll know it's time to. . ."

- A verbal reminder to individual children lets them know that circle time is starting soon.

"In five minutes we'll be starting circle time in the loft, Tina. You need to finish your block building."

In order to help the children focus, the teacher might initiate a song, fingerplay, chant, or dance in which all perform a similar act. Many circle leaders then build a sense of enthusiasm in one another by recognizing each child and adult. An interesting roll call, a "selecting nametags" activity, or a simple statement like "Who are friends at circle time today?" are good techniques. Children enjoy being identified.

"Bill is wearing his red shirt, red shirt, red shirt...
Bill is wearing his red shirt at circle time today.
Katrina has her hair cut, hair cut. . ."

To build motivation or enthusiasm, some teachers drop their voice volume to a whisper. Others "light up" facially or bodily, showing their enthusiasm. The object is to capture interest and build a desire in the children to want to know or find out. Statements like:

"We're now going to read a story about. . ."

or

"You're going to learn to count to six today. . ."

do not excite children. In contrast, statements like:

"There's something in my pocket I brought to show you. . ."

or

"Raise your hand if you can hear this tiny bell. . ."

build the children's interest and curiosity. Tone of voice and manner will be a dead giveaway as to whether wonder and discovery is alive in the teacher. Teachers should use natural conversation. Unfortunately, sometimes a television voice or a forced enthusiasm occurs. Presenting material or topics (of an appropriate age level) close to the heart of the presenter is a key element. Experiences from one's own love of life can be a necessary ingredient. New teachers and student teachers should rely on their own creativity and use circles to share themselves rather than try to follow someone else's script.

PRACTICE If memorized songs, fingerplays, or chants are part of the circle, practice is necessary. Time spent preparing and practicing will promote a relaxed presenter. Lap cards may be used as insurance if the leader forgets under pressure. These items are suggested if they make a student teacher feel more confident.

Practice sessions often alert the student teacher to whether most of the circle time activity is lead by the teacher, and children do little more than listen. If so, there is time to redesign the activity.

TECHNIQUES A student teacher's circle time awareness and verbalizations promote goal realization and success. Feedback from children and adults needs to be monitored while presenting. For example, seeing a child hesitate may cue the presenter to repeat and emphasize words. It is worthwhile to see what really interests the children and spend additional time with the activity. Sometimes, even the best circle time plans are discarded, revised, or created based on feedback.

One technique that helps recognize individuality is giving credit to each child's idea. "John says he saw a fox in the woods, Mike thinks it was a wolf, and Debbie says it looked like a cat." Bringing a child back to focus by naming him or asking a question is common. "Todd, this dog looks like your dog, Ranger" or "Todd, can you show us. . .?"

Handling child behaviors during circle time can distract a student teacher and upset the sequence of thought. Quick statements such as "If everyone is sitting down, you all will be able to see" or "I like the way Mei-Lee and Josh are waiting for a turn" helps curb distracting behaviors. A circle leader can be very grateful for an alert aide or assistant teacher to handle group or individual behaviors so the circle time can proceed.

TRANSITIONS To end circle times, a transition statement or activity is used. The transition statement should create an orderly departure rather than a thundering herd or questionable ending of circle time. There are thousands of possibilities for disbanding the group one by one. Some examples are:

"Raise your hand if your favorite ice cream is chocolate. Alfredo and Monica, you may choose which area in the room you are going to now."

"People with curly hair stand up."

"Put your hand on your stomach if you had cornflakes for breakfast."

"Peter, Dana, and Kingston, pretend you are mice and quietly sneak out the door to the yard."

EVALUATION If time and supervision permits, you should analyze your circle after you have relaxed and reflected on its particulars. Hindsight is valuable now. If possible, you might consider video taping your circle time. This offers tremendous growth opportunities. Listen closely to the supervisor's and cooperating teacher's objective comments and suggested improvements.

UNIT TEACHING

The unit (theme) approach to child program planning is popular in many early childhood centers. A unit includes a written collection of activity ideas on one subject, idea, or skill such as butterflies, homes, neighborhood, kindness, friendship, biking, swimming, jogging, etc. Activities within the unit encompass a wide range of curriculum areas including art, music, numbers, science, small and large motor development, etc. A unit's course of study involves a day, week, or longer period; one week is typical. Though usually preplanned, units can be developed after a child's or group's interest is recognized. Units differ from teacher to teacher and school to school; each offers a unique collection and presentation of activities.

POSSIBLE INSTRUCTIONAL BENEFITS
There are a number of reasons for using the theme approach in young children's instruction. Some major ideas are as follows:

- A unit tackles instruction through a wide variety of activities which reinforce child learning as the same new ideas, facts, skills, and attitudes are encountered through different routes. Discovery and deductions happen in varied activities, keeping classrooms enthusiastic and alive.
- The classroom environment can be "saturated" with activities and materials on the same subject.
- A unit approach lets children gather, explore, and experience the theme at their own pace and level of understanding because of the number of choices in room activities and materials.
- Planned group times offer shared experiences and knowledge.
- Teachers can identify and gather unit materials for future use, saving time and energy.
- Teachers can guide child discovery better through knowledge gained from their own research during unit preparation and construction.
- Community resources become classroom materials, and community uniqueness is incorporated into instruction.
- The teacher is aided in collecting and developing audiovisuals and "real objects," figure 5-2.

Fig. 5-2 The subject of butterflies is a possible study theme which will interest the children. (Courtesy of San Jose City College Child Development Center)

Fig. 5-3 Class pets can lead to a unit about animals.

- A theme can evolve from the unplanned and unexpected, giving curriculum flexibility.
- The teacher's and children's creativity and resourcefulness are encouraged and challenged.
- Once the environment is set, the teacher is free to help uninvolved individuals and interact intimately with the highly focused children.
- The classroom environment becomes a dynamic, changing, exciting place for both children and adults, figure 5-3.
- A unit can provide a security blanket for new teachers outlining a plan for one week's activities.

POSSIBLE LIMITATIONS OR WEAKNESSES
Critics of unit teaching mention several limitations of this type of program.
- Once developed, units tend to become a teacher-dictated curriculum.
- A reliance on this crutch produces dated programs.
- Units may not be closely evaluated or critically analyzed for appropriateness during construction.
- Unit teaching promotes the copying of teaching techniques rather than the developing of individual styles.
- A dependence on commercial materials can add expense and lose child interest.

- Unit teaching promotes the idea that preplanned units are a preferred way to teach.
- Units often overlook geographic, socioeconomic, and cultural factors.
- Units impose one child's or teacher's interest upon the whole group.
- Units may be used to compare teachers.

UNIT SUBSECTIONS Units have many subsections. Based on teaching preferences and teacher decisions, each section is either present or absent. Subsection listings contain a description of contents:
- *Title page* includes theme identification, author's credit line, ages of children, classroom location, and descriptive and/or decorative art.
- *Table of contents* lists subsections and beginning pages.
- *Instructional goals description* contains author's identification of concepts, ideas, factual data, vocabulary, attitudes, and skills in the unit.
- *Background data* is researched background information with theme particulars useful in updating adults on the subject. Technical drawings and photos can be included.
- *Resource list* includes teacher-made and commercial materials (names and addresses) and/or supplies. Also contains audiovisuals, community resources, consultants, speakers, field trip possibilities, and inexpensive sources of materials.
- *Weekly time schedule* pinpoints times and activities, supervising adults, and duration of activity.
- *Suggested activities* uses activity plans, procedure descriptions, and/or plans room settings, centers, and environments.
- *Children's book lists* identifies the theme of children's books.
- *Activity aids* describes patterns, fingerplays, poems, storytelling ideas, recipes, chart ideas, teacher-made aids and equipment, ideas and directions, and bulletin board diagrams, figure 5-4.
- *Culminating activities* offers suggestions for final celebrations or events which have summarizing, unifying, and reviewing features.

Fig. 5-4 Children helped paste the giant apples which were part of a unit on kinds of fruit.

- *Bibliography* lists adult resource books on unit subject.
- *Evaluation* contains comments concerning instructional value, unit conduct, and revisional needs.

HOW TO CONSTRUCT A UNIT Initial work begins by choosing a subject. Then data is collected and researched. Next, brainstorming (mental generating of ideas) and envisioning "saturated" classroom environments take place. Instructional decisions concerning the scope of the proposed child course of study are made. The search for materials and resources starts. Instructional goals and objectives are identified, and activities are created. A tentative plan of activities is compiled and analyzed. After materials, supplies, and visual aids have been made or obtained, a final written plan is completed. The unit is conducted, concluded, and evaluated. Each aspect of instruction is assessed. Notes concerning unit particulars are reviewed, and unit revisions, additions, or omissions are recorded. The unit's written materials are stored

in a binder for protection. Other items may be boxed.

Units can be an individual, team, or group effort. Developing a unit during student teaching creates a desired job skill and may aid in preparing for the first job. A written theme, finished during student teaching, can display competency and become a valuable visual aid for job interviews.

SATURATED ENVIRONMENT Thinking up ways to incorporate a unit's theme into the routine, room, yard, food service, wall space, etc. means using your creativity. Background music, room color, the teacher's clothing, and lighting can reflect a theme. The environment becomes transformed. Butterfly-shaped crackers, green cream of wheat, special teacher-made theme puzzles, face painting, and countless other possibilities exist. Do not forget child motor involvement, and child and adult enactment of theme-related concepts and skills.

A student teacher-authored unit found in the Appendix shows creativity in unit construction. Figure 5-5 shows one school's planning for unit instruction for the calendar year.

Summary

Each classroom's circle times differ in intent and purpose. Student teachers plan and present circle times after carefully analyzing the goals of circle time and the group's particular dynamics, needs, and learning level. Many decisions affect the smooth, successful flow as different stages evolve. Technique, preparation, presentation, and goal realization are all factors which should be evaluated.

Unit teaching is a popular instructional approach. However, there are different views of the benefits and limitations of unit teaching. Construction of a teaching unit includes theme identification, research, decisions concerning instructional objectives, activity development in a wide range of curriculum areas, and gathering of materials, supplies, and teaching aids. Each unit is a unique collection of activities planned for a specific group of young children, and should take into consideration their particular geographic,

Preschool themes		Themes for toddlers and two-year-olds	
Jan. 30–Feb. 3	Color in My World	Jan. 30–Feb. 3	Getting Reacquainted (getting used to school)
	Groundhog Day		
Feb. 6–Feb. 10	Color in My World	Feb. 6–Feb. 10	Ourselves (our names and body parts)
	National Dental Week		
	Getting ready for Valentine's Day	Feb. 13–Feb. 17	Ourselves (body parts)
		Feb. 20–Feb. 24	Sounds and Sights
	Chinese New Year	Feb. 27–Mar. 3	Textures and Touch
	Abraham Lincoln's Birthday	Mar. 6–Mar. 10	Farm Animals (horse, cow, sheep, chicken)
Feb. 13–Feb. 17	Black History Week		
	Valentine's Day	Mar. 13–Mar. 17	Pet Animals (dog, cat, rabbit, hamster)
	George Washington's Birthday		
		Mar. 20–Mar. 24	Spring Vacation
Feb. 20–Feb. 24	International Friendship Week	Mar. 27–Mar. 31	Insects and Spiders (bees, spiders, ladybugs)
Feb. 27–Mar. 3	Five Senses		
Mar. 6–Mar. 10	Transportation	Apr. 3–Apr. 7	Zoo Animals (lion, tiger giraffe, elephant)
Mar. 13–Mar. 17	Easter, St. Patrick's Day		
Mar. 20–Mar. 31	Weather, Japanese Am. Wk.	Apr. 10–Apr. 14	Fruits (apple, orange, banana, pear)
Apr. 3–Apr. 7	Planting Seeds, Flowers	Apr. 17–Apr. 21	Vegetables (carrot, zucchini, celery, lettuce)
Apr. 10–Apr. 14	Birds		
Apr. 17–Apr. 21	Bugs & Insects	Apr. 24–Apr. 28	Colors (red, blue, green, yellow, brown)
Apr. 24–Apr. 28	Animals of the Woods		
	Arbor Day	May 1–May 5	Colors (continued from Apr. 24–28)
May 1–May 5	Lei Day, May Day	May 8–May 12	Families (Mother's Day)
	National Be Kind to Animals Week	May 15–May 19	Sizes (large, small, in-between)
	Cinco de Mayo, Japanese Boys Day		
May 8–May 12	Mother's Day		
May 15–May 26	Community Helper		

Fig. 5-5 Sample of theme curriculum

socioeconomic, and cultural setting. The choice of unit sequence and subsectioning is up to the individual. After a unit is presented, it is evaluated by the author for improvement.

Suggested Activities

A. Plan and present a circle time activity. Use figure 5-6 as a guide.

1.	Topic?	6.	Materials?
2.	Time and place?	7.	Preparation and practice?
3.	Number of children?	8.	Circle sequence?
4.	Adults present?	9.	Evaluation?
5.	Goals?		

Fig. 5-6 Circle time planning guide

B. List the advantages in conducting a circle time with seven to ten children rather fifteen to twenty children.

C. Visit a student teacher's classroom to observe a circle time. Time its length. Analyze its goals and success. Keep the discussion confidential.

D. In groups of five to six, discuss ways to increase children's active participation in circle times.

E. In groups of five to six, develop a list of themes which you feel would interest the children at your placement site.

F. After the class has been divided in half, select either the "pro" or "con" views of unit teaching as an instructional approach. Use twenty minutes to plan for a debate in a future class. Invite four or five parents of preschoolers to react to the debate.

G. Interview three practicing teachers concerning their views of unit teaching.

H. With a group of three others, identify five instructional objectives for the following themes: friendship, pets, automobiles, things that taste sweet, grandparents.

I. Develop a unit individually, in pairs, or with a group of others. Prepare copies to present to the class, and discuss sharing and trading units.

J. Examine figures 5-7 and 5-8, and develop a flowchart on the concepts of boats, vehicles, houses, or a subject of your own choosing.

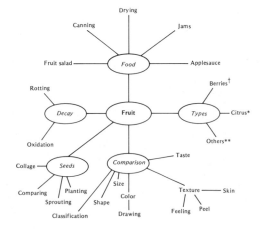

*Citrus fruits include oranges, tangerines, lemons, limes, and grapefruit.
**Others include apples, bananas, plums, peaches, cherries, pears, apricots, raisins, figs, grapes, and nectarines.
†Berries include blueberries, raspberries, strawberries, and boysenberries.

Fig. 5-7 Conceptual flowchart on fruit (From *Teaching Young Children* by Joan M. Bergstrom and Rose K. Margosian. Columbus, OH: Charles E. Merrill Publishing Co., 1977.)

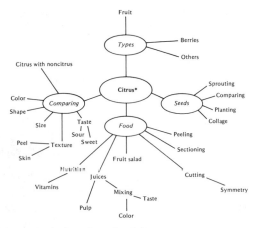

*Citrus fruits include oranges, tangerines, lemons, limes, and grapefruit.

Fig. 5-8 Flowchart of the emerging curriculum related to the concept "fruit" (From *Teaching Young Children* by Joan M. Bergstrom and Rose K. Margosian. Columbus, OH: Charles E. Merrill Publishing Co., 1977.)

Review

A. List subsections of common circle times.

B. Describe five important considerations when a student teacher is planning to conduct a twenty-minute circle time with fifteen four-year-olds.

C. Complete the following statements.
1. Two ways to improve a teacher's skills in conducting circles are. . .
2. Activities which approach the same knowledge through art, music, science, cooking, measurement activities, and language activities can reinforce. . .
3. A "saturated" environment might be described as. . .
4. Using a unit developed in another section of the country is probably. . .

D. List possible unit subsections.

E. Identify the items listed below as subsection (S) or part of a subsection (P).
1. child activities
2. child skill level
3. adult/child ratio
4. teacher evaluation
5. weekly time schedule
6. furniture and comfort
7. child safety
8. index
9. culminating activity
10. table of contents
11. artistic decoration
12. instructional goals description
13. resource list
14. cultural values
15. background data
16. audiovisuals and real objects
17. title page
18. balance of curriculum areas
19. book lists
20. bibliography

F. List what you believe are two benefits and two limitations of unit teaching.

G. Describe the use of unit teaching in your future teaching responsibilities.

Section 3
Guidance Revisited

Unit 6
Guidance Goals and Techniques

OBJECTIVES

After studying this unit, the student will be able to:

- List three major guidance areas.
- Discuss classroom environmental factors which influence child behaviors.
- List and describe five common guidance techniques.
- Define rapport and its relationship to child guidance.
- Identify child behaviors used in resisting adult authority.
- List the seven elements of a behavior modification plan.
- Design, implement, and evaluate a behavior modification plan.
- Analyze what guidance techniques work best and state why.

THE GUIDANCE FUNCTION

When we think of the guidance function in the classroom, what do we mean? Guidance can be the act or function of guiding; it can mean leadership or directing someone to a destination or goal. In the classroom, guidance is the teacher's function of providing leadership. In particular, it is the act of assisting the child to grow toward maturity. This is the major goal.

There are many functions for the teacher to perform in order to achieve this goal. Each choice regarding curriculum, for example, can be seen as one part of the total guidance function. What materials you set out for the children to explore is another; whether materials such as puzzles and blocks, scissors and paste pots, crayons and paper are used only under your direction is a third. The physical arrangement of the classroom is another. Are the play blocks easy to reach? Is your housekeeping corner attractive? Do you have enough dress-up clothes to stimulate a variety of role plays in sociodramatic play? Is there a quiet corner where children can look at books (figure 6-1)? Is there plenty of space, especially outside, for active play? Do children have an opportunity to climb, run, and ride wheeled toys without endangering each other's safety?

Perhaps the guidance function about which you hear the most is discipline. Like guidance, discipline is frequently misunderstood. Seen most commonly in a negative way, discipline has its positive meaning. Instruction and training in proper conduct or action is one meaning; it is, perhaps, more positive than the more common meaning — punishment. Discipline can also be seen as the training effect of experience and as learning a set of rules and regulations.

Teachers often use the word *undisciplined* in describing a child who does not know how to control behavior, usually aggressive. The timid, shy child can also be undisciplined in that the child is overly controlled. This child has learned as little about self-discipline as the underdisciplined child. Neither child knows how to regulate behavior according to social norms or standards. Both children need instruction and training in proper conduct. The question arises regarding how to provide such instruction and training. Very young children learn to behave according to societal standards through the

Fig. 6-1 **A book can be enjoyed in a quiet, comfortable area.**

training received at home. However, many parents simply do not know how or are unwilling to do the early training that produces a self-disciplined child by age three. Even parents who understand some things about their children's needs may fail to maintain the consistency of adult behavior that is essential to the children's positive growth.

So, what is the teacher to do? One set of guidelines is the 4 c's: *consistency, considerateness, confidence,* and *candor.* What is meant by consistency? Consistency of adult behavior, consistency of expectations, consistency of limits and rules. Consistency means that you understand yourself well enough so that you can respond to children in a fair and impartial manner. It also means reliability; your behavior does not change from day to day and remains reasonably predictable to the children. For children, there is safety in knowing that the adults in their lives are predictable. Such reliability gives children feelings of security and safety. This becomes especially important when you, as a student teacher, are responsible for children who may be inconsistent and unpredictable.

The second "c" is considerateness. This means that you are considerate of the children you teach and of the adults with whom you work. You respect the children, and are aware of their needs, their likes, and dislikes. You are considerate by taking time to listen, even to the child who talks constantly. It means watching all of the children closely, and noting which child needs an extra hug and which one needs to be removed from a group before a temper tantrum erupts. All of these actions show children that you care, and will help you establish a warm relationship with them. Considerateness helps to build rapport.

The third "c" is confidence. You need confidence to make decisions that reflect careful thought on your part, decisions that are free of bias and based on all evidence. Confidence implies that you realize you like some children better than others, and you know why you react differently to identical actions involving different children. Confidence is knowing when to stand up for your opinions and decisions and when to compromise. It means understanding when to be silent, knowing that waiting is the more mature action to take.

Candor, the fourth "c," means that you are open and honest in your interactions with the children, your fellow workers, and yourself. It means being frank and fair; you may inevitably "put your foot in your mouth," but you will gain a reputation for being honest in your relations with others. Candor is the ability to admit a mistake and being unafraid to apologize.

The four c's can perhaps be spelled CARE. As Rogers (1966) wrote, good teachers possess three qualities: congruence, acceptance of others, and empathy. These can easily be expanded to four: congruence, acceptance, *reliability*, and empathy, figure 6-2.

Congruence is Rogers' term for understanding yourself. Always remember that with truly great teachers, their teaching is such an extension of themselves that you see the same person whether that person is in the classroom, the office, the home, or the supermarket. These people radiate self-confidence in knowing who they are and what they want from life. It is sometimes difficult for the student teacher to copy the congruent teacher, for the methods the teacher uses are so much a part of that person that the student teacher may not be able to emulate. This is related to the second goal of guidance — knowing yourself.

What you as a student teacher must learn is what methods are congruent with your inner self. The best methods are always those which seem natural to use,

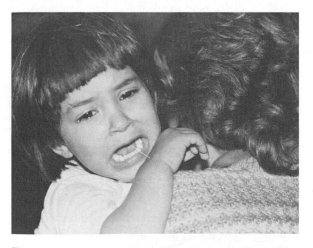

Fig. 6-2 Student teaching offers many opportunities to show children you CARE.

those which are an extension of how you feel about yourself.

Acceptance in the Rogerian sense means truly caring about each child you teach. It means all children deserve your respect regardless of how they act. The aggressive, "acting-out" child is just as deserving of your acceptance as the star pupil of the class.

As mentioned, reliability means that your children know you and the routine for the class. Being reliable also implies fairness.

According to Rogers, empathy implies being able to place yourself in the child's shoes, of seeing from that perspective. It is the ability to see that the hostile, aggressive child needs love and acceptance more than the happy, easygoing child does. Empathy also means knowing that the happy child needs attention even though it is not demanded. Learn to be empathetic; it is worth the effort.

Let us assume that you have learned how to CARE. Does that mean you will not have any behavior problems? Does that mean you will automatically have rapport with all your children? Of course not. It only means that you can, perhaps, understand children's behavior more easily and plan to teach self-discipline to those who need to learn.

GUIDANCE TECHNIQUES

Now let us look at specific techniques you might use to manage some of the problems you will encounter in any classroom. At the same time, do not forget the broader meaning of the term guidance.

In its narrower sense of classroom or behavior management, guidance refers to those things you do to teach or persuade the children to behave in a manner of which you approve. There are many ways to manage behavior; but there are four which have proven to be more effective than others: (1) behavior modification; (2) setting limits and insisting they be kept; (3) labeling the behavior instead of the child; and (4) teacher anticipation and intervention.

BEHAVIOR MODIFICATION In terms of behavior modification, it is important to be objective. The term has acquired a negative connotation that is unfounded. Everyone uses behavior modification, whether it is recognized or not, from turning off the lights when children are to be quiet to planning and implementing a behavior modification plan. In any plan, there are seven steps:

1. Keep a log of observations on the child. Really look at what the child is doing. Do this at least five times a day, for at least three days in a row, figure 6-3.
2. Read your observations; look for patterns. Is this child predictable? Does he or she usually have a temper tantrum around 9:30 a.m.? Does the child often fight with another in late afternoon?
3. Look for the reinforcers of the behavior noted in your observations. Does the child misbehave in order to get attention from the adults in the room? Do friends admire the behavior?

4. Decide on a schedule of reinforcement after finding the current reinforcer.
5. Implement the new reinforcement schedule. Give it time. Many teachers fail to use a reinforcement plan for a long enough period of time. Try a minimum of two weeks to two or three months. (Behavior that has taken two or three years to develop will not change in one or two days.)
6. Keep a second log of observations. On the basis of your study of the initial observations, analyze this second series and note whether your reinforcement schedule has worked.
7. Stop your planned reinforcement schedule. See if the child goes back to the former pattern of behavior. If so, go back to the second step and start over.

Student Teacher: _____

Name of School: _____   Date: _____

Identity Key (do NOT use real name)	Description of What Child is Doing	Time	Comments
M – Maria T – Teacher ST – Student Teacher S – Susie J – Janine B – Bobby Sv – Stevie	M arrives at school. Clings to mother's hand, hides behind her skirt. Thumb in mouth.	9:05	Ask T how long M has been coming. I bet she's new.
	M goes over to puzzle rack, chooses a puzzle, goes to table. Dumps out, and works puzzle quickly and quietly. B & Sv come over to work puzzles they've chosen. M looks at them, says nothing, goes to easles, watches S paint. S asks M if she wants to paint. M doesn't answer.	9:22 9:30	Her eye/hand coordination seems good. I wonder why M doesn't respond. Ask T if M has hearing problem.
	M comes to snack table, sits down where T indicates she should. Does not interact with other children at table.	10:15	Is M ever a quiet child!
	M stands outside of playhouse, watches S & J. They don't ask her to join them.	10:47	She looks like she'd like to play.
	M goes right to swings, knows how to pump.	10:55	Nothing wrong with her coordination.
	During Hap Palmer record M watches others, does not follow directions.	11:17	Hearing? Maybe limited English? (She looks of Spanish background.)

Fig. 6-3 Anecdotal record form

Look at the second and third steps. You have completed your observations and now you need to find the reinforcers of the observed behavior. The behavior must bring some kind of reward to the child. As the teacher, you job is to discover what the reward is.

Many student teachers fail to understand the nature of a child's reward system. You look at what an adult perceives as negative behavior (hitting another child, for example), and may decide to institute a schedule of reinforcement or a behavior modification plan without taking that first step, understanding why the child hits.

Study step 4; planning a reinforcement schedule. Look at the child in the sample log (figure 6-3). Assume that the description of behavior is typical of Maria's everyday behavior.

In your analysis of the log, what do you see? Three questions have been raised: Is Maria fairly new to the school? Does she have a hearing problem? Is she bilingual or does she have limited understanding of English? The answers to these questions come during the discussion of observations. Yes, Maria is new to the school. This is only her second week. No, she does not have a hearing problem, but she is bilingual. In fact, the cooperating teacher suspects that Maria may be less bilingual than her mother claims. What has reinforced Maria's behavior? First, she is unfamiliar with English. Second, her cultural background is different. Girls of Spanish background are often expected to be quiet, helpful around the house, and obedient to their elders. Certainly, this explains Maria's behavior, for she willingly helps with clean-up. What are appropriate goals for Maria? Assume that you and your cooperating teacher decide that the most appropriate goal is to help Maria feel more comfortable in the room and that adult approval is the most logical reinforcer to use. Your reinforcement schedule might start by greeting Maria at the door every day when she arrives. Smile at her and say, "Buenas días Maria. It's nice to see you today." Take her by the hand and go with her to a different activity each day. (If Maria seems uncomfortable changing activities so often, stay with the activities she enjoys at first.) Introduce her to the other children at the activity she chooses. Take advantage of the fact that Susie is one of the more mature, self-confident children in the room, and quietly ask her to include Maria in some of her activities. Instead of allowing Maria to watch Susie paint, go to Maria with her painting smock, put it on her, and suggest that she try the activity. When she does pick up the brush and experiment with painting, compliment her action.

Do not worry about Maria's lack of knowledge of the English language. When Maria hesitates, use pointing and naming to help her. Accept the fact that Maria may always be a shy child; do not push her to be outgoing if that is not her nature.

Continue these activities every day. After a few weeks, make another set of observations. (You may not need this step; you may already see the difference.) Still, it is good practice to do the second observation just to check on your feelings. It is more than likely that Maria is already greeting you with a smile as she enters, and that she is beginning to play with Susie and some of the other more outgoing children.

Do you believe that changing Maria's behavior was easy? A more difficult example could have been chosen. However, cases like Maria's are common. You should become aware of these common problems in order to become sensitive about your potential power in the classroom. The word "power" is deliberately being used because, next to the parents or primary caretaker, you, as teacher, are the second most important person in the child's life. You have tremendous potential for influencing the child.

Let us now observe the negative-acting child. What motivates the negative-acting child? An easy answer is adult attention. Many, if not all, children want adult attention so much that they will deliberately misbehave to get it. Normally, this is fairly simple to change. When the child is doing something of which you approve, go to the child and compliment the good behavior. In many cases, praising good behavior does change negative attention-getting behavior.

Some children, however, are so conditioned (from their upbringing and inadequate early child-care experiences) that the only way they know to get attention is to misbehave. They do not understand why you praise them for being good. First, it is difficult to catch them in the act of good behavior. Second, their negative behavior is often *so* negative you cannot afford to ignore it because it is endangering the welfare of other students. Finally, negative-acting children misinterpret the teacher's attempts to be warm, gentle, and caring as weaknesses; their acting-out, aggressive behavior gets worse as you try to give them positive attention. These children gradually become more and more obnoxious until you finally snap and give them the negative attention they want. Look at their faces when you lose your temper and chastize them. They smile! What are you going to do? A clue is to CARE; be congruent, acceptant, reliable, and empathetic. You also need to be firm, yet fair and try, even with the acting-out child, to be friendly.

SETTING LIMITS   Rules must be stated, repeated, and applied consistently. The aggressive acting-out child must often be reminded of these rules over and over again. You may have to repeatedly remove the acting-out child from the room or to a quiet area in the room. You may have to insist firmly and caringly that the child change the negative behavior. A technique that works one day, removing the child to a quiet corner, may not work the next. A technique that works on one child may not work on another.

There are several difficulties facing the student teacher regarding behavior management. One of the difficulties is the problem of developing a repertoire of techniques with which you are comfortable. A second difficulty is developing the awareness or sensitivity to children so that you can almost instinctively know which technique to use on what child. The third difficulty is understanding, usually through the process of trial and error, what techniques are congruent with your self-image. If you see yourself as a warm and loving person, do not pretend to be a strict disciplinarian. The children will sense your pretense and not behave.

Perhaps the most critical error made by many student teachers is confusing the need to be liked by the children and the fear of rejection with their need for limits. As a result, the student teacher may fail to set limits or interfere in situations, often allowing the situation to get out of hand. When the student teacher must finally intervene, the student teacher may forget to CARE; he or she may fail to be congruent and not accept the child causing the problem. The student teacher may not be consistent from day to day or child to child, and may not take the time to develop empathy.

The children, in contrast, know perfectly well the student teacher's need to be liked, but they do not know whether the student teacher can be trusted. Trust is acquired only when the children discover that the student teacher CAREs. It is more important that the children respect, rather than love, the student teacher. In fact, no child can begin to love without having respect first.

It is easier to explain your limits at the beginning of your student teaching experience than to make any assumptions that the children know them. They know what limits your cooperating teacher has established, but they do not know that you expect the same. In order to reassure themselves that the limits are the same, they test them. This is when you must insist that your rules are the same as the children's teacher. You will have to repeat them often. Most children will learn rapidly that your expectations are the same. Others will have to be reminded constantly before they accept them.

LABELING THE BEHAVIOR   What is meant by the phrase "labeling the behavior, not the child"? Essentially, we are referring to what Gordon (1974) calls "I" messages in contrast to "you" messages. In an "I" message, you recognize that it is *your* problem rather than the child's. For example, if one of your three-year-olds accidentally spills the paint, you are angry not because the child spilled the paint, but because you do not want to clean up the mess. Unfortunately, you may lash out at the child and say something like "For goodness sake! Don't you ever look at what you're doing?" or "Why are you so clumsy?" The result is that the child feels that spilling the paint is the child's fault when it is possible that it is your fault. The paint may have been placed too close to the child. The spilled paint is your problem, not the child's. How much better to say something like "I really hate to clean up spilled paint!" This is what is truly annoying you, not the child. Even children can understand a reluctance to clean up a spill. How much better it would have been to label the behavior, not the child.

There are times, of course, when you will honestly feel you do not like the child, and it is especially important then to let the child know that it is the behavior you do not like, rather than the child. Saying "I don't like you when you hit" is often more effective than saying "I don't like you." The latter statement covers all of the child's behaviors, the former relates only to the behavior of which you disapprove. Children do not make this distinction easily and will accuse you of not liking them. Do not let this worry you; look for the first opportunity to compliment the child. Go to the child and say, "I really do like the way you are building with the blocks today." Continue to look for other times when you can give an honest compliment. Do not try to use positive reinforcement unless the child's behavior warrants it. All children know whether they deserve a compliment; do not try to fool them.

Sending "I" messages is a technique that even young children can learn. As the teacher, you can ask children to say "I don't like it when you do that!" to other children instead of shouting "I don't like you!" By labeling the action that is disliked, the child who is being corrected learns what is acceptable behavior without being made to feel bad. The children who are doing the correcting also learn what is acceptable. Eventually, they also learn how to differentiate between who a child is and how the child behaves. It is a lesson even adults need to practice.

ANTICIPATING BEHAVIOR The technique that takes time and experience to learn is anticipating aggressive behavior and intervening before the situation erupts, figure 6-4. By studying patterns in the child's behavior, you can learn to anticipate certain situations. Many children are quite predictable. Some children can be in a social atmosphere for only a short time before being overwhelmed by the amount of stimuli (sights, sounds, and actions), and reacting in a negative way. If you conclude, from observing a child, that the child can play with only one other child before becoming aggressive, you can take care to allow that child to play with only one child at a time. If you know that another child really needs time alone before lunch, you can arrange it. Likewise, if you know a third child becomes tired and cross just

Fig. 6-4   Intervening is sometimes necessary to promote sharing and prevent disagreements. (Courtesy of Jim Clay)

before it is time to go home, you can provide some extra rest time for that child.

Learning to anticipate behavior is not easy. You will require much practice. Keep trying; it is worth the effort, and the children will be happier.

ADDITIONAL GUIDANCE STRATEGIES

Child behavior may always remain puzzling and challenge your efforts to help each child learn socially acceptable behaviors. A review of common strategies used by other teachers may be helpful. Naming strategies, describing them, and discussing when they are most appropriate and effective will sharpen your professional guidance skills.

In this unit thus far, you have studied goals and techniques, the origins of behavior, and ways to promote self-control in children. One goal in guiding child behavior is the idea that the child will learn to act appropriately in similar situations in the future. This can be a slow process with some behaviors, speedy with others. There is a change from external "handling" of the child, to the child monitoring his or her own progress, and then acting and feeling that it is the right thing to do.

ENVIRONMENTAL FACTORS It is easy to conclude that it is the child who needs changing. A number of classroom environmental factors can promote inappropriate child behaviors in group situations. A dull variety of activities, an "above comprehension" program, meager and/or frustrating equipment, and a "defense-producing" teacher elicit behavioral reactions to unmet needs. Close examination of the classroom environment may lead to changing causative factors rather than attempts to change child behavior. School programs, room environments, and teaching methods can fail the children rather than the children failing the program.

As a student teacher, you should carefully examine the relationship between the classroom environment, the daily program, your teaching style, and children's reactions. Fortunately, your training program has developed your teaching skill as well as an understanding of quality environments. An analysis of your placement may lead you to discover that child appeal is lacking. Rearranging and/or creating new areas may add interest. Remember, however, that any changes need the cooperating teacher's approval.

RAPPORT This is an important element of guidance. Trying to develop rapport, trust, a feeling relationship with each child can be tricky. Mitchell, the active, vigorous explorer, may be hard to keep up with — even talk with! He may prefer the company of his peers, so how can one establish rapport? When it does happen you will be aware of the "you're O.K., I'm O.K." feeling, and experience pleasure when he says "I enjoy being with you" with his eyes.

SAME BEHAVIOR, DIFFERENT STRATEGY Child individuality can still result in unexpected reactions. The boy who finally swings at another child after letting others grab his toys, and the child who slugs at every opportunity, are performing the same act. You will decide to treat each incident differently. The age of children, their stage of growth, and the particulars of the situation will be considered. You have already learned that what works with one will not necessarily work with another. You will develop a variety of strategies, focus often on the child's intent, and hypothesize underlying causes.

You will be able to live with child rejection, come to expect it, and realize it is short-lived. Act you will, and react the child will. Sometimes you will choose to ignore behavior and hope it goes away. You will find ignoring is appropriate under certain conditions.

OTHER COMMON STRATEGIES All rules in an early childhood center are related to four basic categories of actions: (1) children will not be allowed to hurt themselves; (2) children will not be allowed to hurt others; (3) children will not be allowed to destroy the environment; and (4) everyone helps with clean-up tasks. You will keep tabs on whether rules are reasonable and/or too numerous. *Stating rules in a positive way* serves two purposes. It is a helpful reminder and states what is appropriate and expected. "Feet walk inside, run outside" is a common positive rule statement. Statements such as "Remember, after snack you place your cup on the tray" or "towels go in the waste basket" clearly indicate the child's task.

Cause and effect and factual statements are common ways to promote behavior change. "If you pick off all the leaves, the plant will die." "Sand thrown in the eyes hurts." "Here's the waiting list; you'll have a turn soon, Mark." Each of these statements gives information which helps children decide the appropriateness or realize the consequences of their current actions.

Using *modeling* to change behavior entails pointing out a child or teacher example:

"The paint stays on the paper. That's the way, Kolima."

"See how slowly I'm pouring the milk so it doesn't spill."

"Nicholas is ready, his eyes are open, and he is listening."

These are all modeling statements, figure 6-5.

Always using the same child as a model can create a "teacher's pet." Most teachers try to use every child as a model. When children hear a modeling statement, they may chime in "me, too" which opens the opportunity for recognition and reinforcement of

Fig. 6-5 "See how carefully Kathy is using the glue" is an example of a modeling statement. (Courtesy of Jody Boyd)

another positive model. "Yes, Carrie Ann, you are showing me you know how to put the blocks in their place on the shelf. Good job."

Redirection is another behavioral strategy which works by redirecting a child to another activity, object, or area.

"Here's a big, blue truck for you to ride, Sherilyn."

"While you're waiting for your turn, Kathleen, you can choose the puzzle with the airplane landing at the airport or the puzzle with the tow truck."

"That's your big outside voice, Marta. You can use it when you're outside."

These are redirection statements.

Statements like "Let's take giant steps to the door. Can you stretch and make giant steps like this?" and "We're tiptoeing into snack today; we won't hear anyone's footsteps" may capture the imagination and help overcome resistance. The key to redirection is to make the substitute activity or object desirable. A possible pitfall in using this strategy too frequently is that it may give the child the idea that something better will be offered every time the child cannot have or do as the child wishes. Offering a pleasurable alternative each time a difficulty arises may teach the child that being difficult and uncooperative leads to teacher attention and provision of a desirable activity or object.

Younger preschoolers (two- and three-year-olds) intent on possessing toys and objects usually accept substitutions, and their classrooms are equipped with duplicate toys to accommodate their "I want what he has" tendency.

Giving a choice of things you would like the child to do appeals to the child's sense of independence. Some examples are:

"Are you going to put your used napkin in the trash or on the tray?"

"Can you walk to the gate yourself or are we going to hold hands and walk together?"

"You can choose to rest quietly next to your friend or on a cot somewhere else in the room."

Setting up direct communication between two arguing children works as shown in the following:

"Mike, you're telling Brian you had it first. Did you hear Mike, Brian?"

"Use your words, Xitlali. 'Please pass the crackers'."

"Look at his face; he's very unhappy. It hurts to be hit with a flying hoop. Listen, he wants to tell you."

Taking a child by the hand and helping confront another to express the child's wishes or feelings lets the child know you will defend his or her rights. It also lets the child know that you care that rules are observed by all.

Self-fulfilling statements such as "I know you can share, Molly. Megan is waiting for a turn" and "In two minutes, it will be Morris' turn" intimate it will happen. Hopefully, you will be nearby with positive reinforcement statements, helping the child decide the right behavior, and feel good about it. *Positive reinforcement* of newly evolving behavior is an important part of guidance. It strengthens the chances that a child will repeat the behavior. Most adults will admit that, as children, they knew when they were doing wrong, but the right and good went unnoticed. The positive reinforcement step in the behavior change process cannot be ignored if new behavior is to last. Positive reward can be a look of appreciation, words, a touch, or a smile. Often a message such as "I knew you could do it" and "I know it wasn't easy" is sent.

Calming-down periods for an out-of-control child may be necessary before communication is possible. Rocking and holding helps after a violent outburst or tantrum. When the child is not angry anymore, you will want to stay close until the child is able to become totally involved in play or a task.

Ignoring is a usable technique with new behaviors which are annoying or irritating but of minor consequence. Catching the adult's attention or testing the adult's reaction may motivate the behavior. One can ignore a child who sticks out the tongue or says "you're ugly." Treating the action or comment matter-of-factly is ignoring. Answering "I look ugly first thing in the morning" usually ends the conversation. You are attempting to withhold any reaction which might reinforce the behavior. If there is definite emotion in the child's comment, you will want to talk about it rather than ignore it.

When all else fails, the use of *negative consequences* may be appropriate. Habit behavior can be most stubborn, and may have been reinforced over a long period. Taking away a privilege or physically removing a child from the group is professionally recognized as a last-resort strategy.

Short periods of supervised chair-sitting and isolation can change behavior. Teachers need to be careful not to shame or humiliate the child in the process. Statements such as "You need to sit for a few minutes until you're ready to. . ." allow the child an open invitation to rejoin the group and live up to rules and expectations. The isolation area needs to be supervised, safe, and unrewarding. Teachers quickly reinforce the returning child's positive, socially acceptable new actions.

Removal of privilege can restrict the child's use of a piece of play equipment or use of a play area for a short period. After the "off-limits" time, the child is encouraged to try again, with a brief positive rule statement to remind the child of limits.

CHILD STRATEGIES   Child strategies to remain in control are natural and normal. Rules can be limiting. Crying, whining, pleading, screaming, and arguing are common. Anger, outrage, and aggression may occur. Suddenly going deaf, not meeting adults' eyes, running away, holding hands over ears or eyes, becoming stiff, or falling to the ground may help the child get what is wanted. The child may also use silence, tantrums, changing the subject, name-calling, threats to tell someone, or threats to remove affection. Even "talking them to death" or ignoring rules are not uncommon strategies. Much of the time, young children function in groups, showing consideration for others. Empathetic and cooperative interaction of preschoolers within classrooms leads adults to admire both their straightforward relationships and their growing sensitive concern for others.

Summary

Throughout this unit, you have been able to formulate an idea of the scope of the guidance function. Remember that in actuality everything you do — planning activities, arranging the environment, planning the length of activities, planning how much direction you will provide — are parts of the guidance function.

Another part is managing behavior. In this unit, you were given two cues to use in managing behavior: the four c's of consistency, considerateness, confidence, and candor; and CARE — be congruent, acceptant, reliable, and empathetic. In addition, four specific techniques were explained: behavior modification, limit setting, "I" messages, and anticipating behavior. Try them; experiment with others of your own. Discover which techniques work best for you and analyze why they work best.

Helping children satisfy needs in a socially acceptable way and feel good about doing so is a guidance goal. Classroom environments can promote self-control, especially when rapport, caring, and trust are present. Examination of behavior — its intent and circumstance — may lead student teachers to different plans of action with different children. There is no "recipe" for handling guidance problems. A review of common strategies was contained in this unit. They are as follows: positive rule statements; cause and effect and factual statements; modeling; redirection; giving a choice; setting up direct communication; self-fulfilling statements; positive reinforcement; calming-down periods; ignoring; and negative consequences.

Children's strategies to circumvent rules and limits cover a wide range of possible actions; yet, an obedience to rules and sensitivity to others is present most of the time.

Suggested Activities

A. Use an anecdotal record form similar to figure 6-3. Experiment with one of your own. Use and evaluate both. Discuss your results with your peers, cooperating teacher, and supervisor.

B. Read Carl R. Rogers' "To Facilitate Learning." Write a review of the major points Rogers makes regarding the qualities of a good teacher. How do you feel you compare on these points?

C. Read Dr. Thomas Gordon's *T.E.T.: Teacher Effectiveness Training.* Discuss the techniques with your peers, cooperating teacher, and supervisor.

D. Describe a technique which you have used to successfully change behavior. Share the experience with another student.

E. Read "Classroom Discipline Problems? Fifteen Humane Solutions" by Marjorie Hipple, *Childhood Education Magazine*, February, 1978.

F. Analyze your placement classroom's rules. Do many rules fall into the four basic areas mentioned in this unit? Are there any rules which need a new category?

G. Are there times during your student teaching day when inappropriate child behaviors tend to increase? Share your ideas with your cooperating teacher, and report the outcome to the class.

H. On a separate sheet of paper, complete the following story with names of appropriate techniques discussed in this unit. Compare your answers with those of a classmate.

SHE TRIED THEM ALL!

Snack time went well until Elmo started blowing bubbles in his milk. Using (1). . ., she said, "Rayleen, I like the way you finished all the milk you poured in your glass." Elmo still blew into his milk. "Milk is for drinking, Elmo," she said, trying (2). . .Elmo kept blowing, and Trina joined him. "You can blow bubbles after your snack, Elmo. Drink the milk, and then you can blow lots of big, sparkly bubbles at the water table. Finish, and then you and I can look for the straws." She was sure that this (3). . .would work. Elmo (4). . .her and kept blowing. "Elmo, you can drink the milk, or you can leave the snack table." This was her attempt to use (5). . .to stop Elmo from blowing bubbles in his milk. "I know you can drink that milk, Elmo. You'll drink it down while I count to three. One. . .two. . .three," she counted, trying (6). . ."Elmo, you must drink, or leave the table. We eat and drink at the snack table. Blowing bubbles in milk is playing. We play in the classroom and yard." She tried using (7). . .Elmo blew in the milk and said, "This is the way I drink," which showed he wanted to (8). . .rather than stop blowing bubbles.

"Elmo, I think you need to sit over here for a minute until you can return to the snack table and drink the milk." She took Elmo by the hand to a chair in an adjacent room. She waited, hoping (9). . . would change his behavior. "You're a milky dummy," Elmo said. She felt it best to (10). . .this comment.

Another student teacher who had watched the whole incident walked over to Elmo and whispered briefly in his ear. Elmo quickly returned to the snack table, and carefully finished all the milk in his glass. What do you think the student teacher said to Elmo? (11). . .Before Elmo left the table one of the student teachers needed to say (12). . .to Elmo.

Review

A. List four classroom factors which might promote inappropriate child behaviors.

B. Complete this statement.
The reason teachers may use different techniques in guiding aggression is. . .

C. 1. List four positive rule statements.
2. List four redirection statements.
3. List four modeling statements.

D. There are seven steps in planning and implementing a behavior modification plan. Arrange these steps in their proper order.
1. Plan a schedule of reinforcement.
2. Make an educated guess as to what is reinforcing the child's present behavior.
3. Analyze your log of observations.
4. Observe current behavior.
5. Observe current behavior again.
6. Stop reinforcement.
7. Implement schedule of reinforcement.

E. List six strategies a child may use to "get around" an adult who has just announced that it is time for all the children to come inside.

F. Select the answer that best completes each statement.
1. Roberta, a student teacher, feels sure a textbook or a practicing teacher will be able to describe guidance strategies which work. Roberta needs to know that
a. children are different but the same strategies work.
b. teachers handle behaviors based upon examples their parents and teachers modeled in their own childhood.
c. there are no techniques that always work.
d. books and practicing teachers agree on best methods.
e. None of these

2. Withholding of privilege is
a. a technique that may work.
b. used before rule statements.
c. not very effective.
d. a rather cruel punishment.
e. All of these

3. When a teacher notices inappropriate child behavior, the teacher should immediately realize that
a. parents created the behavior.
b. children may need to learn school rules.
c. the teaching technique is ineffective.
d. the director should be consulted.
e. None of these

G. Complete the following statements. Analyze your responses and discuss them with your peers and supervisor. What have you learned about yourself?
1. The ideal classroom should. . .
2. When a fight breaks out, I want to. . .
3. As a teacher, I want to. . .
4. Aggressive children make me. . .
5. Shy children make me. . .
6. Children who use bad language ought to be. . .
7. Little boys are. . .
8. Little girls are. . .
9. Whiny children make me. . .
10. Stubborn children make me. . .

Resources

Gordon, Thomas. *T.E.T.: Teacher Effectiveness Training.* New York: David McKay Co., Inc., 1974.
Rogers, Carl R. "To Facilitate Learning," from *Innovations for Time to Teach,* ed. M. Provus. Washington, DC: National Educational Association, 1966, pp. 419–443.

Unit 7
Analyzing Behavior Origins

OBJECTIVES

After studying this unit, the student will be able to:

- Identify what motivates children to act as they do.
- Analyze behavior using Maslow's hierarchy of needs.
- Analyze behavior using Erikson's psychosocial theory of development.
- Recognize the similarities, as well as the differences, between the highly controlled and disciplined child and the under controlled, undisciplined one.

In order to analyze the origins of any behavior, you, as the student teacher, need to remember two important concepts:

1. All behavior is meaningful to the child, even that which an adult might call negative.
2. All behavior is reinforced by the environment (people, places, and things).

Let us begin this unit by looking at some of the typical reinforcers of behavior. Perhaps the easiest ones to understand are physiological in nature: the need to eat when hungry, drink when thirsty, sleep when tired, dress warmly when cold, stay out of the sun when hot, etc. It is less easy to understand the psychological ones, although they control more of our actions.

MASLOW'S HIERARCHY OF NEEDS

Maslow (1968) attempted to develop a hierarchy of needs by which people are motivated.

Growth Needs
- Aesthetic needs
- The need to know and understand
- Self-actualization

Deficiency Needs
- Esteem needs
- Need to belong and be loved
- Safety needs
- Physiological needs

Maslow grouped these needs according to whether they were "deficiency" needs or "growth" needs; whether or not the individual was growing in a positive direction. For anyone to grow positively, Maslow felt that the deficiency needs must be filled in order for the growth needs to be met.

The implications for the children you teach are multiple. The child who is hungry, cold, and, more importantly, unloved may not be able to grow and learn as we would wish. This child may be afraid to grow for fear of losing the known. Regardless of how inclement and/or unwholesome that child's current environment may be, there is a certain safety in the known. For this child, growth can be full of anxiety.

Anxiety and fear in the child are often seen in the classroom as opposites. One fearful, anxious child will withdraw physically from the environment, figure 7-1. The child may cling to the mother or the teacher, refuse to try a new activity, and limit participation to what the child knows and can do best. Another fearful, anxious child will lash out verbally or physically, sometimes both.

Maslow's hierarchy of needs is one way of looking at what motivates behavior. The child who is hungry, poorly clothed, and unloved may have difficulty in becoming self-actualized. The same child may have difficulty in developing the natural desire to explore, know, and understand the environment. The overtly aggressive child and the fearful child are both under-disciplined or undisciplined.

ERIKSON'S THEORY OF PSYCHOSOCIAL DEVELOPMENT

Erikson's (1963) theory of psychosocial development is also relevant. According to Erikson, there are three different stages the child goes through from birth to school age. Each stage has its developmental task to achieve.

FIRST STAGE OF DEVELOPMENT For the infant (birth to approximately one and one-half to two years), the task is to develop basic trust. If the infant is fed when hungry, changed when wet, dressed to suit the weather, and given much love and attention, the infant will learn that adults can be trusted.

Fig. 7-1 When mom leaves, there may be a period of uneasiness.

(Maslow would suggest that the child's deficiency needs have been met.) The infant who is not fed regularly and feels rejected or neglected may learn that adults cannot be trusted. (According to Maslow, the infant's deficiency needs have not been met.)

SECOND STAGE OF DEVELOPMENT As the child becomes mobile and begins to talk, the child enters the second stage of development. Erikson calls this the locomotor-genital stage. Two-year-old children are motor individuals; they love to run, climb, ride, move, move, and move. They are so active, they almost seem like perpetual motion machines! The developmental task of the two-year-old toddler is learning autonomy and self-discipline. It is this age in particular that is so trying for both the parents and preschool teachers.

Why? It is important to understand that the healthy toddler wants to explore. Many parents and teachers mistake the mobile young toddler's desire to explore with a willfulness to go beyond the established limits. What often happens then is a coming together of two opposite ways with which the child's exploration needs are handled. On the one hand, the parents and teacher are delighted to have this curious child trying out new-found motor abilities — walking, running, climbing, manipulating (picking up) small objects, tasting the objects, and turning them over and over in the hands. Adults, for the most part, approve of this behavior, and encourage the efforts to go up and down the front porch steps when there is supervision. We find the toddler's delight with new toys a joy to watch. The child is encouraged through our approval (hand clapping, smiles, and other verbal and nonverbal forms of behavior) to try other things. This is where the child gets into trouble and so, incidentally, do the parents and teacher. Not knowing what is safe or acceptable, the toddler tries to do many things that are both unsafe and unacceptable. The curious, mobile toddler pokes fingers into light sockets; finds electrical wires fascinating; picks up dog or cat food from the pet's dish, smells it, tastes it, manipulates it; twists the TV and stereo knobs; opens kitchen cupboard doors and dumps out the contents of the shelves; and shakes bottles of cleaning fluid, trying to open them to taste. This child also picks up rocks and dirt, pulls flowers from the neighbor's garden, walks into the street, and runs away when called. When these behaviors are met with disapproval, handspanking, or a firm no, the child does not understand. When the toddler wanted to climb the front porch steps, and adults had time to be near, it was okay. Now, at the end of the day when the parents are tired, the child still wants to practice going up and down stairs. The toddler cannot understand why the parents say no and become angry when the crying starts.

One concern we, the parents and teachers (caregivers), have is that the young toddler often seems to be deliberately breaking limits. We fail to understand that one of the ways the child can be reassured that we care is to repeatedly test the limit to see if we really mean what we say. What sometimes happens is, on days when we are rested and time is plentiful, we tolerate behavior that would not be tolerated under different circumstances.

If it is okay to throw a ball to another child, why is it wrong to throw a rock? If it is okay to run down the driveway in one instance, why is it wrong in another? (Boundaries are not understood very well, especially since the child can go somewhere with supervision but not without it.) In the toddler's mind, these are seen as inconsistencies regarding adult expectations. The child cannot differentiate safe from unsafe, so for parents and preschool teachers/day care workers, it means repetition of rules and limits. Eventually, of course, the child does learn. "I don't go down the driveway without holding Mom's hand" or "I don't leave the yard unless Miss Jan holds my hand."

For some parents and teachers/day care workers, the two-year-old child becomes too difficult to handle in a caring way. Two courses of action are frequently taken. Some parents confine the child rather than tolerate the need to explore. As a result, the child's basic motor needs are squelched, and the child becomes fearful and distrustful of his or her motor abilities. The child also learns to feel guilty about the anger felt toward the adults. Since these adults are still responsible for the child's primary care (food, water, love), the child feels that there must be something wrong with him or her if the adults prevent

the natural desire to explore. Thus, the child feels guilty and learns to be ashamed of the anger and represses it. In the classroom, this child is the timid, shy, fearful one with poor motor abilities due to a lack of opportunities to practice them.

Other parents may refuse to assert their responsibilities, and allow the child to do anything. (Think of how terrifying it is for the child to have such power over the parents!) As a result, the child's behavior becomes progressively worse until the parents finally have had enough and resort to punishment. A different result may be a child who fights against any kind of limits and becomes shameless in attempting to do the opposite of what an adult expects or wants, especially regarding motor restrictions. Just as the physically restrained child learns to feel ashamed and guilty, so does the unrestrained child. This child really wants to have reasonable limits set but cannot accept them without a struggle. This struggle of wills makes the unrestrained child feel just as guilty as the overly restrained child. Both children lack the inner controls that the emotionally healthy child has developed. Both lack self-discipline; the overly restrained child through a lack of opportunities to practice, the under-restrained child through a lack of learning any standards.

THIRD STAGE OF DEVELOPMENT   The next stage roughly approximates the usual preschool years of three to five. Erikson believes that the developmental task of the preschooler is to develop initiative, to learn when to do something by oneself and when to ask for help. The result of practice in asserting one's initiative results in a self-confident, cheerful child.

Again, as with the overly restrained toddler, the five-year-old who has been denied a chance to exert initiative learns instead to be ashamed. The child learns that any self-made decisions are of no importance; the adults in the child's life will make decisions. For example, if the child attempts to dress without help, the parents are likely to criticize the result. "Your shirt's on backwards. Don't you know front from back?"   Sometimes the correction is nonverbal; the parent or teacher will simply reach down toward the child, yank the T-shirt off the arms, turn it, and put the arms back through the sleeves. The child learns that he or she does not know how to dress and eventually may stop trying altogether. As the teacher, you then see a child of five who cannot put on a jacket without help, who mixes left and right shoes, and who often asks, "Is this the way you want me to. . .?" This child needs constant reassurance that the assigned task has been completed the way the adult wants it done. Given an unstructured assignment, such as a blank piece of paper on which to draw, this child looks first to see what the other children are doing. Because the child has no self-confidence, the child frequently comes to you for ideas.

The under-restrained toddler grows to be an under-restrained preschooler, and becomes your most obvious classroom problem. This child enters preschool like a small hurricane, spilling blocks, throwing down a difficult puzzle, and tearing a neighbor's drawing because it is "not as good" as the child's own. This child is the one who pushes another off the tricycle to ride it, and grabs the hammer from another when the child wants to use it.

The under-restrained child is also undersocialized. This child has never learned the normal "give and take" of interpersonal relationships, and does not know how to take turns or share, figure 7-2. This child has had few restrictions regarding what to do, when to do it, and where. At the same time, this child often wanted the parents, caregivers, and teachers to instruct what to do and what not to do. A word of caution: Some perfectly normal children who have little or no preschool experience will act like the undersocialized child simply because they lack experience. They learn rapidly, however, and soon become quite acclimated to the classroom procedures and rules. The under-restrained, undersocialized child does not learn rules and procedures easily, and continually pushes against any restrictions.

Remember: The child who is most unlovable is also the one most in need of your love. What are some of the ways you can help this child? Use the four c's and CARE. It is difficult to accept this child; all children deserve your respect and acceptance regardless of how unlikable they may be. In fact, this particular child will probably sense your dislike; therefore, it is important to be scrupulously fair. Do not allow yourself to be caught in the trap of assuming that this child will always be the guilty party in every altercation. It does not take other children long to realize that they have the perfect scapegoat in their midst; it is too tempting for them to break a rule and blame it on the child who is expected to break rules. Remember to be firm. The under-restrained child needs the security of exact limits. They should be repeatedly stated and enforced.

Check the child's family background. You are likely to discover there is little security. Bedtime may occur whenever the child finally falls asleep, whether it be on the floor in front of the television, on the couch, or in bed with an older brother, sister, or cousin. You may discover that mealtimes are just as haphazard. Breakfast may come at any time in the morning and only if there is food in the house. You may find out that family members eat as they each become hungry. This child may open a bag of potato chips for breakfast and eat whatever can be found in the refrigerator for dinner. Sometimes the child's only meal is the one served at school. Life, for this child, simply is not very safe or predictable. Mom may or may not be home when the child returns from

Fig. 7-2 Learning to wait for his turn is not easy.

school. Dad may come home and may work or not as the opportunity presents itself. There may be no one primary caretaker for this child. It is even possible that this child has always been an unwanted child and has been sent from relative to relative.

In terms of Erikson's theory, this child, being unwanted, may never have learned to trust. This possibility is easy to check. As you try to be friendly, does this child's behavior worsen? As you reach out, does the child draw away and/or wince? Think of the consequences of not being wanted. If the child perceives that no one, especially the significant adults in the child's life, likes him or her, how can the child learn to like his or her own self? How can the child learn self-discipline if no one has cared enough to take disciplinary measures? How can a child learn to love without first receiving love from others, preferably from the significant adults in the child's life? The child cannot do these things. An unwanted, unloved child is a real challenge to any caring teacher. Because the child feels so little self-worth, attempts of friendliness on your part will be seen as weakness. To deal with this child you first will have to acquire a tough skin. This child has learned how to "read" adult behavior. This is the child's form of protection. This child knows what you are going to do before you even do it. On the other hand, the child's behavior will seem less predictable to you. One day the child will obey the rules of the classroom; another day the child will not. This youngster will make friendly overtures to another child in the morning and kick that same child in the afternoon. The child will help a group of peers build a city with the blocks, only to knock them down when the project is finished.

You will have to repeat the limits and rules continuously. You will continually have to physically remove this child from the center of action to a quiet corner or room. There is no magic wand which can change this child overnight. In fact, you have to remember that it has taken two, three, or four years to shape the child into the person you are seeing. It may take weeks, even months to change the child. In rare cases, it may even take years.

Uncaring, neglectful families may have been warm and loving, and this child may have learned how to trust at least in part. Still, if this child has not resolved Erikson's second task of early childhood, learning autonomy, the child may frequently get into trouble. Never having learned how to set limits, this child is constantly going beyond limits. The roof is off limits? This child finds a way to climb on the roof. The kitchen is off limits? This child continually goes into the kitchen. The child will continue the escapades even if an injury results. The child accepts hurt as the correct punishment. In fact, this child seeks punishment. When you speak to the child's family, the answer often given is "Just give him a good spanking. He'll behave then!"

Children with this type of behavior test every resource you have. Again, remember to use the four c's and to CARE even though it may be difficult. Repeat the limits and expectations over and over. Physically remove the child whenever necessary; isolation sometimes works best.

Another technique is to say what the child is thinking, figure 7-3. "You want me to tell you that I hate you, but I'm not going to." Sometimes the shock of hearing you put into words what the child is thinking is enough to change the behavior. It may work for a day anyway. You will have to do this repeatedly. When the child hits another, you can say, "You expect me to yell at you for hitting Joey. Well, I'm not going to. I'm going to ask you to sit with me

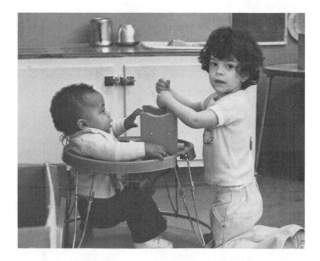

Fig. 7-3 "Janine, I know you'd like to tease Robbie by taking his toy." (Courtesy of Jody Boyd)

in the corner here until you think you can go back with the other children. You know we do not hit in this room." Insist again that limits be respected; the child must follow the rules just like everyone else.

Speak to the parents but be careful. Try not to speak down to them or in an accusing manner. Try to use the "I want to help your child" approach. Most parents want to help their children; however, many do not know how. You may have to explain why you have limits and rules, and suggest that the parents have some limits for the child at home. You may have to give many tips to some parents, and you will have to be tactful and show them that you care. If you sense a noncaring attitude, you can easily understand why the child has problems. In this case, you will have to work with the child only, but keep trying.

One technique that sometimes works with the aggressive, underdisciplined child is to "call" the child on the behavior. What is meant by "call?" One way to look at interactions between two or more children is to find the underlying motivators. Does this sound familiar? Some children are motivated by a desire to control, for they have learned that their only safety lies in their ability to control their environment. This can provoke a tug of war between the child's need to control and yours. At this point, there is no sense in trying to reason, especially verbally. Simply isolate the child, repeat the rules or limits, and leave. Tell the child as you leave that you know what the child is doing and why. Be specific. "I'm not going to argue with you" or "Sit here until you feel ready to rejoin us."

Be prepared to understand that you will not be successful with every child. There will always be one or two children who will relate better to another teacher.

Once in a while you will see a child who is so psychologically damaged that the regular classroom is not an appropriate setting. Using the Maslow hierarchy, you can easily understand that very few of this child's deficiency needs have been met. The child may be underfed, poorly clothed, uncared for, and unloved. Erikson would suggest that this child has never resolved the task of basic trust as an infant, much less having resolved the tasks of autonomy and

initiative. Being unwanted and unloved makes it extremely difficult for a child to acquire any sense of self-worth.

As the teacher, your job is to provide the kind of environment in which the child is able to resolve these early developmental tasks, even if the child has not yet done so. It is never too late to learn to trust or to develop autonomy; it is never too late to satisfy the deficiency needs so that the growth needs can be encouraged.

ANALYZING BEHAVIOR

Let us look at a sampling of behavior, and see if you can apply Maslow's and Erikson's theories. More importantly, see whether knowing the theory helps teach the child.

Chris is a four-year-old in your morning nursery school group. You noted when he was enrolled that his mother looked much older than the others. Under "Reason for Enrollment," his mother wrote, "To give me a rest, and to give Chris a chance to be with children his own age."

Later, in your conference with her, Chris' mother confessed, "You know, Chris was such a surprise to his father and me! After twenty years of being married, we never thought we'd ever have children. I thought I was going through the 'change,' you know, when I found out I was pregnant. What a shock! My husband and I lead such busy lives, you can imagine what having a baby did!"

Upon further discussion, you discover that Chris was carried full-term, the delivery was normal, and his arrival home was uneventful. Chris' mother assured you that her son has always been well cared for. "After all, my husband has a good income from his business (he's a CPA), and I used to run his office before Chris came. I'm a financial secretary, you know, and a good one."

When you asked about Chris' eating habits and sleeping patterns, she responded, "Well, of course, Chris doesn't have many regular habits. According to Mattie, my housekeeper, Chris eats when he wants to. Mattie takes care of

Chris while my husband and I work. We don't see too much of him, you know, especially during tax season. But Mattie assures me Chris eats well, and I know he sleeps well when he finally goes to bed."

Upon further questioning, you find out that Chris "has a TV in his bedroom and usually falls asleep with it on. My husband or I turn it off when we go to bed."

Later, the mother volunteers, "Chris is such an active child that his father and I sometimes go nuts on the weekends. We tried locking Chris in his bedroom. That worked until he found out how to open his window screen and crawl out. Can you imagine that? And, only three years old at the time. I can tell you we paddled him good for that!"

You wonder what Chris' behavior is going to be like in the classroom, and you invite his mother to bring him for a visit. Unfortunately, your worst fears are realized. Chris is like a tornado. In less than ten minutes, he has knocked down one child's block tower, smeared another's painting with dark blue paint, smashed three clay sculptures which were drying on the windowsill, raced outdoors and grabbed a hammer from one child, and was threatening another when you intervened.

Why do you think Chris acts the way he does? What hypotheses or educated guesses can you make? Was he a wanted child? Do his basic physiological needs seem to be met? (The answer to that question is obvious. Chris is clean, well dressed, and large for his age. He shows no signs of malnutrition.) Moving to the next level on Maslow's hierarchy, safety needs, you can only guess at this point. Looking at his rather awkward large motor coordination and lack of ease in handling his body, it becomes apparent that Chris does not seem comfortable in the physical environment. Moving to the third level, the need to belong and be loved, you are no longer so sure. Chris parted from his mother as soon as he came into the room. You already knew, however, that he was used to being with a housekeeper, not his mother. Her comment regarding Chris' behavior was "Good lord! Sometimes he acts this way when we visit friends. I was really hoping he might be different at

school!" Then she screamed, "Chris! How many times have I told you to leave other people's things alone? You behave yourself!" Upon intervening, you grabbed Chris' arm and said firmly, "Chris, we never use tools except at the workbench. Come over here and I'll give you a piece of wood and some nails, and you can hammer all you want."

Looking at the fourth level of the Maslow hierarchy, do you think Chris has feelings of self-esteem? Is it likely that a child who destroys other children's work has good self-esteem? The answer is no. What are the chances then of Chris being able to self-actualize? At this point, they are probably not too good. Chris is typical of the underdisciplined child, cared for in a material way but not in a loving way.

What would Erikson's theory reveal? Has Chris resolved the tasks of infancy and toddlerhood? Is he ready to work on the task of preschoolers? It is possible that, before Chris became an active crawler, his mother did love and accept him. She had reported a normal delivery and a healthy baby. In telling of his birth, she commented about what a pretty baby Chris was, and how she and her husband used to take him everywhere because he'd go to sleep anywhere as long as he was in his bassinet. You suspect that it was only after Chris began to crawl that he began to pose problems. You feel that Chris probably has some level of basic trust.

Autonomy, though, is another question. You already know that Chris was locked in his bedroom so his parents could rest. When asked, Chris' mother admitted that she generally kept him confined to the playpen while in the house or yard. "I couldn't have him get into my collection of miniatures or into his father's rose garden!" When asked if Chris had space in the yard for a swing set or other play equipment, Chris' mother said, "Heavens, no! My husband and I like to entertain in our yard in the summer; we can't have play equipment cluttering it up!"

It seems apparent that Chris has not had the kind of gross motor experiences of most preschoolers. In fact, you already noted during Chris' visit that he ran awkwardly as though he did not have much practice running in the past. Another observation was that Chris' mother took off his jacket for him; the boy did not do it for himself. When asked whether Chris dressed himself, his mother stated, "Oh no, I always put his clothes on for him." When asked if Chris chose what to wear, she replied, "No. Chris wouldn't know what to choose! He'd end up with a blue plaid shirt and his green overalls when he ought to be wearing his gray pin-striped shirt and black jeans!"

You realize that Chris has had little experience in making the usual choices common to many preschoolers. Has he resolved the question of autonomy? It seems unlikely. What does this mean for you in terms of having Chris in your nursery school? First, it means a lot of close watching, restating rules, calm insistence of acceptable behavior, and gradual choices. You know it also means a lot of tactful, gentle education for Chris' parents.

Summary

In this unit we have presented two different theories, Maslow's and Erikson's, to help you analyze a child's behavior. We also presented an actual case study of a child, Chris, and demonstrated how to apply Maslow's and Erikson's theories to the analysis of his behavior. In addition, we showed you how to take the results of an analysis and apply these to guidance techniques and curriculum decisions.

Suggested Activities

A. Read Erik Erikson's *Childhood and Society.* In particular, read those chapters covering the first three stages of psychosocial development. Write a review of your reading, and discuss it with your peers and supervisor.

B. Read Abraham H. Maslow's *Towards A Psychology of Being.* Write a review of the book, and discuss it with your peers and supervisor.

C. Keep a log of observations on a child, and analyze the behavior according to Maslow and/or Erikson. Discuss your analysis with your peers, supervisor, and cooperating teacher.

Review

A. List Maslow's hierarchy of needs.

B. According to Erikson, what are the first three stages of psychosocial development. What are the tasks associated with each?

C. Read the following description of behavior. Then answer the questions at the end.

Cindy, an only child, is a bright-eyed, small, three-and-a-half-year-old attending your day care center for the first time. Her family recently moved to your community. Her mother and father are both teachers in local school districts. Her mother reported that Cindy's birth was normal, and she has had no major health problems. Coming to your day care will be her first experience with children her own age except for religious instruction school.

Cindy appears to like day care very much. She is a dominant child despite her small size, and rapidly becomes one of the leaders. She plays with just about all of the toys and materials supplied at the center. Her favorite activities, however, appear to be the playhouse and easel painting when inside, and either the sandbox or swings when outside. She occasionally gets into arguments with her peers when they no longer accept her leadership. Cindy has difficulty resolving these conflicts, and frequently has a tantrum when she is unable to have her own way.

1. Would you guess that Cindy has basic trust? What evidence suggests this?
2. Do you think Cindy has resolved the task of autonomy? What evidence suggests this?
3. Erikson would suggest that Cindy's task at age three and one-half is to learn to use initiative. What evidence is there in the brief description of her behavior that suggests she is going through this phase of development in a positive or negative way?
4. Using Maslow's hierarchy of needs, at which level would you place Cindy? Why?

Resources

Erikson, Erik H. *Childhood & Society,* 2nd ed. New York: W.W. Norton and Co., Inc., 1963.

Maslow, Abraham H. *Toward A Psychology of Being,* 2nd ed. Princeton: Van Nostrand Reinhold Co., 1968.

Unit 8
Promoting Self-Control

OBJECTIVES

After studying this unit, the student will be able to:

- Understand the relationship between Erikson's task of autonomy and the ability of the child to learn self-control.

- Identify two phases of development which are critical in terms of developing self-control according to Burton White.

- Discuss the relationship between the guidance function and the ability of the child to learn self-control.

Earlier, we discussed the theorists Maslow and Erikson, who have studied behavior and suggested that there are stages and levels of development through which we all pass with age. In order to discuss self-control and to understand how it is acquired, we are going to take a second, closer look at Erikson. We are also going to study two new theorists and observers of young children — Burton White (1975) and Robert White (1959).

ERIKSON AND SELF-CONTROL

This unit will begin with a second look at the first two stages of development according to Erikson, and the tasks associated with each. The oral-sensory stage, with its task of resolving whether other persons can be trusted, is easy to understand.

Look at a small baby. What do you see? If the child is younger than six months, you will notice almost immediately that this infant is constantly using the senses and the mouth. The presentation of a toy brings a multiple reaction. The child puts it into the mouth, tastes it, takes it out of the mouth, looks at it, turns it over in the hands, shakes the toy, listens to see if it will make a noise, and holds the toy to the nose to see if it smells. The child uses all of the senses to understand this toy which has become a part of the immediate environment, figure 8-1. Eyes (seeing), mouth (taste), hands (touch), nose (smell), and ears (hearing) all come into action, figure 8-2.

What does this have to do with learning self-control? Think about the interaction between the infant and the toy, as well as between the infant, toy, and significant adult, usually the mother. Think also

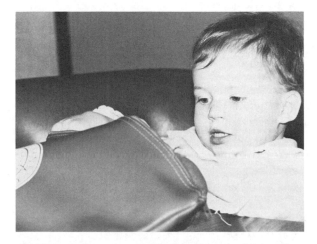

Fig. 8-1 Infants and toddlers will thoroughly explore whatever captures their attention.

Fig. 8-2 "This is so much fun to touch!"

about why the infant uses all of the senses to learn about a new toy or, indeed, about anything in the environment. Why is learning about one's surroundings important? When one learns about the environment, one feels safe in that environment and learns to control it. Can you see why it is important for the infant to sense some control over the environment? How does the child feel when experiencing cause and effect relationships? What does the child learn from tasting, shaking, looking at, and manipulating an object? The child is learning that he or she has some influence upon what is happening. It is this feeling of influence or control that is important to the child's learning of self-control.

Think about what can happen if the child feels no control over the environment. Suppose the significant adult in the infant's life holds out a new toy toward the child, shakes it in front of the eyes, and, as the infant reaches for it, takes it away? Suppose the infant reaches for an object over and over only to have it always withdrawn? How long do you think the child will continue to reach? The child will ultimately stop trying. The child will also learn to feel helpless and not in control over the environment. This child, then, will have difficulty in acquiring self-control. This is the child who becomes either underdisciplined or overdisciplined.

Experiencing some influence on the environment leads the child to understand that he or she affects the environment. An awareness of cause and effect relationships develops in this manner.

LEARNING AUTONOMY   Let us move on to the second stage of development according to Erikson — toddlerhood, with its task of learning autonomy in contrast to shame and doubt. This stage coincides with two physiological events in the toddler's life: the ability to crawl and walk and learning how to use the toilet.

There has been much written about the problems of training a child to use the toilet. Many parents, day care workers, and family day care providers do not understand that most children will essentially train themselves, especially if given an appropriate model such as an older sibling who is toilet trained or a loving, caring parent who anticipates the child's need to use the toilet and, in an unthreatening way, sits the child on the seat and compliments the child upon success. The adult needs to allow the child to look at, and even smell, what his or her body has produced. It is not uncommon for toddlers to play with their bowel movements, an action sure to bring the wrath of the adult down upon them. What needs to be remembered is that the child is pleased and curious about what the body has done. Instead of becoming angry, adults should understand the child's interest, stating simply that playing is not approved of and direct attention to playing with clay, for example, as a substitute.

Problems arise when adults overreact to the child's playing with fecal matter. Many parents who try to toilet train what appears to be a stubborn, willful child fail to understand that the child is simply attempting to develop control — over the parent, in part, but over his or her own self as well.

At this time, the child reinforces the sense of having an effect on the environment. Assume that the toddler, as an infant, was allowed some degree of freedom in which to crawl and explore safely, that within this safe environment the infant had a variety of toys and objects with which to play and manipulate and a loving adult to supervise. This infant then becomes an active, curious toddler, ready to expand his or her environment. Assume also that the parents, day care workers, and family day care providers with whom this toddler comes into contact continue to provide a safe environment in which the child can explore. What is the child then learning? At this particular age, the child is continually learning that he or she has control over the immediate environment. The child can learn only when given practice in self-control. In order to allow for practice, the environment must be physically safe, stimulating, and offer choices.

It is this third factor — offering choices — that is critical in terms of helping a child acquire self-control. Even an infant crawling around in a playroom can make choices about which toys he or she will play with and when. As the child begins to feed himself or herself, the child can make a choice between slices of apple or orange as a snack. The toddler can make the choice between two shirts that may be laid out. In the day care setting, the toddler can easily make the choice between playing with clay or climbing on a play gym. As we talk about older infants and toddlers, we are also talking about allowing the child a choice between two alternatives chosen by the adult, figure 8-3. The young child cannot handle a choice of six different activities; this is overwhelming. Too much choice is as bad as none. In either case, one child may become confused, anxious, and angry while another will withdraw and do nothing.

MASLOW AND SELF-CONTROL

In studying Maslow's hierarchy of needs, remember that one goal is to help the child become self-actualizing; the child's deficiency needs must be met. The child's belongingness, love, and esteem needs must be met. Belongingness carries the implication of family identity, of belonging to a particular adult or group, and feeling that one is a part of this group. There is psychological safety in having a group to belong to. This group is the one which takes care of the physiological needs and makes sure that the environment is safe. This group also allows the growing child to develop self-esteem.

How is self-esteem developed? According to Maslow, it is developed in interaction with the important people in the environment. Look at the

Fig. 8-3 "Shawn, you can choose to hold the squash or place it here on the table."

following sequence of events: It is morning. The infant cries; the mother goes to the crib, smiles, speaks softly to the baby, and picks the baby up. She changes the diaper, goes to the kitchen to warm a bottle or sits down in the rocking chair to nurse. As the infant feeds, she coos and speaks to the child and plays with the hand. What is the infant learning? Besides learning that this mother is reliable and loving, the baby is learning that he or she is important to the mother. Later, the child turns over from the stomach onto the back. The mother smiles, claps her hands, and says, "My, aren't you getting big! How smart you are to turn over!" The child is learning that he or she is physically competent. Self-esteem is developed through the continual interaction between the parent, day care worker, and child. Every time you praise the child, smile, and clap your hands at achievements, you are helping to build the child's self-esteem.

The child from this type of environment will have no difficulty in becoming self-actualized. In contrast, the child whose home environment has *not* provided for these deficiency needs will have difficulty. For this child, you will need to provide those experiences which the child has missed: attention to physiological needs, safety needs, and the need to belong. The loving day care worker or family day care provider can do much to help the child whose own family group has been unable to help.

Children are remarkably resilient; they can survive situations which seem almost impossible. Even given a poor beginning, if a child comes into contact with a warm, loving, acceptant adult, the child will still be able to self-actualize. Children who seem invulnerable or untouched by negative family environments (alcoholism, criminality, poverty, and/or mental illness) are also those children who, during their first year, had at least one significant adult in their lives who cared (Pines, 1979). This adult could be trusted, thus enabling the children to resolve the question of basic trust. According to Pines, these children are able to find other adults to whom they can relate in terms of resolving the other tasks of early childhood. These adults meet the children's deficiency needs so that they can self-actualize in spite of negative environments.

How does self-actualization relate to self-control? One aspect of self-actualization *is* self-control. The child who is able to self-actualize is able to make choices and accept leader or follower roles, and has a good sense of self, figure 8-4. Having a sense of self

enables the child to be assertive when appropriate or to accept directions from another.

BURTON WHITE AND SELF-CONTROL

White (1975) divides the child's first three years into seven phases, each with its unique characteristics, needs, and preferred child-rearing practices.

Phase I: Birth to six weeks
Phase II: Six weeks to three and one-half months
Phase III: Three and one-half to five and one-half months
Phase IV: Five and one-half to eight months
Phase V: Eight to fourteen months
Phase VI: Fourteen to twenty-four months
Phase VII: Twenty-four to thirty-six months

According to White, during Phase I the primary needs of the infant are to feel loved and cared for, and to have the opportunity to develop certain skills such as holding up the head while on the stomach and tracking objects held eight to twenty-four inches from the face. The new-born baby does not need much stimulation other than a change of position from back to stomach to the mother's arms.

During Phase II, helping the infant achieve certain skills such as holding up the head becomes more important than during Phase I. Phase II infants also need hand-eye activities such as crib devices.

Phase III infants have attained head control and are beginning to attain torso control. At this age, the child learns to turn from stomach to back and back to stomach. Also, the child's leg muscles are strengthened. Infants at Phase III enjoy being held so they can press their feet against a lap and practice standing. They are quite social, and respond to tickling and smiling with their own coos and smiles. The infants "soak up" all the attention from family and strangers alike, and respond easily.

Phase IV infants begin to show an understanding of language. *Mama, daddy, bottle,* and *eat* may all be understood by the child. The child cannot say the words but can respond, indicating a knowledge of the words. Phase IV babies are beginning to develop real motor skills such as sitting independently, getting up on hands and knees, and rocking. A Phase IV child

Fig. 8-4 Children develop the ability to assume the roles of both leader and follower. (Courtesy of Steve Howard)

may even pull to a standing position. Phase IV babies need freedom in which to move and practice these growing skills. They can also grasp toys quite well and need suitable small objects with which they can practice picking up and holding. Toys such as crib devices to kick at, stacking toys, stuffed toys, balls to pick up, objects which are two to five inches in size so they cannot be swallowed all help the Phase IV child learn about the world and gain mastery over the immediate environment.

During Phase V, the infant usually comes into direct conflict with significant adults for the first time. This is due to the child's growing mobility. Soon there is no area in the house or day care center that is safe from the child's active exploration. Knickknacks, books, ashtrays, electric cords, pots and pans, utensils, and pet food dishes are stimuli to the active Phase V child, and bring the child into conflict with the parents or care givers.

It is at this age that the child begins to develop self-control. It is important that the child has a childproof area in which to play. Parents, day care workers, and family day care providers need to know that the Phase V child can be safe from harm in that area.

If the Phase V child does not get into trouble, the Phase VI child will. At this point, mobility has been established. Phase VI children can walk and begin to run, climb, ride, push and pull objects, reach for and pull down, and talk. "No" becomes a favorite word, mostly because they hear it so often. Mama, daddy, bye-bye, and baby are spoken. The Phase VI child begins to pay less attention to the people in the environment and spends more time looking, listening, practicing simple skills, and exploring.

It is the exploring that causes difficulty for both the Phase V and the Phase VI child. Most houses and yards are not childproof. Children will pull flowers off stems, grab dirt pebbles and throw them, toddle down driveways and out into streets, climb up ladders, and push and pull at furniture. This struggle to experiment with growing motor skills comes into continued conflict with parental and center needs for the child's safety. Instead of complimenting the climber who has mastered the front steps and is now crying to be picked up so he or she can start over, we scold the child, saying the steps are off limits. The Phase V and Phase VI child simply cannot comprehend

this. It would be more beneficial to our peace of mind and the child's need to climb if a portable gate is placed across the third stair and the child is allowed to practice going up and down. If the child falls down the three steps, he or she will not be hurt, and will approach the climb more carefully the next time.

Self-control grows from experiences like these. The Phase V and Phase VI child will become an autonomous, able Phase VII preschooler if allowed to experiment with what the body can do, and given opportunities to practice growing motor skills. As a Phase VII preschooler, the child will be able to:

- Get and hold the attention of adults.
- Use adults as resources after first determining that a job is too difficult.
- Express affection and mild annoyance.
- Lead or follow peers.
- Compete with peers.
- Show pride in accomplishments.
- Engage in role playing activities.
- Use language abilities with increasing competence.
- Notice small details or discrepancies.
- Anticipate consequences.
- Deal with abstractions.
- See things from another person's viewpoint.
- Make interesting associations.
- Plan and carry out complicated activities.
- Use resources effectively.
- Maintain concentration on a task while simultaneously keeping track of what is going on (dual focusing).

According to Burton White, most babies grow at essentially the same rate until Phase V. Most family environments provide reasonably positive experiences for Phase I through Phase IV children. As mentioned, conflicts arise as the child's mobility increases. As a teacher of young children, you must provide the kind of environment in which the children have as much opportunity as possible to grow and learn about their environment and themselves.

ROBERT WHITE AND SELF-CONTROL

Robert White (1959) was concerned with how children are motivated to act as they do. From his studies, White concluded that children are motivated by the desire to gain mastery over the environment or to become competent. He used the word "effectance" to explain why children will repeat an action as they learn something. They are learning to become effective.

We are not going to discuss Robert White and his effectance motivation in detail. The implications for teachers, day care workers, and parents seem obvious. It is normal for children to do the same thing over and over again as they attempt to know all they can about something or to master it. It explains why, after initial experimentation with an activity, the child varies actions and will then repeat the variation over and over again.

IMPLICATIONS FOR TEACHERS To summarize what these four theorists believe regarding the promotion of self-control, let us briefly look at each. Erikson relates self-control with resolving the question of autonomy, the task of toddlers. According to Maslow, self-control relates to the resolution of deficiency needs and the beginnings of self-actualization. Burton White's theory indicates that self-control develops as the child passes from Phase V to Phase VI in a healthy, positive environment with caring, loving parents. Robert White relates self-control to effectance; the child who has gained mastery over the environment gains self-control, figure 8-5.

What does this mean to you as a teacher? First, you will need to provide the kind of environment in which the children feel safe. Second, you must also provide the kind of personal environment in which the children can grow positively. You must use guidance techniques and recognize, through keen observation, which children need more help than others to learn self-control.

What is meant by saying that you must provide for a safe environment? The physical arrangement of the rooms must be safe. It also means consistency of behavior expectations and predictability regarding the schedule and your own behavior. You must remember and use the four c's of discipline. You must CARE so that the psychological climate is warm and loving. It means recognizing a child's development level in terms of self-control.

If the child has not learned to be autonomous, you will need to provide the kinds of opportunities which allow the child to do so. As mentioned, it means providing guided choices and allowing practice in decision making. Does the child have a low self-image? Is the child's need to belong unfulfilled? You will need to provide success experiences for this child and a lot of tender, loving care (TLC as it has been called). If this child has at least a sense of belonging in class, this is a start.

Is this a negative-acting child who appears to be at Burton White's Phase V and Phase VI stages? What has happened to this child? Most likely, if you check with the parents or other primary caretakers, you will find that the child's attempts to develop major interests at Phase V were thwarted. This child was not encouraged to explore the physical environment and master newly emerging motor abilities. This is the child who becomes too fearful or shy or too aggressive. This child needs opportunities to explore and use motor abilities but needs to be told the limits over and over. This child must be urged ever so gently to try again.

Fig. 8-5   This child has gained mastery over his environment.

Self-control, or self-discipline, is learned only through the initial imposition of controls from the significant adults in the child's life and the opportunity to practice the child's own controls secondarily.

Summary

In this unit we have attempted to explore the different theories of self-control and their practical applications for the teacher, day care worker, etc. We studied the theories of Maslow and Erikson, especially Erikson's concept of autonomy. Children who are allowed to explore within safe limits and to practice their motor abilities become autonomous. Children who are over-restricted or under-restricted fail to become autonomous. It takes gentle persuasion, careful arrangement of opportunities, and positive reinforcement to help these children succeed.

Two new theorists were introduced: Burton White and Robert White. Briefly, Burton White believes there are seven phases of development during the child's first three years. Phase V and Phase VI, covering the ages between eight and twenty-four months, are the periods during which conflicts arise due to the child's increasing motor ability. Given appropriate toys and the freedom to explore within safe limits, the child develops into a healthy, happy preschooler.

Robert White's theory of competence motivation makes sense to anyone who has watched a child do the same thing over and over until the task has been mastered.

Suggested Activities

A. Read Burton L. White's *The First Three Years of Life.* Give close attention to Chapters 6 and 7. Discuss your readings with your peers, cooperating teacher, and supervisor.

B. Read Robert W. White's "Motivation Reconsidered: The Concept of Competence." Write about your reaction to the article. Discuss your readings with your peers, cooperating teacher, and supervisor.

C. Observe one child in your classroom closely and analyze the child's level of self-control. Discuss your observations regarding whether you feel the child has resolved the task of autonomy, feels competent, and is becoming self-actualized. State specific actions which reinforce your conclusions.

Review

A. List the seven phases of development that occur during the child's first three years according to Burton White.

B. What does Robert White mean by "effectance?"

C. Complete the following statements.
1. Shy, timid, and fearful children are. . .
2. Aggressive, acting-out children are. . .
3. The infant who is fed, diapered, kept comfortable, and loved has probably resolved the task of. . .
4. A child needs the opportunity to make choices and explore within safe limits in order to become. . .
5. According to Robert White, children strive for. . . over their environment.
6. According to Burton White, the phase of infant development most distressful to parents is either . . .or. . .
7. According to Maslow's hierarchy, the child who feels a strong identification with the family probably has reached at least the level of. . .
8. Deficiency needs must be at least partially satisfied in order to. . .
9. In the research on invulnerable children, Pines related that they had learned to. . .adults.
10. According to Burton White, the primary need of an infant is. . .

D. List five characteristics of an autonomous, able three-year-old child.

E. Rate each of the following actions with a plus (+) if it would help a child develop self-control or a minus (–) if it would not help. If the action would neither help nor hurt, rate it with an x.
1. Smiling each morning when the child enters
2. Picking up and isolating the child who is fighting
3. Spanking the child

4. Setting strict limits and frequently reminding the child of them.
5. Asking the child who is fighting to please stop.
6. Moving toward a group of arguing children
7. Complimenting the child when successful at a new task
8. Applying the same standards to all the children
9. Gently persuading the child
10. Pairing a shy child with an outgoing one
11. Ridiculing a naughty child
12. Redirecting the attention of a child engaged in a potentially dangerous activity

Resources

Pines, Maya. "Super Kids: The Myth of the Vulnerable Child." *Psychology Today* (Jan. 1979).

White, Burton L. *The First Three Years of Life.* Englewood Cliffs, NJ: Prentice-Hall, Inc., 1975.

White, Robert W. "Motivation Reconsidered: The Concept of Competence." *Psychological Review,* 66 (1959), pp. 297-333.

Section 4
Communication

Unit 9
Common Problems of Student Teachers

OBJECTIVES

After studying this unit, the student will be able to:

- Identify five common student teacher problems.
- List areas of possible conflict between student teachers, supervisors, and cooperating teachers.
- Describe courses of action which lead to solutions of typical problems.

This unit is not intended to solve problems encountered during student teaching. It will probe possible reasons for difficulties and help alert the student to possible courses of action. Knowing that problems are going to occur is stress reducing. You will relate strongly to some ideas and vaguely to others. Knowledge hopefully may help you escape some problems, confront others, and cope with ones that cannot be changed.

KINDS OF PROBLEMS

Do you know of any human relationship that is problem-free and always smooth sailing? Student teaching, involving close human interaction and communication, is no exception. Pressures, feelings, desires, needs, risks, and possible failures are inherent.

STRESS During the first days and weeks of student teaching, stress arises usually from student teachers' desire to become good practicing teachers, and feelings of self-doubt and lack of confidence. As you grasp the challenges through watching your cooperating teacher and attempt to put your own theory into practice, the task seems monumental. Frances Fuller (1969), who summarized eleven studies related to the concerns of teacher education students, pinpointed three sequential stages in teacher training: (1) focus on self or self protection; (2) focus on pupils (children); and (3) focus on outcomes of teaching.

ANXIETY An early focus on self may produce anxiety. A student teacher can feel uncomfortable until there is a clear feeling of exactly what is expected (Danoff, 1977). One can react to stress in a number of ways. In student teaching, reactions could be:

- Becoming defensive
- Concentrating energies on passive, shy children

- Becoming extremely authoritative — giving directions in every situation
- Talking too much
- Looking for fault in others
- Becoming overly critical of the student teaching situation
- Withdrawing into busy work or room maintenance
- Seeking additional written or oral guidelines
- Organizing tasks into time blocks
- Clearly outlining assignments on a calendar, file, or binder system
- Seeking the supervisor to communicate anxieties
- Using stress-reduction techniques

The first seven reactions can lead to immediate additional difficulties. The other reactions confront and possibly reduce tension. Anxiety may occur when there are changes in a person's life. Change for student teachers occurs with their increasing responsibilities. Also, anxiety can stem from feeling of doing the wrong thing.

> I was convinced that in every situation there was a "right" and a "wrong" thing to do, and I was deathly afraid of doing the wrong thing. (Burnett, in *Roles in Off-Campus Student Teaching*, 1967)

Typically, this feeling disappears with experience.

> I found that I could be firm and quick and calm, and that it wasn't so much a matter — of luck or a stroke of genius — making the "right" decision, as it was of simply doing something that would work. (Burnett, in *Roles in Off-Campus Student Teaching*, 1967, p. 44)

Sometimes extreme reactions to student teaching happen.

> The situation is complicated by biases and stereotypes each of us may have about the teaching role. You may find yourself saying, "All teachers are bad. . . .I will save these children and protect them from the teacher. I will do the opposite of what she does. . ." Or you may say, "All teachers are wonderful, superior people. . . .I will copy the words, phrases, voice

quality, and gestures of this teacher. Then I, too, will be marvelous." (Danoff, et al., 1977)

Even extreme feelings can be accepted as natural and to be expected. Once accepted, there is the chance to move on and get past them or at least cope.

> First of all, students can expect to feel inadequate when they begin participating in the school and probably for some time after that. They cannot possibly be prepared for all that may happen. No one can give instructions that will cover everything, certainly not in the time there may have been for preparation. Of course, students will not feel sure of what is expected of them or of what they are supposed to do. The teacher who is guiding them may not be sure of these things herself, as she does not know them yet or know what is possible for them. What we can do about the feeling of inadequacy at this point is to feel comfortable about having it. (Read and Patterson, 1980)

Another common panic feeling during first days is expressed in the following:

> The material in Introductory Educational Psychology courses has slipped from memory. How is all that stuff about learning theory going to help you survive tomorrow? Gone are all the professors who told you of the excitement, challenge, and satisfaction of teaching. (Brooks, 1978)

You will find it is possible to be excited, eager to try your ideas and activities, eager to develop your own teaching style, and still be somewhat apprehensive. Dr. Joanne Hendrick states, "One of the outstanding characteristics of beginning teachers is the caring and involvement that they bring with them to their work," and that these will promote their success in student teaching (1975, p. 16).

In contrast to the anxious approach to student teaching is the relaxed, confident one. Danoff, Breitbart, and Barr (1977) suggest this happens after your first successes. Self-confidence and self-esteem are important primary goals of student teaching. They evolve in student teachers as they do in children through actions resulting in success and through the feedback received from others. A strong feeling of success through child interactions is described by Read and Patterson:

> A child's face lights up when he sees us come into the room, and we know that our relationship with him is a source of strength. He is seeing us as someone who cares, who can be depended on, and who has something significant to give him. It makes us feel good inside to be this kind of person for a child. It gives us confidence (1980), figure 9-1.

Hints for dealing with anxiety suggest trying not to worry about being the teacher and, instead, reflecting on teachers you liked and why (Brooks, 1978, p. 2). Another method is to relax and treat children your own way, the way you really think about them. This will give you the confidence required to give more, try more, and be more effective (Lewis and Winsor, 1968).

Not only will you enjoy your developing confidence, but your cooperating teacher will also be pleased. One cooperating teacher described her memorable experiences in the following:

> My best experience has been throwing a student teacher into a classroom teaching situation despite reservations and lack of confidence on the part of that student teacher and seeing him emerge as a capable, confident, successful teacher. (Tittle, 1974)

Putting student teaching in perspective, while being able to laugh at one's self, helps reduce anxiety. This is something each student teacher needs to consider.

SEEKING HELP

It is difficult for some student teachers to ask for help or suggestions. The risk involved is having either the cooperating teacher or supervisor realize one's limitations. Therefore, student teachers sometimes turn to other student teachers. Trust is an important element in this dilemma. Fortunately, one builds trust through human interaction and seeking help usually becomes easier as time passes.

It is important to seek help quickly in many instances and to use consultation times and meetings to pick the brains of others and seek assistance.

> The biggest threat to good communication is that the student teacher believes that any questions they ask the supervising teacher will reflect a lack of preparation which might be interpreted as not being motivated. (Brooks, 1978)

The role of both the supervisor and cooperating teacher includes on-site support and advice, figure 9-2.

Fig. 9-1 "Come and see what I just made, teacher!" (Courtesy of Nancy Martin)

Fig. 9-2 Seeking advice and assistance becomes easier as time passes.

Lillian Katz (1972) notes that a beginning teacher needs encouragement, reassurance, comfort, guidance, instruction in specific skills, and insight into the complex causes of behavior. Stevens and King (1976) point out that in the English primary school system, it is usual practice that a beginning teacher receives advice and supportive assistance on a daily basis throughout the first full year of teaching!

THE HALF-A-TEACHER FEELING During their experiences, many student teachers are led to feel, either by their students or cooperating teachers, that, because of their position, they are not quite students and not quite teachers yet. Because of this "neither-here-nor-there" attitude, student teachers are not always treated as figures of authority. Read the poem in figure 9-3. It may bring a knowing smile. "My worst experience took place because the students in many instances did not recognize me as a teacher but referred to me as a student teacher." (Tittle, 1974) Some student teachers have had the experience of being treated as a "gopher." "I do not think that a student teacher should be made to do what a teacher is not required to do. I hate being given errands and 'dirty work' to do just because I'm a student teacher!" (Tittle, 1974, p. 37) Sometimes early in student teaching, a strong team feeling has not been developed. Its development is critical for all involved. It may be best to consult with one's supervisor first. Cooperating teachers have a number of factors to consider in relinquishing control of their classroom. Often they feel uneasy about their routines and classroom behavior standards being threatened. They also may feel they are asking too much too soon of their student teachers, and may be unclear of their role in giving assignments. It may be difficult for cooperating teachers to interchange their roles and become co-teachers instead of lead teachers. They can also be worried about child safety.

Cooperating teachers get a real sense of teaming with students as the semester progresses. Tittle describes her finest experience as follows:

> My best experience was with a student who adjusted herself to classroom routines and was so perceptive that she would anticipate without having to ask her to do things. As a result, we worked as a team and the pupils really accomplished a great deal. (1974, p. 40)

GUIDANCE Student teachers often find that the children will obey the rules when the cooperating teacher is present or asks them, but not when they ask them. Children test and question the authority of this new adult. Student teachers tend to force issues or completely ignore children when classroom rules are broken. These situations may be temporarily troublesome to student teachers. In time, the children will realize the student teacher means what is said. Consistency and firmness will win out.

When student teachers feel they cannot deal with these situations, they tend to stay close to self-controlled or affectionate children. This type of behavior indicates a possible withdrawal from the total room responsibility.

ATTACHMENTS At times a child may form a strong bond and liking to a particular student teacher. The child may be inconsolable for a period after the student's departure. Most students worry about this

---

STATUS

This room is hers
This is *her* class-
This much is established
Clearly. . .
And,
As if by decree,
I am classified,
Categorically,
As an "almost,"
A "not-quite,"
A neophyte,
Labeled simply
"Wait-and-see."
But —
What else *can*
A student teacher be?

Fig. 9-3 "Status" by Anthony Tovatt (Reprinted by permission of the publisher, *The Indiana Teacher*, Jan. 1958, 102:207.)

behavior, and their supervisors' and cooperating teachers' reaction to it. It is an important topic for team meetings.

Male student teachers can have a unique experience during student teaching based on children's past experiences or lack of experiences with males. The male student teachers' reactions can range from expecting roughhousing to expecting clinging behavior or fear. After a short period, the children will see the male student teacher as just another teacher with his own individuality.

PHILOSOPHIC DIFFERENCES   Student teaching provides the student teacher with a growing experience. Sometimes the cooperating teacher's view of child education and how children learn is quite similar to the student's; in other placements, it is not. Understanding of methods, techniques, curriculums, and goals and objectives of classrooms is the task of the student. When conflicting views are present in a supportive atmosphere, they are respected. Student teachers gain a chance to clarify their own ideas when confronted with differing ones. New and diverse views result in the growth and clarification of a student's idea of what is best for children and families.

It is disconcerting and uncomfortable for both students and cooperating teachers when their teaching styles clash. Open discussion is the best course of action, particularly if it is done in a caring way which preserves the dignity of each teacher's opinions.

Students should not surrender their philosophical values, but tenaciously retain what they feel is best for children. Every wave of newly trained preschool teachers has its own contribution to make. The old or established way is always subject to questions in education. Practicing teachers continue to try innovative approaches; some are used in a complete or modified form, others are discarded. Thoughtfulness and open-mindedness help student teachers as does an "all win" attitude. Remember: Everybody learns and grows!

PERSONALITY CONFLICTS   Whether or not you believe everyone has their own "vibes," you probably readily admit that you work much better with some people than with others. Carol Tittle describes one of her experiences:

> I had a student teacher who was very cold. She did an excellent job of teaching, but seemed to have created a wall between myself and the class by her very presence. I do not mind a student teacher that cannot teach a lesson. That comes with experience and I can help her. (1974)

Communication skill is critical in working relationships. Fortunately, student teaching is only a temporary assignment. Most difficult situations can at least become bearable through communication.

BEING HELD BACK   Very often, student teachers are not given the opportunity to work with children as much as they would like. As a result, they can become frustrated and feel that their potential for growth as teachers is being stifled. This can also happen when a cooperating teacher steps in during an activity or incident and assumes the student cannot handle the situation. These occurrences reduce the student's opportunity to work out of tight or uncomfortable spots. In the first example the student is not allowed to start; in the second, to finish.

The student needs to know the "why's" behind the cooperating teacher's behavior; the cooperating teacher needs to grasp the student's feeling. Neither can happen without communicating.

> Your master teacher is not able to read your mind. The only way he is going to know the things you are worried about, any feeling of inadequacy or uncertainty you may have, as well as your positive feelings, is to tell him. (Gordon-Nourok, 1979)

TIME AND ENERGY   Time seems to be a problem for many students — enough time and organization of time. Cooperating teachers sometimes complain that students are not prepared, are tardy, or are unreliable. Working while student teaching limits the hours necessary for preparation of activities. Student teachers must learn to manage their time. This involves planning ahead and analyzing task time lengths.   Poor time management increases tension, destroys composure, and creates stress. Only the student teacher can make adjustments to provide enough time and rest necessary for student teaching. Standards of teacher training are rarely relaxed for just one individual. Figure 9-4 offers time management hints.

SITE POLITICS One of the most difficult placement situations is one which is consumed with conflicts. Power struggles between teachers, the director, parents, community, or any other group makes the student feel as if he or she is walking a tightrope, afraid to join either faction and trying to be a friend to all. This situation should be discussed with your supervisor quickly.

Summary

Student teaching is a miniature slice of life and living. Problems arise and are common to all. Some situations change with time, others need extended communication to be resolved.

Growth and change are experienced sometimes easily, sometimes painfully. It is helpful to maintain a caring and sharing feeling, open communication, and a sense of humor. Time and successful experience take care of most initial difficulties. The supervisor's and cooperating teacher's role is to provide supportive assistance. Team status may evolve slowly, and depend on student effort.

What you *can* do is make better use of the time you do have through planning and organizing your workdays.

First, analyze the way you spend your work hours over a three-day period. Keep a log and record what you did, how much time you took doing it and whether or not the time was spent productively. Your log should help you get a better grip on your workday and boost your efficiency.

Some other potentially useful time tips are:

- *Start the day with at least 10 minutes of an activity you really enjoy.* Exercise, read the newspaper, linger over a second cup of coffee. This should give you the positive attitude you need to face the day.

- *Set priorities.* Determine what you must accomplish today. Follow up with a list of tasks you might get to if things go well, put the others on hold.

- *Set time limits.* Be realistic, wary of tasks that take up more time than they are worth.

- *Speed up decision-making.* Define the problem, generate a reasonable number of alternatives with relevant staff and reach a decision. Don't waste time mulling over an infinite number of alternatives.

- *Beware of perfectionism.* It causes defeatism and stress. Count your imperfections and mistakes as learning experiences. Try to do better next time.

- *Keep your desk clear.* Don't handle papers more than once. Read a paper through the first time and, if possible, take action then. If you have to put it in your in-box, dispose of it next time around. Do it, delegate it, file it, or throw it away.

- *Periodically re-evaluate goals*, both short and long term. Keep a handle on deadlines and objectives that must be met within specific amounts of time.

Fig. 9-4 Avoid the time crunch [By Bettye W. McDonald in *Keys to Early Childhood Education*, Vol. 2, No. 2 (Feb. 1981), Washington, DC: Capitol Publications, Inc.]

Suggested Activities

A. Interview three practice teachers about their joys and problems in student teaching.

B. With other student teachers, make a list of problems not mentioned in this unit.

C. Rate the following situations as M (major problem) or m (minor concern). Discuss the results in small groups.

1. A student teacher is placed in a class that the child of a best friend is attending. The best friend asks for daily reports.

2. Little Johnny tells a cooperating teacher that he is afraid of the student teacher.

3. Bonnie, a student teacher, finds she is susceptible to colds and infections.

4. Children do not respond to the student teacher's rule statements.

5. The student teacher has had no background experience with children of the ethnic group where placed.

6. The student teacher is used as an aide in the classroom.

7. A child's mother tells the cooperating teacher she does not like the idea of a student teacher taking over the classroom.

8. The supervisor rarely visits the classroom.

9. Jane and Mary, two student teachers, are placed in the classroom. Mary feels that she is doing the bulk of the preparation of activities.

10. A classroom assistant teacher feels threatened by a student teacher in the same room.

11. Debra is placed in a classroom where there are so many adults that there does not seem to be enough work or children to occupy her time.

12. A student gets tongue-tied when presenting an activity for the first time.

13. One of the student teacher's planned activities ends in pandemonium. Paint is all over the walls and floor, and the children are uncontrolled.

14. Steve is told he is doing very well student teaching, but is experiencing nervousness, fatigue, and distress.

15. A student teacher has difficulty planning activities that suit the children's age and interest level.

16. Bob, a student teacher, watches children near him, but rarely scans the room to see where his services are most needed.

17. Megan breaks down and cries as soon as she gets into her car after her first day of student teaching.

D. Identify some student teacher problems that might be occurring because of our society's changing male and female sex roles, single parent families, or cultural and ethnic differences.

E. In groups of two, dramatize one of the problems presented in this unit for the class. Let your partner guess the problem.

F. List briefly three possible courses of action for the following student teacher situations. Of the three, what do you feel is the best course of action?

1. Amy, a fellow student teacher, confides in you that she objects to the way her cooperating teacher punishes children.

2. Joey, a four-year-old, says, "You're not the teacher. I don't have to do that" when you ask him to return blocks he has played with to the bookcase.

3. You have a great idea about rearranging the room, and do so in the morning before the children or cooperating teacher arrive. The cooperating teacher is obviously upset upon entering the room.

4. You tried very hard to encourage Tommy to complete a task, and the cooperating teacher quickly finishes the task for him to make sure he is not late for snack.

5. You cannot seem to get any feedback on your abilities as a student teacher from either the cooperating teacher or the supervisor.

6. You notice you are spending an increasing amount of time straightening, table wiping, sink cleaning, and with block area maintenance.

7. You realize you do not know any parents' first names, and half of the semester is over.

8. Manuela and Colleen are student teaching in the same classroom. Manuela feels Colleen is insensitive to Mexican cultural events and rarely builds a sense of ethnic pride in the children.

9. Carol, a student teacher, plays the guitar and is a talented folksinger. She has not planned a classroom activity to share her talent.

10. Your supervisor gives you credit for setting up a new activity area which the children are exploring with enthusiasm; however, the cooperating teacher was the one who set up this activity. Since your supervisor has encouraged you to add new activities, you did not correct the mistake. The next day you feel badly about taking credit, but are reticent to approach your supervisor with the truth.

G. Select the answer which best describes your probable reactions to the following situations.

1. Your cooperating teacher compliments you enthusiastically about knowing where you are needed most.
   a. You thank your cooperating teacher.
   b. You say, "I really appreciate you telling me."
   c. You smile and say nothing.

2. Your cooperating teacher just finished what you felt was a great interaction with a child. The child really learned from the incident.
   a. You remain silent, making a mental note of the teacher's approach.
   b. You quickly make a note to bring it up at a staff meeting so you can ask more about what the teacher said to the child.
   c. You tell the teacher on the spot that you learned from the incident.

3. You learn from Linda, a fellow student teacher, that your break time was too long.
   a. You tell Linda you will be more careful in the future.
   b. You deny it.
   c. You tell Linda things that she does wrong.

4. Your supervisor suggests you assume more teaching responsibility.
   a. You follow your supervisor's suggestion.
   b. You tell your supervisor you are not ready.
   c. You ask for clarification.

H. Which of the following best describes your behavior.

1. Preparation:
   a. You prepare in detail in advance.
   b. You wing it.
   c. You rush around at the last minute.

2. New ideas:
   a. You are eager to try new ideas.
   b. You have good ideas but are scared to try them.
   c. You are slowly trying ideas.

3. Compatibility:
   a. You get along well with a few people.
   b. You find it difficult to get to know people.
   c. You get along well with most people.

4. Pressure:
   a. Student teaching makes you tense.
   b. You are relaxed when student teaching.
   c. You are uneasy about 50% of the time.

5. Sense of humor:
   a. You can laugh at yourself.
   b. You are serious most of the time.
   c. Student teaching is not very funny.

6. Communication:
   a. You talk about yourself and your interests easily.
   b. You strain to make small talk.
   c. You are more talkative after you have known people for a while.

7. Interests of others:
   a. You usually know about the interests of others.
   b. You sometimes know about the interests of others.
   c. You rarely know about the interests of others.

8. First day:
   a. Your first day was anxious.
   b. Your first day was scary.
   c. Your first day had its share of ups and downs.
   d. Your first day was relatively calm.

9. Differing opinions:
   a. You tend to argue with people if they have different views.
   b. You carefully defend your opinions.
   c. It does not bother you when others disagree.

10. Problems:
    a. You take problems to friends.
    b. You speak up when something bothers you.
    c. You remain silent, hoping things will change without having to talk about them.

11. Confidence:
    a. Others see you as self-confident.
    b. Others do not notice your capabilities.
    c. You gain confidence slowly.
    d. You lack confidence in new ventures.
    e. You are neutral — neither highly confident nor unassured.
12. Feedback:
    a. You need a lot of reassurance and positive comments.
    b. You are eager for people to recognize your capabilities.
    c. You know your talents and skills will be recognized.
13. Trust:
    a. You are very trusting.
    b. You wait to decide who can be trusted.
    c. People have to earn your trust.
14. Sensitivity:
    a. You are sensitive to others.
    b. Your focus is usually on yourself.
    c. You roll with life's punches.
    d. You are easily hurt.
15. Interaction:
    a. You would rather mix paint than mix with children.
    b. You look forward to working with children on a joint project.
    c. You are more of a guidance figure than a companion.

Review

A. List common student teacher problems.

B. Briefly describe what you feel are prime areas or issues of conflict in student teaching?

Resources

Brooks, Douglas M. *Common Sense in Teaching and Supervising.* Washington, DC: University Press of America, 1978.

Burnett, Jeanne Kendall. "A Student Teacher Speaks," from Kraft, Leonard E., and Casey, John P. *Roles in Off-Campus Student Teaching.* Champaign, IL: Stipes Publishing Co., 1967.

Danoff, J., Breitbart, V., and Barr, E. *Open for Children.* New York: McGraw-Hill Book Co., 1977.

Fuller, Frances. "Concerns of Teachers: A Developmental Conceptualization." *American Educational Research Journal,* 6 (March 1969), pp. 207-226.

Gordon-Nourok, Esther. *You're a Student Teacher!* Sierra Madre, CA: SCAEYC, 1979.

Hendrick, Joanne, Ph.D. *The Whole Child.* St. Louis: C.V. Mosby Co., 1975.

Katz, Lillian. "Developmental Stages of Preschool Teachers." *Elementary School Journal* (1972), pp. 50-54.

Lewis, Claudia, and Winsor, Charlotte B. "Supervising the Beginning Teacher." *Educational Leadership,* Vol XVII, No. 3, (1968).

Read, Katherine, and Patterson, June. *The Nursey School and Kindergarten,* 7th ed. New York: Holt, Rinehart & Winston, Inc., 1980.

Stevens, Joseph H., Jr., and King, Edith W. *Administering Early Education Programs.* Boston: Little, Brown and Co., 1976.

Tittle, Carol K. *Student Teaching.* Metuchen, NJ: The Scarecrow Press, Inc., 1974.

Unit 10
Developing Interpersonal Communication Skills

OBJECTIVES

After studying this unit, the student will be able to:

- Describe the goals of interpersonal communication during the student teaching experience.
- Identify communication skills which aid in sending and receiving messages to and from others.
- Define "authenticity" of communication.
- Describe the atmosphere necessary for promoting student teaching growth.

Clear, authentic communication of feelings, done with skill and sensitivity, is not often taught at either home or school. The student teaching experience puts student teachers, children, and other adults in close human contact, and adds the anxiety-producing procedure of observing and assessing the student teacher's competency development. If you have already acquired the abilities of speaking openly and frankly without alienating, being a skillful listener, and receiving and accepting suggestions, this unit will serve as a review, perhaps giving additional insights and communication techniques.

COMMUNICATION

Communication is a broad term, defined as giving and/or receiving information, signals, or messages. Human interactions and contacts are full of nonverbal signals accounting for 60% to 80% of most human encounters. Lynne De Spelder and Nathalie Prettyman (1980) have identified some of the more easily recognized nonverbal communications:

- facial expression, figure 10-1
- body position
- muscle tone

- breathing tempo
- voice tone

A two-way process of sending and receiving (input and output) information occurs in true communication. Communication skills can be learned; however, it is not easy (Sciarra and Dorsey, 1979). It is imperative

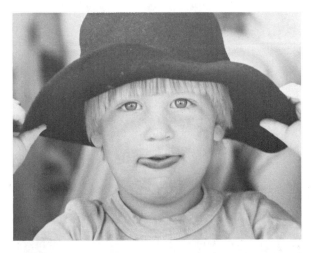

Fig. 10-1 Reading the expressions in children's eyes and faces is a nonverbal communication skill. (Courtesy of Nancy Martin)

that all participants in the student teaching experience have good communication skills. This idea cannot be overemphasized. The whole climate of interpersonal relationships in an education center can be affected by an individual's ability to communicate. As Sciarra and Dorsey point out:

> The director has the major responsibility for creating a climate of care, trust, and respect. This climate can best be achieved by demonstrating caring behaviors, by taking steps to build feelings of community, and by developing good communication skills among and between all members of the center community. (1979, p. 3)

Student teacher growth and self-realization can depend on the communication skills of the student teacher and others. According to Carl Rogers, "It is through a mutually supporting, helping relationship that each individual can become better integrated and more able to function effectively." (1961) Student teachers can model appropriate communication behaviors, increasing effectiveness for other adults and children. Since every family encounters differences in opinion and values at times, a child center can expect disagreements between adults, between children, and between children and adults. This is why good, effective communication skills are essential.

CARING AND SHARING: A FIRST STEP IN COMMUNICATING

What makes a person interesting or easy to talk with? Why do we discuss problems with some individuals and not with others? Perhaps it is because that person with whom we can talk freely loves and accepts us as we are at that moment. Love and acceptance can be demonstrated a number of ways. Saying it may be the easiest way, showing it through actions may be the toughest. With children, giving attention and not interfering with their freedom of choice helps develop their feelings of self-worth and value. Touching also usually reinforces rapport; a pat, hug, or open lap expresses love and acceptance. A wink, a notice of accomplishment, or a sincere recognition of a special uniqueness in an individual helps feelings of caring and sharing grow, setting the stage for easy approaching and interacting.

Respecting an individual's needs, feelings, and desires and building a support system based on love and respect may, as Hans Selye suggests, promote security and freedom from distress which hinders the attainment of potential (1974).

Student teachers work and plan ways to establish rapport with children and adults on their first working days, figure 10-2. Communications depend on first contacts and interactions. Mary Weir and Patricia Eggleston (1975) suggest there are definite skills, based on perseverance and know-how, beginning teachers can acquire to establish an easy flow of daily conversations with children.

- Offer a personal greeting to each child.
- Take time to listen and respond to the child who is bursting to tell a story.
- Make a point of giving a special greeting to the shy child; verbalize the child's actions.
- Introduce new vocabulary.
- Help children plan for the day, building on prior experiences and introducing new ones.
- Permit children to solve their own problems through language.
- Find time to talk personally with each child during the day about important events or experiences in their lives.
- Find opportunities to elaborate and expand children's language.

Fig. 10-2 Being together and enjoying a brief walk can enhance communication.

- Explain requests or demands to children so that they will understand. Avoid repeating what children already know.
- Avoid expressing shock or punishing children for asking questions about physical functions.
- Talk to the children more than adults.

AUTHENTICITY Much has been written about being *real* with children and adults. This means sharing honestly your feelings without putting down or destroying feelings of competency and self-worth. The term *congruent-sending* was coined by Dr. Thomas Gordon, who is well known for his work in human communication. His definition follows:

> Congruence refers to the similarity of what a person (the sender) is thinking or feeling, inside, and what he communicates to the outside. When a person is being congruent, we experience him as "open," "direct," or "genuine." When we sense that a person's communication is incongruent, we judge him as "not ringing true," "insincere," "affected," or just plain "phony." (1972)

The resulting risk in sending real messages without skill is that we may experience rejection. Student teachers can learn to express a wide range of real feelings in a skillful way. Anger is perhaps the hardest to handle skillfully. Haim Ginott has advice for dealing with anger:

> The realities of teaching make anger inevitable. Teachers need not apologize for their angry feelings. An effective teacher is neither a masochist nor a martyr. He does not play the role of a saint or act the part of an angel. He is aware of his human feelings and respects them. Though he cannot be patient, he is always authentic. His response is genuine. His words fit his feeling. He does not hide his annoyance. He does not pretend patience. He does not demonstrate hypocrisy by acting nice when feeling nasty.
>
> An enlightened teacher is not afraid of his anger because he has learned to express it without doing damage. He has mastered the secret of expressing anger without insult.

> . . .When angry, an enlightened teacher remains real. He describes what he sees, what he feels, and what he expects. He attacks the problem, not the person. He protects himself and safeguards his students by using "I" messages. (1972)

A student teacher's idea of the perfect teacher as being always calm and cool may inhibit communicating and produce feelings of guilt. A multitude of emotions will be present during student teaching days; a daily diary helps students pinpoint feelings in early stages, and written expression is often easier than oral sharing with a supervisor. Usually, pleasant feelings are the ones most easily described and orally transmitted. Recognizing the build-up of bad feelings may take a special tuning into the self. Common tension signals include:

- Shrill, harsh, or louder voice tone.
- Inability to see humor in a situation.
- Withdrawal and/or silence.
- Continual mental rehashing of an emotionally trying encounter.

Richard Abidin states that sharing feelings, including those you consider negative, can help develop a closeness to others.

> "Sharing yourself" is a method of building a better relationship and we know that people with close relationships will take into consideration the feelings, ideas, values and expectations of people they love and feel close to. "Sharing yourself" is a way in which close families influence the behavior of each other, but the object of the method is developing closeness, understanding, and love, not power, over one another. (1976, p. 41)

"I" MESSAGES "I"-message sending takes practice, and is only one part of a communication sequence — input or sending. A series of teacher-sent "I" messages follow. You will probably be able to picture the incident which evoked them.

> "I'm very sad that these pages in our new book about horses are torn and crumpled. Book pages need to be turned with care, like this."

"I am angry, Alphonso. I saw that block you threw at Jake. People are not targets for throwing."

"I get so upset when materials I planned to use with the children disappear."

"Wait a minute. If all the student teachers take a break together, there will be only one adult in the classroom. I'm frustrated; I thought there was a clear statement about taking separate breaks."

"I'm confused about this assignment. I feel like I missed an explanation. Can we talk about it sometime today?"

"I'm feeling very insecure right now. I thought I sensed your disapproval when you asked the children to stop the activity planned for them."

Abidin suggests one should guard against "I" messages that are destructive; they sometimes send solutions or involve blaming and judgmental phrases. These are false "I" messages:

"I feel frustrated when you behave so stupidly."

"I am angry when you don't keep your promises. Nobody will be able to trust you." (1976, p. 41)

The ability to send "I" messages is a communication skill which follows recognition of feelings and an effort to communicate directly with individuals concerned. At times we provoke strong feelings within ourselves, and an "inner" dialogue ensues. "I" messages do not tend to build defensiveness as do "you" messages. The communication starts on the right foot.

LISTENING: THE ABILITY TO RECEIVE

We listen with our ears, of course,
But surely it is true
That eyes, and lips, and hands, and feet
can help us listen, too.

Though commonly used with children, this poem may aid student teachers' communicative listening skills. The poem is describing "active listening," a term also attributed to Dr. Thomas Gordon:

In recent years psychotherapists have called our attention to a new kind of listening, "active listening." More than passively attending to the message of the sender, it is a process of putting your understanding of that message to its severest of tests — namely, forcing yourself to put into your own words to the sender for verification or for subsequent correction. (1972)

The active listening process is probably more difficult to learn than that of "I"-message sending. Most individuals have developed listening habits that block true listening. Sara W. Lundsteen has labeled four chief listening distortions:

1. *Attitude cutoff* blocks the reception of information at the spoken source because expectation acts on selection. For example, if a student has a strong negative reaction every time he hears the word *test*, he might not hear the rest of this message: "The test of any man lies in action."

2. *Motive attributing* is illustrated by the person who says of a speaker, "He is just selling me a public relations line for the establishment," and by the child who thinks, "Teachers just like to talk; they don't really expect me to listen the first time because they are going to repeat directions ten times anyway."

3. *Organizational mix-up* happens while one is trying to put someone else's message together — "Did he say 'turn left, then right, then right, then left,' or...?" or "Did he say 'tired' or 'tried'?"

4. *Self-preoccupation* causes distortion because the "listener" is busy formulating his reply and never hears the message: "I'll get him for that; as soon as he stops talking, I'll make a crack about how short he is, then. . ."

Preoccupation with one's own message is a frequent distortion for young listeners. Hanging on to their own thoughts during communications takes a great deal of their attention and energy. Some teachers help out by suggesting that young listeners make small, quick pictures to help cue their ideas when their turn to speak arrives. That way they can get back to listening. Older children may jot down "shorthand" notes to help them hold on to ideas and return to the line of communication. (1976)

New active listening habits can change lives and communicating styles, giving individuals a chance to develop closeness, insight, and empathy.

> To understand accurately how another person thinks or feels from his point of view, to put yourself momentarily into his shoes, to see the world as he is seeing it — you as a listener run the risk of having your own opinions and attitudes changed. (Gordon, 1972)

To develop new listening habits, it is necessary to make a strong effort. The effort will pay off dramatically, as it provides an opportunity to know others at a deeper level. It is a chance to open a small inner door and catch a glimpse of the "authentic" self. By listening closely, a new perception of an individual can be revealed; our own thoughts about how we are going to answer are secondary.

> Before that, when I went to a party I would think anxiously "Now try hard. Be lively. Say bright things. Don't let down." And when tired, I would drink a lot of coffee to keep this up. But now before going to a party, I just tell myself to listen with affection to anyone who talks to me, to be in their shoes when they talk; to try to know them without my mind pressing against theirs, or arguing, or changing the subject. No! My attitude is: "Tell me more. This person is showing me his soul. It is a little dry and meager and full of grinding talk just now, but presently he will begin to think, not just automatically talk. He will show his true self. Then he will be wonderfully alive ..."(Ueland, 1941)

The student teacher hopes others will recognize his or her teaching competencies. Being anxious to please and display what one knows, one can focus communication on sending messages and convincing others of one's value. New listening skills will take conscious practicing. To gain skill in active, reflective listening, an exercise called "mirroring" is often used.

The examples below (Abidin, 1976, p. 36) mirror back to the child the feeling the listener has received.

1. Child, pleading: "I don't want to eat these baked potatoes. I hate them."
   Listener: "You don't like potatoes."
2. Child, pleading and forlorn: "I don't have anything to do today. What can I do? I wish there was something to do!"
   Listener: "You're bored and lonely."
3. Child, angry and confused: "I hate Julie. She always cries and tries to get her way. If I don't do what she wants, she goes home."
   Listener: "You're angry and confused," figure 10-3.
4. Child, stubborn and indignant: "I don't want to take a bath. I'm not even dirty. I hate baths anyway. Why do I have to take a bath every day?"
   Listener: "You don't want to take a bath."
5. Child, crying: "Fran won't let me play with her dolls. She's mean. Make her give me some of them to play with."
   Listener: "You're angry with Fran."
6. Child, crying because of hurt finger: "Ow! Ow! It hurts! Ow!"
   Listener: "It sure hurts!"

Adults find mirroring and reflecting back feeling statements easier with children than adults. With

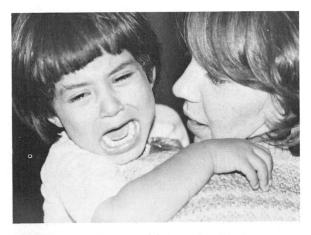

Fig. 10-3 "You're feeling angry right now."

use, mirroring statements feel more comfortable and the sender, whether a child or an adult, feels he or she has been heard. With adults, clarifying mirroring-type questions seem more natural and are conducted in the following fashion:

"Am I hearing you say you're really angry right now?"

"Is frustration what you're feeling?"

"You're saying you don't want to be told what to do?"

Summary

Skill in sending and receiving oral and written messages is a necessary skill for student teachers. The whole sharing and caring climate of the student teaching experience depends in part on communication know-how. Developing rapport with adults and children during early days helps people become relaxed and comfortable, promoting student teacher attempts to display emerging competencies.

Love and acceptance is established in a variety of ways, figure 10-4. Authenticity in communication is deemed highly desirable and effective to earn acceptance during student teaching. "I" messages are an integral part of effective communication skills. Skill in sending "I" messages and active, reflective listening increases with practice, becoming a natural part of the student teaching experience.

Suggested Activities

A. Identify the following statements as either true or false. Note the statements which you felt were controversial. Share your results with the class.

Being Real (Adapted from Greenberg, 1969)

1. I should behave calmly and coolly at all times.
2. I never feel helpless or angry with children in my care.
3. In classroom interaction, children's feelings are more important than teacher's feelings.
4. A competent teacher keeps emotions under control at all times.
5. I love all the children in my care equally.
6. I treat all children alike.
7. Children are handled individually and differently by most teachers.
8. A continuous, positive, warm, affectionate adult/child relationship is easily maintained on a day-to-day basis.
9. A teacher's emotions are easy to hide from children and other teachers.
10. A teacher should try always to be positive rather than negative even if feelings toward a child are negative.
11. Continuous positive comments are not real and sincere, and children know it.
12. Children appreciate being treated honestly, and are encouraged to deal more honestly with their own feelings, thereby being able to control them.
13. Each teacher has certain personality traits they favor in children.
14. Some teachers favor boys over girls.
15. I have no prejudices.
16. As we get to know adults and children, our prejudices often disappear.
17. A good teacher knows about all new methods and teaching techniques.

Fig. 10-4 Physical comforting is one way to establish bonds of acceptance between children and adults. (Courtesy of Nancy Martin)

18. Teachers often live with confusion and uncertainty about what exactly the children in their care are learning.

19. Learning rarely involves struggle and conflict.

20. A well-adjusted teacher is always in balance, with little stress, struggle, conflict, or anxiety because that teacher has figured out the right way to handle children.

21. A child's physical appearance and mannerisms can influence whether the teacher likes or dislikes that child.

22. Almost all teachers lose their tempers at one time or another while in the classroom.

23. Teacher anger often occurs as the result of accumulated irritation, annoyance, and stress.

24. A child usually responds to anger with anger.

25. A teacher who faces his or her own anger and expresses it without hurting the children can help the children learn to face and accept their own anger.

26. Children should know that adults can get angry and still like them.

B. Read the following essay. Write a short paragraph describing your reactions to it and how it relates to a student teacher's communication skills.

PLEASE HEAR WHAT I'M NOT SAYING

Don't be fooled by me. Don't be fooled by the face I wear. For I wear a thousand masks; masks that I'm afraid to take off. Pretending is an art that's second nature with me, but don't be fooled. My surface may seem smooth, but my surface is my mask. Beneath this lies no complacence. Beneath dwells the real me in confusion, fear, and aloneness. But I hide this. I don't want anybody to know it. I panic at the thought of my weakness, and fear being exposed. That's why I frantically create a mask to hide behind, a nonchalant, sophisticated facade, to help me pretend, to shield me from the glance that knows. But such a glance is precisely my salvation, that is, if it is followed by acceptance and love. It's the only thing that will assure me of what I can't assure myself, that I am worth something.

But I don't tell you this. I don't dare. I'm afraid to. I'm afraid your glance will not be followed by acceptance and love. I'm afraid you'll think less of me, that you'll laugh at me. And your laugh would kill me. I'm afraid that deep down I'm nothing, that I'm no good, and that you will see this and reject me. So I play my game, my desperate game, with a facade of assurance outside, and a trembling child within.

And so begins the parade of masks. And my life becomes a front. I idly chatter to you in the suave tones of surface talk. I tell you everything that is really nothing and nothing that is really everything, of what's crying within me. So when I'm going through my routine, do not be fooled by what I'm saying. Please listen carefully, and try to hear what I'm not saying, what I'd like to be able to say, what I need to say for survival, but what I can't say. I dislike hiding. Honestly, I dislike the superficial game I'm playing, the phony game. I'd really like to be genuine and spontaneous and me. But you've got to help me. You've got to hold out your hand, even when that's the last thing I seem to want. Only you can call me into aliveness.

Each time you are kind, gentle, and encouraging, each time you try to understand because you really care, my heart begins to grow wings. Very small wings, very feeble — but wings nonetheless. With your sensitivity and sympathy, and your power of understanding, you can breathe life into me. I want you to know that. I want you to know how important you are to me, how you can be the creator of the person that is me if you choose to. Please choose to. You alone can break down the wall behind which I tremble. You alone can release me from my world of panic and uncertainty, from my lonely person. Do not pass me by. PLEASE — DO NOT PASS ME BY. It will not be easy for you. A long conviction of worthlessness builds strong walls. The nearer you approach me, the blinder I strike back. I fight against the very thing I cry out for. But I am told that love is stronger than walls, and in this lies my hope. Please try to beat down those walls with firm but gentle hands. Who am I, you may wonder. I am someone you know very well. FOR I AM EVERY MAN YOU MEET, AND I AM EVERY WOMAN YOU MEET.

C. Form groups of six for the following role playing activity. Select two members to role play; others will be observers. Switch role playing until all group members have had two turns.

"Role Playing in Reflective Listening"

Directions: Analyze each of the following role-played statements or situations. Offer suggestions for active listening responses.

1. Student teacher to cooperating teacher: "Your room needs more organization."
2. Cooperating teacher to student teacher: "Mary, have you been having problems at home lately?"
3. Irritated cooperating teacher to student teacher: "John, you've been ill too often. We must be able to rely on our student teachers to be here every day."
4. Critical parent to student teacher: "My daughter needs her sweater on when she goes out of doors."
5. One student teacher to another: "Mrs. Brown, the director, only sees what I do wrong, not what I do right."
6. One student teacher to another: "You always leave the sink a mess."
7. John, a preschooler, is dumping paint on the floor.
8. Student teacher to child who is not going to wash area: "It's time to wash hands."
9. Mary, a-four-year-old, hit you because you insisted that she share a toy.
10. College supervisor to student teacher: "Filomena, I'm confused. Your assignments are always late. Weren't my directions clear?"
11. Cooperating teacher to student teacher: "I don't believe you're trying very hard to gain new skills, Tisha."
12. Cooperating teacher to student teacher: "When you were doing your activity, I had a difficult time not stepping in. The boys were destroying the girls' work."

D. In three conversations during the coming week, inhibit your responses and focus on listening. What happened? Share your experiences with the group.

E. With a classmate, describe incidences during student teaching when "listening with affection" would be most difficult.

F. Closely observe the conversations of others. (Television conversations are usable.) Have you observed any skilled listeners? Were there any glimpses of inner self? Report your findings to the group.

Review

A. Write a student teacher "I" message for each of the following situations:

1. Fred, your cooperating teacher, does not have his usual warm greeting and has barely spoken to you all morning.
2. Your supervisor has given you a failing grade on an assignment. You spent many hours on that assignment, and you feel like dropping the class.
3. You cried during the staff meeting when other adults suggested one of your activities with the children was a flop.
4. Another student teacher in your classroom is not living up to assigned duties, making it twice as difficult for you.
5. A child says to you, "I wish you were my mommy."
6. Your cooperating teacher has asked you not to pick up and hold a particular child. You feel the child needs special attention.
7. An irate parent says to you, "This school policy about bringing toys from home is ridiculous."
8. Your neighbor says to you, "I hear you're going to college to become a babysitter. How wasteful of your talents."

B. Define the following terms:
   authentic communication
   nonverbal messages
   rapport
   congruent sending
   active listening
   motive attributing
   self-preoccupation listening

C. Give an example of an appropriate student teacher verbalization for each of the following:

1. Offer a personal greeting to each child.
2. Help a child plan for the first activity choice, building on a prior experience.
3. Avoid expressing shock when a child asks about genitalia seen on another child.

D. Choose the best answer to complete each statement.

1. Your cooperating teacher has informed your supervisor that you were not prepared for class on the preceding day. This is not the first time it has happened. Your supervisor seems upset since you two have already discussed this problem. In talking to your supervisor, you want to use active listening techniques in communicating. You say,
   a. "You need to explain assignment dates again, please."
   b. "She's always criticizing me; I'm really upset."
   c. "But I was prepared. I brought in two flannelboard stories and a music game!"
   d. "I can see you're disappointed and perhaps a bit angry, too."
   e. "Isn't there any way I can please the two of you?"

2. Your cooperating teacher is always stepping in and taking over in guidance situations. You have pleaded to be allowed to follow through so children will know you mean what you say. You decide to send a congruent feeling statement at a staff meeting. You say,
   a. "I'm really frustrated. You always take over."
   b. "I've had it. Can't you let me finish what I start?"
   c. "I'm confused. I want the children to know I mean what I say, but it's just not happening."
   d. "You need to step back and let me follow through with the children."
   e. "I know you're trying to help me, but I don't need your help."

3. You feel you can easily handle the whole day's program, but you haven't been given the opportunity. You say to your supervisor,
   a. "Please help me. The cooperating teacher doesn't give me enough to do."
   b. "I feel I'm competent enough to handle a whole day's program."
   c. "I'm just doing clean-up and housekeeping most of the time."
   d. "You could ask my cooperating teacher to give me more responsibility."
   e. "I'll sure be happy when I finish and have my own class."

4. Mrs. Schultz is angry and yells, "Janita wet her pants again. I don't think any of you remembered to remind her!" You respond by saying,
   a. "You're upset because you don't think we reminded Janita."
   b. "They all wet sometimes, Mrs. Schultz!"
   c. "I didn't see her wet today."
   d. "We remind all the children right before snacks."
   e. "My child wets at school also!"

5. Congruent sending and authentic sending are
   a. very different.
   b. easy skills for most adults.
   c. similar to active listening.
   d. very similar.
   e. similar to parcel post sending.

E. Complete the following statements.
1. To immediately verbalize the feelings which I sensed during a conversation with someone seems. . .
2. The hardest thing about practicing "I"-message sending will be. . .

Resources

Abidin, Richard R. *Parenting Skills: Trainers' Manual.* New York: Human Sciences Press, 1976.

De Spelder, Lynne Ann, and Prettyman, Nathalie. *A Guidebook for Teaching Family Living.* Boston: Allyn and Bacon, Inc., 1980.

Ginott, Haim. "I'm Angry! I'm Appalled! I am Furious!" *Teacher and Child.* New York: Macmillan Publishing Co., Inc., 1972. Reprinted in *Today's Education Magazine,* NEA Journal (Nov. 19, 1972).

Gordon, Thomas, Ph.D. "The Risks of Effective Communication." *Parent Notebook,* a publication of Effectiveness Training Associates (1972).

Greenberg, Herbert M. *Teaching with Feeling.* New York: Macmillan Publishing Co., Inc., 1969.

Lundsteen, Sara W. *Children Learn to Communicate.* Englewood Cliffs, NJ: Prentice-Hall, Inc., 1976.

Rogers, Carl. *On Becoming a Person.* Boston: Houghton Mifflin Co., 1961.

Sciarra, Dorothy Jane, and Dorsey, Anne G. *Developing and Administering A Child Care Center*. Boston: Houghton Mifflin Co., 1979.

Selye, Hans. *Stress Without Distress*. New York: The New American Library, 1974.

Ueland, Brenda. "Tell Me More." *Ladies Home Journal* (Nov. 1941), 58:51 as quoted by Clark Moustakas in *The Authentic Teacher*. Cambridge: Howard A. Doyle Printing Co., 1966.

Weir, Mary K., and Eggleston, Patricia J. "Teacher's First Words." *Day Care and Early Education* (Nov./Dec. 1975).

Unit 11
Problem Solving

OBJECTIVES

After studying this unit, the student will be able to:

- Identify a sequential approach to problem solving.
- Describe three alternatives when faced with problems.
- Use alternative solutions.
- State both sides of a problem.

Conflicts are a part of life. Resolving these conflicts depends largely on individuals' reactions to them. You have already developed a style of reacting; it varies according to the age, sex, dependency, and love you have for the other persons involved. Problem solving becomes easier when an established, trusting relationship exists between people.

Clark Moustakas has identified two ways teachers and children establish relationships.

Two ways in which teachers may establish significant bonds in their relationships with children are the confrontation and the encounter. The confrontation is a meeting between persons who are involved in a conflict or controversy and who remain together, face-to-face, until feelings of divisiveness and alienation are resolved and replaced by genuine acceptance and respect, even though differences in belief and attitude may continue to exist. The encounter is a sudden spontaneous, intuitive meeting between teacher and child in which there is an immediate sense of relatedness and feeling of harmony and communion. (1966)

THEORIES IN PROBLEM SOLVING

Glickman (1981) has pinpointed three distinct styles which school administrators or directors,

who often face staff conflicts, use in human interactions, figure 11-1. At one end of Glickman's continuum is a nondirective style of relating; collaborative or joint problem solving is seen in the middle; directive style at the other extreme. You may function according to each of these styles when faced with conflicts, figure 11-2.

In your attempts to solve problems, you will want to adopt a planned approach rather than a random one. Glickman's "planful" responses (1981, pp. 10–11) are as follows:

- *Listening:* saying nothing, perhaps nodding, being attentive, waiting for the speaker to finish.
- *Clarifying:* replying with questions intended to give a fuller understanding of the problem.
- *Encouraging:* talking at great lengths about other problem factors.
- *Presenting:* offering your thoughts on the situation or behavior.
- *Problem solving:* initiating the discussion with statements aimed at exploring solutions.
- *Negotiating:* attempting to quickly reach a settlement.
- *Demonstrating:* physically showing how to act, what to do, or what to say.
- *Directing:* detailing what one must do.

	1 Listen- ing	2 Clarify- ing	3 Encourag- ing	4 Present- ing	5 Problem Solving	6 Nego- tiating	7 Demon- strating	8 Directing	9 Standard- izing	10 Rein- forcing	

s _____ t

T   S

Orientation
  to
Supervision: Nondirective   Collaborative   Directive

Key: T = Maximum teacher responsibility   S = Maximum supervisor responsibility
      t = Minimum teacher responsibility   s = Minimum supervisor responsibility

Fig. 11-1 The Supervisory Behavior Continuum (Reprinted with permission of the Association for Supervision and Curriculum Development and Carl D. Glickman. Copyright © 1981 by the Association for Supervision and Curriculum Development. All rights reserved.)

Nondirective	*Collaborative*	*Directive*
Help another by	With one or more individuals	Help another by
Listening	Talk it out	Telling them what to do
Asking clarifying questions	Name and describe conflict	Showing them what to do
Encouraging to find one's own solution	Give and take	Making a rule to follow
	Mediate and show ideas	Commanding that it be done in a
Help yourself by	Negotiate	certain way
Self-analysis	Form a pact	
Self-assessment	Come to agreement	Help yourself by
Finding your own solution	Contract with one another	Making a clear rule about your own
		conduct

Fig. 11-2 Problem solving

	Magical problem-solving	*Naive problem-solving*	*Critical problem-solving*
Naming the problem	No problems seen, or accepted as facts of existence	Individual's behavior deviates from ideal roles or rules	Unjust or conflict-producing rules and roles of the system
Analysis of causes	External, inevitable: God, fate, luck, chance	Individual inadequacies in self or others	Historical causes; vested interests of groups; internalization of roles and rules by others
Acting to solve the problem	Passive acceptance, conformity	Reform individuals	Transform one's internalized roles and rules and change the system's roles and rules.

Fig. 11-3 Aspects of problem solving [Reprinted from "Education for What?" by A. Alschuler, et al., in *Human Growth Games*, J. Fletcher (ed.), 1978, with permission of the publisher, Sage Publications, Beverly Hills, California.]

- *Reinforcing:* delineating the conditions and consequences of the solution.

Freire (1970, 1973) has identified three aspects of problem solving: naming the problem; analyzing the causes; and acting to solve the problem. In addition, Freire has identified three stages of consciousness in problem solving: magical problem solving; naive problem solving; and critical problem solving. Personalizing this theory, figure 11-3, for student teachers as it relates to problem-solving styles involves answering the following:

- Do you passively accept problems as just your luck without trying to change them? (*Magical:* "That's just the way it is; I'm unlucky.")
- Do you realize problems exist, putting the cause on your own shoulders? (*Naive:* "If I did this or that, it would have been okay.")
- Do you tend to blame the system, the process, or the situation rather than yourself or others? (*Critical:* "No one can pass student teaching; it's just too hard.")

Examining problem-solving theories may help you understand yourself and your problem-solving style.

A PROBLEM-SOLVING PROCESS

Most problems can be faced in a sequential manner. This text suggests problem solving in a rational manner, when emotions are under control. Take some time alone to cool down or physically burn off excessive tension before you try to use it. Substituting new behaviors into your problem-solving style takes time and effort. Practice is necessary.

Sending "I" messages and active listening will avert problem build-up. However, you do have the choice of living with a problem and not working on it. This can work for short periods, but usually erodes the quality of your relationship with others or with yourself. Alienation occurs in most instances, but you may prefer this course of action and be prepared for its consequences. Most often you will choose to confront others or yourself and work toward solutions which eliminate the problem. Familiarize yourself with the following. It suits many different situations.

Step 1. Recognition of tensions, emotions, or the problem.

Step 2. Analysis. (Who and what is involved? When and where does it occur? Whose problem is it?)

Step 3. Sending "I" messages. (Active listening and reflecting messages.)

Step 4. Discussion. (Probing; getting more data. Who owns the problem?)

Step 5. Stating both sides of the problem clearly.

Step 6. Proposing and finding possible solutions.

Step 7. Agreement to try one of these solutions. Agreement to meet again if the solution does not work.

Step 8. Consideration of willingness, time, and effort to solve the problem.

This process can be attempted but will not work if one party refuses to talk, mediate, or look for courses of action which will satisfy everyone involved. Refusing to act on solutions also hinders the process. Problem solving is two sided even when you are the only one involved. At Step 2, one sometimes realizes the problem belongs to another, and the best course of action is to help that person communicate with someone else. Often a problem may disappear at Step 3.

The discussion, Step 4, can include "I'm really interested in talking about it" or "Let's talk; we'll examine just what's happening to us." However, there is a tendency to blame rather than identify contributing causes. Getting stuck and not moving past Step 4 hampers resolution of the problem. Statements like "You're right; I really avoid cleaning that sink" or "I'm really bothered by interruptions during planned group times" all involve owning the problem.

Before possible solutions are mentioned, a clear statement of conflicting views, Step 5, adds clarification.

With a child: "You'd like to paint next, and I told Carlos it's his turn."

With a fellow student teacher: "You feel the way I handle Peter is increasing his shyness, and I feel it's helping him."

With a cooperating teacher: "I think my activity was suitable for the group, but you think it didn't challenge them."

With a supervisor: "You feel I tend to avoid planning outdoor activities; I think I've planned quite a few."

Your confrontation might start at Step 6. ("Let's figure out some way to make the noisy time right before nap a little calmer and quieter.") Finding alternate solutions admits there are probably a number of possibilities. "Together we'll figure a way" or "That's one way; here's another idea." A do-it-my-way attitude inhibits joint agreement. Thinking alternatives over and getting back together is helpful at times. Seeking a consultant who offers ideas can aid problems which participants see as hopeless.

When all parties decide to try one solution, Step 7, consideration should be given to meeting again if that particular alternative does not work. ("We'll try it this week, and discuss whether it's working next Monday, okay?")

Step 8 reinforces both sides. "Good job. We figured it out." "Thanks for taking the time to solve this." "I appreciated your efforts in effecting a solution." This process is not to be used as a panacea; rather, it contains helpful guidelines.

Classroom problems can involve any aspect of the student teaching situation, figure 11-4. Interpersonal conflicts will take both courage and consideration of the proper time and place to confront.

The teacher is sometimes afraid to confront a child who is hostile, caustic, or vengeful. Such a teacher avoids and avoids until the accumulation of feelings becomes so unbearable an explosion occurs, and the teacher loses control. Once the self is out of control, there is no possibility to bring about a positive resolution of the problem. But when the hateful, rejecting emotions subside, there is always hope that the teacher can come to terms with the child and reach a depth of relatedness and mutuality. (Moustakas, 1966, p. 23)

Arrange to problem solve when participants have no classroom responsibilities, and where there will not be any interruptions or noninvolved observers.

RESISTANCE Resistance of rules and not conforming to what is expected can be seen in both children and adults. It is usually viewed as negative behavior. Moustakas believes it is healthy.

Resistance is a way for the child to maintain his own sense of self in the light of external pressures to manipulate and change him. It is a healthy response, an effort of the individual to sustain the integrity of the self. (1966, p. 31)

Resistance and controversy can become challenges that develop our understanding and let us know others at a deeper level, figure 11-5. Though confrontations

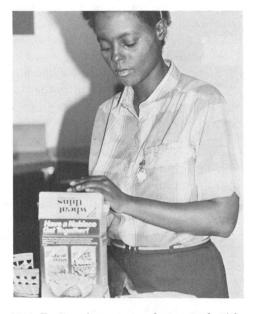

Fig. 11-4 Feeling that you are always stuck with snack preparation is a problem.

Fig. 11-5 Through problem solving, we can actually understand a child at a deeper level.

may frighten student teachers in early days, later they are seen as opportunities to know more about the children and adults.

The threat of anxiety in facing an embittered, destructive child can be eliminated only in actual confrontation with the dread child because until we actually meet him, we cannot know him. (Moustakas, 1966, p. 24)

Summary

Problem-solving skills are important for student teachers, figure 11-6. There seem to be definite styles of relating to others during problem-solving situations. Students are urged to practice new techniques in problem solving. Early fears of confronting tend to disappear as communicative problem solving becomes a way to know and understand others. In problem solving, teachers model the skills for children; therefore, the children can learn these skills.

Fig. 11-6 Woodworking is often a favorite activity, but it may require problem-solving conversation. (Courtesy of Jim Clay)

Suggested Activities

A. Choose a partner, and discuss your style of solving problems or getting your own way with your family. List techniques that you believe help individual solutions, but are destructive to joint solutions. After five minutes, discuss this with another partner. Report back to total group.

B. In the following situations, state as clearly as possible what you think are both sides of the problem. Then describe two alternatives which you feel might satisfy both parties of each conflict.

1. Cecelia has been assigned to student teach from 9:00 to 2:30 on Tuesdays. Her cooperating teacher notices she has been leaving early. Cecelia has been arriving ten to fifteen minutes early each day. Mr. Kifer, the cooperating teacher, confronts Cecelia one day before she departs. "Leaving early, Cecelia?"

2. Henri, a four-year-old, has been told repeatedly by the student teacher that he must put the blocks he used back on the shelf. Henri has ignored the request continually. The student teacher requests the cooperating teacher to ask Henri to replace the blocks since he does not respond to the student teacher.

3. The cooperating teacher has been silent most of the morning. The student teacher can feel tension mounting and says, "I'm really feeling uncomfortable because I sense there is something wrong." The cooperating teacher ignores the remark. At the end of work, the student discusses the situation with the supervisor.

4. Christopher, a student teacher, is fuming. "After all the work I put into the activity, she didn't even mention it," he says to Charlotte, another student teacher.

5. "I'd really like to present this new song to the children," says Robin, a student teacher. "You didn't put it in the plan book, Robin, and I have a full day planned," the cooperating teacher says. "Let's talk about it; I can see the disappointment on your face." Robin replies, "It's not disappointment. I can't see why the schedule is so inflexible." "Let's talk about that after the morning session, Robin."

6. "I sure needed your help at circle today," the cooperating teacher said. "I was in the bathroom with Anthony; he's got those pants that button at the shoulders," the student teacher answers.

7. "I'm really tired today, Mrs. Cuffaro," the student teacher answers when asked why she stayed in the housekeeping area most of the morning. Mrs. Cuffaro says, "There were lots of other children who could have used your assistance, Annette. Will you have time to talk when the children are napping?" "Sure," Annette replies.

8. Miriam, an attractive student teacher, is assigned to an on-campus laboratory school. Male friends often hang around the lobby or ask the secretary to give her messages and notes. The secretary has told Miriam this is bothersome. Miriam tells the secretary the notes often concern getting a ride home since she does not have a car.

C. Read each statement. Of the two courses of action, select the one you feel is appropriate. In small groups, discuss your choices.

1. Some of your money has been missing from a locker you share with another student teacher.
   A. You should consult with your supervisor.
   B. You should ask the other student about it.

2. You have spoken sharply to one of the children.
   A. You ask your cooperating teacher if you can step out of the room for a minute.
   B. You ask your cooperating teacher to move the child into the cooperating teacher's group.

3. You do not feel comfortable singing; you feel your voice is "toad-like."
   A. You should use a record to teach the song.
   B. You should say, "I'm a real toad at singing."

4. Your supervisor expected you at a meeting, and you forgot to attend.
   A. You suggest you pick the next meeting time.
   B. You confess to forgetting.

5. An aide in the classroom seems very competent to you. You feel she has more skills than the cooperating teacher. She makes a remark about the cooperating teacher's lack of patience with a particular child.
   A. You agree with her.
   B. You ask, "Have you and Miss Tashima ever discussed child-handling techniques?"

6. Vicki, a student teacher, is friendly, attractive, and charming. She has barely passed her previous classes, and has used her personal charm more than study skills. In student teaching, she's sliding, doing only the minimum amount of work. She feels both her supervisor and resident teacher are aware that she is "trying only to slide by."
   A. Vicki should drop out.
   B. Vicki should admit her past actions have caught up with her.

7. Leticia works in a community preschool. She feels that the theory in classes has focused on the ideal rather than the practical. Her supervisor has warned that her methods produce child behaviors which are negative and growth limiting.
   A. Leticia says, "You know what is in the books isn't real; that's not the way it is in preschool."
   B. Leticia asks, "Exactly which of my behaviors produce those child behaviors?"

8. Although Gloria knows spanking children is against the law, she is reluctant to tell her cooperating teacher in the church-affiliated preschool. Everyone who works at the school accepts it as appropriate. Gloria can see the children's behavior changing for the better. (Gloria is a member of the church.)
   A. Gloria should keep silent.
   B. Gloria should consult with her supervisor.

9. Sydney has been placed in a preschool where the cooperating teacher often leaves the room, leaving her in full charge of twenty preschoolers. Sydney handles it well, and has planned many interesting, exciting activities for the children.
   A. She should talk to her cooperating teacher about her responsibility.
   B. She should consult with her supervisor.

10. Connie has been placed in a preschool that handles children of an ethnic group different from her own. She feels excluded and out of step, even though her cooperating teacher has been friendly.
    A. She should discuss the problem with the cooperating teacher.
    B. She should wait and see if the feeling subsides. If not, she should talk to her supervisor.

11. The cook at the center where Teresa has been placed is never happy about the way Teresa cleans the tables after lunch.
    A. She should ask the cook to show her how it should be done.
    B. She should ask her cooperating teacher about the cook.

12. A parent compliments Peter, a student teacher, about activities he has planned which are multicultural. "You offer the children so many activities that Mrs. Bridgeman, the cooperating teacher, would never have thought of! I'm glad you're a student teacher in this classroom!"
    A. Peter should smile and discuss the remark with the cooperating teacher.
    B. Peter should defend the cooperating teacher because he knows the classroom is full of multicultural materials.

Review

A. Arrange the following problem-solving steps in order, based on the eight-step sequence. You may find that more than one applies to the same step.

1. Cooperating teacher: "We'll put paintings without names in this box this week and see what happens." Student teacher: "Okay."

2. Student teacher: "You feel children's art work should always have the child's name printed in the upper left corner."

3. Cooperating teacher: "You could put names on the art work when you're the adult in the art area."

4. Student teacher: "I feel the child's name should be put on the art work only when the child gives permission to do so. If the children don't ask to have their names put on it, they will learn the consequences when it's time to take the art home.

5. Student teacher: "I could tell each child what will happen if there is no name on his or her painting."

6. Cooperating teacher: "There's been quite a bottleneck when parents try to find their child's art work at departure time. Sometimes there are no names printed in the upper left corner."

7. Student teacher: "You would like to put each child's name on his or her art work, and I think each child can learn something if I don't print his or her name when he or she does not give me permission to do so."

8. Student teacher: "I appreciate your understanding my point of view."

9. Cooperating teacher: "You could write the child's name lightly if that child said no.

10. Cooperating teacher: "I think the lesson to be learned isn't worth the commotion at closing."

11. Student teacher: "This is the way I feel about names on art work."

B. Using Glickman's "planful" responses, identify the following statements. (Example: "Tell me more about it." *Encouraging*)

1. "Do you mean you're feeling angry?"

2. "Just stop helping the child."

3. "The way I look at it, you've been asking for a lot of direction from the cooperating teacher."

4. "I'll put the chairs up on Tuesdays; you can do it on Thursdays."

5. "Tell her it's her turn."

6. "If you straighten the closet every day, he'll get the message and do it too."

7. "I think I hear anxiety in your voice."

8. "Looking the speaker in the eyes."

9. "There's more, isn't there?"

C. Briefly answer the following questions.

1. How can facing a defiant child be considered a challenge?

2. What is positive about a child resisting expectations, and doing something his or her own way and in his or her own time?

D. Match items in Column I with their *opposites* in Column II.

I	II
1. Silence and withdrawal	a. Scaring your opponent
2. Problem solving	b. Focusing on your verbal defense
3. Listening	c. Blowing up
4. Self-solution	d. Out of control, irrational
5. Early "I" message	e. Avoiding confrontations
6. "Planful"	f. Alienation, and living with the problem
7. Encounter	g. Being given a command
8. Using tears	h. Talking too much
9. Ignoring child behavior	i. Confronting a child for hitting another

E. Complete the following statements.
1. If a person refuses to talk about a problem. . .
2. One can resign oneself to alienation when. . .
3. The hardest part of problem solving for me is. . .
4. Some techniques for problem solving which were not encouraged in this unit are. . .

5. One problem that is probably going to occur in student teaching that was not mentioned in this unit is. . .

F. List as many possible alternative solutions as you can for the following problem.

Winona has been placed with a cooperating teacher who she feels has created a classroom environment which offers the children few play choices. She has communicated this idea to her cooperating teacher who then asks Winona for suggestions. Winona's suggestions might include. . .

Resources

Freire, Paulo. *Pedagogy of the Oppressed.* New York: Seabury Press, Inc., 1970.

_____ . *Education for Critical Consciousness.* New York: Seabury Press, Inc., 1970.

Glickman, Carl D. *Developmental Supervision.* Alexandria, VA: Association for Supervision and Curriculum Development, 1981.

Moustakas, Clark. *The Authentic Teacher.* Cambridge: Howard A. Doyle Printing Co., 1966.

Section 5 The Child

Unit 12
Observation and Assessment

OBJECTIVES

After studying this unit, the student will be able to:

- Use at least three different types of observation forms: narrative (anecdotal), event sampling, and fixed interval (time sampling).
- Analyze a child's behavior from information gathered through observation.
- Develop an individual learning plan for the observed child.
- Describe the difference between observation and conjecture.

OBSERVATION FORMS

In this unit, we are going to go beyond our earlier description of behavior and observation in order to help you understand how to use different types of observation forms and, more importantly, how to use the information learned to develop learning plans for the observed child. (A developmental checklist can be found in the Appendix.)

NARRATIVE   This is one of the simplest forms to use when observing children. A narrative describes the child's behavior as it occurs. As the observer, you can sit to one side of the room or yard with a small notebook, figure 12-1. Pick a child to observe, and simply record what you see. Your narrative might look something like this:

Stevie, one of the new children in the room of four-year-olds at the ABC Nursery School, enters

Fig. 12-1 Observation can take place inside the class-room.

the room and hangs onto his mother's coat, with his finger in his mouth. He looks unhappy as his mother says impatiently, "Let go, Stevie; you're too big to act like a baby. You know I'm in a hurry to get to work this morning." Stevie looks at another child, Sammy, who is playing with the blocks. "Look at how nicely Sammy is playing! Why don't you go over and play with him."

Stevie begins to cry as his mother attempts to drag him over to the block area. He whines, "Don't wanta stay today, Mama. Wanta go home!"

Mrs. Thomas, the teacher, intervenes. "Mrs. Con—way, could you stay awhile today? I know Stevie would like to show you the dinosaur he made yesterday. It's drying on the shelf over by the window. Stevie, why don't you show the dinosaur to your Mom?"

(Mrs. Thomas really knows how to handle Stevie's reluctance to separate from his mother, doesn't she? Look at how happy he is now, showing his dinosaur to his Mom! I remember how much time he took yesterday when he made it; I didn't think he'd ever finish! But Mrs. Thomas let him take as much time as he needed to feel satisfied. I guess she knew that if he got started describing the dinosaur to his mother, he'd forget about her having to leave. I wonder why Mrs. Conway doesn't give Stevie a little extra time each day when she brings him instead of hurrying him so. She knows he hates to be left in a hurry!)

After a minute or two of describing the dinosaur and its ferocity, Stevie goes to the door with his mother. "Bye, Mom. See you this afternoon." Stevie runs off. "Sammy, let me play with some of the blocks!" "Ok, Stevie. Wanta help me build a garage for the big trucks?"

"Sure."

Stevie and Sammy work quickly and build a garage for three of the big trucks.

Davie and Mike come in together with Mike's older brother.

"I'll be back at 3:30 when school gets out. Be ready, you two."

"Mrs. Thomas will see we're ready, Joe; you know we'll be ready," says Mike.

Davie goes over to the garage Stevie and Sammy have built. "I want the red truck," he demands. "Can't have it. We need it," protests Stevie. Davie grabs the truck. Stevie gets to his feet and shouts, "Gimme it back!" Stevie tries to grab the truck

from Davie. A tug-of-war begins as both boys shake the truck between them. Sammy says to Stevie, "Aw, let him have it. We got enough trucks anyway." Stevie lets go of the truck, sits back down on the floor, puts his finger in his mouth, and sulks.

How might this same interaction appear if you were using a different observation form? (However easy the narrative is to read, it does remove you from the classroom action while you are writing.) The narrative can be abbreviated somewhat through the use of the anecdotal record form. Figure 12-2 illustrates this narrative in anecdotal form.

EVENT SAMPLING FORM In contrast to the narrative and anecdotal forms, an event sampling form, figure 12-3, might be used. In this form Stevie's play behaviors are being observed. In addition, the times of each observation are indicated to provide additional information. Two theorists lend themselves to a consideration of children's play behaviors in terms of an observation model. They are Parten (1932) whose play categories have been useful for many years and Piaget (1962).

Parten divided play behaviors into the following categories: *Onlooking* (observing, talking, but not participating), *solitary* (play without reference to another child), *parallel* (play in which two or more children may be using similar materials without personal interaction), *associative* (play in which two or more children may be using the same materials but each child is doing a separate activity; for example, each child may be using blocks, building separate towers), and *cooperative* (play in which there is a common goal toward which two or more children are working; for example, the children are using blocks to build one house (1932, p. 244).

Piaget suggested that there are three types of play which are common among preschoolers: *symbolic* (play in which the objects with which the child is playing become something else; for example, blocks become a garage or a house), *practice* (play in which the child continuously repeats an activity as though to master it; for example, in block play, trying over and over to build an ever taller structure without calling it a tower), and *games* (play

Student Teacher:	MB

Name of School: ABC School, Day Care Center

Date: 16 September

Identity Key (Do NOT use real names)	Description of What Child Is Doing	Time	Comments
S – Stevie	S enters, clings to M's coat. Finger in mouth.	8:03	S looks unhappy.
M – S's Mom	M, "Let go, S. You're too big to act like a baby. I'm in a hurry; you know it!		I wish S's M wouldn't do that!
T – Teacher	Lk how nice Sa plays by self!		
Sa – Sammy	Why not play w/him?		
D – Davie	S cries.	8:05	
Mi – Mike	T suggests S show M dinosaur fr yesterday.		I wish I'd thought of that; S is really proud of his dinosaur.
J – Joe, Mike's brother	S and M go to see dino.		
	S says "Bye" to M; goes to Sa, "Lemme play w/you."	8:08	
	Sa says, "Let's build a garage for the trucks."		Good for Sa; he always has good ideas!
* * * *	* * * * * * * *	* *	* * * *
	D, Mi, & J come in.	8:47	
	D says, "I want the red truck."		
	S, "No; we need it."		
	D grabs the truck.	8:55	Oh oh, I better watch & see what happens.
	Sa says, "Let him have it. We have enough trucks."		I love kids like Sa! He is so mature!

Fig. 12-2 An anecdotal record form

Child: Stevie

Date: 16 September

	Symbolic	Practice	Games
Onlooking:	Watching M & J in playhouse (9:45 am)		
Solitary:	Pretending to be Superman on jungle gym (10:23 am)	Putting puzzles together (8:35 am) On swg. Trying to pump self (10:40 am)	
Parallel:	Bldg rd for car in sandbox (3:20 pm)	Dumping H_2O fr 1 container to another at H_2O table (2:57 pm)	
Associative:		Bldg towers w/sm blks next to Sa (8:30 am)	
Cooperative:	Bldg garage w/ lrg blks w/ Sa (8:12 am)		Following Sa's directions for card game, "War" (4:10 pm)

Fig. 12-3 A two-dimensional play model, combining event and time sampling

in which the children follow a set of agreed-upon rules).

In looking at the anecdotal record and narrative account of Stevie's early-morning activities, it would be noted on the event sampling form that he was involved in cooperative-symbolic play with Sammy. If, however, Stevie was followed throughout the day, observations might look more like the rest of the event sampling form in figure 12-3.

FIXED INTERVAL MODEL Only a small portion of Stevie's total activities were recorded using the event sampling form. If more than a sampling is needed, a *fixed interval* or *time sampling* model might be used, figure 12-4.

OBSERVATIONS

As you can see, each type of observation form produces a slightly different picture of the child being observed. In addition, each form takes a different amount of time to complete. With both the narrative and time sampling models, time is needed to sit and observe. If you are involved actively in the room with the children, you do not often have the freedom to do this. (One of the reasons we have used the opening hour for our example is that often there are fewer children present at that time; thus, it is easier to take the time to observe just one child.)

Event sampling with a model, such as the one on play behaviors, may be somewhat easier to complete because you are not limited by time. The observation form can be placed on a clipboard and carried everywhere. You can enter remarks quickly, especially if you code and abbreviate. Children can be easily coded by initials. Activities can be easily abbreviated: building can be bldg; painting can become ptg; water can be H_2O; swinging can become swg, etc. Once you begin to use abbreviations, you will find your observations are simplified. Always remember that you can go over your observations after the children leave or during nap time and make any necessary notations. If you noted a question such as the one in figure 12-4 (Deliberately?), and if you asked Stevie if his action was deliberate and he said yes, this can be entered on the form in a different colored ink. By

---

Child: Stevie   Date: 16 September

8:05 a.m.	S showing off dinosaur to his Mom.
8:10 a.m.	S building garage for trucks w/Sa.
8:15 a.m.	Still building garage w/Sa.
8:20 a.m.	Driving trucks around garage w/Sa.
8:25 a.m.	Placing sm blocks in dump truck; driving to side of block area, dumping blocks. Building tower. Tries to build tower taller than Sa's tower.
8:30 a.m.	Still bldg tower w/Sa.
8:35 a.m.	Runs over to puzzle table. "This one's easy," he says. Dumps it out, puts it together easily. Picks a second one; does the same.
8:40 a.m.	Back w/Sa building another garage for the large trucks (three of them); asks, "Can I use a big book for the roof?" When told "No," improvises w/piece of cardboard box from playhouse.
8:45 a.m.	Still bldg garage w/Sa.
8:50 a.m.	After argument w/D, gives D truck; goes back to play w/Sa. (What a pleasure to have a child as mature as Sa in the Center!)
9:00 a.m.	Joins rest of children on rug for opening "good morning" song. Sings loudly and off-key. (Deliberately?)

Fig. 12-4 Five-minute time sampling model

using a different color, you can quickly and easily differentiate between an original comment and a follow-up comment.

You may have already realized that event sampling and time sampling can be combined. Look at figure 12-3. It was easy to indicate the time of day that each activity was observed.

You can now see that you have a sampling of eight play behaviors of Stevie and that these are scattered throughout the day. If you want to observe Stevie again in order to get a better picture, you can easily note that you have no observations between 10:40 a.m. and nearly 3:00 p.m. Using the same observation form another day, you can concentrate on Stevie's behaviors during the missing times. After three or four days in a row, you will begin to have a good picture of what Stevie's play behaviors are like, figure 12-5.

The best method, however, is to combine forms, using different ones for different purposes. Although they take the most time, the narrative and anecdotal forms provide the most information. Forms such as the two-dimensional play model are handy to use when time is limited. They also supplement the narrative forms well and provide much information relevant to their single purpose. We have used the example of play behaviors, but you might want to use social behaviors or attending behaviors.

Fig. 12-5 A child's motor skill can be observed by watching the use of play materials.

When working with a child who is asocial or anti-social, social behaviors become more important to observe. One such form, figure 12-6, was developed by Goodwin and Meyerson for use in the classroom, and is called the Teacher/Pupil Interaction Scale (TPIS). The scale measures four types of teacher behavior and four types of student behavior on another two-dimensional form. The teacher behaviors are as follows: (1) instruction; (2) reinforcing; (3) nonattending; and (4) disapproving. The student behaviors are: (1) attending; (2) scanning; (3) social; and (4) disruptive. Both teacher and student behaviors are defined as follows.

Teacher Behavior

Instruction: Makes explanation, talks to pupil, gives directions, asks questions, etc.

Reinforcing: Dispenses praise, smiles, nods, makes physical contact by patting, touching; dispenses material rewards (candy, tokens).

Nonattending or neutrals: Withholds attention, sits passively, attends to personal notes, works with other pupils, attends to activities which do not include the pupil being observed.

Disapproving: Criticizes, corrects, admonishes, reproves, expresses generally negative feelings, statements, etc.

Pupil Behavior

Attending: When receiving direction or instructions, maintains eye contact or heeds direction. When performing desk work, attends to work (turns pages, uses pencil, looks at paper). When addressed by teacher, child attends.

Scanning: Looks about room; watches other children; daydreams; makes no verbal or physical contact with other children.

Social contacts: Teaches other children; talks to others; walks about room interacting with others but does not attract the general attention of the class with noise or disturbances.

Disruptive: Calls attention to self by behaviors which are audible/visible throughout the room, e.g. tapping with pencil, throwing objects, shouting.

Pupil: Stevie
Observer: Student teacher
Teacher: Cooperating teacher

Date: 16 September
Times: 9:00 a.m.
10:05 a.m.
2:32 p.m.
4:47 p.m.
5:35 p.m.

	1	2	3	4
A	1			
B	1			
C	1			
D	1			
E	1			
F	1			
G	1			
H				1
I				1
J				1
K				1
L				1

Activity: Opening exercises — "good morning" song.

pt where S began to sing off-key & loudly (T continued to lead group, ignored S)

	1	2	3	4
A	1			
B		1		
C		1		
D			1	
E			1	
F			1	
G				4
H				4
I	1			
J	1			
K		2		
L	1			

Activity: T reading to group after outdoor play. Stevie begins to daydream. (Lks like he's sleeping.) T asks him to pay attn. S lks startled; begins to listen again. T thanks S. (Q: How much sleep does he get?)

	1	2	3	4
A			3	
B			3	
C			3	
D			3	
E			3	
F			3	
G				3
H				3
I				4
J		4		
K		4		
L		4		

Activity: Sitting w/Sa in sandbox, talking, not playing w/any of the sandbox toys.

Threw sand at D as he walked by; continued to throw sand until T reprimanded him.

	1	2	3	4
A			3	
B			3	
C			3	
D			3	
E			3	
F			3	
G			3	
H		3		
I		3		
J		3		
K		3		
L				3

Activity: S & Sa are talking. Sa suggests they play "War." S says, "No." Boys continue to talk; Sa continues to urge S to play "War;" S agrees; boys begin game.

S loses temper because he thinks he's going to lose; throws cards. Sa picks them up.

	1	2	3	4
A	1			
B	1			
C	1			
D	1			
E			3	
F			3	
G		2		
H		2		
I			3	
J			3	
K			3	
L			3	

Activity: T giving directions on how to paint dinosaur; compliments S. T left to go to other group. Stevie continued to paint until Sa came by the table. Then talked to Sa.

Fig. 12-6 Teacher/Pupil Interaction Scale (TPIS)

It is difficult to think that all teacher/pupil interactions could be reduced to only four actions by each. If you use the scale, you will discover that many actions can be comfortably placed in one of the four categories.

The real advantage of the TPIS is that the observer records interactions for only one minute at a time. Thus, it lends itself to the busy teacher who does not have the leisure to complete a narrative, anecdotal, or play model form. Rating procedures are as follows:

1. The observer makes a judgment each five seconds for a one-minute sample of teacher/pupil interaction. Three five-minute blocks taken during an hour over a three-day period provide a reliable basis for judging the typical behavior of a pupil. A five-minute block consists of five one-minute samples, with a one-minute pause between each sample.
2. Pupil behavior is designated by the column in which the rating is made.
3. Each row indicates a single five-second sample.
4. The teacher behavior is designated by a number (1 through 4), and is entered in the column which describes what the pupil is doing.

Please note in Figure 12-6 that the example does not include a five-minute block of time but rather includes five one-minute samplings of behavior taken at times when the student teacher found a minute in which to record. You may find for your own purposes that taking one-minute samplings throughout the day gives you as much information as you need in order to develop a picture of what the child you are observing is like. Also, please note that we included a brief description of the action in order to help clarify the coding. Remember that the horizontal numbers at the top refer to pupil behavior; the numbers entered by the observer refer to teacher behavior.

ANALYZING OBSERVATIONS One reason, perhaps the main reason, for observing children is to help you, as the observer, better understand the child. This is why we used one child to illustrate each of the observation techniques covered in the unit.

What have we learned about Stevie just from observing him in action? What questions have we raised? Let us start with our opening narrative observation.

Stevie has difficulty in separating from his mother when she brings him to the day care center. The narrative describes typical behavior, not exceptional. If we caught Stevie on an exceptional day, we would have noted that this was not his usual behavior. We can also surmise that Stevie's mother almost seems to encourage his desire not to have her leave; in spite of reminding him that she has to leave quickly, she takes time to listen to Stevie describe his dinosaur. Stevie then seems quite happy to let his mother leave, especially since his friend Sammy is playing with the large blocks, which Stevie enjoys. In the later interchange between Stevie and Davie, we might guess that Davie is the more aggressive since he simply tells Stevie that he wants the red truck and takes it. We might also guess that Stevie does not know how to solve his problem as smoothly as Sammy, as he enters into a tug-of-war with Davie over the truck. Sammy, in contrast, recognizes that even if Davie takes the red truck, he and Stevie still have two trucks with which to play; arguing over the third truck is not worth it. A later indication of Sammy's social maturity (and leadership ability) occurs in the incident of the card game. Sammy knows how to play "War" and patiently explains the rules to Stevie. Even when Stevie loses his temper and throws the cards because he thinks Sammy will win, Sammy does not lose his temper but, instead, quietly picks up the cards.

An analysis of Stevie's play behaviors tends to show that, except for his play with Sammy, Stevie prefers solitary or parallel play to cooperative or associative play. He also appears to use symbolic and practice play more than play involving rules, such as the card game. We might surmise that Stevie, intellectually, is not at the stage where he can understand or internalize what rules mean. Perhaps giving him some of the Piagetian tasks, measuring his ability to classify and conserve, would be of value in understanding Stevie more fully. This idea may be pursued later.

In looking at the results of the TPIS, we can see that Stevie is reasonably attentive when involved in an activity he enjoys, as noted in the sampling of his painting of the dinosaur. Likewise, we can also note that when large-group activities were going on, Stevie's attention wanders. During the opening exercises, Stevie is not paying attention at first; later, he appears to sing off-key deliberately. We may want to ask him why, or we may feel that it is best to ignore the behavior just as the cooperating teacher did. Better yet, we may want to talk to the cooperating teacher and ask why Stevie's actions were ignored.

Our five-minute samples also raise a guess that while Stevie likes Sammy, he does not like Davie. There appears to be no outward aggressive behavior on Davie's part which would provoke Stevie to throw sand at Davie. However, the throwing of sand could have been related to the argument over the truck. We might want to ask Stevie why he threw the sand at Davie.

One last guess we might want to pursue is based upon the observation that Stevie appears to fall asleep during storytime in the late afternoon. Again, if this was not usual behavior, we would have made some comment about its being atypical. It raises a question about how much sleep Stevie gets at home. We make a note to question his mother on this point.

Let us assume that we talked to Stevie about his actions, discussed our guesses with the cooperating teacher, and also spoke to his mother, Mrs. Conway. We will now summarize the questions and their respective answers.

First, where is Stevie in terms of the ability to classify and conserve? In administering some of the Piagetian tasks, we discover that he can arrange objects from small to large, and that he can, with difficulty, classify by color or shape but not by both. In terms of conservation, Stevie is a nonconserver. You can well imagine his older brothers teasing him about his thin, little dime being worth less than one of their big, fat nickels!

Second, in talking to the cooperating teacher about Stevie's large-group behavior, we discover that the cooperating teacher chooses to ignore most of Stevie's attempts to gain attention by loudly singing off-key. The cooperating teacher feels that asking him to stop will reinforce his behavior, especially since he seems to be doing it for the attention. Some of the other children oblige by "shushing" him and laughing at him. When this occurs, Stevie usually giggles and sings even louder and more off-key. At times, the teacher cannot totally ignore Stevie, and

may tell him to leave the circle if he cannot behave, a move which usually quiets the boy.

Third, regarding sand throwing, we may ask Stevie why he did it. The answer may be "Because I felt like it." Indirect attempts to discover if Stevie deliberately threw the sand at Davie because he was angry when Davie took the red truck may prove fruitless. When asked point blank, however, if he threw sand at Davie because of his anger, Stevie is likely to answer yes. He may not understand that his anger is related to the incident of the truck, though, since that happened a while before.

Last, in talking with Stevie's mother, we discover that since she and her husband are renting a small house with only two bedrooms, Stevie and his two brothers sleep in the same room and go to bed at the same time. "After all," she says, "the boys are only four years apart in age. They go to bed between 8:00 p.m. and 9:00 p.m., depending on what's on television. Their father and I let them watch one show each evening if they've been good and if Tommy, the eight-year-old, has done his homework." When asked when the boys are awakened, she replies, "We have to be up at 6:00 a.m. so we can get breakfast and still get to work on time. And you might know that Stevie knows every trick in the world to make us get a late start!" The mother states that she believes the boys get enough sleep, especially with the nap the two younger ones receive at the center each day. (The middle boy, a first grader, comes to the center after school each day as does the older boy.)

Stevie's father works at a local foundry; his mother is a clerk-typist in a county office. Although Mr. Conway works 8:00 a.m. to 4:00 p.m. and could pick up his sons at approximately 4:45 p.m., he firmly believes that their care is his wife's responsibility. Thus, the three boys have to wait until about 5:45 p.m. when their mother can pick them up. Efforts on the part of the center staff, director, and teachers to persuade the father to attend parent/teacher/staff conferences have met with flat refusals and the statement that "raising kids is a woman's responsibility, not a man's; you speak to my wife."

The effect of the father's attitude is apparent in the behavior of the three boys, Stevie in particular. Smaller than most of the other four-year-olds at the center, Stevie tends to be slyly aggressive rather than overtly. He seems to know that in a one-to-one argument with any of the other boys in the room, he would lose. So, he throws sand or blocks, trips another, or knocks over another child's block tower. "But, teacher, it was an accident," he'll insist when confronted. Another effect of his father's attitude is seen in Stevie's choices for play — large blocks, trucks and cars, swings and jungle gym, tricycles, wagons, puzzles, and clay. But, go in the playhouse? Paint at the easel? Stevie calls these activities "sissy," and refuses to play.

His attachment to Sammy seems to be related to the fact that Sammy is the tallest and best coordinated boy in the room. Sammy appears to understand Stevie's need to be associated with him and cheerfully accepts Stevie's company. It is difficult for Stevie when Sammy is absent. On those days, Stevie stays by the teacher's side or stands along the wall, with his finger in mouth, and just watches what is going on.

Stevie's mother has been asked about his playmates at home. "Why, with two older brothers to play with, he doesn't need anybody else!" she replies. The teacher gently points out that Stevie seems "lost" when Sammy is absent, and suggests that maybe Stevie could invite a child home to visit him on the weekend. The mother's reaction to this suggestion is as though the teacher has taken leave of the senses. "With three young ones already, you're telling me I should have another one over? What's wrong with Stevie playing with his brothers? They play real nice together, hardly ever any arguing!" The teacher realizes that one of Stevie's problems socially is the fact that he does not need to make friends in order to have someone with whom to play. The teacher also realizes that Stevie's friendship with Sammy may be related more to the fact that Sammy is bigger and more mature and may remind Stevie of his next older brother. The teacher also realizes, after talking with Stevie's mother, that his parents do not share the concern with Stevie's lack of sociableness.

Finally, the teacher decides to have you, her student teacher, make several observations of Stevie. In this way she hopes to develop a learning plan for

Stevie through which she can encourage him to greater sociability.

DEVELOPING A LEARNING PLAN   Since the goal or objective for Stevie is to increase his sociability, what social behaviors have been observed? There is his social behavior toward his mother as he shows her his dinosaur, describes it, and acts out its ferocity. Next, there is his accepting Sammy's invitation to build a garage with the large blocks and his cooperative play with Sammy in building towers of small blocks as well as a garage of large ones. Later, there is his cooperative play with Sammy, as they play the card game. In every case of positive social interaction recorded, Stevie was interacting only with Sammy. In terms of other social behaviors, Stevie interacted with the class, Davie, and Sammy in negative ways.

Also noted through the observations is the pride with which Stevie talks to his mother about his dinosaur and the care with which he paints it. The teacher thinks that perhaps having the children who made dinosaurs talk about them would be a way in which Stevie could make a positive impression upon the other children.

How will the learning plan look? As with any lesson plan, a learning plan for even one child should contain five elements: 1.) the name of the child for whom the plan is being developed; 2.) the objective for the plan; 3.) any materials or equipment necessary; and 4.) teacher and student activities, as well as a time estimate and an evaluation of the plan's effectiveness, figure 12-7.

Since Sammy is one of the "stars" in the room of four-year-olds, you might also plan to ask another child or two to join Stevie and Sammy as they play with the blocks. Stevie may not want to share but the chances are that Sammy will. In this way, Stevie will be playing with two more children other than Sammy. Why two more? It is easier to exclude one child from play than two children. Also, if Stevie does not want to play with anyone but Sammy, the other two can play together *parallel* to Stevie and Sammy.

Another ploy might be to ask Stevie to introduce a new child, assuming a new child enters the center. In

---

Name: Stevie   Date: 25 September

Objective: Stevie will show off his dinosaur to the other children. He will name it, describe its appearance, and pretend to be a
           dinosaur.

Materials and Equipment: The dinosaurs the children have made.

Procedures:

Teacher Activities	Student Activities	Time
1. During morning circle time, ask the children who made dinosaurs if they would like to share them with the others.		
2. Wait for answers.	Most children will enthusiastically say "Me! I want to show mine!"	5 min.
3. If Stevie doesn't respond, ask him directly.		
4. Compliment Stevie on what a good dinosaur he made.		
5. Compliment another child or two.		
6. Have children get their dinosaurs.	Children go to shelf where dinosaurs are drying. (Make sure they're dry	2 min.
7. Ask who wants to go first.	first.) After one or maybe two children share, have Stevie share.	5 min. for each child
8. Unless Stevie volunteers, pick a more outgoing child to start.		
9. If Stevie forgets, remind him that he knows the name of his dinosaur, its size, what it eats, etc.		
10. Thank the children who shared. Remind the rest that they'll have time tomorrow.		

Evaluation:

Fig. 12-7 An individual learning plan

this way, Stevie could learn to feel important to another child in much the same way Sammy feels important in his relationship with Stevie.

Still another idea might be to ask Stevie to bring one of his favorite books from home to share during storytime. The teacher would have determined, of course, that Stevie has some books at home. She may also have asked his mother if Stevie has one favorite book. Similar to this idea is the sharing of a favorite toy. However, this is not always an appropriate idea, especially if one of the children has no toy to share; a

teacher should be careful about encouraging children to bring toys from home. In addition, some children are possessive about their toys and become upset if another child plays with them. Some centers encourage the sharing of toys; once the toy has been displayed and explained, it is put away until the child leaves for home. At other centers, if a child brings a toy, then that child is expected to share it. A breakable toy might be shown but it would not be shared.

Let us now assume that our interventions regarding the development of Stevie's sociability have met with some success. What are the next steps? Perhaps we will no longer need to develop an individual learning plan for Stevie. It is quite possible that he will continue to make progress without any special attention. It is also possible that, having made progress in social development, we would want to turn our attention to his emotional or physical development. In order to get a clearer picture of Stevie's development, we might want to use a developmental checklist or a standard test or inventory. (Both a checklist and a list of standard tests can be found in the Appendix.)

OBSERVATION AND CONJECTURE

At the beginning of this unit, we listed, as an objective, the ability to describe the difference between observation and conjecture. We deliberately used both throughout the various observations.

Study the narrative in the first pages of this unit. The observation starts with a simple description of Stevie entering the day care center one morning. As soon as we state, "He really looks unhappy," however, we are no longer simply describing; we are making an inference about how Stevie must feel based upon how he looks. We are giving an opinion about the child. Opinions based on evidence are conjectures.

Later, we made a statement about the supervising teacher that is also an opinion. We placed the comment in parentheses in order to separate it from the narrative observation.

On the anecdotal record form (figure 12-2), the column labeled "Comments" is for your conjectures or guesses as to why a child or another person may have done something. The column labeled "Description of What Child is Doing" is for description only. Notice that there are no value terms used; any value words are saved for the "Comments" column.

In the time sampling model (figure 12-4), notice that value terms or conjectures ("What a pleasure to have a child as mature as Sa in the Center!" and "Deliberately?") are separated from the description with parentheses. Using parentheses is an easy way to differentiate between your observation and your opinions about the observation. A similar technique

is used in the TPIS (figure 12-6). Opinions are placed in parentheses; descriptions of what is being observed, for the most part, are not. The one exception is the comment about the teacher continuing to sing the "Good Morning" song when Stevie began to sing loudly and off-key. However, since the description deals with what the teacher, not Stevie, is doing, it seems appropriate to place it within parentheses.

Summary

In this unit we presented several examples of observation techniques. The simplest is the narrative but it also requires the most time. Although it is more complicated, the Teacher/Pupil Interaction Scale (TPIS) takes little time, can be put onto a 3 x 5 index card, is inconspicuous, and can be supplemented with comments to the side describing the action being noted. Also introduced were the two-dimensional play model and a time sampling model; an anecdotal record form was reviewed. No one form is any better than any other, and student teachers are urged to use their own creativity to devise forms for their own specific uses.

Suggested Activities

A. Choose, with your cooperating teacher's permission, a child on whom you will make several observations. Try out the different techniques; do a narrative description, a time sample, and an event sample. Try the Teacher/Pupil Interaction Scale (TPIS). Discuss your results with your cooperating teacher, your supervisor, and your peers.

B. Try developing your own observation form. Discuss its effectiveness with your cooperating teacher, college supervisor, and peers.

C. Read *The Children We See* by Betty Rowen. Try out some of the observation forms presented. Again, discuss the results of data gathered in terms of effective information received.

D. Complete the following exercise, "Inference-Observation Confusion." Decide whether the statements following the story are true or false; the validity of some statements may be unknown. (An answer key is found at the end.) Were you able to separate inference from observation? Are you able to separate inference from observation with your students? Write a paragraph in which you present an observation of a child in one column and inferences as to what the behavior means in another column. For example:

<table>
<tr><td align="center">Observations</td><td align="center">Inferences</td></tr>
<tr><td>Susie came into class this a.m. with a frown.</td><td>Maybe Susie's mother yelled at her on the way to school. This has been true before.</td></tr>
</table>

INFERENCE-OBSERVATION CONFUSION (Haney, 1960)

A business man had just turned off the lights in the store when a man appeared and demanded money. The owner opened a cash register. The contents of the cash register were scooped up and the man sped away. A member of the police force was notified promptly.

Statements About The Story

1. A man appeared after the owner had turned off his store lights.
2. The robber was a *man*.
3. The man did not demand money.
4. The man who opened the cash register was the owner.
5. The store owner scooped up the contents of the cash register and ran away.
6. Someone opened a cash register.
7. After the man who demanded the money scooped up the contents of the cash register, he ran away.
8. While the cash register contained money, the story does *not* state *how much*.
9. The robber demanded money of the owner.
10. The story concerns a series of events in which only three persons are referred to: the owner of the store, a man who demanded money, and a member of the police force.
11. The following events were included in the story: someone demanded money, a cash register was opened, its contents were scooped up, and a man dashed out of the store.

Answer Key

1. True
2. ?
3. False
4. True
5. False or ? (Listen to arguments for both possibilities.)
6. True (The owner is "someone;" this is a confusing question.)
7. False or ? (You do not know who scooped up the contents; you do know the man sped away. Listen to arguments for both possibilities.)
8. False (The story does not state that the contents were money.)
9. ? (You do not know whether the *man* was a robber; there could have been a woman or another man who was the actual robber.)
10. ? (Again, you do not know if the man who demanded money was alone or not.)
11. True

Review

A. List examples of observation techniques, and state at least one reason why each technique is effective.

B. Read the following descriptions of behavior. For each child, analyze and develop a learning plan which contains at least one general behavioral objective.

1. Denise (five years old) is sitting on the swing. "Teacher, come push me," she demands. "Try to pump, Denise," responds the teacher. "Don't know how," Denise whines. "Push me, Susan," Denise says to a child going by on a tricycle. "Can't now. Push yourself," answers Susan. Pete comes up to the swing. "Get off and let me swing," he states. "No! My swing!" Denise cries. (Denise looks like she is going to cry.) The teacher's aide comes over and asks, "Do you want me to show you how to make the swing go?" Denise answers, "Please."

2. The following chart was developed by Greg, a student teacher, who was interested in Penny's attending behavior. Starting with the TPIS, he adapted it into a simpler form on which he could check off observations as he noticed them throughout the 9:00 a.m. to 10:00 a.m. activity hour. On a 3 x 5-inch card which he could hold in the palm, Greg drew a vertical line, dividing the card in half lengthwise. He then wrote "Attending" on the one side, "Nonattending" on the other. His final results looked like this:

		Attending	Nonattending
Mon.	9:05	yes (t.i.)*	
	9:16		no
	9:27		no
	9:40		no
	9:52	yes (t.i.)	
	*t.i. = teacher initiated		
Tues.	9:07		no
	9:18		no
	9:25	yes (t.i.)	
	9:34	yes	
	9:40		no
	9:47		no
	9:55		no
Wed.	9:02		no
	9:12	yes (t.i.)	
	9:20		no
	9:35		no
	9:42		no
	9:58		no
Thurs.	9:05		no
	9:15		no
	9:33	yes (t.i.)	
	9:48		no
	9:55		no
Fri.	Penny was absent.		

Question: How much attending behavior should the teacher expect of a three-year-old during an activity period?

3. Johnny, a three-and-a-half-year-old in a morning preschool, is the subject of the third observation. The two-dimensional play model, combining event and time sampling, was used to gather data.

Child: Johnny   Date: 17 Nov.

	Symbolic	*Practice*	*Games*
Onlooking:	Watches 3 girls in playhouse, when asked to join, shakes hd No. (9:35 a.m.)	Watches children go up & dwn slide (10:22 a.m.)	
	Watches J & A at easels. T asks, "Do you want to paint, J?" "No." (11:05 a.m.)	Watches children in sandbox, filling cups & pails over & over. (10:35 a.m.)	
		Watches children on swing. (10:45 a.m.)	
Solitary:	"See my cracker? It's a plane!" Zooms cracker thru air; makes plane sounds. (10:03 a.m.)	Sits on swing while teacher's aide pushes. (10:50 a.m.)	
Parallel:	Picks up egg beater at H_2O table. Beats H_2O. Says, "I'm making eggs for breakfast." (11:12 a.m.)	Picks up paint brush at easel; lets paint drip. Picks up next brush. Repeats w/remaining brushes. (11:35 a.m.)	

No examples of associative or cooperative play

Question: Do three-year-olds do as much onlooking and solitary play as Johnny? Should you be concerned?

4. Jimmy is a four-year-old at a private day care center/nursery school. The following is a time sample of his behavior during outside free play.

10:05 a.m.:	J runs stiffly toward two of his friends on tricycles. "Let me ride!" he shouts.
10:10 a.m.:	J is happily riding on the back of E's tricycle. E had to stop to let J climb on. J first placed his left foot on, lifted it off, placed the same foot on again, took it off; finally he put his right foot on and then successfully put his left foot on.
10:15 a.m.:	J is still riding on the back of E's tricycle.
10:20 a.m.:	J and E have switched places. J had difficulty pedaling up the slight grade. E pushed from behind.
10:25 a.m.:	E has suggested that he, J, and S go to the work bench. J picks up the hammer and a nail. He hits the nail awkwardly into a block of wood. E says, "Hey, watch me! Hold the nail like this!"
10:30 a.m.:	E is holding J's hands with his, showing him how to drive the nail into the block of wood.
10:35 a.m.:	J is sitting in the sandbox, shoveling sand into a bucket. E is still at the work bench.
10:40 a.m.:	J is putting sand into another bucket. He looks surprised when the bucket overflows. He reaches for the first bucket. S says, "I'm using it now," and pushes a third pail toward J.
10:45 a.m.:	J and S are smoothing down the sand, calling it a road. They go and get a couple of cars to run on their road. E joins them, having completed his project at the work bench.
10:50 a.m.:	When called to clean up for activity time, J climbs out of the sandbox. As he does this, his foot catches on the edge and he falls down. He gives the sandbox a kick, and joins the others to come inside.

Question: Is Jimmy's poor gross motor coordination something about which the teacher should be concerned?

C. Identify each of the following statements as either inferences or observations.

1. Johnny likes to read.
2. Susie has a new dress.
3. Sammy is a mean boy.
4. Betty has emotional problems.
5. Janine has a smile on her face.
6. George hit Stevie on the playground.
7. Mary had a frown on her face.
8. Mark looks unhappy.
9. Kathy likes to play with clay.
10. Vickie is an affectionate little girl.

Resources

Haney, William V. *Communications: Patterns and Incidents.* Homewood, IL: Richard D. Irwin, Inc., 1960.

Parten, M. B. "Social Participation Among Preschool Children." *Journal of Abnormal and Social Psychology,* 33 (1932), pp. 243-269.

Piaget, J. *Play, Dreams and Imitation in Childhood.* New York: W. W. Norton & Co., Inc., 1962.

Unit 13
Individual Plans, Conferencing, and Referral

OBJECTIVES

After studying this unit, the student will be able to:

- Develop an individual learning plan for a child.
- Discuss the role of the school and parents in working with a child.
- Discuss the role of the student teacher in developing an individual learning plan and conferencing with parents.

THE INDIVIDUAL LEARNING PLAN

In preparing an individual learning plan, you must always remember the child's total environment. Do you remember Maria, the subject of our observations in Unit 6? Let us observe her again. Is her behavior a cause of concern? It is important to consider what is normal. Assuming that it is early in September and that Maria is a new student in the center, her behavior of watching others from a distance and playing by herself, figure 13-1, may not be unusual for a marginally bilingual child from a culture in which females are expected to be quiet and nonassertive. If Maria had been in school for seven or eight months, she might have become more social, acquiring a greater knowledge of English. (We are assuming Maria is attending a preschool in which competence in speaking English is encouraged. Some preschools attempt to preserve the child's original language rather than to encourage the use of English.)

What does our observation of Maria suggest in regard to planning for her education? First, it suggests that we want to answer our questions: Is she hard of hearing? Is Spanish her dominant language? Is she encouraged to be obedient and well-behaved at home? Let us assume that she is not hard of hearing; Spanish is her dominant language; and she is encouraged to be quiet and obedient at home. Now, what are our goals for Maria?

We might want to encourage Maria's interaction with Susie and Janine, two of the more outgoing

Fig. 13-1 When Maria is not watching others play from a distance, she is playing by herself.

children in the center, figure 13-2. Because Susie can easily think of something to play with another child, we might suggest that Susie ask Maria to join her in an activity. We should, however, be more cautious with Janine. We know we can pair Maria with Janine at the easels or at the puzzle table, but it might not be a good idea to pair them together at activities such as sociodramatic play unless Susie is present. Janine might be less tolerant of a child who is not familiar with the English language. In contrast, Susie might even know some Spanish, if there are a number of Spanish-speaking children at the center.

THE STUDENT TEACHER'S ROLE   One of the roles of a student teacher is that of an observer. During the first days of placement, the student teacher will often be given time to observe. This is an especially valuable time for both the student teacher and the cooperating teacher. Take advantage of this period. Observe several children carefully; confer with your cooperating teacher and college supervisor regarding which children to observe. After you have completed your observations, discuss them with your cooperating teacher, supervisor, and peers. It is fascinating to listen to someone else's perceptions of your observations.

Fig. 13-2 These two children are good friends and will accept Maria and play with her.

Often we become emotionally involved with the children whom we observe; thus, we can receive a different perspective from those who do not know them as well, including our cooperating teacher. This situation can be reversed. Many cooperating teachers know that their judgment of children can be obscured by knowledge of the children's backgrounds. A student teacher's judgment, in contrast, is not affected by this factor.

We are reminded of a time when we were new to a community and had, as one of our students in a parent cooperative, a four-year-old named Tony. Not knowing Tony's background, we evaluated his behaviors based on our expectations of four-year-olds. Tony was quite ordinary and average. His intellectual, linguistical (language), physical, social, and emotional development were appropriate for his age. He was, in many ways, typical in comparison to other four-year-olds. Later, during our first parent conference, we discovered that Tony's father was the president of a local college. If we had known that fact, it is likely we would have treated Tony as if he was an exceptional child. His physical development was perhaps more advanced; at four, he could skip well, pump himself on a swing, and was beginning to learn how to jump rope. (Tony had ample opportunity to swing, jump rope, and learn how to skip because he had an older brother who encouraged him to learn these skills.) We might have expected Tony's language development to be advanced; he was exposed to a sophisticated level of language every day through contact with his father and mother. Regarding social and emotional development, Tony again seemed to be average for his age; he had several friends among the boys of his own age group; he seemed to have the usual amount of curiosity and competence for boys of his age.

If we had known that Tony's father was a college president, we often think that we would have expected more from Tony than what he could deliver. What are the results of expecting more than a child can deliver? The child may stop trying to succeed. Another result is that the child may become aggressive and frustrated when asked to accomplish more than the child is able to do.

Assume that Tony is a current student of ours. Should an individual learning plan be developed for

Tony? The activities offered to the other children would most likely be appropriate for Tony. Let us also assume we had a conference with his parents. From this meeting, we discovered that they have high hopes for Tony's success in school. In fact, they placed him in the preschool to increase his "readiness" for school. Tony's mother told us that they expect Tony to achieve several goals this year. They expect Tony not only to learn the alphabet but also the sounds of the alphabet. They also expect Tony to learn to count to 100 and to be able to name all of the primary, secondary, and some of the more obscure tints and shades of the various colors. They want Tony to become more attentive, to increase his attention span. Tony's parents expressed no interest in Tony's physical learning experiences. They feel that he does not need any specific teaching in terms of physical ability; that, since he has a play gym at home, he receives all the physical exercise he needs.

In this hypothetical situation, some of Tony's parents' goals will be met through the regular curriculum. We might honestly feel that some of their other goals are more appropriate for kindergarten. Should we tell his parents this? Will they listen?

We can reassure Tony's parents that we share many of the same goals. We can show them a brochure or flyer describing our curriculum. We can stress to Tony's parents that helping Tony feel good about himself is a worthwhile goal as is allowing him time to explore different activities.

What is the student teacher's role in working with Tony? It could be to give him a one-to-one learning opportunity. The cooperating teacher could decide that Tony should know his alphabet, and might assign you to help Tony first learn the letters of his name. The cooperating teacher may also decide that the parents' expectations are not appropriate. In the meantime, however, in order to let the parents feel more confident in the school, the cooperating teacher might assign you to work with Tony on a one-to-one basis. The cooperating teacher may feel that in time Tony's mother will realize that her expectations are unrealistic.

We have suggested thus far that the student teacher has a role in observing children who are chosen by the cooperating teacher and those of the student teacher. A second role is that of working on a one-to-one basis with an individual child, figure 13-3. The student teacher is also a participant in parent conferences and in-school and out-of-school activities.

Student teachers quite naturally are invited (and urged) to attend functions such as parent education meetings, staff conferences, parent or school-sponsored dinners, and fund-raising events. The student teacher should become a part of the life of the school or day care center.

CONFERENCING As a student teacher attending a parent conference, you will want to defer to your cooperating teacher for the most part. Naturally, if you are asked a direct question by either the parent or teacher, you should answer. Primarily, however, your role will be that of observer rather than participant. You should remember that statements made at a parent conference are confidential. The privacy of parents and children should be respected. Do not repeat anything that was said with others except when appropriate. For example, if your cooperating teacher asks you for your opinions after a conference, you would naturally discuss them. Also, the cooperating teacher might assign you the task of reporting on the conference.

Fig. 13-3 Working on a one-to-one basis

One exception to this rule of confidentiality occurs in student teaching seminars. It is appropriate to discuss your student teaching assignment with your peers and supervisor.

REFERRAL RESOURCES Many schools and day care centers have a list of local resources which a student teacher may examine. Most have the names of one or several physicians to whom parents are referred if they do not have a medical doctor. Frequently, low-cost clinics are used for referrals. The same is true for dental care. Many schools and day care centers also refer children for testing or evaluation by psychologists or psychiatrists, and will have names of one or more psychological or counseling referral services.

Two other frequently used resources are county child care referral services and child abuse centers. Your local telephone book will have county office listings. In California, for example, most counties have a Child Care Coordinating Council, or Four C's as it is widely known. Four C's is a resource for all parents and schools, day care centers, and day care homes. They maintain up-to-date lists of licensed nursery schools, day care centers, family day care homes, etc. Four C's will also assist the newcomer who wants to inquire about licensing a new family day care home. They can provide information on local resources which is not available from other sources. For example, a newcomer with a health handicapped child may know of a national organization but not a local one. Many parents may not know of local chapters because they do not know about the national organization itself.

Other referral sources are public and private social services. These services can offer a wide variety of help ranging from food stamps to foster home care to financial aid to Alcoholics Anonymous.

DEVELOPING THE INDIVIDUAL LEARNING PLAN

At this point, we would like to present a few other models of individual learning plans so that you can try out different forms to see which works best.

Study figure 13-4. It is a lesson plan for two-year-olds, focusing on the topic of birds. Let us assume that one of the two-year-olds in the group is Alan, who has been referred to the center by Child Protection Services. His mother just gave birth to a baby girl. Alan's father did not accept the new baby as his, and deserted the family. Alan's mother, an alcoholic, blamed Alan for his father's desertion and started beating him. Neighbors called Child Protective Services, who threatened to take Alan away. Alan's mother, a recipient of AFDC (Aid to Families with

Age Group: Two-year-olds

Time	Activity	Materials	Value to Child	Limits
7:45	Set up room			
8:00–9:00	Greet children; put on nametags	Nametags (on bird forms)	Makes children feel welcome	None
8:00–9:00	Free play, art table	Precut birds, paper, paste	Learn about color; eye-hand coordination	Paste, monitor
8:00–10:00	Prereading; matching birds	Tchr-made lotto	1:1 correspondence; problem-solving skills; left/right concept	Lotto stays on table
8:00–10:00	Science/social science: places where birds live	Bird cage & bird, bird's nest, birdhouse	Investigation of materials; acquisition of vocab.	Bird stays in cage; items stay on table

Fig. 13-4 Lesson plan (Adapted from "Unit Plan — Topic: Birds" by Claudia Warren and Linda L. Reynolds, University of South Carolina. Distributed at NAEYC Conference, November 6, 1981.)

Dependent Children), does not want Alan taken away because she needs the money. She has promised her social worker that she will go into counseling and stop beating Alan.

Alan comes into the center like a small hurricane. Highly aggressive, he is difficult to leave unattended. More than once he has bitten and/or hit another child. He seems to have no understanding of rules. Mrs. Smith, the cooperating teacher, is especially worried about studying the unit on birds. She is afraid that Alan will try to hurt her parakeet, which she has brought to the center so the children can observe. She asks Amy, the student teacher, to develop an individual learning plan for Alan that will dovetail with hers. The student teacher has prepared the learning plan in figure 13-5. Notice that the student teacher made use of the regular activities and modified some. For example, Alan's nametag has been made of cloth so that it will be difficult for him to tear it. Notice also that the student teacher stays

Time	Activity	Materials	Value to Alan
7:50	Greet Alan, help him w/coat	None	Greeting Alan & calling him by name may help establish rapport.
7:55	Pin on nametag	Nametag (made of cloth; he has torn paper ones)	May help him learn to recognize his own name; may help him feel valued.
8:00	Free play; suggest art table	Precut birds, paper & paste	Name colors to Alan; eye-hand coor. practice; vocabulary building.
8:10	Watching bird	Bird in bird cage	Talk about homes; bird cage is home for bird; Alan's home is apartment. Talk about color of parakeet, sounds parakeet makes.
8:15	Free play	Blocks and/or trucks	Follow quiet, passive play with active, noisy play. Uses large muscles; helps in coordination.
8:45	Toileting	Bathroom	Since Alan usually has to use bathroom before 9:00, ask him to go at this time unless he is still engrossed with the blocks/trucks and playing w/o biting.
8:55	Free play, matching birds	Tchr-made game	Reinforces names of colors; helps him learn left/right progression; eye-hand coordination; visual discrimination. *Caution:* Help Alan to succeed; he hasn't got much patience for seat work.
9:10	Free play, water table	Apron; water table toys	Experimentation w/quantity; vocabulary building; change of pace. (Besides, I know Alan enjoys the water table; if I stay w/him, he won't splash s/one or spill water.)
9:25	Toileting (if Alan didn't go earlier)		
9:35	Group time, fingerplay "5 Little Birds"	None	Alan needs social experiences (show him how to hold up fingers; sit him on lap to keep him in group but away from someone else)

Fig. 13-5 Learning plan for Alan — Topic: Birds

with Alan especially during potentially difficult activities. She stands with him as they both look at the parakeet. She holds him on her lap during group time, and moves his fingers during the fingerplay. She assists him with the pasting if he needs it, and stays near him during block play to prevent his biting any of the other children who are playing with the blocks at the same time. She asks Alan if he needs to go to the bathroom, and assists him with his toileting needs. At the water table, she directs him to get his apron, and she stands near him, talking to him about what he is doing in order to help build his vocabulary. (*Note:* On the student teacher's individual plan for Alan, she omitted the "limits" column since she would be overseeing all of the action.)

The cooperating teacher and student teacher hope that all the extra attention will help Alan learn more acceptable behavior. It is also hoped that he will form an attachment to the student teacher so he can begin to experience some of the loving care that has not been received from his mother. The cooperating teacher knows that the student teacher will only be around for a short while, but she is hoping that Alan will learn to trust the student teacher. She realizes that once the child can begin to relate to and trust one adult, he will be able to relate to and trust another.

Another example of an individual plan for Alan can be found in the Appendix.

It is in working with the "different" child that the individual plan becomes more essential. Figure 13-6 presents a model plan for use with a child who has exceptional needs. Again, we have illustrated our model with goals and objectives for Alan, mostly

---

DISTRICT/SCHOOL ABC Day Care Center **STUDENT'S NAME** Alan K. **C.A.** 2-3 **DATE** 14 Oct

LONG-RANGE GOAL Alan will learn what is and is not acceptable social behavior.

PERIODIC OBJECTIVE Alan will stop biting and hitting others. He will hit Bobo instead.

FUNCTIONAL DESCRIPTION OF PROBLEM See above **BEHAVIORAL STRENGTHS** Agile and well-coordinated

SHORT-TERM OBJECTIVES (Section 3153 Proposed Title V Regulations)	INTERVENTION ACTIVITIES AND MATERIALS	MONITORING OF OBJECTIVES
(Specify time, specific behavior, evaluation conditions, and criteria)		Person(s) responsible for implementation:
1. By holding Alan in lap during group time, Alan will learn to sit quietly. (4 months)	ST or aide will hold Alan, and speak quietly to him. ST or aide will manipulate Alan's hands to demonstrate fingerplays.	Teacher, with assistance from ST & aide ———— Reviewed
2. Alan will learn 5 fingerplays and 3 songs. (6 mo.)	ST or aide will sing songs to Alan so he may hear them more clearly.	Date ———— ———— Achieved
3. Alan will stop hitting others. (2 mo.)	ST or aide will remove Alan from room when he hits, and ask him to hit Bobo clown instead.	Date ———— ———— Revision Recommended
4. Alan will stop biting others. (2 mo.)	Tchr, ST, or aide will direct Alan to bite leather strap ea time he bites or tries to bite anyone else.	———— ————
5. Alan will listen during storytime. (4 months)	Tchr, ST, or aide will hold Alan on lap during storytime, "ohing" and "ahing" to hold his interest.	————

Fig. 13-6 Individual instructional plan

because he does have exceptional needs and because we feel it is helpful to see data used in different ways.

PARENT INVOLVEMENT We have not discussed in detail the parents' role in the development of an individual learning plan. The best plans are those which are made with the parents' approval and support. Certainly in the case of Stevie (Unit 12), the mother seems to care and be concerned. Although she may not see any reason to worry about Stevie's social behavior at home, she may be easily persuaded that he could be more social at school.

In Maria's case, her mother might want Maria to learn both English and Spanish. That could be her reason for placing Maria in a "bilingual" center. In writing an individual learning plan for Maria, then, the mother's concern that Maria retain her knowledge of Spanish while learning English must be respected.

In the example of Tony, the problem is possibly that the parents' goals are different than those of the school, at least initially. Assigning the student teacher to work with Tony on a one-to-one basis might be all that is necessary, especially since he is typical for his age.

We have provided some models of individual plans for an abused, aggressive child (Alan) who needs special help and one-to-one teaching. We can guess that Alan's mother is not too concerned about what happens to him at school. If this is the case, the teacher should ask his social worker to become involved, or the court might appoint a surrogate parent.

You should note in all of our examples that the goal of the school is parent education, as well as child education. Especially in Stevie's and Tony's cases where the parents' perceptions of the children differ with those of the school, it is important for the teacher and/or director to enable the parent to see more clearly what the child's needs are at school. This is not always easy to accomplish. Sometimes compromises must be made. One such compromise is suggested in the example of Tony by teaching him the letters in his name. (Most educators would agree that learning the alphabet is not a particularly worthwhile activity. However, teaching the alphabet pleases parents.)

Summary

We discussed the development of an individual learning plan for a child. We presented several types of individual plans, and attempted to illustrate how an individual plan dovetails with a class plan. In addition, we discussed the roles of the parent, school, and student teacher in developing and implementing such a plan.

Suggested Activities

A. Select a child, with your cooperating teacher's approval, for whom you will develop an individual learning plan. Implement the plan, and evaluate its effectiveness. Use either of the forms in figures 13-5 and 13-6.

B. For an overview of how the exceptional student is defined and for activity ideas, read *The Special Student* by C. M. Charles and Ida M. Malian. Discuss "special" students with your peers, cooperating teacher, and supervisor. Do you think you have some "special" students in your school or center?

Review

A. Read the following statements. Determine whether each statement identifies a responsibility of the school, teacher, student teacher, or parent, or whether it is a responsibility shared among all of them. (*Note:* Assume that the school is not a parent cooperative.)

1. Planning the curriculum
2. Buying supplies
3. Observing children
4. Arranging parent-teacher conferences
5. Arranging fund-raising events for the school
6. Sending out publicity about school functions
7. Arranging transportation for a field trip
8. Teaching a child on a one-to-one basis
9. Hiring new personnel
10. Disciplining the child
11. Developing an individual learning plan for a child
12. Evaluating the success of an individual learning plan

B. Read the following situations. Then read the statement made by a parent. What would you consider to be an appropriate response? Discuss your responses with your peers, cooperating teacher, and supervisor.

1. One day Tony gets into a fight with Adam. As you know, Tony's father is a college president, and his mother a well-educated housewife; however, he is from a single-parent family. He also belongs to an ethnic and religious minority. The fight was provoked by Adam, who perceives Tony as stuck up. Your cooperating teacher calls both of Tony's parents and asks for a conference. Tony's mother responds immediately and says, "What's going on in your school? How come Tony got assaulted? What are you going to do about it?"

2. Donna Farmer arrives at school one morning with bruises on her arm. Later, she winces when you put your arm around her shoulders. You call the school nurse who takes Donna into her office and examines her. She returns Donna to your room and says, "You'd better call Child Protective Services. I think Donna's mother beat her up this morning." You tell the nurse you would like to speak to Donna's mother first; you do not believe that she is the type of person who would beat her child. The nurse suggests that you will not get the truth out of the mother but agrees to wait to call Child Protective Services until after you talk to her. You begin your conversation with Donna's mother by saying, "Good evening, Mrs. Farmer. I'm glad you could stop by after work today. I'm concerned about Donna. The bruises on her arm seem to really hurt her, and she moaned during naptime today." Mrs. Farmer screams, "Are you telling me I beat up on my own kid?"

3. You are concerned about Mark's apparent neglect. He arrives at preschool in dirty, torn clothing. His hair would never be combed if it were not done at school; he often smells of stale urine and fecal matter. You discover that his underpants look like they have been worn for a month without having been washed. You ask the mother if you can make a home visit. She says, "No. The mister don't want no one to come when he ain't home." You finally persuade her that it is important to talk about Mark. She reluctantly agrees. After the usual opening remarks, you ask, "Do you have a washing machine at home?" Mark's mother responds negatively, eyes you suspiciously, and asks, "What business is it of yours whether the mister and me has a washing machine?"

4. Kathy Mumford caught your attention for two reasons. First, she is always cocking her head to one side and holding it close to paper when she draws, and you noticed that she frequently squints to see pictures that are held up during storytime. You also have to repeatedly tell her to put toys away, wash her hands, etc. You do not have the services of a school nurse, so you call Kathy's mother and ask if she can come to the school for a short conference. In the meantime, you look at Kathy's entrance form and doctor's statement. The doctor has noted a slight nearsightedness but no apparent hearing problem. You suspect that Kathy has deficiencies in both, yet you hesitate to contradict Kathy's pediatrician. When Mrs. Mumford arrives, you decide to ask about Kathy's behavior at home. Mrs. Mumford admits that Kathy does sit close to the television and does not seem to hear at times. "Mr. Mumford put an end to Kathy's problem of not hearing. You know what he did? He sat in the kitchen while she was in the family room and whispered, 'Kathy, do you want some ice cream, honey?' Well, Kathy answered right away! Mr. Mumford and I both think Kathy just gets too involved in things. She's not deaf!"

5. Joe is one of those students who never sits still for a minute. He moves around constantly from the moment he enters the day care center until naptime, when he must be urged strongly to lie down. Naptime is agony for Joe; he twists and turns, grumbles, sighs to himself, and disturbs everyone around him. You think perhaps Joe eats too much sugar, and you decide to ask his mother about it. "Mrs. Jackson, what are Joe's favorite kinds of food? We have trouble at the center persuading him to try some things."

Mrs. Jackson answers, "Well, if you'd feed him something like hamburgers or hot dogs and baked beans, he'd eat okay. But you keep giving him junk like that dark bread. He don't like nothing but white bread! And you don't ever have candy and chocolate! Joey really loves chocolate, you know, not those carrot and celery sticks and fruits. He don't go for them."

C. For each of the five children in the preceding review activity, write an appropriate behavioral objective for an individual learning plan in the curriculum area indicated.

1. Tony will be able to. . .
   (An objective related to learning the letters in his name)

2. Donna will be able to. . .
   (An objective related to recognizing the shapes of a circle, square, triangle, rectangle, and oval)

3. Mark will be able to. . .
   (An objective related to washing his hands after using the bathroom without having to be reminded)

4. Kathy will be able to. . .
   (An objective related to classifying at least five common fruits and vegetables in the proper class)

5. Joe will be able to. . .
   (An objective related to trying at least two or three foods which are new to him)

Unit 14
Working with the
"Special" Child

OBJECTIVES

After completing this unit, the student will be able to:

- Define "special."
- List at least five characteristics of "special" children.
- State the categories of "handicap" according to the Education for All Handicapped Children Act, PL 94-142.
- Discuss the concept of "least restrictive environment."
- Discuss the implications of "least restrictive environment" to the teacher of an early childhood program.

HANDICAPPED CHILDREN AND PUBLIC LAW 94-142

We know that most of you think that all children are special; we do also. However, it is important to recognize that some children have needs beyond those of the average child; some have needs which can be met only by a team of specialists working together for the welfare of the children. To meet the needs of "special" children, the federal government passed into law the Education for All Handicapped Children Act, Public Law 94-142, in 1975. Every state was given a deadline of Fall 1977 to implement this law with legislation of their own.

According to PL 94-142, handicapped children are defined as follows:

Sec. 121a.5 Handicapped children.
(a) As used in this part, the term "handicapped children" means those children evaluated in accordance with sections 121.a.530-121.a.534 as being mentally retarded, hard of hearing, deaf, speech impaired, visually handicapped, seriously emotionally disturbed, orthopedically

impaired, other health impaired, deaf-blind, multi-handicapped, or as having specific learning disabilities, who because of those impairments need special education and related services.

(*Note:* To obtain a copy of PL 94-142, write to your local congressman. More information on this law can be found in *Exceptional Children and Youth: An Introduction* by Edward L. Meyen.)

Public Law 94-142 provides a "free, public education" for all handicapped children between the ages of three and twenty-one. The law further guarantees the right of every citizen to have available a "full educational opportunity" (Section 613).

What are the mandates of PL 94-142?

- A free and appropriate public education, including special education and related services, for all handicapped children ages three to twenty-one.

    Special education is defined as instruction specially designed to meet the unique needs of handicapped children. It may include classroom instruction, physical education, home and hospital instruction, and institutional instruction. (Physical education was often omitted from the curriculum in special classes, especially those for children with orthopedic handicaps. It was felt that the physical and/or occupational therapy they received was equivalent to physical education. According to the intent, it is not.)

Related services are those commonly referred to as support services: speech therapy, psychological counseling, vocational counseling, transportation, etc.

- The law makes a distinction between *first priority* and *second priority* children. First priority children are those with severe handicaps within any disability who are not receiving an adequate education. For example, local public education districts traditionally did not educate the severely emotionally disturbed, the severely mentally retarded, or even the deaf, blind, or deaf-blind. These children were normally educated, if at all, in state or private institutions.

- Parents must be informed about projected evaluation of their children. This must be done in writing and in the parents' native language. The parents must be involved and give permission at every step of the process of identification, evaluation, educational placement, and evaluation of that placement. They have the right to see all files, observations, tests, etc. administered to their children. They may question an evaluation and ask for a second opinion. (The law is unclear about who is responsible for a second evaluation, the district or the parent.)

- Each child identified as needing special education or related services must have an Individual Education Program (IEP) approved by the parents. This program includes short- and long-range objectives for the child, specific materials which will be used, the time in which the objective is to be accomplished, and the name of the individual responsible for its implementation and evaluation. The IEP must be evaluated at least once each year.

- Each child is to be placed in the "least restrictive environment," figures 14-1, 14-2, 14-3. What is

"least restrictive" for one child may not be for another. For example, a child with severe cerebral palsy of the athetoid type (limp, twitchy muscles) who is strapped into a wheelchair and cannot talk may not belong in a regular classroom until that child acquires the ability to talk. At this point, assuming the child can communicate with peers, the child might properly be placed in the regular class and receive the related services of speech therapy, physical therapy, occupational therapy, and adapted physical education. Assuming no mental defect, the regular classroom teacher may need no special materials in the classroom other than a book holder and a raised desk that would fit over the child's wheelchair, with a clasp to hold the child's papers.

- Due process is guaranteed for every child and family. The parents have the right to sue the district if they feel that the best interests of their child are not being served. For example, a mentally retarded child could be recommended for placement in a special day class. The parents may feel that the child can remain in the regular class for many activities such as art, music, physical education, lunch, and recess; the district may feel otherwise. The parent then may sue the district for what they perceive to be the inappropriate placement of the child.

- Evaluation of the child must be done with instruments which are nondiscriminatory in terms of race and ethnicity. Testing must also be in the child's dominant language, if he or she has a limited knowledge of English or is non English speaking.

- Provisions are included for the appointment of a *surrogate* or substitute in cases when a parent refuses to participate or is unable to participate in the process.

IMPLICATIONS OF PUBLIC LAW 94-142

It is clear that PL 94-142 includes early childhood education. For this reason, you may find some "special" or handicapped children at your school or center. If you are in a Head Start class, for example, it is important to remember that they must serve identified handicapped children.

Fig. 14-1 The "least restrictive environment" may be having the child sit in a special chair. . .(Courtesy of Jody Boyd)

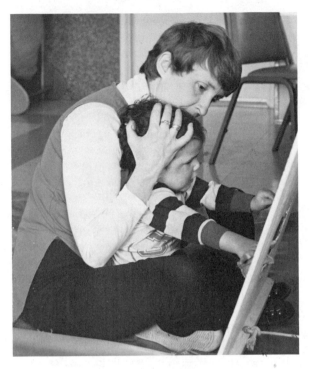

Fig. 14-2 . . .or it may be having the physical therapist position the child's head while the child uses the arms. . .(Courtesy of Jody Boyd)

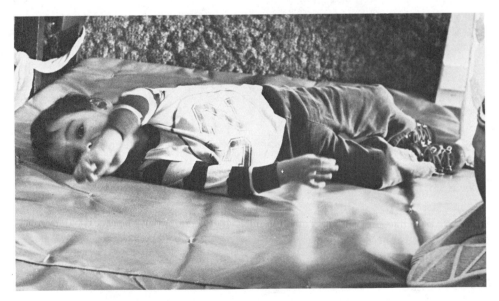

Fig. 14-3 . . .or it may be letting the child roll free on a mat. (Courtesy of Jody Boyd)

The preschool classroom is appropriate for many "special" children. Children with orthopedic problems can fit quite comfortably into a regular classroom as long as the classroom is accessible. (Accessibility is covered by PL 93-380, Section 504.) A lack of wheelchair ramps is not considered to be a valid excuse for not admitting a child in a wheelchair. Children with partial sight, children who are hard of hearing, and children with mild retardation and emotional problems can be placed in a "normal" preschool class. They can overcome their limitations, figure 14-4.

Both the "special" and "normal" child profit from association with each other. In one case involving a child who was hard of hearing, all of the children learned sign language in order to communicate better with that child. In fact, the children learned sign language faster than the teacher! In another example, a severely emotionally disturbed (depressive) child was placed in a regular preschool. The children quickly learned to tolerate temper tantrums and screaming. To a visiting stranger, they would explain, "Don't worry about Richie. He just needs to be alone now." In many ways the children were more tolerant than some of the parents.

Special children are no different than any other child; if you meet them with kindness and CARE, they will reciprocate. Mentally retarded children often integrate well into the preschool setting. They often have very good social development, and their physical development is almost normal. Their language may be simpler than that of peers, but they often make their needs known through body language. They may not be able to do some of the cognitive tasks well, but they can derive as much pleasure from painting, role playing, and playing with clay, blocks, and trucks as any other child. Knowing that this child is less able cognitively than some of the other children, you can work with activities the child *can* do successfully and reduce the amount of stress associated with goals that are too high. One private preschool had a policy to integrate "special" and "normal" children. The director allowed four identified "special" children in a class of twenty-four. Over the period of five years since this policy had been in effect, the school has taught mentally retarded children, children with orthopedic problems, and partially sighted, hard of hearing, emotionally disturbed, speech-impaired, and health-impaired children, as well as other children who were not as yet identified as having specific learning disabilities.

Study figure 14-5. You will note that there are more children with speech or language handicaps, more mentally retarded, emotionally disturbed, and learning disabled children than children who are orthopedically, visually, or hearing impaired. You are more likely to have a speech or language impaired, emotionally disturbed, learning disabled, or mentally retarded child in the preschool than one with the other types of problems.

SPECIAL CHILDREN "Special" children are as different from each other as are "normal" children, but not all "special" children are easily recognizable, figure 14-6. There are signs which can help you identify a "special" child. Does "Johnny" hold his head to one side constantly? Does he squint? (He may need glasses.) Does he ignore directions unless you are close to him and facing him? Is his speech unclear? (He may have a hearing problem.) Does the child have frequent bouts with *otitis media*, a middle ear infection?

Is the child not learning to talk at the same rate as his peers? (He may have a problem of language delay.) Is he still using baby talk when most of his

Fig. 14-4 Children can overcome physical limitations. (Courtesy of Jody Boyd)

Handicap	Percent of Population	Number of Children Ages 5 to 18**
Visually impaired (includes blind)	0.1	55,000
Hearing impaired (includes deaf)	0.5–0.7	276,000–385,000
Speech handicapped (includes language delay)	3–4	1,650,000–2,200,000
Crippled and other health impaired	0.5	275,000
Emotionally disturbed	2–3	1,100,000–1,650,000
Mentally retarded (both educable and trainable)	2–3	1,100,000–1,650,000
Learning disabled	2–3	1,100,000–1,650,000
Multihandicapped	0.5–0.7	275,000–385,000
Gifted, talented, and creative	2–4	1,100,000–2,200,000
Totals	12.6–19	6,931,000–10,450,000

*Figures obtained from Bureau for the Education of the Handicapped.
**Based on 1980 population estimates.

Fig. 14-5 Prevalence of "special" children in the United States*

Fig. 14-6 Not all "special" children are easily recognizable.

peers have outgrown it? (He may have a speech problem.) Is he frequently out of breath? Does he sneeze often? (He may have an allergy that should be properly diagnosed by a doctor. Fortunately, most health problems are diagnosed by family doctors; your role might simply be to monitor the child's medication if the doctor asks you. Children taking medication often have to be observed to decide if the dosage is appropriate; doctors must know if the child's behavior changes in any way, such as increased drowsiness or irritability.)

Is the child extremely aggressive or withdrawn? (He may be emotionally disturbed.) Is the child extremely active? Does he have a short attention span? Is he easily distracted? Does he have problems with cause and effect relationships? Does he have difficulty in putting his thoughts into words? (He may have a learning disability.) Is the child much slower than his peers in talking and completing cognitive work such as classifying objects? (He may be mildly mentally retarded.) It is important to note that these characteristics are only indications of the problem, not solid evidence that the problem does exist. Only a qualified person can make the actual determination.

Do you have a child at your center who is talking in sentences at age two or two-and-a-half? Is this child larger, taller, and heavier than other children of the same age? Does this child enjoy excellent health? Does he or she already know the names of the primary and secondary colors? Does the child already know the letters in his or her name? Does this child see relationships between seemingly unrelated objects? This child may be special in the sense of being gifted or talented.

WORKING WITH THE "SPECIAL" CHILD

In general, working with the "special" child is not much different than working with the "normal" child. Your cooperating teacher will, in most instances, give you cues for teaching a "special" child.

The child with a speech or language impairment may need one-to-one tutoring, figure 14-7. An early indication of a hearing impairment is lack of language

skills or unclear speech. If you suspect a child has a hearing loss, you should recommend to the parent that the hearing be checked. If the child is experiencing language delay, it may be because the parent has not spent much time talking to the child. Indeed, some children speak in what sounds like "television language." You should provide these children with opportunities to use verbal language. You may need to name objects for them and provide them with descriptive adjectives. You may play several language activities with these children such as feelie-box games and guessing games in which they describe one child to another. The other child tries to guess the name of the first.

The mentally retarded child may need no special attention beyond your being attuned to activities which may be frustrating. Your teacher may ask you to assist the child in certain activities which are known to be more difficult. For example, during a fingerplay, you may be asked to hold the child on your lap and to manipulate the child's fingers. The mentally retarded child might also need some extra help in language; slow language development is often a characteristic of a mentally retarded child.

You may experience greater difficulty in working with the emotionally disturbed and the learning disabled child. This is because it is difficult to identify a child who has emotional problems or a

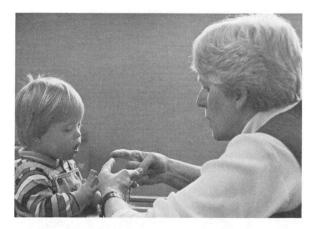

Fig. 14-7 It is common to work one-to-one with a "special" child. (Courtesy of Jody Boyd)

	Estimated Number of Children Age 0–19*	Percent of All U.S. Children Age 0–19*	Number of Children Identified Age 3–21, 1977–78**	Percent of All U.S. Children Served Age 3–21, 1977–78**	Est. of % Unserved
Mentally retarded	1,507,000	2.300	944,980	1.84	20
Deaf and hard of hearing	377,000	.575	87,146	.17	70
Speech impaired (includes language delayed)	2,293,000	3.500	1,226,961	2.39	32
Visually impaired	66,000	.100	35,717	.07	30
Emotionally disturbed	1,310,000	2.000	288,634	.57	72
Orthopedically and other health impaired	328,000	.500	224,237	.43	14
Learning disabled	1,966,000	3.000	969,423	1.89	37
Totals	7,847,000	11.975	3,777,098	7.36	275

*Estimated by Bureau of Education for the Handicapped, 1977.
**Identified under provisions of PL 94-142 and PL 89-313. From Bureau of Education for the Handicapped, 1979.

Fig. 14-8 Prevalence of handicapped children in the United States

learning disability. Look at figure 14-8. It is estimated that more than 70% of emotionally disturbed and hard of hearing children are unserved. Note the high percentage of mentally retarded and orthopedically handicapped children who are served. The logical reason for this gap is that obvious disabilities are more likely to be diagnosed. The exception is the case of the mentally retarded child. For example, a child with Down's Syndrome is easily recognized.

Retardation is easily measured with any well-known standard intelligence test. Despite the fact that intelligence testing (often called IQ testing for Intelligence Quotient, a figure derived from a comparison of mental age with chronological age) has come under fire over the past fifteen to twenty years, its use is still widespread. As a tool in understanding the child's intellectual development in regard to predicting possible success in school, the IQ test provides valuable information. Combined with other measures of a child's development (such as the checklist previously referred to and found in the Appendix), the IQ test provides a differential picture of the child's

drawback, other than the fact that many of its items are somewhat dated, is its verbal emphasis. The Wechsler Intelligence Scale for Children and the Wechsler Preschool/Primary Intelligence Scale attempt to provide both verbal and performance measures of intelligence. However, both of these tests may discriminate against a child from a racial and/or ethnic minority. Even though both have been translated into other languages, there is still the question of appropriateness. For most preschools, a developmental checklist provides as good or better information than an IQ test. The major advantage to the IQ test, of course, is in its use in diagnosing mental retardation. It seldom, however, provides clues regarding how to work with the child who is diagnosed as retarded.

If we use a developmental checklist or an instrument such as the Brigance (see Appendix for more information) which relies upon our observation of the child, we can develop a learning plan based upon what we see. Noting that a child can walk upstairs alternating the feet, but walks downstairs one foot at hold our hand at first. Then we can have the child hold onto a railing. Finally, we can urge the child to try without any support. If we note that a child is still speaking two-word sentences, we can provide for more language experiences on a one-to-one basis. In every case we should not urge the child to accomplish tasks that are not appropriate to his or her developmental level. The child who cannot gallop will not learn to skip; but perhaps the child is ready to learn how to slide one foot after the other sideways.

There is probably no area more controversial than that of emotional disturbance. Many teachers may think a child is emotionally disturbed but do not know how to approach the parent. Very often, if you see a young child with emotional problems, you will see a family with emotional problems. To many parents, even the suggestion of emotional disturbance in their child brings about a reaction such as "Are you telling me that I'm responsible for my child's emotional problems?" Many teachers and administrators have been known to avoid using the term "emotional problems," and to suggest that the child "acts out," "has no friends," "daydreams," or is "aggressive" or "withdrawn." We have to understand how difficult it is for a parent to accept the possibility that something may be wrong with the child. If the parents have no idea that the child is not perfectly "normal," it becomes extremely difficult to convince them that there may be a problem.

Facing the possibility that their child may not be perfect, some parents actually grieve for the lost image of what their child was to have been. They grieve in much the same way they would grieve if the child had died. They become angry and accuse us of prejudice, of not really knowing their child. Some parents verbally attack our skills and suggested diagnosis; others deny that anything is wrong. Most go through a period in which they blame themselves for causing the child's problems. In some instances, we may feel that they are indeed responsible for the problems of the child.

The emotionally disturbed child may or may not present a problem in the classroom. Certainly the aggressive child presents a challenge and must be watched closely. For this reason, it is not uncommon for the teacher to assign an aide or student teacher to work on a one-to-one basis with the child to try to control the child's outbursts. Holding the child on your lap, allowing the child to hit a weighted clown doll instead of a child or adult, having the child bite on a leather strap when he or she feels like biting, having the child run around the playground when he or she feels like exploding are all good techniques. Remember that behavior modification works well with children who are emotionally disturbed.

You should be aware that as the withdrawn, depressed child becomes better, he or she is likely to become aggressive. This is known as the pendulum effect. When a depressed child reaches this stage and begins to act out, some parents become angry and fearful; they stop therapy, not understanding that the child must release the pent-up anger. They do not understand that it will take time for the child to learn how to deal with anger in socially acceptable ways. We can reassure the parent that this phase is normal for the child. We can also be alert for signs that the child needs to be alone to stomp, yell, throw, and hit without hurting anyone. In some preschools, the child may be directed to go to another room where the child can throw nerf balls, pound on clay, or hit a weighted clown doll. In others, there may be a "time out" corner in which the child will be told to sit until he or she feels ready to rejoin the group. Whatever the technique used, you may be asked to remain with the child for safety purposes. At the same time, you can admire the child's anger and suggest ways in which the child can channel it in a positive direction.

The child suspected of having learning disabilities presents a challenge. While some parents are willing to accept a diagnosis of possible learning disabilities, others are not. What is a learning disability? It is commonly defined as a significant discrepancy between the child's measured ability and the child's actual classroom performance. For example, the learning disabled child has average or better intelligence but has not learned to read, write, or cipher. Reading and/or writing are usually involved; mathematics is frequently involved also.

Several labels have been applied to the learning disabled in previous years: aphasic, dyslexic, language disabled, educationally handicapped, developmental aphasia, emotional blockage, hyperactive, and hyper-kinetic. There was an accepted belief that a learning disabled child had suffered some minimal brain damage, generally at birth, or due to post-birth trauma (injury, high fever, accidents involving injury to the head, etc.). The idea led to the common usage of MBD to indicate such a possibility. In recent years, however, a growing number of educators believe that learning disabilities are not a true category but rather a diverse set of residuals or leftovers from other categories. The thinking of educators is as follows: "If we can't call this child emotionally disturbed because the parents won't accept it, let's just say he's learning disabled. After all, he isn't really badly disturbed; he does know what reality is."

Other investigators and researchers, notably Kirk (1972), Cruikshank (1977), and Kephart (1967) strongly believe that learning disabilities are a true category. Kirk even defined them as a disturbance in the perceptual processes of the child; the child's vision is fine but what the child sees is distorted in relation to what others see. Likewise, another child might hear perfectly well but does not process or attend to auditory stimuli. Still another child might not have good coordination; thus the child's kinesthetic sense seems disturbed. There is some evidence to suggest that the learning disabled child may have perceptual deficits, but there is also evidence to suggest that diet (Feingold, 1975), disorders of input and/or output, disorders of verbal and nonverbal learning (Meyen, 1978), and even brain functioning may be at fault (Strauss, et al., 1947).

Given the many theories as to what causes learning disabilities, what is the teacher to do? Among the several techniques proven effective with the learning disabled are:

- Structure. A well-planned classroom. Classroom rules are posted for older children and repeated often to younger ones so they understand the limits.
- Consistency of discipline by the teacher.
- Behavior modification.
- CARE. Be congruent; acceptant; reliable; and empathetic. It works with all children, especially the learning disabled child.

- Alternate quiet and active activities. Provide for enough physical exercise to tire the active child; allow the child enough freedom to move around often. Do not expect the child to sit still unless you are there.
- Love. A family medicine specialist, Lendon Smith, M.D., made the following statement (1981) to an audience of early childhood educators. "We have 5,000 children on stimulants to calm them down. All that 4,995 of them need is a little love." Smith was decrying the tendency of parents and teachers to ask medical doctors to place the seemingly overactive child on stimulants or drug therapy. He advocates instead that we use diet, physical exercise, relaxation exercises, and proven educational techniques such as those previously mentioned. We urge you to do the same.

Summary

In this brief introduction to the "special" child, we presented an overview of current thinking regarding the integration of the "special" child into the regular classroom. We attempted to show that, in many instances, the "special" child can do very well in the regular room. Such integration has almost always been successful. Of course, there were awkward moments initially, but the other children proved more tolerant than adults in accepting the "special" child.

We presented an overview of PL 94-142, and listed some of its major provisions. We discussed the term "least restrictive environment," and emphasized that what is least restrictive for one child may not be for another.

Finally, we offered some practical suggestions for working with the "special" child. We tend to agree that these techniques seem appropriate for all children. Methods that work well with one population are often applicable to another. For more specific ideas, you may wish to refer to the Suggested Readings list in the Appendix.

Suggested Activities

A. Visit a preschool that has "special" children in attendance. Spend at least one morning watching the "special" children, taking notes as you observe. What similarities and/or differences do you find between the "special" children and the "normal" children? Discuss your answers with your peers and supervisor.

B. Visit a preschool for "special" children. Again, take notes on your observations. In what ways is this "special" class different from or similar to the regular classroom? Discuss your answers with your peers and supervisor.

C. Visit a residential center for the "special" child. Discuss your observations with your peers and supervisor.

Review

A. Write your own definition of "special."

B. What are five characteristics of a "special" child?

C. According to PL 94-142, what are the eleven categories of "handicapped" children?

D. Read the following descriptions of behavior. Identify the child in each situation as "special" or "normal." Discuss your answers with your peers and supervisor.

 1. Ladan is a new child in your room of four-year-olds. Her mother says that the family speaks English in the home; however, you have doubts. In the classroom Ladan seems to be more of a spectator rather than a participant. You note that when playing "Simon Says" Ladan does not appear to know what to do, but copies her neighbor.

 2. Richie is an abused two-year-old who has recently been placed in a foster home. He enters preschool every morning like a small whirlwind, running around the room, kicking at block structures other children have built, knocking over puzzles others are making, and screaming at the top of his lungs.

 3. Even though Tommy has been in your kindergarten class for nearly the entire year, his behavior

has not changed noticeably from the first day. He still clings to his mother's hand when she brings him to school, and cries for three to five minutes after she leaves. He has only one friend in the room, and efforts to persuade him to play or work with another child are met with tears.

 4. Sally is a pretty, blonde three-year-old in your day care center. Lately, she has been complaining about her head hurting every afternoon. On several days, she has complained about feeling sick to her stomach. You have suggested to her mother that she may be coming down with a cold, but the doctor's exam shows that Sally is in good health except for a possible nearsightedness.

 5. Joey has started kindergarten but does not yet talk. However, he does appear to understand when someone talks to him. When his mother is questioned, she says that she is not concerned because Joey's older brother did not talk much until after he started school also. When you check on the older brother, you note that he is in a special class for the mentally retarded.

Resources

Cruikshank, William M. "Myths and Realities in Learning Disabilities." *Journal of Learning Disabilities,* 10 (1977), pp. 51–58.

Feingold, Ben F. *Why Your Child Is Hyperactive.* New York: Random House, 1975.

Kephart, Newell C. "Perceptual Motor Aspects of Learning Disabilities," from Frierson and Barbe, eds., *Educating Children with Learning Disabilities.* New York: Appleton-Century-Croft, 1967.

Kirk, Samuel A. *Educating Exceptional Children.* Boston: Houghton Mifflin Co., 1972.

Meyen, Edward L. *Exceptional Children and Youth: An Introduction.* Denver: Love Publishing Co., 1978.

Smith, Lendon. "Mind, Body, Diet, Behavior." Presentation at the California Association for the Education of Young Children Conference, March 15, 1981.

Strauss, A.A., and Lehtinen, L.E. *Psychopathology and Education of the Brain Injured Child.* New York: Grune and Stratton, 1947.

Section 6 Parents

Unit 15
Parents as Volunteers

> **OBJECTIVES**
>
> After completing this unit, the student will be able to:
>
> - List at least five ways in which parents can serve as volunteers.
>
> - State a minimum of five precautions to remember when working with parents.
>
> - Design a plan for parent participation in any school or center in which the student hopes to be employed.

HISTORY OF EARLY CHILDHOOD EDUCATION

In 1856 the first kindergarten was established by Margarethe Schurz and her husband, Carl, in Wisconsin. Elizabeth Palmer Peabody, a wealthy woman dedicated to bettering society and education, was so impressed with the Schurzes that she became a self-appointed spokesman for kindergartens. Her interest and sponsorship coincided with several factors: the first compulsory attendance laws, opposition to child labor, a sharp rise in the number of children in relation to the total population, and a growing number of immigrant children of working parents. Many educators viewed the kindergarten movement as a vehicle to aid in the acculturation of the immigrant child (Osborn, 1975, pp. 22, 32).

By 1900 John Dewey had convinced the administration at the University of Chicago to open a laboratory school, containing a class for four- and five-year-olds which he called the "Sub-Primary." In 1907 Maria Montessori opened the *Casa dei Bambini* in Rome. In 1909 the first White House Conference on Children was held; its concerns were child care and development (Osborn, 1975, pp. 34–35).

In 1912 the Children's Bureau (now a part of the Office of Child Development) was established, and the first cooperative nursery school was opened in 1916 by a group of faculty wives at the University of Chicago. Soon many major universities had child development laboratories, and private parent-cooperative nursery schools were established in most large cities (Osborn, 1975, pp. 35–36).

During these early years, some nursery classes were sponsored by settlement houses, church groups, and other organizations in many of the big cities. Educating the young child "had been seen as a vehicle for reaching and influencing immigrant families isolated by language and cultural barriers who were clustering in what were rapidly becoming big-city ghettos. Hull House in Chicago and Henry Street Settlement in New York were typical. . . ." (Goodlad, et al., 1973, p. 5.)

For the most part, though, the education of young children was an opportunity available only to those who could afford it, primarily the middle and upper-middle classes. It was also available in college communities and suburban cities. During World War II, one exception to this pattern emerged. Child care centers, such as the Kaiser Centers, located near war-related industries operated twenty-four hours each day, provided medical care for the sick child, gave a hot meal which could be taken home with the parent after a long day at the shipyard, and offered other services such as counseling. After the war, the centers closed.

With the advent of Head Start and the concept of compensatory education, the federal government entered the field of early childhood education; that influence is still felt today. Legislators passed the Economic Opportunity Act of 1964 and the ESEA of 1965, which funded "early intervention" programs; many still exist today (Goodlad, 1973, pp. 8–14). Written into these acts were provisos for active parent participation. Parents from poverty backgrounds with little or no education were presumed to be knowledgeable. In particular, they were knowledgeable about their children and community. No longer would an upper-middle class "do-gooder," usually white, come into a minority neighborhood and tell parents how to raise and educate their children. It was a major step forward to where we are today, with Parent Advisory Committees and parent volunteers.

Where are we today? Throughout the 1970's, there was a growing trend to full-time day care. As inflation problems hit more families, more mothers joined the work force. This created a need for extended day care, which led many former nursery schools to offer after-school care. It has also led to franchised operations, such as Kindercare and Mary Moppets. Still, the number of children being cared for in licensed centers remains small. Many mothers choose, instead, the licensed family day care home or a relative or neighbor.

The 1980's have seen a gradual increase in the number of employers entering the day care field, particularly those who employ a large number of women. Some employers have established their own day care center. Others have provided vouchers for employees with children, which are redeemable at certain day care centers in the community.

PARENTS AS VOLUNTEERS

In many ways the well-educated, middle- and upper-middle-class parent has often been involved as a parent volunteer. Prior to World War II, few married women worked, and there were few single parents. Because of the depression during the 1930's, there were no paid aides in most elementary schools. Teachers who wanted to individualize programs often asked parents for help. Others felt parents did not belong in the classroom, although they were welcome at PTA/PTO meetings and at school fund-raising events.

The compensatory education programs brought a new focus on the parent (Evans, 1971, pp. 12–13). The findings of many studies on class size and the effects of the teacher:pupil ratio on learning are in favor of smaller classes. A review of fifty-nine studies revealed that lowering the teacher:pupil ratio led to better results on cognitive measures and favorable effects on both teachers and students in terms of higher morale, more positive attitudes, self concepts, etc. (Smith and Glass, 1980, pp. 419–433). One of the easiest ways to lower the teacher:pupil ratio is through the use of parent volunteers.

With young children, many states limit class size to 15:1 for four-year-olds, 12:1 for three-year-olds, and as low as 3:1 for infants. It is presumed that the younger the child, the more the child needs adult attention. One way to provide for this need is to use parent volunteers, figure 15-1. While this concept works in theory, in practice there are many limitations. Many mothers are currently working and do not have the time to volunteer; others, particularly low-income and/or minority parents, may not feel welcome or needed.

What is a teacher to do when federal and state mandates require parent participation? As always, there is less of a problem with the nonworking

Fig. 15-1 Parent volunteers often help with instruction. (Courtesy of Jody Boyd)

parent. There may be many reasons why the parent does not work, and you need to be sensitive to them. One parent may not work because there is a baby at home and no one with whom the baby can be left. Another may be disabled or have problems with mobility.

In most communities in past years the administration of school programs was left to the professionals — the principal and teachers in a public school, the director or teachers in a preschool. Most of these professionals were middle class, often white. They perceived their role as one of informing parents about their children's behaviors, especially learning behaviors. Thus, parent-teacher conferences were held at regular intervals. During these conferences, teachers told parents what their children had been doing on various measures of learning and classroom behavior. The professionals sometimes felt that the parent did not know how to parent; they sometimes looked down on the parent whose English was different and whose clothing was old, torn, and unstylish. Parent-teacher organizations were usually led by middle-class, nonworking mothers. Lower-class parents tended to be ignored if they attended. Soon they stopped coming, and unkind teachers and other parents would say, "Well, what can you expect of parents with no background in school who speak broken English? They just don't care." Fortunately, federal compensatory education programs demanded

parent participation. It is recognized that almost all parents love and care for their children and want what is best for them. Of course, there are those to whom children are a nuisance, but this is a phenomenon found across all social classes. There are neglectful upper-class parents, as well as uncaring middle- and lower-class families.

HOW TO MOTIVATE PARENTS TO VOLUNTEER One might say that anything a parent does of his or her own free will to be of some service to the teacher is being a volunteer. Parents have been baking cookies for classroom parties for years. They have also sewn bean bags, mixed homemade clay, and brought old toys for a toy share-in. Parents have built climbing structures and house equipment, put up fences, installed swings, and cleaned yards and rooms. Many of these activities have been done at home on the parents' free time, figure 15-2. These are volunteer activities.

How do you persuade nonparticipating parents that they are needed? Guides are available to teachers which provide helpful hints. They often include communication strategies and specific techniques and activities useful in working with parents.

One way in which you may encourage a parent to participate is to speak to the parent about your expectations of his or her involvement when the child is being registered. Some centers have a list of

Fig. 15-2 This father enjoys volunteering at the center on his day off. (Courtesy of Jody Boyd)

activities in which the parent may participate; the parent is asked to check those activities which he or she feels comfortable doing. The teacher then calls upon the parent when needed, and asks the parent to help out.

The home visit can lead to better rapport between the parent and school. It is possible for a discerning teacher to note special talents on a home visit (hand-sewn curtains or drapes; potted plants; newly painted walls which the parents did themselves; cooking abilities). The teacher can follow up with a request of the parent to use that talent on a school project, figure 15-3. Parents who protest that they have no skills may think the teacher means teaching skills, and may not realize that wielding a paintbrush can sometimes be of more value. Gardening skills are also frequently overlooked. Parents may not realize how much care goes into maintaining the landscape of a center, and may be delighted to spend an afternoon digging the ground for a garden the children will be planting during the next week. A teacher might

Fig. 15-3 A creative parent volunteer designed and posted this bulletin board.

want to sprout beans and peas and then transfer them into a vegetable garden, allowing the children to weed and water the beans and peas, watch them grow, and finally pick, cook, and eat the fruits of their labor.

STUDIES OF PARENT PARTICIPATION A friend who is a Head Start teacher visits the home of every incoming child during the late summer. She always brings a simple toy to entertain the child and to make the child feel important. With the child busily occupied, the parents then feel more relaxed, rapport is easily established, and requests for help are met with a more positive frame of mind. This teacher usually has between one-fourth and one-third of parents unable to help out during the school day due to work or school commitments. The remaining parents are expected to donate at least one morning or afternoon each week to the program. Even knowing that they are expected to assist once each week, many parents are relatively inactive. Of twenty-four parents, this teacher knows she will be fortunate if four or five assist regularly. More likely than not, assistance will be limited to out-of-school kinds of assistance (baking cookies, making bean bags) rather than in-school assistance (Leviten, 1978).

Studies have indicated that teachers who work with parent volunteers place much value in the parents and in their labor. In her research, Elizabeth C. Buchanan (1978) found that teachers who made regular use of parent volunteers were more apt to have positive attitudes about the value of the parents to the classroom. Teachers in districts where volunteers received some training were also more favorable in their attitudes. Teachers who did not feel threatened by the presence of volunteers tended to use them more in instructional activities. Teachers with negative perceptions of the value of volunteers were more likely to use them less and to use them in activities such as running a copy machine and yard supervision.

Generally, there are advantages for everyone involved in parent participation programs. Teachers have the additional resource of the volunteer's time, energy, and talent; parents have the satisfaction of knowing that they are making an active contribution to their children's learning; and children feel that their parents care more, and they achieve more in school.

Summary

Parent participation is a many-faceted phenomenon. Volunteering includes assisting in the classroom, as well as baking cookies for snack time, helping build climbing structures, attending parent education meetings, sewing bean bags, and many more activities.

The historical use of parents as volunteers was discussed and some studies on the use of parents as volunteers were reviewed. Remember: Do not be discouraged if parent participation in the classroom is low. It takes time to establish rapport with parents, especially those from different cultures.

Suggested Activities

A. Visit three or four different types of preschools, such as a publicly supported day care center, a proprietary day care center, an adult education-supported nursery school, the preschool associated with your college. Talk with the teachers and directors of these centers about how they involve parents in their programs. Discuss your findings with your peers and supervisor.

B. With your cooperating teacher, develop a list of activities for volunteers for use in your own classroom.

Review

A. What are five different ways in which parents can serve as volunteers?

B. Name five precautions to keep in mind when working with parents.

C. Design a plan for a parent education meeting. What are your objectives? What materials or equipment will you need? Describe the procedure. Discuss your plan with your cooperating teacher, peers, and supervisor. Implement the plan, and evaluate its effectiveness.

Resources

Buchanan, Elizabeth C. *Parent Volunteers in California's Early Childhood Education Schools.* Master's Thesis, California State University, Hayward, 1978.

Evans, Ellis D. *Contemporary Influences in Early Childhood.* New York: Holt, Rinehart & Winston, Inc., 1971.

Goodlad, John I.; Klein, Frances M.; Novotney, Jerrold M.; and associates. *Early Schooling in the United States.* New York: McGraw-Hill Book Co., 1973.

Leviten, Ruth. *Ways to Involve the Non-Participating Parent in the Preschool Program.* Master's Project, California State University, Hayward, 1978.

Osborn, D. Keith. *Early Childhood Education in Historical Perspective.* Athens, GA: Early Childhood Education Center, University of Georgia, 1975.

Smith, Mary Lee, and Glass, Gene V. "Meta-analysis of Research on Class Size and Its Relationship to Attitudes and Instruction." *American Educational Research Journal,* 17 (Winter 1980), pp. 419–433.

Unit 16
Parents and Student Teachers

OBJECTIVES

After studying this unit, the student will be able to:

- Name at least five techniques to use when interacting with parents.

- Listen to and/or watch an audio/videotape of a parent-teacher conference and analyze the interaction according to a theory of communication such as the Johari model.

- Participate in a mock parent-teacher conference, role playing both parent and teacher.

- Discuss the different types of parent interactions.

INTERACTING WITH PARENTS

Most interactions with parents are informal, figure 16-1. The most frequent interaction occurs when parents bring and pick up their children from the center. The parents will say something to the teacher or smile and nod. These constitute interactions. Often when we have noted that children have done something commendable during the day, we will mention it briefly to the parents when the children are picked up. Likewise, if we think there has been a problem, we often take a few minutes to explain what has happened. Communications such as these are typical of the informal kind.

More formal communications consist of scheduled parent-teacher conferences and home visits, figure 16-2. In each case the parents will have prior notice about the conference or home visit. They can then plan ahead of time. The house or apartment can be cleaned; clutter can be put out of sight; other children can be warned to behave; other adults living in the house can be asked to be present or leave. If the meeting is to take place at school, the parents can plan the conference ahead of time, anticipating ques-

tions which may be asked and preparing answers. Thus, the parents may tell what they think we want to hear rather than the truth.

MODELS OF COMMUNICATION

One communication model compares the process of communication to a telephone call in which there is a caller who is sending a message through a specific channel — the telephone — to a receiver, who has to decode the message (Berlo, 1960). Whether the message is understood depends upon five variables: the communication skills and the attitudes of both the receiver and sender, their knowledge, the social system to which each belongs, and their cultures, figure 16-3. Any differences between the sender and receiver on any of the variables can lead to misunderstandings.

Let us study a hypothetical situation involving Stevie; his mother, Mrs. Conway; and Mrs. Thomas, the teacher. Mrs. Thomas thinks that Stevie is not getting enough sleep, and telephones Stevie's mother to ask if she can stay for a brief conference when she

Fig. 16-1 Most interactions with parents are informal.

Fig. 16-2 The development of friendships may be discussed at parent-teacher conferences.

picks up her children. Stevie's mother reluctantly agrees. Before the teacher and mother meet, they may already be processing information.

Stevie always looks tired when his mother brings him to school every morning. During naptime, he really falls asleep. Not many four-year-olds do. For most of them, in fact, naptime is "squirm" time. It seems that we hardly even begin to turn on the music on the tape recorder before Stevie falls sound asleep. I've also noticed that Stevie is hard to awaken after naptime is over. I think he'd like to sleep

for a longer period of time than we give him. I bet he doesn't get enough sleep at home. I think I'll talk to his mother about it.

After making an appointment with Stevie's mother for that evening, Mrs. Thomas may begin plans on how to approach the subject of Stevie's sleep schedule. Her thoughts may be as follows:

I've always believed that the best approach in working with parents is to first let them know that I have the welfare of their child on my mind. I think I'll start by stating how much I

Sender	Message	Channel	Receiver
Communication skills Attitudes Knowledge Social system Culture	Content Structure	Eyes (seeing) Ears (hearing) Hands (touching) Nose (smelling) Mouth (tasting) Body in space (kinesthesia)	Communication skills Attitudes Knowledge Social system Culture

Fig. 16-3 Variables in a communication model

enjoy having Stevie attend school. Then, let me see, should I come right out and ask how much sleep he gets? Maybe, it would sound better if I ask when he goes to bed and when he gets up. If I don't think he's getting enough sleep, I can ask Stevie's mother how much sleep she thinks Stevie should get. Wait a minute, maybe I can ask her how much sleep her other children, Tommy and Bobby, used to get when they were four. No, I think asking when Stevie goes to bed and gets up is a better approach. Mrs. Conway seems like a knowledgeable and caring mother. Certainly, Stevie arrives clean and well-dressed every day.

In the meantime, Stevie's mother may be thinking along these lines:

Now why would Stevie's teacher want to talk about Stevie? I thought I filled her in on everything she needed to know when I enrolled him. Maybe he's been acting up at school. Maybe he got into a fight with Davie. Goodness knows he talks about beating up Davie if he keeps teasing him. Maybe it's finally happened. Mike (Stevie's father) would surely be proud of Stevie for a change. He's always telling the boy to stop being such a sissy and letting Bobby or Tommy stick up for him! Maybe she wants me to bake something for school or take a day off work to help out. She knows I can't afford to take any more time off.

Perhaps a different approach would have been to ask the question over the telephone. Indeed, many teachers would do exactly this. Why bother a busy parent with a conference if the information can be handled on the telephone? Other teachers, however, prefer to ask any sensitive questions face-to-face in order to watch reactions. (Since many centers ask parents to fill out extensive questionnaires, some parents could feel that, through questioning of this type, their word is being doubted.)

Let us now proceed with the actual interaction between the two parties.

Teacher: "Mrs. Conway, please come into my office where it'll be quieter. Boys, why don't you find something to play with? Stevie, why don't you show Tommy where things are around the room? Bobby, I bet you remember where to find toys, don't you?" (The boys go off to play, and Mrs. Conway and Mrs. Thomas go into the office. Mrs. Thomas asks Mrs. Conway if she would like a cup of coffee. Mrs. Conway accepts.)

"Mrs. Conway, as you know, we are always concerned about the children and want what's best for them." (I wish I could read Mrs. Conway's body language better. She really looks tired this evening.)

Mother: (What's Mrs. Thomas trying to say? Of course the school has the welfare of the children at heart. Why does she suppose I enrolled both Bobby and Stevie here.) "Yes. That's why I enrolled the boys here."

Teacher: "Well, I've noticed that Stevie seems to sleep heavily during naptime. Does he take a nap on weekends?" (That's as good a start as I can think of. Start with an observation; ask the parent if they've noted similar behavior at home. That's worked before.)

Mother: (I wonder what she's angling for?) "Let's see. I think Stevie always takes a nap on the weekend. I like the boys to keep pretty much the same schedule as during the week, you know."

Teacher: "What time does Stevie go to bed? Is it the same time as on weekdays?" (I might as well simply ask her.)

Mother: "We put the boys to bed between 8:00 p.m. and 9:00 p.m. weekdays, and we like to do the same on weekends so Mr. Conway and I can get to a late movie or dinner once in a while." (What does she want? She *knows* what time the boys go to bed.)

Teacher: "Do the boys get up at the same time on the weekend?" (There, maybe that will get at what I'm trying to say. I'd lay odds that they sleep longer in the morning on the weekends.)

Mother: "Tommy is usually up before Mr. Conway and me. He likes to go into the living room and watch television Saturday mornings. When Mr. Conway and I get up, all three boys are usually glued to the television."

Teacher: "What time would that be?"

Mother: "About 9:00 a.m. usually. You see, Saturdays are the only days we get to sleep in, and we know the boys will be fine watching television. Also, their grandmother is usually up around 8:00 a.m., and she keeps an eye on the boys, especially if they go in the yard to play."

Teacher: "Is Stevie ever asleep when you get up?"

Mother: "Once in a while but not usually. If we let the boys watch television Friday evening until 9:00, Stevie's usually still asleep after Mr. Conway and I get up Saturday. Why are you asking me these questions about sleep and bedtime?" (I wonder what she wants to know.)

Teacher: "I've wondered whether Stevie slept more on the weekend than during the week. You see, as I said before, I've noticed that he really falls sound asleep during naptime. You know, some children need more sleep than others. Have you noticed any difference with the three boys?" (Maybe this will give her an idea that Stevie may need more sleep than the others. I hope so.)

Mother: "Let me think. When Tommy was little, he didn't used to sleep too much. I remember it really annoyed me when I was carrying Bobby that Tommy didn't want to take a nap! And he wasn't even two yet! Bobby, though, was taking a nap even after he came to school when he was three." (Mrs. Thomas nods.) "Didn't Bobby take a nap after kindergarten last year?" (Mrs. Thomas again nods.) "Bobby always needed more sleep than Tommy. That Tommy is like a live wire, always sparking!"

Teacher: "What about Stevie?"

Mother: "Stevie always seemed more like Tommy when he was little. But lately he seems more like Bobby. He and Bobby are real close, you know, always playing together. Tommy has his own friends now, especially since he's on the soccer team. Say, why don't you ask Tommy when Stevie gets up Saturday mornings?" (Mrs. Conway's voice trails off.) "I think you're wondering if having all three boys go to bed at the same time is right for Stevie. Is Stevie getting enough rest?"

Teacher: "Exactly. What do you think?"

At this point we are going to analyze the interaction according to the model in figure 16-3. Let us look first at our sender, Mrs. Thomas. What do her communication skills seem like? What appears to be her attitude toward Mrs. Conway? Upon what is she basing her knowledge of the situation? From what kind of social system does Mrs. Thomas come? What is her cultural background? What about Stevie's mother? What is her cultural background? First, we might suggest that Mrs. Thomas' communication skills are reasonably sharp. She starts with an observation of Stevie, and asks Mrs. Conway to confirm or deny similar behavior on weekends. Then Mrs. Thomas attempts to bring Mrs. Conway to the same conclusion by asking if she had noted any differences between one boy and another. Eventually, because her communication skills are reasonably sharp, Mrs. Conway realizes what Mrs. Thomas is asking, and asks the question herself.

Second, in studying the interaction, we might surmise that Mrs. Thomas and Mrs. Conway have smooth lines of communication between them. (You will note your cooperating teacher easily deals with parents who are known from previous experiences. You will also note, as a general rule, that the more a teacher deals with parents, the greater that teacher's skill.)

Next, what can we guess about Mrs. Thomas' social system and culture? Her social system is her school; her culture can be seen most easily as middle class. She may be white or black (or another ethnic minority). These characteristics are not as important as the observation of social class. Mrs. Conway's social system appears to be bureaucratic at work (she is a clerk-typist at a county office). Given Mr. Conway's occupation at a foundry and his views of raising children as being "women's work," we might surmise that the Conways are from the working class. A home visit might confirm many of our surmises. If we make further inquiries, we might discover that Mrs. Conway has had some advanced secretarial training at a local junior college, and she attended a communications workshop for county employees who deal with the public.

Let us now look at the message. What was its content? How was it treated? What structure did it take? Simply, the content involved describing Stevie's naptime behavior at school to his mother. Mrs. Thomas was reporting to Mrs. Conway. The structure involved verbal input, watching nonverbal input closely. It also involved asking questions in order to persuade Mrs. Conway to see that Stevie might need more sleep. Part of the structure was also concerned with arranging the factors in a particular order. First, Mrs. Thomas directed the boys to entertain themselves and suggested to Stevie that he show his oldest brother the location of toys and equipment. In this way, Mrs. Thomas gave Stevie a job to do which would make him feel more competent and give him the opportunity to direct his bossy, oldest brother. Then Mrs. Thomas spoke directly to the second-oldest boy, telling him that he would know where things were and, indirectly, rewarding him for his good memory.

Next Mrs. Thomas arranged for a quiet and private conference. (In a case such as this, Mrs. Thomas would have probably asked her aide to take charge in the room.) Knowing that Mrs. Conway would enjoy a cup of coffee, Mrs. Thomas offered her some. (Having something to drink and/or eat helps establish rapport. It also helps a tired parent relax.) In addition, addition, Mrs. Thomas did not sit behind her desk but, instead, sat on a chair next to Mrs. Conway.

What channels of communication were used during the interaction? Most obviously were the ears for hearing and the eyes for seeing. Since Mrs. Thomas offered a cup of coffee or tea to Mrs. Conway, the mouth or sense of taste would have been involved also. It is difficult not to involve the sense of touch and the kinesthetic sense. Shaking hands involves touch; walking, sitting down, and holding a mug of coffee or tea all involve the kinesthetic sense. It is through these messages from our senses that we interpret the stimuli which form our world. Under many circumstances, each person involved may have separate interpretations of the same set of stimuli; this is where misunderstandings develop. In our multicultural, multiracial culture we are, perhaps, prone to misunderstandings which arise from different interpretations of the same data.

Look at figure 16-3. Let us assume that Mrs. Thomas is a well-educated (master's degree in early childhood education), articulate, middle-class black woman. Let us further assume that she was raised by educated, religious parents. Mrs. Thomas' values will reflect her upbringing. Strict but warm-hearted, she believes in practicing her religion every day. She attempts to see the good in everyone. Even when she disagrees with someone, she tries to see their point. A believer in God and family, Mrs. Thomas also defers to Mr. Thomas in personal family matters.

What would happen if Stevie's mother was a poorly educated single parent who just arrived to this country? Her reaction to Mrs. Thomas might be very different than that which was previously described. First, using figure 16-3, there would be a difference on each of the variables or characteristics listed under Sender and Receiver. These differences in communication skills, knowledge, social system, and culture could make it extremely difficult for Mrs. Thomas to communicate with Mrs. Conway.

Even less obvious differences can block understanding. One such block was suggested in the first description of Stevie's parents. Mr. Conway was described as a foundry worker who thought raising children was women's work. As a result, the boys had to remain at the school an hour longer than necessary because he would not pick them up. It was further suggested that Mr. Conway was proud of his oldest boy, Tommy, because of his size and athletic ability and less proud of Stevie who was small for his age. We might also assume a difference in the way in which Mrs. Thomas and Mrs. Conway view Stevie. For example, Mrs. Thomas might see a sensitive, quiet little boy who needs a lot of loving care. Mrs. Conway might see Stevie as a "sissy" who was afraid to stand up for his own rights. Mrs. Thomas might try to educate the parents to make them change their attitude about what characteristics a boy or man should have. In doing so, it is likely that she might fail. This is because attitudes are resistant to change. Mrs. Thomas might have more success helping Stevie feel better about himself in terms of activities at school. Mrs. Thomas should interfere in the family matter only if she perceives that Mrs. Conway has some doubts about her husband's views. Even then, Mrs.

Thomas should proceed carefully. Changing family attitudes is risky. Regardless of how we might feel about how a father treats his son, it is important to remember that the child has to learn to live with the parent's attitude.

THE JOHARI MODEL Let us now consider a second model of communication: the Johari model, which was named after its two originators, Joseph Luft and Harry Ingham. The Johari model is presented in figure 16-4. In the model there are four "windows." The upper left corner window is "open;" in other words, what is presented to another person is known both to the other person and to the self. The upper right corner is the "blind" window. This window represents those aspects of ourselves which are evident to others but not to ourselves. The lower left corner is the "hidden" window. In any interpersonal exchange, there may be aspects of ourselves which we may want to hide from another person. The last window, on the bottom right side, is "unknown." There are aspects about a person which are unknown to that person as well as to any observer.

Let us use the example of the interaction between Mrs. Thomas and Mrs. Conway to illustrate how the Johari window might look. Before the conference Mrs. Conway might keep the "open" part of her window fairly small. Mrs. Thomas, in contrast, may have a larger "open" window and keep her "hidden" window larger, at least initially. As the two women begin to feel more comfortable, the "open" windows of each will widen, and Mrs. Thomas' "hidden" window will become smaller. Mrs. Conway's "blind" window may become

	Known to self	Not known to self
Known to others	Open	Blind
Not known to others	Hidden	Unknown

Fig. 16-4 The Johari model of communication (From *Of Human Interaction* by Joseph Luft. Palo Alto, CA: National Press Books, 1969.)

smaller as she begins to realize that Stevie may need more sleep, something that she had not thought about before.

The Johari model can be adjusted to increase or decrease various parts according to the situation. For example, as a person grows older, he or she will often learn more about the self; that person's "blind" and "unknown" windows may grow smaller. In a new social situation in which one feels uncomfortable, one's "open" window might be quite small. With a best friend, however, this "open" window might be very large.

NONVERBAL COMMUNICATION We have suggested that nonverbal communication often tells more than verbal communication about how someone feels. In the previous example, the teacher noted that Mrs. Conway seemed tired. Was there any evidence for this? Most likely, it was based upon nonverbal communication. Study figure 16-5. You will note that nonverbal communication involves body talk, such as gestures, facial expression, eye expression, stance, and large body muscles. Motions such as a wave of the hand, a shrug of the shoulders, a smile, standing erect or slumping all send messages. Actions like pushing one's chair closer or away from another, and leaning forward or back also send messages.

Just as nonverbal communications give clues, so does verbal communication. The tone, pitch, rate, and loudness of a person's voice send messages. When a person is excited, the pitch of the voice will rise and the rate of speech will increase. Excitement causes a person to speak louder. Anger often makes a person speak louder and quicker, but the pitch may become lower and the tone hard. As mentioned by Gordon (1974), we should strive to be "active listeners." We should listen to hidden messages, not just to words.

The observation that Mrs. Conway looks tired is based upon her knit eyebrows, turned-down corners of the mouth, slumping shoulders, quiet voice, and slow rate of speech. She may use no words to indicate her fatigue. In fact, listening only to her words does not give us any clue as to how she feels. This is based totally upon nonverbal clues and our active listening.

COMMUNICATION TECHNIQUES In order to fully grasp the different methods of communication,

Message sent through body talk	Specific Physical Expression					
	Gesture	Facial expression	Eye expression	Large body muscles	Stance or posture	Comments

Message sent vocally	Specific Vocal Expression				
	Tone	Pitch	Rate	Loudness	Comments

Fig. 16-5 Nonverbal interaction sheet

it is a good idea to act out situations. You should take turns with your peers role playing parents and teachers. Try this: On a three-by-five card, write a communication problem you have observed at your center. Place all the cards in a box. Pair off with another student teacher, and pick a problem from the box. Discuss and decide how you both would resolve the problem. Present your results to the class. Your peers should use the models of communication to analyze the action of the conference being role played. You and your partner should use the same form so that you can discuss how you both *see* the action. You will find this exercise interesting. It will be helpful to be aware of some specific communication techniques which work in conjunction with the models of communication.

- In working with parents, the first rule is to put them at ease. Sit the parents comfortably. Offer something to eat or drink, especially if the conference is at the end of a workday.
- Try to begin the conference in a positive manner. Even if you need to report a child's negative behavior or ask the parent a difficult question, always start on a positive note. Comment on the child's good behaviors or actions before stating what the child does incorrectly.
- Try to elicit from the parent a description of the child's behavior in school. (This is especially appropriate in a setting such as a parent-cooperative or child development center.) If the parent has not seen the child in action at school, ask about the child's observed behavior at home or in other social settings such as church, if appropriate. This will enable you to study the degree of parental perceptivity regarding the child's behavior.
- Be specific when describing the child's behavior. Avoid generalities. Use descriptive, preferably written, accounts taken over a period of at least three consecutive days, with several samplings per day.
- Keep samples of the child's work in a folder with the child's name and with the date indicating when the sampling was taken. Actual samples of work can speak more loudly and eloquently than words.

- Avoid comparisons with other children. Each child is unique. Most develop in idiosyncratic ways that make comparisons unfair. (If the comparison must be done for a valid reason, do this carefully and only with your cooperating teacher's permission.)
- When you have to present some negative behavior, *avoid*, as much as possible, making any evaluation about the goodness or badness of the child and/or the parent.
- Remember your attitude is important. You can choose to CARE.
- Keep any conference "on focus." Remember that most parents are busy; their time is valuable. Do not waste it. Discuss whatever is supposed to be discussed. Do not stray off course.
- Be cheerful, friendly, and tactful.
- Act cordial; remember your manners even if the parents forget theirs. Remember that it takes two to argue.
- Be honest; avoid euphemisms. Do not say "Tony is certainly a creative child!" when you really mean "Boy! Can Tony ever find ways to bother me!"
- Be business-like, even with a parent who may be a friend. In this situation, you are the professional, not the friend.
- Know your facts and the program so well that you never feel defensive discussing it.
- Be enthusiastic, even if you are tired and feeling down.
- Do not discuss another child unless it is appropriate.
- Do not make judgments before you have had the opportunity to see all the evidence.
- Do not betray confidences. A child will often tell you something which should not be repeated or something about the parents which is best overlooked. If, however, you think the disclosure is important to the child's welfare, discuss with your cooperating teacher and/or college supervisor. Rely upon their recommendations.
- Observe the parents' body language. It will often tell you more about how they are really feeling than the words they say.

Summary

In this unit we discussed interactions between parents and student teachers, and parents and teachers. We have presented you with four models of communication, both verbal and nonverbal. Finally, we presented a list of some specific techniques to use when interacting with parents.

One final word: Most parent-teacher communication is informal in nature. Therefore, it is important to remember that the impression you make in informal interactions may often set the stage for how a parent views and accepts you.

Suggested Activities

A. If your school has videotape equipment, role play a difficult parent conference in which you play the teacher attempting to talk to a mother about her physically aggressive child and she refuses to believe you. Observe yourself during playback. Using figure 16-5, notice your nonverbal communications. Analyze your verbal communication, using either figure 16-3 or 16-4. Discuss your analysis with your peers, supervisor, and/or cooperating teacher.

B. Read Julius Fast's *Body Language.* Replay your videotaped role play and analyze the body language you and the "parent" used.

C. Read Robert R. Carkhuff's, David H. Berenson's, and Richard M. Pierce's *The Skills of Teaching: Interpersonal Skills.* Discuss its concepts with your peers, cooperating teacher, and supervisor. Try some of the suggested exercises. Evaluate their effectiveness.

D. Read "Model for Human Relations Training," in *Human Relations Development: A Manual for Educators* by George M. Gazda, et al. Try some of the exercises suggested in Chapter 13 of the book. Evaluate your responses according to the model. How did you do?

Review

A. List five techniques to use when conducting a parent conference.

B. Match each of the following statements with the Johari model that is most appropriate. Each model may be used more than once.

Key: O – Open
B – Blind
H – Hidden
U – Unknown

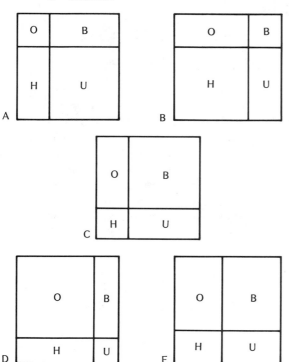

1. How you appear to your best friend.
2. How a young child might appear to his or her parent.
3. Anyone in a new environment.
4. An older person facing a new situation.
5. A student on the first day of class.
6. Someone who is unsure of him or herself.
7. An employee who is unexpectedly asked by the boss to come into the office.
8. Your reaction when the director of your placement center comes into your room unexpectedly.
9. How you may appear to your students on the last day of class.
10. How you may appear to a group of peers whom you know well and respect.

C. Read the following dialogue. Then complete the activity which follows.

Setting: It is early in the year. This is Susie's first experience in preschool. An only child of older parents, Susie always comes to school in clean dresses with ruffles and lace trim. Susie is average in size for her four years. She is attractive and has dark hair and dark eyes. A rather dominant child, Susie has excellent language skills which she uses to boss other children. Because of this behavior, Susie has come into conflict with Janice, a small, wiry child who has been attending the preschool since she was three. Janice is very assertive and clearly resents Susie. Susie does not like Janice. Their mutual dislike has led to a clothes-pulling incident. As a result, the ruffle on Susie's dress was partially torn off and Janice's shirt collar was ripped. As the student teacher, you became involved because the incident erupted on the playground when you were in charge. Mrs. Brown, your cooperating teacher, has contacted both mothers and arranged to see each parent separately. She has asked you to talk to Mrs. Smith, Janice's mother, while she talks to Mrs. Jones, Susie's mother. She explains further that Mrs. Smith is rather proud of Janice's assertiveness and understands that it sometimes leads Janice into altercations with the other children. You have met Mrs. Smith before and have sat in on at least one parent conference with her. You feel comfortable explaining what happened.

Student teacher (ST): "Mrs. Smith, it is good to see you again. Wouldn't you like to come into the office? I think there may be a cup of coffee left in the pot." (You greet Mrs. Smith with a smile. You remember that she likes a cup of coffee after work and had two cups during the last conference. You pour a cup of coffee for Mrs. Smith and a cup of tea for yourself. You sit in the chair at a right angle to her.)

Mrs. Smith (MS): "Thank you. You know how much I enjoy my coffee, don't you? Now, what's happened? I know you wouldn't ask me here without a reason."

ST: "Well, today, when the children were outside for free play, Janice and Susie had an argument." (You say this with a shrug of your shoulders and a slightly nervous smile.)

MS: "I've been wondering when that would happen. You know, Janice often tells me how much she hates Susie!" (She says this looking directly at you. You begin to feel uncomfortable and look away.) "What happened exactly?"

ST: "Well, Janice and Susie got into a clothes-pulling fight before I knew what had happened. Unfortunately, Janice's shirt collar was torn, and the ruffle on Susie's dress was ripped." (You look at the floor as you say this, feeling uncomfortable about not having intervened before the fight erupted.)

MS: "You know, Janice's shirt was new. I should have known better than to let her first wear it to school." (She laughs.) "You know, I sometimes think Janice is more like a boy than a girl! That's why I let her wear pants all the time. Fortunately, a torn shirt is easy to mend, but I hate mending! I never did figure why Susie always has a dress on; it must really hamper her play." (She looks sharply at you.) "Hey, it's okay. These things happen from time to time. I know Janice well enough to know that she's bound to get into a fight once in a while. She's just like her older brother. In fact, I think he's the one she admires most!"

Identify the following statements as either *true* or *false*. If the validity of any statement cannot be determined due to lack of information, identify it as such.

1. Mrs. Smith seems to be more comfortable than the student teacher.
2. The student teacher's approach to the conference was effective.
3. The student teacher watched Mrs. Smith's body language.
4. Mrs. Smith understands the situation well.
5. This was probably one of the student teacher's first conferences alone without the support of the cooperating teacher.
6. Using the model in figure 16-3, both Mrs. Smith and the student teacher appear to have equally refined communication skills.
7. According to the model in figure 16-3, the student teacher and Mrs. Smith are most likely from the same culture.
8. Using the model in figure 16-4, Mrs. Smith reveals a larger "open" window than the student teacher.
9. Based on the model in figure 16-4, the student teacher most likely has a larger "blind" window than Mrs. Smith.
10. The student teacher appears to have a larger "hidden" window than Mrs. Smith.

Resources

Berlo, David K. *The Process of Communication.* New York: Holt, Rinehart & Winston, Inc., 1960.

Gordon, Thomas. *T.E.T.: Teacher Effectiveness Training.* New York: David McKay Co., Inc., 1974.

Unit 17
Understanding Home and School Interactions

OBJECTIVES

After studying this unit, the student will be able to:

- Make a home visit with the approval of the cooperating teacher.
- Write a report on the results of the home visit, and discuss them with peers, cooperating teacher, and supervisor.
- Discuss differences and similarities in parent behavior at home and at school.

In this unit we will present some ground rules for home visits, as well as some ideas for parent involvement in the school.

PLANNING THE HOME VISIT

Some schools have a policy that the family of each enrolled child must be visited at least once during the school year. Others plan home visits only when they are necessary. If you are student teaching in a school where home visits are an accepted feature, planning a home visit usually involves no more than choosing, with your cooperating teacher, which home to visit. Many times the cooperating teacher may ask you to visit the home of a child with whom you are having difficulty establishing rapport. Other times you may be asked to visit the home of a child with whom you have had little interaction. You may be asked to visit the home of a child who needs more attention than another.

Your first step is to contact the parents and let them know you would like to make a home visit. Since most parents will ask why, it is a good idea to discuss the reason for the visit with your cooperating teacher prior to telephoning or speaking to the parents. In many cases your response may be simply that you would like to get to know the child better. Other times the cooperating teacher will suggest you

tell the parents that you were recommended by your cooperating teacher to visit the home. If the school requires home visits, the parents may be more hospitable than those from a center without such a policy.

Another point that should be made concerns planning home visits at homes of parents from different ethnic or social groups. Parents may be suspicious of your motive in wanting to visit, especially at a school or center without a home visitation policy. In this situation, you should defer to the wishes of your cooperating teacher, allowing the cooperating teacher to make the choice and the initial contact with the parents. In some cases you will accompany the cooperating teacher rather than make a solo visit.

Regarding the question of home visits, in most cases it is best to ask the parents when they bring or pick up their child. It helps to watch nonverbal cues to plan how you will ask. (Obviously, if the parents seem tired, cross, and/or hurried, you should wait. It is better to ask when the parents are in a good mood and when they have the time to talk for a few minutes.) Naturally, the longer you are at a center, the better some parents will begin to know you. With one of these parents, you may feel quite comfortable about planning the home visit over the telephone. Your cooperating teacher may even encourage a telephone contact so that you can gain experience making such calls.

Let us assume that you and your cooperating teacher have discussed which child's home that you are to visit. *Your next step is to speak to the parents, preferably in person.* You wait until the parent comes to pick up the child and lingers for a minute or two to inquire how the child behaved that day. At this point, you could ask if there is a convenient time to visit the child at home. The mother will most likely ask why; you and your cooperating teacher may have already agreed that you should say, "I'd like to get to know Sandy better, and Mrs. Smith (the cooperating teacher) suggested a home visit."

Mrs. Campbell, Sandy's mother, may or may not bring up some obstacles. She may work in a 9:00 a.m. to 5:00 p.m. job so that, unless you could plan the visit on the weekend, it would not be convenient for her. (Of course, home visits can be planned at any time, including weekends, evenings, and even holidays.) You may suggest an evening. She may counter with a coming holiday. Naturally, some parents do not work; therefore, they may have more time during the day in which to plan a visit.

After setting the time and day for your home visit, you may want to talk again with your cooperating teacher for guidance. What is the purpose of the home visit? Most commonly, it provides you with the opportunity to become better acquainted with the child. What should you look for? In addition to seeing how the child behaves at home, you are interested in watching the interactions that take place between the child and others in the home — parents, siblings, other relatives, and/or friends. Logically, too, you will want to note what kind of a home it is, whether it is clean, cluttered, old, poor, wealthy, warm, or run-down. (A child may live in a very poor section of town yet have a home that is clean and warm in atmosphere. Another may live in a mansion that is well-kept and beautifully furnished; yet, the atmosphere may be cold and sterile, without love.)

Now you are ready for your home visit. You have talked to Mrs. Campbell, and she has suggested that a week from Saturday at 2:00 p.m. would be best for her. Since you live in a large, urban community, you have to plan on a trip across town. You estimate that it will take about one-half hour to make the trip and allow an extra fifteen minutes in case you get lost.

THE HOME VISIT

You arrive at the Campbells' apartment a few minutes early. You decide to look around before you go into the apartment. The Campbells live in a lower-income area. The streets are dirty and littered with paper, broken bottles, and empty soda and beer cans. There is little grass in front of the apartment house; the yard is generally unkempt and weedy. The apartment house, like the others on the street, is built in motel fashion. It is badly in need of paint, and you surmise that local teenagers have used the walls for graffiti. There are at least two abandoned cars on the street. One has no tires, and its windows are smashed; the other is resting on its rims and is severely dented as though it had been hit in an accident and never repaired. Further down the street, a group of youths are playing soccer in the street. Some of them appear to belong to an ethnic minority. A radio or record player is blaring from one of the apartments; a baby is heard crying.

You get out of your car, lock it, and look at the mailboxes to see which apartment is the Campbells'. They live in Apartment 2E. You begin to make your way through the cluttered hallway and almost trip over a small, grubby child riding a rickety, old tricycle. "Who ya lookin' for?" she demands. You tell her you are going to visit the Campbells. The little girl responds negatively. "Oh them! They're sure stuck up. Why dya want to see them?" You walk past the child, who keeps pestering you with questions. When she sees that you have no intention of answering, she rides off.

You walk up the stairs to the second floor, noting the chipped paint and shaky railings. You go past the apartments with the blaring radio and the crying child, arriving finally at 2E. You ring the bell. Sandy answers. She is spotlessly clean and wearing what appears to be her Sunday dress. She greets you shyly, ducking her head. You enter a sparsely furnished but immaculate apartment. The television is on; Sandy goes into the kitchen and announces your arrival. Mrs. Campbell enters and asks you to sit. She has just made some tea and offers you some. You thank her and accept. She leaves and returns quickly with three steaming mugs, one for you, one for herself, and a small one for Sandy.

Before you can ask anything, Mrs. Campbell hesitantly and nervously says, "I want to apologize for making you come all this way on a Saturday, but I dare not ask for time off from work. And I did think your wanting to visit us was such a nice thing. It's good for Sandy to see you're interested in her like that." You murmur something about wanting to get to know Sandy better as well, figure 17-1. Mrs. Campbell suggests to Sandy that she show you some of her books. "I think books are so important. Sandy and I go to the library every two weeks, and she picks out six books to bring home to read. You know I read to her every night, don't you?"

You wonder if Sandy and Mrs. Campbell live by themselves or if there are any others who share the apartment. You then remember that Mrs. Campbell listed two parents on Sandy's school enrollment form. "Is Mr. Campbell at work?" you ask. Mrs. Campbell sighs. "I only wish he were!" she says. Sandy announces, "Daddy's at the races. He thinks Sandy's Dream is going to win today. He told me my name would bring him good luck." Mrs. Campbell admonishes Sandy. "Now, you be quiet, Sandy. Miss Julie doesn't care about what Daddy's doing." Mrs. Campbell smiles slightly and shrugs her shoulders. "Mr. Campbell has been out of work lately and has been going to the races to pass the time." Without thinking, you ask what Mr. Campbell does for a living. "He's a heavy equipment operator; you

Fig. 17-1 Home visits enable the child, parent, and teacher to get to know each other better.

know, he operates those big road-grading machines they use to build highways. Only, there hasn't been much work lately, and Mr. Campbell doesn't like to take jobs away from home. It makes it real hard on Sandy and me, though, because there's only my salary to live on. You know, we used to have our own home in suburbia but we had to give it up in order to pay our bills after John lost his last job."

You remember that Mrs. Campbell listed her job as billing clerk for a large corporation with headquarters in your area. You get the impression that Mrs. Campbell is trying very hard to maintain her small apartment the same way she kept her former home.

A shout from the apartment from next door can be heard. "You'll have to ignore the Browns," Mrs. Campbell says. "They always fight when he's had too much to drink." Angry voices can be heard screaming at each other.

Sandy has disappeared and returns with a dilapidated rag doll in her arms. "Want to see Lovey?" she asks, thrusting the doll under your nose. "Sandy, don't bother Miss Julie when we're talking," admonishes Mrs. Campbell. "That's okay, Mrs. Campbell." You pick up the doll and look closely at it, smiling at Sandy. "Sandy, I think you love your doll very much, don't you?" Sandy enthusiastically nods her head. Mrs. Campbell gives her a quick look and shake of her head. Sandy goes over to her mother, sits down on the rug, and plays with her doll.

You and Mrs. Campbell continue the conversation for another fifteen or twenty minutes. You wonder if Mr. Campbell will come home from the racetrack before you leave, and you decide that Mrs. Campbell chose this time for you to come knowing that Mr. Campbell would not be there. It makes you wonder about their relationship. Mrs. Campbell has offered no information about Mr. Campbell other than to answer your question about his work. You sense some underlying feelings of anger and despair but also feel that it is none of your business.

You soon rise to leave and thank Mrs. Campbell and Sandy for their hospitality. You hand Sandy your mug. She turns to her mother and asks if she can walk you to your car. Mrs. Campbell replies, "Okay, Sandy, but come right back upstairs. I don't want you playing with those no-good riffraff downstairs."

She turns to you and explains that the children who live below are "real rough and use language I don't approve of so I don't let Sandy play with them." "They swear," Sandy volunteers, "and use words my Momma and Daddy won't let me repeat." Mrs. Campbell glances quickly at you.

"It's not so bad now, but I worry about when Sandy grows a little older. It won't be easy keeping her away from them when they all get into school together." Her face brightens a little. "But maybe we'll be able to move from here by then. We're trying to save so we can move across Main Street." You understand what she means. The houses and apartments across Main Street are cleaner and better kept; most people own their own homes. You also know that there are fewer ethnic and racial minorities living on the other side of Main Street, and realize that Mrs. Campbell would like to be in a less integrated neighborhood.

REFLECTIONS ON THE HOME VISIT

After returning to your own home, you jot down your impressions of the visit with Mrs. Campbell and Sandy. Your first impression is that they seem out of place in the neighborhood. Mrs. Campbell obviously attempts to keep the apartment clean. Sandy is always clean and wears clean clothes to school. At the age of four, she already knows to wash her hands when she goes to the bathroom; you have not had to remind her as you have the other children. You also noted that Sandy eats slowly and uses good manners, reflecting good training at home.

Your second impression is that Mrs. Campbell is under great strain where Mr. Campbell is concerned. You understand why Sandy is such a quiet child. Mrs. Campbell is a quiet woman who is training Sandy to be a quiet child at home. You also understand why Sandy rarely mentions her father. It is obvious that Mrs. Campbell disapproves of her husband spending so much time at the races. You suspect that Mr. and Mrs. Campbell have probably had many arguments about this matter, especially since their finances seem somewhat precarious. You may have also surmised that the couple has had many arguments about Mr. Campbell's unemployment. These disagreements may be another reason why Sandy is quiet and subdued.

Sandy may blame herself for the difficulties her parents express between themselves. You begin to realize why Sandy needs emotional support before trying something new and much praise when accomplishing something that is fairly simple. In addition, Sandy's desire to please her mother is carried into her relationship with adults at school; she is always seeking adult approval. "Is this the way you want it done?" or "Do you want me to help you?"

As you relate your impressions to your cooperating teacher, you have another thought. Not only did the Campbells seem out of place in the neighborhood, but you suspect that Mrs. Campbell has no friends among her neighbors. You wonder to whom she would turn when and if she ever needed help. The cooperating teacher suggests that Mrs. Campbell might receive support from the pastor at her church. She had listed a church affiliation on the questionnaire that she completed when she enrolled Sandy. You and your cooperating teacher agree that Mrs. Campbell probably attends church regularly. Certainly, Sandy has talked enough about Sunday school to confirm this possibility. You are slightly relieved to think that Mrs. Campbell is not quite as isolated as you had thought.

OTHER HOME/SCHOOL INTERACTIONS

At this point we have talked only about two types of home and school interactions: the parent conference (formal and informal) and the home visit. There are many other types of interactions as well. Many preschools or day care centers have a parent advisory board which develops policy and procedures, plans parent education programs and fund-raising events, and even interviews prospective teachers, aides, or parents who wish to enroll their children in the center.

Even if a school or center has no parent advisory board, it may hold regular parent education programs. Some preschools, especially those associated with adult education classes on child development, include parent education as a mandatory part of their program. Other preschools send home checklists of possible topics for parents in planning parent education meetings. Topics may range from discipline and related problems to specific areas of the curriculum to planning for emergencies.

Another form of home/school interaction consists of written communications such as notes informing parents about coming events, requests for used toys or books, requests for help in building equipment, etc., and notes from parents asking specific questions of the teacher or director. Some centers have newsletters which advertise parent education meetings. They frequently include curriculum items for parents to try at home (especially arts and crafts), recipes for snacks, and a question/answer column for parents. Newsletters may also contain a swap column or notices of toys to exchange. They do not have to be printed formally; most are mimeographed or duplicated on copy machines, figures 17-2, 17-3.

In the tenth annual Gallup Poll on attitudes toward the public school (1978), some interesting facts have been revealed. In response to what activities people would include for parents if they were a school

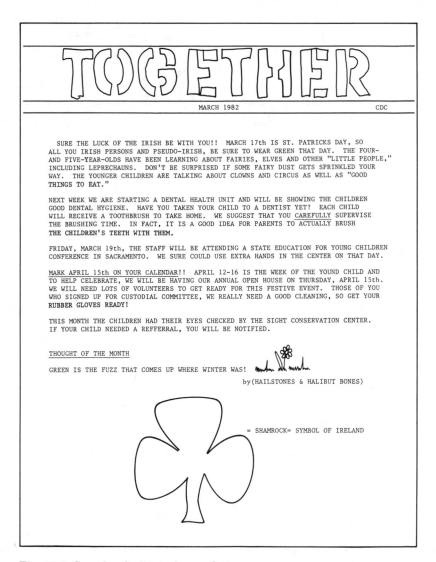

Fig. 17-2 Sample of a center's newsletter

Parkway Art and Garden show 1986

WHERE: Parkway Child Development Center
          180 Fruit Avenue
          San Jose, California
          299-7719

WHEN: April 2nd, 1982
          9:00-11:00 a.m. and 3:00-5:00 p.m.

WHAT
FOR: Celebrate Spring!

WANT TO KNOW
  MORE?:
          Call Ann at 299-0000

Art Work by Renee and Reyna
Age 5

Fig. 17-3 Sample of a center's event bulletin

principal, parent-teacher conferences, parent education, and newsletters were the top three answers. A PTA or PTO (Parent/Teacher Association and Parent/Teacher Organization) and parent volunteers were fourth and fifth respectively. Child care during conferences was listed sixth; after-school programs for working parents was seventh. Special support groups for parents were listed eighth (reflecting the growing number of families with single parents) and Parents Anonymous (a telephone hot line for potential and actual child abusers) came in eighteenth. Interestingly enough, home visits were listed sixteenth; however, this may be because the questionnaire addressed itself to public schools rather than parents with preschool youngsters.

PRECAUTIONS Obviously a survey of parents whose children are enrolled in your center will be of more value than a national survey. You will never truly know what activities the parents perceive as being important unless you ask. If you belong to a racial or ethnic group which is different from that of the parents, you will need to be especially sensitive to the cultural differences. Even social class differences among people of the same racial and ethnic group can lead to communication blocks. Differences in education promote problems also. You need to know whether the parents can read and understand English well enough to answer the survey.

If you have several non- or limited-English-speaking (NES or LES) parents, you may want to have another person translate the survey, either orally or written, so that the NES and LES parents can provide input. If you know of even one parent who has difficulty reading English, you can discuss the questions on your survey in an informal interview, asking the questions orally. With LES and NES parents, it is sometimes of value to ask the parents to spend some time in the room with their child. Then you can ask the child to explain to the parents what is happening in the room. Children, especially preschoolers, acquire a second language much more easily than adults, and they make good teachers for their parents. This is particularly true in centers where there is warmth and respect for everyone.

When there are obvious social class differences, it is important to realize that some parents may not be active in school activities because they do not believe they are wanted or educated enough. This can result in the parents feeling that they are not respected by the teacher, director, or student teacher. This feeling can become more bitter if the teacher belongs to a different race or ethnic group. As you begin to work with minority families, you will need to develop an insight into the problems which may be unique to them.

Single parent families are also prone to stress, some of which is created by the myths surrounding the stereotype of the minority or single parent. It is a myth, for example, that the child from a single parent family will have emotional problems. The truth may be that had the parent remained married to an abusive other parent, the child might have been more disturbed. Likewise, it is a myth that the single parent lacks interest in the school's activities. Since most single parents are women, and women tend to

have lower-paying jobs with less personal freedom, they may not be able to participate in the school program. Be very careful not to interpret this as a lack of interest. The truth may be that single parents cannot take time off from work in order to be more active. The single parent may compensate by talking with the child every evening and sending notes when questions arise. The single parent may not have time to bake cookies for a party, but may be willing to buy napkins.

Be aware that single parents may need a support group, especially if they have no family members living close by. If you have several children from single parent families, you might even want to plan a parent education meeting devoted to their needs.

Be sensitive, especially if you are in an infant/toddler center; understand that the mother may feel guilty at leaving her child every day to go to work. Even parents of older children can feel this way, as can parents from families in which both parents work. Remember that most mothers work, not because they want to, but because they have to. Many of them might be happier to be home with their child.

Unfortunately, many families cannot exist without the income from two working parents. Be sensitive to ways in which they can involve themselves in the life of the center without taking away from their limited time. Parent education meetings are fine, but not if a parent of limited income has to hire a baby-sitter. Knowing this, your cooperating teacher or director may make arrangements for children to be cared for on site. Many families may not have a car and must rely on public transportation. Find out when buses travel and what routes are available. Make sure the meetings end on time so a parent does not miss the bus.

Remember that parent education, however important it may seem to you, may not be as valuable to every parent. Many will choose to attend when the topic presented meets their needs and be absent when it does not. Others may find it too hectic to try to attend a meeting held in the evening. They may reason that there is not enough time after getting out of work, picking up the children, arriving home, fixing dinner, and eating.

There will always be one parent upon whom you can rely regardless of the circumstances. Do not take advantage of this. Some parents cannot say no.

Summary

In this unit we have attempted to detail a home visit as seen from the student teacher's perspective. We included illustrations not only of the physical description of the parents' home but also of the feelings experienced by the student teacher. We also discussed other home and school interactions — from the informal and formal interview to the newsletter and parent education meeting. Finally, we have cautioned you to be aware of cultural, familial differences, pointing out that these exist even within what appears to be a single culture.

Awareness of the parents' communities can be obtained through procedures as simple as a drive through the neighborhood or as complex as a formal written survey for parents to answer. Such knowledge will make you more sensitive to the parents and help you communicate with them. The parents will then be more interested in what is going on at the school and will be more willing to become active in its support.

Suggested Activities

A. With your cooperating teacher's permission, interview some of the parents at your center. What kinds of support systems do they appear to have? In what type of activity at the center do they enjoy participating or do they prefer not to participate? Why?

B. Check the mode of transportation used by the parents at your center. Do most of them have their own cars? Do many of them use public transportation? Do some of them walk? What are the implications for parent education meetings regarding the most common mode of transportation? Discuss this with your peers, cooperating teacher, and supervisor.

C. How are local schools in your community helping to assimilate newly arrived immigrants into the system? What kinds of specialized materials are being used, if any? What kinds of specialized services are offered? Discuss your findings with your peers and supervisor.

D. Interview a single parent. Find out some of the advantages and the disadvantages of raising a child alone. What support system does the parent need? What are some of the resources they use? Have they been satisfied with the services?

E. Take a poll of your fellow student teachers. What kinds of life-styles are represented? Discuss your findings.

Review

A. What are the three most common types of home/school interactions?

B. Name five precautions to take when working with parents.

C. Using one of the communication models presented in Unit 16, analyze the home visit reported in this unit. Ask the following questions of yourself.
1. Were the communication skills of the student teacher and Mrs. Campbell equally sharp?
2. Did the student teacher and Mrs. Campbell seem to have similar attitudes? Did they have similar values? Is it likely that they came from similar cultural backgrounds?
3. Using the Johari model, describe the communication skills of the student teacher and Mrs. Campbell.

D. Read the following statements. Determine whether they are effective communication statements or blocks to effective communication. If any statement is neither, identify it as such.
1. To parent who picks up child late: "Mrs. Jones, you know you're supposed to pick up Susan before 6:00 p.m."
2. To parent about an upcoming parent education meeting: "We've followed up on your request and, at Tuesday's meeting, one of the county

social workers will talk about applying for food stamps and AFDC. We hope you'll be able to attend."

3. To parent bringing child to center in the morning: "Why don't you go with Randy to the science corner? He has something to show you. Randy, show your Dad what you found yesterday."

4. To parent with limited skills in English: "Mrs. Paliwal, we hope you'll be able to stay today so you can see the kinds of things we do here at ABC School. You know, we think it's important for the parent to become involved in the school's activities, and Anil seems so shy. I think he might feel better if you could stay with him for a few minutes. How about it?"

5. On the telephone to parent whose child has been involved in a fight at school: "Mr. Smith, we're hoping you might stop by early this evening to pick Steve up. We know how busy you are, but we're busy too and Steve needs you."

6. To a mother who is berating a child other than hers: "You know we never raise our voices to the children, Pat."

7. To parent reading story to own child during free play: "Mrs. Smith, would you please watch the children at the waterplay table? Johnny, why don't you play with Sammy over at the puzzle table?"

8. To harried parent who arrives with crying child later than usual; mother is late for work and is blaming the child: "Mrs. Baker, would you like to call and tell your boss you've been held up this morning?" To child: "Richie, I know you like to play with clay; why don't you go over to the clay table and ask Miss Susan what she is doing?"

9. On the telephone to parent whose daughter wet her pants and has no dry ones at school: "Mrs. Carter, Kathy wet her pants this morning. I hope you won't mind that we put her into a spare pair we had on hand. Tomorrow you can bring an extra pair so if Kathy has another accident, she'll have her own clothes to wear."

10. Across the playground to parent pushing own child on a swing: "Mrs. Koster, come over here please. Mary knows how to pump herself. Don't baby her."

Resources

Gallup, George. "The tenth annual Gallup Poll of the public's attitudes toward the public schools." *Phi Delta Kappan* (Sept. 1978), pp. 33–45.

Section 7
Knowing Yourself and Your Competencies

Unit 18
Being Observed

OBJECTIVES

After studying this unit, the student will be able to:

- List important goals of observation, evaluation, and discussion.
- Describe five observation techniques.
- Identify five possible student teacher observers.

Although the primary focus of student teaching is on the student teacher, all adults involved experience change and growth. A process combining observation, feedback, and discussion is often necessary to acquire new skills or expand existing skills. Methods of observation vary with each training program, but they all are basically a record of what was seen and heard. An analysis of this record is called an assessment or evaluation. Observation, analysis, `evaluation, and discussion can be described as a continuous and ever-growing cycle, figure 18-1, that starts during student teaching and ends at retirement.

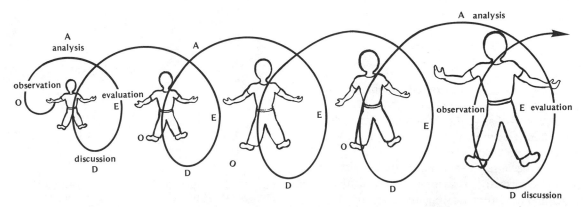

Fig. 18-1 Cycle of growth which starts in student teaching

Professional teaching involves lifelong learning and continuous efforts to improve. As more discoveries are made about the process of human learning and as our society changes, teachers assess existing teaching methods, try new ones, and sometimes combine elements of both new and old methods. Observation is important to this process. The student teacher begins by being watched, and ends up watching him or herself as a practicing teacher!

GOALS OF OBSERVATION, EVALUATION, AND DISCUSSION

Important goals of the observation/evaluation/discussion process for student teachers follow:
- To give student teachers valid assessments of their level of performance through specific, descriptive feedback.
- To allow suggestions and helpful ideas, which aid students' acquisition of skills, to flow between participants.
- To create a positive attitude toward self-improvement and self-knowledge.
- To establish the habit of assessing performance.
- To maintain the standards of the teaching profession.

Through observation and evaluative feedback, the student teacher receives objective data that the student teacher cannot collect, figure 18-2. Levin and Long describe the developments which follow:

Students receive evidence about whether they have reached the set standard, what they have learned successfully, and what they still need to learn. As a result, students begin to develop a positive view of their own learning abilities.

Students who have more self-confidence and a greater desire to learn become more involved as they progress in their learning. Gradually, they need less external help to reach a defined standard and may even take over the corrective procedures themselves. Effective use of feedback corrective systems helps teachers develop more confident students who not only achieve at a higher level but who also learn how to learn. (1981)

Evaluation may sound ominous to the student teacher because it is usually connected to a grade or passing a class or training program. A breakdown in trust may occur. Actually, evaluation is a chance for improvement, a time to realize that all teachers are a combination of strengths and weaknesses. Adopting a new view of evaluation will allow trust to remain intact:

While in the past, evaluation has been conceived mainly as a process of passing judgment, nowadays it is seen as a continuous process of collecting information and supplying feedback for improvement. (Levin and Long, 1981, p. 39)

The quality of the feedback given to a student teacher is an important factor.

Feedback information can be effective if and only if it is followed by corrective procedures which correct weaknesses of learning and instruction. (Levin and Long, 1981, p. 25)

Feedback needs to be consistent and constructive throughout a student teacher's placement.

Fig. 18-2 You will be observed working with your own group of children.

In most teacher-training programs, great importance is attached to the practicum's end-of-the-day conference. These conferences generally include how the day went, how particular children behave, and what plans should be made for the next day. It is also the time for the master teacher to evaluate the student teacher's abilities and recommend improvement.

Feedback as a teaching procedure has received considerable attention in the brief literature of research on teaching. In general, feedback does change or influence an individual's performance *if* given meaningful interpretation, and *if* delivered consistently and constructively. (Thompson, et al., 1978)

Student observational feedback may sensitize and pinpoint behavior the student can then examine while teaching, figure 18-3. Feedback is information, which the reporter believes to be true and accurate, on an individual happening or interaction. Discussions following observations include constructive criticism, praise, descriptive analysis, examination of situational factors, the creation of action plans, further analysis of written records, child behavior particulars, action/reaction relationships, and any other feature of the observation that is important.

METHODS OF OBSERVATION

Training programs collect data on student teachers' performances in many different ways. Among the most common collection techniques are:

DIRECT OBSERVATION Usually a recorded specimen description, time sampling, and/or event sampling. This can be either obtrusive (the observed individual is aware of the process) or unobtrusive (collecting data without the subject's knowledge, perhaps from an observation room), figure 18-4.

- Time sampling: An observer watches and codes a set of specific behaviors within a certain time.
- Specimen description or narrative: A "stream-of-consciousness" report that attempts to record all that occurs, figure 18-5.

Specimen description involves recording everything that the individual does or says with as much information about the context (people involved, circumstances that might be influencing the behavior, and so on) as possible. (Irwin and Bushnell, 1980)

- Event sampling: A detailed record of significant incidents or events.

Fig. 18-3 Another student teacher can observe a peer and give valuable feedback.

Fig. 18-4 Observation rooms usually have one-way windows and counter top writing desks.

March 3, 1980
Candy Nicholetti
Campbell Head Start
10 children, 2 adults
Windy-fair

You're fixing snack, and you seem to have developed a good relationship with your cooperating teacher. You talk briefly and warmly, smiling often.

Interaction in classroom. Clear, concise, enthusiastic speech model. Enthusiastic and expressive voice. You use positive reinforcement for child's sharing. ("I like the way you gave Sally a turn.") Some language expansion and attempts to help child put ideas in words ("Tell me what you think about. . ."). A child comes up to you readily and leans against you, showing that she finds you accepting and comforting. Room is set with inviting activity areas, and children are busily engaged.

In play area a child sits on your lap. Interactive in dramatic play. Now you remove yourself after trying to motivate child to participate in housekeeping center.

"Wait a minute. You've got some stuff on your face. Do you know what it's called?" "Corn-meal." You mention specific descriptive characteristics. You converse easily, and develop new concepts during your interaction. Nice enjoyment of joke ("Good to see you laugh, Candy").

"John, could you please not run inside?" Your behavior change statement was a request rather than a restatement of rules.

Back in the housekeeping area with Tommy on play telephones. "Did you hear that it's time to clean up?" you ask after clean-up time is announced. You offer to help child put away blocks. Let's see if you really follow through. Other child offers to help the first child. "You are a good helper. You're going to help your friend Sam put the blocks away." Your cooperating teacher means what she says. The children will know this soon also. What she expects to happen, happens. Your supervision is still total room supervision. You hear what's being said to you by children, and you respond appropriately. You're not afraid to stop behavior, as with milk episode, and you make instant decisions in difficult situations, as seen in the sweater incident.

John: "I want a ride on that, and they already had a ride."

You: "Who wants to share with John?"

This worked, and John was included. You used redirection as a technique.

"Don't throw sand" you say, and then relate to past experience, sand in eyes.

Your work shows both flexibility and assertion, particularly in the situation where you let a child finish her puzzle before lunch.

Modeling how to put away materials encourages the children to follow suit. You're after Richard again; you are going to be consistent and follow through in expecting acceptable behavior. You often use positive reinforcement. You promoted independence in the crayon clean-up and waited to see if the child could figure out the problem for himself.

You did change Richard's behavior, and rewarded him immediately. Motivational redirection techniques: "Let's put them away quicker than a jackrabbit." Not afraid to restrain children physically if necessary, which you did in the toy disagreement.

Again, you promote independence and task completion in art area project. You showed concern over a stepped-on finger, and the child's face showed he knew that you valued his feelings. Snack is prepared; there is no waiting on child's part. Child pours, serving himself. You seem to see what needs to be done and do it without the cooperating teacher's suggestions.

Fig. 18-5 Sample specimen description #1

December 12, 1980
Maria Jimenez
Post Street Child Development Center
15 children, 2 adults
Overcast

You are conducting a circle time. Children are pushing and poking each other at times. You ignore. The book is read enthusiastically. You nonverbally move children with your hand when they crowd together. No attempt is made to involve children in the book other than listening. Children are restless; the book is long, and children have been sitting for a while. The story and word level seems above their understanding. You ignore children's feedback. Few children are interested now or after the story. "Cook," child says. "Right," you say. You end the book, and do a Santa finger-play. Children participate actively, enjoying. Snowmen are passed out to each child rather silently. Your voice is low during the snowman game. No transition is planned. "We're going to make noodles." Children crowd through the door. Barbara has to remind you to excuse them. Positive reinforcement and child behavior guidance has been almost nonexistent. Little promotion of child conversation. You silently help a child with noodle making. Although you help actively, you are verbally passive. You silently clean table. You sit briefly. Now, you push chairs around table. You leave room to do yard supervision. Bending down, you attempt to engage children in conversation while they play in sand. You ask questions with one-word answers, and your focus is close. Often, you reach for things in children's hands, sometimes removing them. Child speaks to you. You ignore or speak in a very limited fashion.

Fig. 18-5a Sample specimen description # 2

CRITERION-REFERENCED INSTRUMENT
An analysis of whether the subject can perform a given task or set of tasks. (An example can be found in the Appendix.)

INTERVIEW   Usually a specific set of questions asked in a standard manner, figure 18-6.

RATING SCALE   The observer sets a point value on a continuum in order to evaluate a characteristic or skill, figure 18-7.

VIDEOTAPING   A video camera records a student teaching sequence.

TAPE RECORDING   Only sound is recorded.

FILMING   A sound or silent record.

Combinations of these methods are frequently used. Some cooperating teachers work alongside their student teachers, and take mental notes rather than written ones.

RELIABILITY

Observations must serve as a reliable and accurate source of information. In student teaching, the participants understand that each observation record covers only a short space of time compared to the length of the student teacher's placement. Each individual will have a slightly different perception of what was seen and heard. Areas of competence that receive similar interpretations from different observers over a period of time should be of special interest to student teachers.

> Reliability refers to the extent of observer agreement or consistency in recording observational information. (Irwin and Bushnell, 1980, p. 182)

The similarity of information in data gathered in different observations confirms the reliability of the measurement. For example, if both a videotaped observation and a time sampling seem to point to the same measurement of skill or teaching behavior, the reliability of the data will increase.

Area	Percentage				
	Almost always	Usually	Undecided	Sometimes	Seldom
1. Does the student teacher plan adequately for classroom experience?					
2. Does your student teacher utilize modern teaching methods effectively?					
3. Does your present student teacher provide adequately for individual differences?					
4. Is your student teacher able to control the behavior (discipline) of students?					
5. Does your student teacher meet class responsibilities on time?					
6. Is your student teacher able to evaluate students adequately?					
7. Does your student teacher cooperate with you?					
8. Is your student teacher willing to do more than minimum requirements?					
9. Does your student teacher attend extraclass social and professional functions? (Clubs, sports, PTA, faculty meetings, etc.)					
10. Does your student teacher seem ethical in his relationships with faculty and students?					
11. Is your student teacher able to motivate students to a high level of performance in a desirable manner?					
12. Does your student teacher demonstrate facility in oral communication?					
13. Is your student teacher able to organize?					
14. Does the student teacher seem to possess an adequate subject matter (content) background?					
15. Does your student teacher demonstrate that he has received an adequate, liberal (well-rounded) education?					

Fig. 18-6 Sample of interview instrument used for cooperating teacher's evaluation of student teacher (From *The Student Teacher's Reader* by Alex Perrodin. Chicago: Rand McNally & Co., 1966.)

NAME _____

The professional qualities of each student teacher
will be evaluated on the following criteria:

A four-point rating scale is used:
(1) needs improvement
(2) satisfactory
(3) very good
(4) outstanding

	1	2	3	4

PERSONAL QUALITIES

1. Attendance and punctuality
2. Dependability
3. Flexibility
4. Resourcefulness
5. Self-direction, sees what needs to be done
6. Sensitive to other people's needs and feelings
7. Tact, patience, and cooperation with others
8. Sense of humor
9. Attitude toward children
10. Attitude toward adults
11. Attitude toward administration
12. Well-modulated voice, good use of language
13. Ability to evaluate self and benefit from experiences

WORKING WITH CHILDREN

1. Aware of safety factors
2. Understands children at their own levels
3. Finds ways to give individual help without sacrificing group needs
4. Skill in group guidance
5. Skill in individual guidance
6. Listens to children and answers their questions
7. Consistent and effective in setting and maintaining limits
8. Encourages self-help and independence in children
9. Sensitive to children's cues in terms of adding to their knowledge or encouraging verbal skills
10. Aware of total situation, even when working with one child
11. Sensitivity to a developing situation in terms of prevention rather than cure

WORKING WITH OTHER TEACHERS, PARENTS, AND VOLUNTEERS

1. Willingness to accept direction and suggestions
2. Is friendly and cooperative with staff members
3. Observes appropriate channels when reporting on school matters
4. Respects confidential information
5. Establishes good working relationships
6. Does not interfere in a situation another teacher is handling
7. Shows good judgment in terms of knowing when to step into a situation

Fig. 18-7 Student teacher responsibilities and evaluation form

The degree of obviousness of the collection method also merits consideration. Videotaping may produce unnatural behavior. Hidden cameras and tape recorders raise ethical questions. Observation rooms and one-way screens are familiar and unobtrusive methods commonly used in laboratory training centers. Objective recording of teaching behavior is a difficult task. Observations can be subjective and reflect the observer's special point of view.

It is easy to make inferences about behavior or situations we have observed. In part, we do so as a shorthand means of communication. It is easier to say that "She sat dejectedly at the end of the table" than to say that "She sat by herself at the end of the table and the corners of her mouth drooped." In part we infer feelings or motives because it is the message we get when we observe. Sometimes, however, these messages are more a reflection of our own feelings than they are of the feelings of the person being observed. Sometimes we are lacking important information which would change our perception, and sometimes we are just plain wrong. (Irwin and Bushnell, 1980, p. 70)

Supervisors and cooperating teachers try to keep all observations objective during student teaching. Discussions between the observed and observer can add additional factors for consideration before analyses and evaluations occur.

To remove subjective comments from teacher observation, Bernard Oliver advocates the use of "ethnographic methods." He suggests observers should attempt to describe precisely teaching episodes using extensive note-taking which leaves little doubt and allows "others less knowledgeable to see qualities and aspects of the classroom that are not readily discernible." Oliver suggests that observers use the following steps as observation guidelines.

1. *Casing the Room:* The initial minutes of the observation revolve around "casing the room" or "shagging around." This involves mapping the physical layout of the class, noting such items as the arrangement of tables, learning aides (bulletin boards, resource centers, etc.), and storage area for student materials.

2. *Entering Interactions:* The second stage emphasizes the cordiality of verbal greetings between teacher and student. How teacher and students enter the room, exchange greetings, and prepare for the instructional process is a valuable source of information for supervisors and teachers. Additional data on the number of students in the class, sex of the student, and ethnicity of students add further value in clarifying entering interactions.

3. *Trafficking:* Once the instructional episode has started, noting the patterns of action in the classroom (i.e., how students move about the room getting water, etc.) provides critical information regarding the organization and management of instruction.

4. *Communication:* The verbal and nonverbal interaction between teacher-student and student-student are a crucial part of this supervision-observation process. How does the teacher call on or make contact with students? What tone of voice and choice of words does the teacher use? What is the reaction of the students? Noting student ethnicity and sex of teacher-directed comments provides additional information which highlights the ecology of the classroom.

5. *Rule Structure:* How is the rule structure established and adhered to? How does the teacher respond to disruptive behavior? What preceded the behavior? How do students respond to the teacher's actions? This recounting of events aids in clarifying the labels and the underlying scheme of social judgments.

6. *Beginnings, Ends, Transitions:* One important aspect of classroom life that appears crucial to teacher performance is that of tracking time and the sequencing of activities. In addition to noting time devoted to activities, off-task and on-task behavior of pupils helps to provide a clearer picture of what happens in the classroom. What do teachers do during transitions? What is the frequency and duration of transitions?

How much time is allotted for the activity? Clearly, the importance of time is a salient variable in the observation of the instructional process.

7. *Post-Observation Conference:* As in most supervisory settings, the importance of the post-observation conference cannot be overstated. The teacher should present his/her personal impressions of the lesson prior to discussing the ethnographic observation. This facilitates self-evaluation and recall of the salient aspects of the lesson. The additional information provided by the ethnographic narrative aids the teacher in clarifying and understanding the antecedents and the consequences of classroom events. This multimodality of ethnographic narratives provides the teacher and supervisor with an excellent tool for increasing teacher effectiveness. (1981)

OBSERVERS AND EVALUATORS

It is possible to be observed and assessed by many people during your student teaching experience. Some students prefer only supervisor's and cooperating teacher's assessments. Others actively seek feedback from all possible sources. A wide base of observational data on competency seems best. Other possible observers in most student teaching placements are:

- self, figure 18-8
- classroom assistants, aides, and volunteers
- other student teachers
- the center's support staff (cooks, nurse, secretary, etc.)
- children
- parents
- community liaison staff
- center administrative staff or consulting specialists, figure 18-9

Student teachers can develop their own rating systems based on teaching characteristics that are important to them. Simple tallies are helpful in recording changes in behavior.

DISCUSSION Discussions held after data is collected are keys to growth. The meeting's feeling tone, its format, location, time of day, and degree of comfort can be critical. The communication skills of participants contribute to success in promoting student teacher skill development.

Two types of discussions, formative and summative, occur during student teaching. An initial formative discussion sets the stage for later discussions. Goals, time lines, and evaluative procedures are explained. Additional formative discussions will follow placement observations. A summative conference finalizes your total placement experience, and scrutinizes both the placement site and your competency.

During the discussion, you will examine the collected data, add comments about extenuating circumstances, form plans to collect additional information, and consider initiating new actions which could strengthen your existing skills through change or modification. Suggestions for improvement are self-discovered and formed jointly with the cooperating teacher or supervisor.

Child behavior resulting from student teacher behavior is a focal point for discussions, figure 18-10. Influencing factors such as room settings, routines, child uniqueness, and the student teacher's technique, method, and behaviors are examined closely.

Discussions which are descriptive and interpretative and involve value judgments about child education and professional teaching are common.

DEALING WITH EVALUATIONS   Student teachers should try to develop a positive attitude about what may appear to be an emphasis on their weaknesses. However, this attitude may come slowly for some student teachers. Conferencing covers student teachers' strengths but sometimes promotes a "report card feeling tone" which is hard to shake. Dr. Leslie Nelson and Dr. Blanche McDonald have the following advice for student teachers.

1. The student teacher should:
   a. Anticipate criticism and welcome its contribution; take a positive attitude toward any advice which is offered by the principal, college supervisor, training teacher, and even from the pupils; expect to have

INSTRUCTIONS

1. As you study the grid, circle each description you feel makes a fairly accurate statement of an attitude, skill, or preference of yours.
2. From the choices you make, write a paragraph or two describing yourself.

If you follow these instructions thoughtfully and honestly, you will have a relatively clear idea of how you see yourself in relation to your effectiveness as a teacher of young children.

Plans ahead, wants to know schedule	Versatile, spur-of-the-moment okay	Prefers to work out own problems	Good under supervision
Trusts own judgment	Often seeks advice	Friendly, open personal life	Friendly but personally reserved
Good at delegating and organizing responsibility	Prefers to let others do the organizing	Best with older children and adults	Best with young and very young
Works well with parents	Prefers to work without help	Liberal, likes new ideas	Conservative and slow to change
Skilled in many areas	About average in abilities	Remembers names, dates — uses her knowledge	Not particular about details — takes what comes
Prefers to share responsibility	More efficient when working alone	Patient, does not rush others or self	Impatient, prefers to get things done fast
Likes to take risks	Cautious, prefers proven methods	Efficient, likes order	Casual, can muddle through
Hates to be late	Relaxed about time and schedule	Active in many outside interests	Prefers audience/bystander role
Often relates physically	Usually relates with words only	Friends with everyone	Prefers a few close friends
Has many ideas	Initiates little but will join in	Positive, optimistic	Somewhat negative, cynical
Works best when job roles well-defined	Prefers flexible job roles	Prefers to be boss	Prefers to be subordinate
Keeps things neat and clean	Messiness no problem	Prefers to work with things	Prefers to work with people
Feelings hurt easily	Pretty thick-skinned	Stable, consistent background	Diverse background
Determined, persistent, stubborn	Easy going, will give up fairly easily	Likes to be in on everything	Prefers to mind own business and not get involved
Likes routine and willing to do same things over and over	Likes variety	Likes working on many projects at same time	Likes to work on one thing at a time
Relaxes by doing something active	Relaxes by resting, sleeping	Needs very little sleep	Feels best with plenty of sleep
Easily satisfied	Somewhat particular	Likes competition and challenge	Prefers noncompetitive work
Introversive, introspective	Outgoing, extrovert	Nonconforming	Adaptive, complaisant

Fig. 18-8 Student teacher self-rating sheet (From *Be Honest With Yourself* by Doreen Croft © 1976 by Wadsworth Publishing Company, Inc. Reprinted by permission of Wadsworth Publishing Company, Belmont, California 94002.)

Emotionally mature and well-adjusted personality
Alert and enthusiastic
Professional competency
Genuine interest in people, children, teaching
Professional attitude
Good appearance and grooming
Above-average scholastically
Wide interest and cultural background
Leadership qualities
Sense of humor
Willingness to learn and desire to grow professionally
Success in directed teaching
Creativeness
Understanding of children
Interest in community participation
Moral character
Cooperative
Good health
Ability to communicate effectively
Good penmanship
Interest in curriculum development
Flexibility
Sincerity
Appropriate humility
Ability to organize

Fig. 18-9 Administrators' responses to the question "What would you like to know about teacher candidates?"

Fig. 18-10 A student teacher's planned activity that captures and holds interest is the focus of discussion.

efforts improved; accept all criticism without permitting feelings to be upset.

b. Develop a feeling of security in the things in which one knows to be correct, but never to be so confident that one cannot see the other person's point of view.

c. Evaluate and criticize one's own efforts. Often one can soften necessary criticism by anticipating one's own weaknesses and discussing them with a supervising teacher.

d. Be consistent in acting on suggestions which are made. One should not make the same mistake day after day.

e. Not alibi or defend mistakes which were made. One's greatest improvement will be made by overcoming deficiencies, not by defending them.

f. Not argue the point when one feels that a criticism has been unjustly made; rather one should govern further actions and the injustice will usually automatically vanish.

g. Use judgment in interpreting criticisms. Sometimes a criticism is made to fit a particular occasion and a student teacher, without using judgment, applies the rule to every situation with which s/he is confronted. This often results in difficulty and confusion. Whenever criticisms seem to conflict, it is quite necessary that the student use a great deal of common sense in interpreting their application.

h. Keep one's poise and sense of humor; one should not become so emotionally disturbed that one cannot act intelligently on the problem at hand.

i. Assume that the teachers are friends; one should understand that they are trying to help one to learn correct procedures and techniques. They are not merely trying to make one miserable. (Nelson and McDonald, 1952)

John Devor has compiled a listing of cooperating teachers' comments concerning the strengths and weaknesses of their assigned student teachers, figure 18-11.

Discussions can describe a wide range of student and teacher behaviors. Clarification of terms can be helpful to student teachers. Keeping records of discussions will aid your planning. They can be reviewed prior to follow-up conferences. Action plans resulting from previous discussions are usually the primary focus of later ones.

Summary

Observation, evaluation, and discussion are integral parts of student teaching. Different methods are used to observe the student's progress. The realization of professional growth through the use of an evaluative method and subsequent discussion depends on a number of different factors, including the process and method of measurement and the people involved. It is important for the student teacher to maintain a positive attitude and consider self-evaluation a

FAVORABLE COMMENTS	WEAKNESSES INDICATED
1. Excellent lesson plan and lesson preparation	1. Difficulty in responding to questions and in giving clear and explicit answers to students.
2. Good discipline — class well in hand.	2. Weak in conducting discussions where all participate.
3. Good rapport with students.	3. Lesson plans not mastered.
4. Good detail in lesson planning.	4. Timing of lesson is a problem, does not fit the lesson to the class time. Loose ends.
5. Good evaluation of students' work.	5. Amenities of written and spoken language need strengthening.
6. Invites questions from students.	6. Eye contact poor; looks at ceiling and floor.
7. Helps students formulate problems that will challenge them beyond the scope of the lesson being taught.	7. Needs to be aware of nervous mannerisms.
8. Inspires students to learn.	8. Should bring all students into group discussion.
9. Shows special interest in individual students.	9. Class is not challenged to its fullest capacity.
10. Forceful voice.	10. Stronger discipline needed at times.
11. Expresses thoughts forcefully and well.	11. Needs to learn to adjust pace of teaching to the learning pace of the class.
12. Student teacher is punctual.	12. Assumes *all* understand when only a *few* understand.
13. Student teacher is dependable.	13. Needs to refrain from using "O.K."
14. Student teacher is cooperative.	14. No enthusiasm: takes teaching as a chore.
15. Superb motivation of students.	15. Needs to give more explicit instructions.
16. Takes suggestions and criticism well.	16. Does not enlist student cooperation.
17. Is well-groomed, neat appearance.	17. Fails to show grace, courtesy and consideration.
18. Excellent speech habits.	18. Is absent without letting supervising teacher know about emergency.
19. Spends much time in planning work.	19. Is not open and aboveboard.
20. Explanations are explicit and definite.	20. Sits on desk, dangles foot, slumps and shows no excitement for teaching.
21. Encourages comments from students.	
22. Time awareness not apparent, but always ends on time.	

Fig. 18-11 Cooperating teachers' comments about their student teachers (Reprinted with permission of Macmillan Publishing Co., Inc. from *The Experience of Student Teachers* by John W. Devor. Copyright © 1964 by John W. Devor.)

vehicle for improvement. Both formative and summative discussions are part of an analysis of the student teacher and the placement experience. Planning to enhance strength and overcome weaknesses takes place during discussions and is a growth-promoting part of student teaching.

Suggested Activities

A. Form groups of four. On slips of paper, write down your fears about being observed and evaluated. Put the slips in a container. Each student takes a turn drawing a slip of paper and describing the fear and the possible cause.

B. Develop your own rating sheet for assessing student teacher performance.

C. Identify to the class some important questions which you would like your cooperating teacher to answer during your summative discussion.

D. As a class, vote on the validity of the following statements. Use a "thumbs up" signal if the statement is true; remain silent if you believe the statement is false. When voting on the more controversial statements, ask your teacher to turn from the class, elect a student to count the votes, and record the final tally.
1. It is unfair to compare one student teacher with another.
2. It is a good idea to have one student teacher tutor another.
3. Peer evaluations should be part of everyone's student teaching experience.
4. Confidentiality in rating student teachers is imperative.
5. Sharing discussion notes with other student teachers may be helpful to both students.
6. Evaluations by supervisors or cooperating teachers should never be shown to employers of student teachers.
7. A student teacher's placement could inhibit the growth of professional teaching competencies.
8. One can experience considerable growth without evaluative feedback.

9. Criticism is threatening.
10. Being observed and evaluated is really a game. Self-discovery and being motivated to do your best is more important.
11. An individual's manner of dress, hair style, etc. should not be included in an evaluation because this has nothing to do with effective teaching.
12. Observation and evaluation can increase professional excellence.
13. Every student should receive a copy of all written evaluations of his or her performance.

E. As a class, discuss peer observations. Answer the following questions.
1. Is peer observation, evaluation, and discussion valuable? Would peer observation be desirable and practical for your training group?
2. Are there any guidelines that should be established for peer observation?

F. Identify the conflicting views of professional image that are shown in the following student teacher recommendation:

I can heartily recommend Beatrice Santelli for a teaching position. Miss Santelli was a student teacher in my class for ten weeks during her last year in college, and I found her to be a most interesting person, and one who has much to offer to teaching.

Her manner with children was excellent, and the children adored her. She always had time for them, and when it came to understanding children and helping them with their problems, Miss Santelli was the most empathetic person I have ever known. I can honestly say that she helped two or three children that I had thought were beyond help. She showed an interest in their problems and their work; and their achievement went up amazingly as a result.

Miss Santelli is bursting with good ideas, and she is able to interest children in even the most routine activities. She brought many extra materials and resources to our classroom; she tried some really ambitious projects that were on a high intellectual level, and always managed to make them understandable to the youngsters. She knew how to go after important concepts rather than rote facts, and I can honestly say that I learned as much from Miss Santelli's teaching as she did from mine.

Miss Santelli is not a conventional person and her dress can be described as somewhat unusual, or bohemian. At times, she seemed rather thrown together, and it would not be uncommon for her to have ripped seams, or hanging hems, and her stockings were seldom straight or without runs. Her hair, which she wore in rather an odd style, usually appeared to need combing. I mention all of this because a potential employer might be put off by her appearance.

Miss Santelli does not put much stock in having a spotless classroom with neat bulletin boards. In my classroom she had many activities going on, and the least of her emphasis was on cleaning up. However, she put so much effort into the real learning of the children, and into working with ideas, that I never minded the looks of the room.

If I were an administrator, I would not miss the chance of hiring Miss Santelli, despite her departure from what we think of as the usual school teacher. (Hunter and Amidon, 1964)

Review

A. Name three methods of observational data collection. Give examples.

B. Select the answer that best completes each statement.

1. The process of observation, evaluation, and discussion
   a. includes observations from supervisors and employers.
   b. usually ends when the student teaching experience ends.
   c. continues after the student teacher graduates and is valued by teachers and employers.
   d. ends when improvement occurs.
   e. can be best performed by the student teacher alone.

2. One of the primary goals of observation, evaluation, and discussion is to
   a. stress the student teacher's weaknesses through peer evaluation.
   b. increase control.
   c. judge how quickly a student can respond to suggestions.
   d. criticize student teachers.
   e. None of these
   f. All of these

3. Feedback can be defined as data that
   a. is collected through observations, and is to be evaluated and communicated to the one being observed.
   b. is recorded by a student teacher during discussion.
   c. includes a free lunch.
   d. is withheld from a student teacher.
   e. None of these

4. If interviews are used to collect data on student teaching, each interviewee should
   a. answer only the questions he or she wishes to answer.
   b. always be asked the same questions in the same manner.
   c. be asked for factual data only.
   d. be asked for opinions only.
   e. be given a specified length of time to answer each question.

5. One benefit of videotaping for the purpose of observation is
   a. the student teacher and supervisor can evaluate the tape together.
   b. it is less frightening than other methods.
   c. a camera captures a more natural view of a student teacher.
   d. it saves time.
   e. All of these

6. If a student teaching skill is evaluated using three different observational methods and each confirms the same level of competency, the three tests would probably be
   a. rated as reliable.
   b. rated as highly valid.
   c. rated as accurate.
   d. standardized.

7. The collection technique which records a series of significant incidents is called a(n)
   a. time sampling.
   b. rating sheet.
   c. specimen description.
   d. event sampling.
   e. questionnaire.
8. An unobtrusive method of observation might involve
   a. hidden microphones.
   b. an observer with a tape recorder.
   c. an observer viewing from a loft.
   d. an observer in an observation room.
   e. All of these
9. If one was trying to assess the rapport that a student teacher developed with a group of children, one could
   a. observe how many children initiated conversation with the student during a given time period.
   b. record and analyze what the children say.
   c. count how many times a child touched the student teacher during a given time period.
   d. observe how many times a child shares an interest or concern with a student teacher.
   e. All of these
10. A final discussion which informs the student teacher about his or her teaching skills is a(n)
    a. formative discussion.
    b. initial discussion.
    c. summative discussion.
    d. incidental discussion.
    e. alternate discussion.

C. Complete the following statement.
   The five individuals who could probably provide the most reliable and valid data concerning my teaching competency are. . .

D. Using another source of reference, write a definition of reliability or validity of assessment methods or instruments. Cite the author and publication date of your reference material.

E. Five individuals observed the same traffic accident. Match the person in Column I to the feature in Column II that he or she would be most likely to observe.

I	II
1. Car salesman	a. driver's license and/or license plate numbers
2. Police officer	b. children involved in the accident
3. Doctor	c. damage to the automobiles
4. Teacher	d. make and model of the automobiles involved
5. Insurance adjuster	e. injuries to those involved

F. What five skills would most cooperating teachers observe before a summative discussion?

G. Write three pieces of advice to student teachers to help them accept constructive criticism.

Resources

Hunter, Elizabeth, and Amidon, Edmon. *Student Teaching — Cases and Comments.* New York: Holt, Rinehart & Winston, Inc., 1964.

Irwin, Michelle, and Bushnell, Margaret M. *Observational Strategies for Child Study.* New York: Holt, Rinehart & Winston, Inc., 1980.

Levin, Tamar, and Long, Ruth. *Effective Instruction.* Alexandria, VA: The Association for Supervision and Curriculum Development, 1981.

Nelson, Leslie, Ph.D., and McDonald, Blanche. *Guide to Student Teaching.* Dubuque, IA: William C. Brown & Co., 1952.

Oliver, Bernard. "Evaluating Teachers and Teaching." *California Journal of Teacher Education*, Vol. VIII (Spring 1981).

Thompson, Carolyn L.; Holmberg, Margaret Cooper; and Baer, Donald M. *An Experimental Analysis of Some Procedures to Teach Priming and Reinforcement Skills to Preschool Teachers.* Monographs of the Society for Research in Child Development (University of Chicago Press), No. 176, Vol. 43 (1981).

Unit 19
Values Clarification for Student Teachers

OBJECTIVES

After completing this unit, the student will be able to:

- Define the role of personal values in teaching.
- Describe how values influence what happens in the classroom.
- Describe how the activities the student teacher enjoys reflect personal values.
- List at least five values which guide the student teacher's lessons and activities.

KNOWING YOURSELF AND YOUR VALUES

We will begin this unit with an exercise. On a separate sheet of paper, number the spaces from 1 to 20. Then list, as quickly as possible, your favorite activities. Do this spontaneously; do not pause to think.

Now go back and code your listed activities as follows.

- Mark those activities you do alone with an *A*.
- Mark those activities that involve at least one more person with a *P*.
- Mark with an *R* those activities which may involve risk.
- Mark those in which you are actively doing something with a *D*.
- Mark with an *S* those activities at which you are a spectator.
- Mark activities that cost money with an *M*.
- Mark activities that are free with an *F*.
- Mark with a *Y* any activity you have not done for one year.

Now that you have coded your activities, what have you learned about yourself? Are you more a spectator than a doer? Do you seldom take risks? Did you list more than one activity in which you have not participated for more than one year? Do you

frequently spend money on your activities, or do most of your activities cost little or nothing? Were any of your answers a surprise? We hope you learned something new about yourself.

Let us try another exercise. Complete the following sentences as quickly as possible.

1. School is . . .
2. I like . . .
3. Children are . . .
4. Teaching is . . .
5. Little girls are . . .
6. I want . . .
7. Children should . . .
8. Little boys are . . .
9. Parents are . . .
10. Teachers should . . .
11. I am . . .
12. Fathers are . . .
13. I should . . .
14. Mothers are . . .
15. Teachers are . . .
16. Parents ought to . . .
17. School ought to . . .
18. Aggressive children make me . . .
19. Shy children make me . . .
20. Whiny children make me . . .

Did you find this activity easier or more difficult than the first? This exercise is less structured than the first. You had to shift your thinking from statement to statement. We hope it made you take a thoughtful pause as you were forced to shift your thinking as verbs changed from simple or declarative to the more complex conditional or obligatory forms. Present tense forms such as "is" or "are" encourage concrete, factual responses. With the conditional "should" or obligatory "ought," your response may have become more a reflection of what you feel an ideal should be. In addition, with the present tense, a response is usually short whereas with the conditional "should" or obligatory "ought," you may have used more words to explain your response.

Look at your answers. Do you find you have different responses depending upon whether the present tense, the conditional tense, or the obligatory form of the verb was used? What do these differences tell about yourself?

Return to the Review in Unit 6 where this last exercise first appeared. Did you write the same responses in each exercise? It is more likely that you did not since the stimuli (sentence fragments to complete statements) are presented in different contexts. However, it is likely that they are somewhat similar; opinions are not likely to change too easily. Does this difference or similarity tell you anything about yourself? Does it say anything about your attitudes toward different kinds of students? Does it say anything about the kind of student you like best or least?

THE ACQUISITION OF VALUES

Let us reflect on how we acquire our values. Logically, many of our values reflect those of our parents. As children, we naturally absorbed our first values through observing our parents and family members and direct parental teaching, figure 19-1. Few children are even aware that they are being influenced by their parents; they take in parental attitudes and values through the processes of observation and imitation. We want to be like our fathers and mothers, especially since they appear to have the power over the rewards we receive. Smiles when we

Fig. 19-1 Family teachings and traditions influence children. They absorb values through observation and imitation. (Courtesy of Nancy Martin)

do something of which they approve, hugs, and "that's right" said over and over shape our behavior so that we begin to accept what our parents accept.

Why are you attracted to the profession of teaching? Is there a teacher in your family? Does your family place a value on learning? Did you enjoy school yourself? Were your parents supportive of school when you were young? The chances are that you answered positively to at least one of these questions. One reason many people teach professionally is that they truly enjoyed being a student themselves, figure 19-2. Learning has been fun and often

Fig. 19-2 Teachers often value education because they received pleasure and reward from learning activities. (Courtesy of Nancy Martin)

easy. As a result, an education is highly valued. Teachers frequently come from families in which the profession was valued not because it pays well but, more likely, for the pleasure received in working with young children and the intangible experience of influencing young lives.

One problem many teachers face is accepting negative attitudes from parents or caregivers who do not place similar values upon education. It is difficult to relate to them. You need to remember that some parents may come from cultures where educational opportunities were denied. In addition, some parents may feel that an education never did them any good; they may be products of education systems which failed them. These parents have different values than you. What can you do? The start is always to show through your actions (they always speak louder than words) that you care for their children, and that you want to help their children. Assuming that the parents want their children to have better opportunities, that they want the best for their children, you can earn the parents' respect and cooperation.

Many of our most enduring values were formed through contact with our family when we were too young to remember. Others were acquired through repeated experience. Let us use an example. Assume that you were raised in the city and lived in apartment houses your entire life. Because you never had a yard of your own, you have had little experience with plants beyond the potted variety. You are now renting a house with a yard, and you enjoy puttering around in the garden. Because your experiences with gardening have been pleasurable, you have acquired a positive value for it. If your experiences had been bad, you could have acquired a negative value just as easily.

KRATHWOHL'S HIERARCHY One way of looking at the acquisition of values is to look at Krathwohl's taxonomy (1964). Krathwohl and his associates were interested in looking at the "affective domain," or the field of knowledge associated with feelings and values. Krathwohl arranged the affective domain into a hierarchy as follows:

1. Receiving (attending)
2. Responding
3. Valuing
4. Organization
5. Characterization by a value or value complex

For you, as a teacher of young children, the first three levels are the most important. Suppose you had not been willing to receive the stimulus of potted plants being a pleasure to see? Being aware of the aesthetics of having plants and enjoying their presence is the first sublevel of receiving — becoming sensitive. Becoming interested in them and enjoying their beauty moves one beyond mere awareness to the next sublevel — willingness to receive. There is a third sublevel of receiving — controlled or selected attention. What does this mean? How is this demonstrated? Looking at potted plants and remarking on their growth, need for water, and flowers are all examples of selected attention.

If you saw that the plant needed water and proceeded to water it, you have moved to the second level of the hierarchy — responding. If you water the plant after being asked to do so, you have reached the first sublevel — acquiescence in responding. If you do it without being asked, you are at the second sublevel — willingness to respond. Noting satisfaction in the growth of the plant because you have been a part of its care moves you into the third sublevel of responding — satisfaction in response.

Valuing, the third level, also has sublevels. The first is acceptance of a value. When you buy your own potted plants, for example, you are revealing a value. You like potted plants enough to buy and care for them. The second sublevel is showing a preference for a value. For example, if you chose to rent a house with a yard instead of an apartment because of the opportunity to work in the yard, you have shown preference for a value. Taking care of the yard then moves you into the third sublevel — commitment.

Let us now study these three levels of value in more specific terms. Try the following exercise (adapted from Biehler, 1971, pp. 301–303). Write your answers on a separate sheet of paper.

Receiving (attending) — The learner becomes sensitized to the existence of certain phenomena and stimuli.

1. Awareness: What types of awareness do you want your students to have? For example, do

you want them to be aware of the books in the classroom? List those things of which you want the children to become aware.

2. Willingness to receive: What types of tolerance do you want your students to develop? For example, do you want your students to sit quietly and listen when you read a book to them? Describe the behavior you hope to see from your students regarding their willingness to receive.

3. Controlled or selected attention: List the things you want the students to recognize that are frequently ignored by trained observers. For instance, do you want your students to recognize the predictability or pattern of repetition of a story?

Responding — The learner does something with the phenomena.

1. Acquiescence in responding: What habits of responses do you want to encourage? Do you want your students to respond to your questions about the story you just read?

2. Willingness to respond: List the voluntary responses you want to encourage. Do you want the students to ask their own questions about a story as you read it?

3. Satisfaction in response: List the habits of satisfaction you want your students to develop. Do you want them to respond with smiles, excitement, or laughter to the story? Do you want them to listen with anticipation, predicting the outcome with pleasure and enthusiasm?

Valuing — The learner displays consistent behavior reflecting a general attitude.

1. Acceptance of a value: List the types of emotional acceptance you want your students to develop. Do you want your students to go voluntarily to the book corner to "read" the same book you just read to them?

2. Preference for a value: What values do you want your students to develop to the point of actively identifying with the stimulus? Do you want them to urge other children in the class to "read" the story? Do you want to see them choose

this book to "read" while role playing school and you as teacher?

3. Commitment: List the behaviors you want your students to develop that will enable you to decide whether they are committed to the stimulus. Do you want them to check out the book from the class to take home? Do you want them to take out the book from the local library? Do you want them to go to the book corner at least three times each week? What evidence of commitment to your stimulus are you looking for?

We will not continue further with this exercise since you may not know if the students have absorbed your stimulus into their values system until after they move on from your class. For yourself, however, go back over this exercise and ask yourself the following:

1. Why did I choose that particular example as the stimulus I wanted my students to receive and respond to?

2. What does this reveal about my own values system?

3. Is this value a part of *me*, a part of my character?

If you cannot answer these questions, we suggest that you go back and repeat the exercise with another stimulus. For example, your choices may range from some facet of the curriculum — storytime and books — to some facet of behavior — paying attention, sharing toys, not fighting, etc.

YOU AND YOUR VALUES

Why is it important for you as a student teacher to be aware of your values? We hope that you already know the answer. In many ways, the answer lies in what Carl Rogers (1966) calls congruence. Self-knowledge should precede trying to impart knowledge to others. By looking closely at your values, you will be able to develop a philosophy of teaching more easily.

Let us move on to another exercise. On a separate sheet of paper, trace the following.

In the top left-hand section, draw a picture of what you believe is your best asset. Next to it in the top right-hand section, draw a picture of something you do well. In the middle left-hand section, draw a picture of something you would like to do better. In the middle right-hand section, draw a picture of something you want to change about yourself. In the bottom left-hand section, draw a picture of something that frightens you. In the bottom right-hand section, write five adjectives which you would like other people to use to describe you. Look at your drawings and think about what your *affective* responses were to this exercise. Did you find it easier to draw a picture of something you do well than it was to draw something that frightens you? Was it easier to draw than to list five adjectives? Did you feel more comfortable drawing or writing your responses? What does this say about you? Were you able to write the first two or three adjectives quickly and then forced to give some thought to the remaining two?

Some of us have more difficulty handling compliments than negative criticism; thus, we find it easier to draw a picture of something we want to do better than to draw a picture of something we do well. Some of us have negative feelings about our ability to draw anything; being asked to do an exercise that asks for a drawn response is a real chore. Did you silently breathe a sigh of relief when you came to the last part of the exercise and were asked for a written response? Does this suggest that you are more comfortable with words than with nonverbal expressions?

If you are more at ease with words, what are the implications regarding any curriculum decisions you might make? Would you be inclined to place a greater emphasis on language activities than on art activities, especially those involving drawing? If you can deal more easily with the negative aspects of yourself than with the positive aspects, what are the implications for your curriculum decisions? Is it possible that you would find it easier to criticize, rather than compliment, a student? Is it possible that you are inclined to see mistakes rather than improvements? Think about this. How do the activities you enjoy reflect your personal values, and thus influence your classroom curriculum, figure 19-3? Go back to the first exercise you completed in this unit. What were the first five activities you listed? List them on a separate piece of paper. Next to this column, write five related classroom activities. Does your list look something like this?

Activity	Related Curriculum Activity
Playing the piano	Teaching simple songs with piano accompaniment
Jogging	Allowing active children to run around the playground
Skiing	Climbing, jumping, gross motor activities

Fig. 19-3 Activities we enjoy may influence classroom curriculum choices. (Courtesy of Nancy Martin)

PERSONAL VALUES AND ACTIVITIES

What is the relationship between activities and personal values? It seems obvious that we would not become involved in an activity that did not bring us some reward or pleasure; we have to be motivated. Usually that motivation becomes intrinsic because significant people in our lives provided an extrinsic reward, usually a smile or compliment. Given enough feedback in the form of compliments, we learn to accept and even prize the activity.

Many of us want to teach young children because we genuinely like them. When did we learn this? Some teachers, as the oldest of many siblings, learned to care for and enjoy being with younger brothers and sisters. Others had positive experiences from babysitting.

Perhaps we want to teach young children because they are less threatening than older children. In addition, young children are often more motivated to please the adults in their lives than teenagers.

Attitudes toward or against something are often formed when we are so young that we do not know their origin. We only know that we have a tendency to like or dislike something or someone. Because these attitudes arouse a strong *affect* or feeling for or against, they can influence our values. People of different backgrounds who do not share similar ideals often find their values being challenged, figure 19-4.

Fig. 19-4   Student teachers from different ethnic groups may find their values challenged at times.

Summary

In this unit we discussed the relationship between attitudes and values, and the curriculum choices which are made as a result. We also discussed how values and attitudes are formed. We included several learning exercises; their aim was to help you define more clearly some of your personal values.

Suggested Activities

A. Complete the following exercise in small groups. Discuss the process involved in making your decision. What did you learn about yourself and your peers as a result?

The Fall-Out Shelter Problem (From Simon, 1972)

PURPOSE

This is a simulated problem-solving exercise. It raises a host of values issues which the student must attempt to work through in a rational manner. It is often a very dramatic example of how our values differ; how hard it is to objectively determine the "best" values; and how we often have trouble listening to people whose beliefs are different from our own.

PROCEDURE

The class is divided into groups of six or seven, who then sit together. The teacher explains the situation to the groups.

"Your group are members of a department in Washington, D.C. that is in charge of experimental stations in the far outposts of civilization. Suddenly the Third World War breaks out and bombs begin dropping. Places all across the globe are being destroyed. People are heading for whatever fallout shelters are available. You receive a desperate call from one of your experimental stations, asking for help.

"It seems there are *ten* people but there is only enough space, air, food, and water in their fall-out shelter for *six* people for a period of *three* months — which is how long they estimate they can safely stay down there. They realize that if they have to decide among themselves which six should go into the shelter, they are likely to become irrational and begin fighting. So they have decided to call your department, their superiors, and leave the decision to you. They will abide by your decision.

"But each of you has to quickly get ready to head down to your own fall-out shelter. So all you have time for is to get superficial descriptions of the ten people. You have half-an-hour to make your decision. Then you will have to go to your own shelter.

"So, as a group you now have a half-hour to decide which four of the ten will have to be eliminated from the shelter. Before you begin, I want to impress upon you two important considerations. It is entirely possible that the six people you choose to stay in the shelter might be the only six people left to start the human race over again. This choice is, therefore, very important. Do not allow yourself to be swayed by pressure from the others in your group. Try to make the best choices possible. On the other hand, if you do not make a choice in a half-hour, then you are, in fact, choosing to let the ten people fight it out among themselves, with the possibility that more than four might perish. You have *exactly* one half-hour. Here is all you know about the ten people:

1. Bookkeeper; 31 years old
2. His wife; six months pregnant
3. Black militant; second year medical student
4. Famous historian-author; 42 years old
5. Hollywood starlette; singer; dancer
6. Bio-chemist
7. Rabbi; 54 years old
8. Olympic athlete; all sports
9. College co-ed
10. Policeman with gun (they cannot be separated)

The teacher posts or distributes copies of this list, and the students begin. The teacher gives 15, 10, 5 and 1-minute warnings and then stops the groups exactly after a half-hour.

Each group can then share its selections with the other groups and perhaps argue a bit more, if there is time. Then the teacher asks the students to try to disregard the content of the activity and to examine the process and the values implications. He asks questions like: How well did you listen to the others in your group? Did you allow yourself to be pressured into changing your mind? Were you so stubborn that the group couldn't reach a decision? Did you feel you had the right answer? What do your own selections say to you about your values? These questions may be thought about or written about privately, or they may be discussed in the small groups or by the whole class.

VARIATIONS

1. Instead of eliminating four people from the shelter, students may be asked to rank order, as in a Forced Choice Ladder (Strategy Number 6), the ten candidates from the most desirable to the least desirable. (There is also nothing sacred about four. It could be three or five, for example.)
2. After each member of the class has ranked the ten people, they can try to come to consensus on who is to be admitted to the shelter.
3. Instead of choosing six candidates for a remote shelter, each group may be instructed to pick four out of the ten to accompany them to their own shelter.
4. Other problem situations may be invented. For example, three (or more) people need a heart transplant and will more than likely die in three weeks if it is not performed. However, only one operation can be performed. The students are to assume the role of the doctor who will perform the operation and must make the decision of who will live.
5. The descriptions of the ten people can be changed to introduce additional values issues. *For example:*
   a. A 16-year old girl of questionable IQ; a high school drop-out; pregnant.
   b. The same policeman with gun; thrown off the force for police brutality (or given a community-relations award).
   c. A clergyman; 75 years old.
   d. A 36-year old female physician; unable to have children (or known to be a confirmed racist).
   e. A 46-year old male violinist; served seven years for pushing narcotics; has been out of jail for six months.
   f. A 20-year old male Black militant; no special skills.
   g. A 39-year old former prostitute; "retired" for four years.
   h. An architect; homosexual.
   i. A 26-year old male law student.
   j. The law student's 25-year old wife; spent the last nine months in a mental hospital; still heavily sedated. They refuse to be separated.

TO THE TEACHER

If one of the fall-out-shelter candidates that we have provided, or that you may create yourself, gets consistently eliminated, simply give that candidate(s) more skills, or make him more attractive in some way; for example, lower his age.

B. Write a paragraph on how you have been influenced by stereotyping and what you have done to counter this. How has this use of stereotyping affected your attitude toward that person who used it? Why?

Review

A. List five personal values.

B. Write an essay describing how the values you listed in review question A influence what you do in the classroom.

Resources

Biehler, Robert F. *Psychology Applied to Teaching.* Boston: Houghton Mifflin Co., 1971.

Krathwohl, David R., et al. *Taxonomy of Educational Objectives: The Classification of Educational Goals. Handbook II: Affective Domain.* New York: David McKay Co., Inc., 1964.

Rogers, Carl R. "To Facilitate Learning," from *Innovations for Time to Teach*, ed. M. Provus. Washington, DC: National Educational Association, 1966.

Simon, Sidney B., Howe, Leland B., and Kirschenbaum, Howard. *Values Clarification: A Handbook of Practical Strategies for Teachers and Students.* New York: Hart Publishing Co., Inc., 1972.

Unit 20
Teaching Styles and Techniques

OBJECTIVES

After studying this unit, the student will be able to:

- Identify at least three different teaching styles.
- Define and describe his or her own teaching style.
- Discuss the relationship between a philosophy of education and teaching style.

TEACHING MODELS

What is meant by teaching style? It is the vehicle through which a teacher contributes his or her unique quality to the curriculum. Much has been written about teaching style, in particular the phenomenon of teachers modeling themselves after their teachers who influenced them in the past.

Placing a student teacher with a "master" or co-operating teacher has its disadvantages as well as advantages. Most college supervisors try to place student teachers with those master teachers who will provide a positive model and are willing to allow the student teacher to practice. However, there are many excellent teachers who are unwilling to work with student teachers. This is because it takes much energy and time to work with student teachers; they have to be watched, referred to resources, conferenced, and encouraged. In addition, most colleges and universities do not compensate the master teacher in any tangible form for their time and energy. As a result, some student teaching placements are less than desirable.

Of course, this situation sometimes works out well. A student teacher with experience as a teacher aide may do quite well in a classroom where the cooperating teacher is less than an excellent model and provides little supervision or guidance. In some cases, the student teacher may even act as a *positive role model* for the mediocre cooperating teacher.

Good cooperating teachers will offer suggestions to student teachers about different lessons to try. They will introduce the student teachers to all areas of the curriculum, usually one area at a time. Most cooperating teachers will allow a certain amount of time for student teachers to observe and become acquainted with the children. Before the end of the student teaching experience, however, most strong master teachers will expect a student teacher to handle the whole day and all parts of the curriculum, figure 20-1. All student teachers will inevitably "borrow" or copy their cooperating teachers' styles; this results from having worked so closely together.

Sometimes, though, a master teacher's style is so unique, so much a part of his or her self that it is too difficult to copy. We are reminded of a male cooperating teacher who stood six feet, four inches tall and weighed around 240 pounds. Female student teachers had problems using his behavior control techniques; the difference in their sizes precluded their use of physical presence as a discipline technique.

One complaint the college supervisor heard regularly was "Of course Mr. Smith has no problems of control! Look at him!" What many student teachers failed to recognize initially was that Mr. Smith used other techniques as well — close observation of the classroom; moving toward the source of potential trouble before it erupted; quietly removing a child from a frustrating activity; and firm and consistent classroom rules.

A master teacher may be so gifted that a student teacher feels overwhelmed. In this situation, the student teacher needs to look at only one facet of the cooperating teacher's expertise at a time. For example, in focusing on how the teacher begins each day, the student teacher may find a model that is not quite so difficult as the total model appears. It may be that the cooperating teacher takes time each morning to greet each child with a smile and a personal comment.

There are also situations where the cooperating teacher is unable to explain how something is done, like the mathematician who can solve a complex problem without knowing how. Intuitive teachers and those who are very involved have this difficulty; they are unable to explain why they do one thing and not another.

Fig. 20-1 At first, student teachers will work in areas where they are most comfortable. Later, they will be expected to handle all parts of the curriculum. (Courtesy of Steve Howard)

Teaching styles are also an extension of the teacher's self. Rogers (1969) contends that the teacher must know the self before effectively teaching another. This means that you have enough self-knowledge to judge from observing your cooperating teacher what activities and techniques will work for you, which ones you may have to modify, and which ones are best not used. Techniques with which you are truly uncomfortable are best put aside until you can become comfortable with them.

SPECIFIC MODELS Mr. Smith is a true master teacher. After having taught every grade in elementary school, he has chosen to teach in a parent-cooperative preschool. Mr. Smith became firmly convinced that working with young children was more rewarding for him than teaching in a public school. Choosing the parent-cooperative preschool reflects Mr. Smith's belief in the importance of the family and his interest in working with parents in the classroom.

Upon entering Mr. Smith's room, a visitor can immediately see that it is arranged into several areas. An entrance area is formed by a desk to the left of the door and the children's cubbies on the right. A parent bulletin board is mounted on the wall by the desk. A large area with shelves housing large blocks, trucks, cars, etc. is found behind the cubbies. An inside climbing structure, built by the parents, is located in the corner. Underneath, there is a housekeeping area complete with stove, sink, cupboards, table, and chairs. In the opposite corner is a quiet area protected by a large, comfortable couch. This area is further defined by its carpet, floor pillows, and bookshelves. On the shelves, there are many picture and story books which Mr. Smith periodically changes for added interest. Three tables with chairs are to the left of the quiet area and straight ahead from the door. Shelves and cupboards along the wall contain small manipulatives — puzzles, cut and paste articles, etc. The window wall opposite the door is the math and science center. In addition, a waterplay area is found here as well as a terrarium and a large magnifying glass, with objects to investigate in a nearby box.

The first impression the visitor has is how busy and happy everyone appears to be. A parent may be found supervising a tissue paper-collage activity at one of the tables; another parent may be supervising at the workbench outside the door, watching as four or five children saw, hammer, and nail a wood sculpture. Mr. Smith may be located at the science center directing two children's attention to their bean plants.

One way of studying Mr. Smith's classroom is to look at his teaching style. It seems very student-centered, which it is. It is highly flexible, changing as student interests change. For example, one day a child brought a chrysalis to school. Mr. Smith immediately asked the children to guess what they thought it might be. He listened intently to every guess, even the wild ones. He asked the child who brought it if she knew what she had found. When the child indicated that she did not, Mr. Smith proceeded to tell the students that they should watch the chrysalis every day to see what was going to happen. He resisted the urge to tell them anything more other than they would receive a big surprise. He placed the chrysalis in a large jar, placed cheesecloth over the opening, and secured it with a rubber band. Fortunately, the butterfly emerged from the chrysalis on a school day, and the children had the excitement of watching it. Mr. Smith allowed the children to watch despite the fact that science had not been scheduled for that particular time. Indeed, the children were so interested that no one wanted to go out to recess when the bell rang!

One might ask whether Mr. Smith's teaching style is congruent with one's perception of him as a person. In talking to him and becoming better acquainted with him, one might find that Mr. Smith sees himself more as a learner than as a teacher. He attends teacher conferences regularly and goes to workshops. He was one of the first preschool teachers in his community to ask that "special" students be placed in his classroom, even before PL 94-142 was enacted. His bias that all students are special and his student-centered classroom make it easy to integrate children with special problems.

Further exploration reveals that he is an avid gardener, likes to fish, enjoys woodwork and would like to enroll in a workshop on stained glass. Mr. Smith appears as gifted outside of the classroom as he is within it.

It is easy to see that Mr. Smith values all the children in his class, figure 20-2. It is one of the reasons why he is so effective, especially in regard to working with "special" children. It also is apparent that Mr. Smith is able to empathize with his children. He is gentle with those who have experienced a serious loss; he refuses to allow an angry child to bait him, and quietly speaks to the child one-to-one; he shares in the excitement of a child who has taken a first train trip, and may urge this child to share the experience with the others. The only times anyone has seen him angry involved a suspected case of child abuse and some of the money-saving policies of the board of education.

If a student teacher were to ask Mr. Smith about his teaching style, he would answer that it is based on his philosophy of education. This, he would continue, is the belief in the inherent goodness of all children and in their innate need to explore the world. He would be able to provide a written statement of his beliefs and curriculum goals for the year.

Mr. Smith's teaching is very much a part of himself — steady and imaginative, with a desire to create a

Fig. 20-2 This teacher values each child and takes advantage of every learning opportunity.

total learning environment for his students. In looking at Rogers' criteria, it is clear that Mr. Smith is congruent, acceptant, reliable, and empathetic, and that his students perceive these characteristics in him as well. One can tell that each child is as important as the next. He uses many nonverbal responses, touching one child on the shoulder as a reminder to settle down and get to work, giving another a sympathetic hug, getting down on his knees to speak directly and firmly to an angry child. From all of his words and actions, it is obvious that Mr. Smith teaches children much more than subject matter.

Let us now look at another teacher, Mrs. Jones. (Although divorced, Mrs. Jones has not adopted the Ms. appellation and corrects anyone who calls her Ms.) A kindergarten teacher for twelve years, Mrs. Jones starts each day by having the children line up outside the door, walk quietly into the classroom, and form a semi-circle around her by the chalkboard. The children sit down, and Mrs. Jones takes the roll. Next, a child announces the day of the week and the date, and places the date on a cardboard calendar beside the chalkboard. Children are assigned this task on a rotating basis. Next comes sharing time, which is also done on a rotating basis with four children sharing each day. The children are then assigned to different tasks. One group of four children may be assigned to the sewing cards. Another group of three may be asked to complete a ditto. A group of six may go to a table and wait for Mrs. Jones to show them how to do a letters/phonics ditto. Two children may be assigned to paint at the easels. Six more children may be assigned to work with the aide on another letters/phonics ditto. The remaining five children may work at a small manipulatives table. Upon questioning Mrs. Jones, one discovers that she schedules the children at rotating tasks throughout the three hours of kindergarten. Mrs. Jones prides herself on the fact that all of her children learn their alphabet letters and corresponding sounds, and their numerals from one to ten. She also points out that she starts approximately one-half of the children in preprimers in January and many of them will enter first grade reading.

A strict disciplinarian, Mrs. Jones does not allow any aggressive acting-out behavior. If a child becomes involved in a fight, that child is quickly reminded that such behavior is not allowed and sent to the principal. Mrs. Jones does not allow a child to interrupt when someone is speaking.

Upon entering Mrs. Jones' classroom, the visitor is impressed by how quiet it is. All of the children seem to be busy at the assignments they have been given. Upon second glance, however, one can notice that one child is only randomly marking the ditto. Mrs. Jones is speaking rather harshly to this child. "You know better than that! Now, get back to work and do it right!" Another child is unenthusiastically stringing beads. A third child is gazing out the window, biting fingernails. A fourth child is sitting glumly at a table where children are completing a cut and paste activity. The visitor wonders why this particular child is so unhappy, and moves closer. The child shrinks down in the chair and slides an arm under the table. The visitor asks, "What's the matter?" Almost in tears, the child looks quickly around to see where Mrs. Jones is and lifts the hidden arm from under the table. The child's hand is stuck in the paste jar. When asked why Mrs. Jones was not informed, the child whispers, "Oh, I couldn't do that!" When asked how the child could hide the stuck hand, the child mumbles, "I don't know." A tear runs down the child's cheek.

What kind of teacher does Mrs. Jones appear to be? Is she congruent, acceptant, and empathetic? It is apparent from looking at the incident of the child and the paste jar that empathy does not exist. An empathetic teacher would have noted the unhappiness on the child's face and would have attempted to find out and solve the problem. Certainly, acceptance also seems to be lacking, especially with the child who was marking up the ditto. Congruence is more difficult to determine, because it depends upon Mrs. Jones' perception of herself.

After talking with Mrs. Jones, it is obvious that she sees herself as a good teacher. After all, her children do well on the tests at the end of the year. Many of them already know how to read. Her children obey class rules. One begins to realize that Mrs. Jones is content oriented rather than student oriented. Hers is a teacher-centered, not student-centered, classroom.

Is Mrs. Jones a congruent teacher? Is her teaching a reflection of her self? If we become friends with Mrs. Jones, we would discover that her small house is immaculate, with everything in its place. She is a person of habit; rising, eating, and going to bed at the same time every day whether it is a school day or not. When meeting for an evening out, her friends know she will be punctual, almost to the minute. They know that she will have only one cocktail before dinner, order a fish special from the menu, and fall asleep at a musical performance because she usually goes to bed at 10:00 p.m. Because her schedule is just as rigid and exact as her teaching, Mrs. Jones is a congruent teacher.

Mrs. Jones is respected by many parents, especially those whose children learned to read in kindergarten. She is less liked by the parents of slower students and students with learning problems; she does not have much patience or understanding of their slow learning patterns. However, they are somewhat in awe of Mrs. Jones because of her reputation as a strict but good teacher.

If one inquired about Mrs. Jones' philosophy of education and curriculum goals, she would most likely answer, "It's simply to direct each of the children, to teach them to behave, read, write, and do simple mathematics." In terms of curriculum goals, Mrs. Jones would state, "I always follow district goals. In fact, I served on the curriculum committee the year the goals were revised." If questioned further, Mrs. Jones would again talk about the importance of reading, writing, and mathematics. Most likely, she will point out that some parents approve of her emphasis upon the basics. (One, of course, will wonder why Mrs. Jones has said nothing about the children!)

Another way of studying these two teachers is to look beyond their teaching styles to their leadership styles. As we know, Mr. Smith runs a student-centered classroom and has a flexible curriculum which changes with student interest and enthusiasm. We also know that the students' needs come first. What is his leadership style? One might say that it is democratic. The students all have a say as to what will happen from day to day. Mr. Smith respects all opinions and ideas, and he teaches this to his students.

Mrs. Jones, in contrast, runs a teacher-centered classroom and has a fixed, rigid curriculum. In terms of her leadership style, one would have to admit that it is autocratic. She is the absolute authority in the classroom.

OTHER TEACHING STYLES

We presented extreme examples of two teaching and two leadership styles. With most teachers, however, you will find variants of these extremes. Between these two contrasting styles, student centered and teacher centered or democratic and autocratic, lie others. The style of most teachers lies somewhere between Mr. Smith's and Mrs. Jones', and a few may even lie at a further extreme. Many teachers follow a more or less set schedule from day to day. Free play always starts the day in preschool; reading activities always start the day in grade school. Sharing activities and attendance follow. Outdoor play and recess follow indoor activities. Quiet play alternates with active, noisy play. Rest follows lunch. Free play and less structured activities such as art, music, or physical education occur before dismissal time.

Many teachers follow a more or less rigid schedule with such curricula as reading and math. These disciplines are sequential; children must know A before they can proceed to B. Many teachers allow more flexibility with activities such as the fine arts. Thus, many curriculum choices may be a reflection of student and/or teacher interest, figure 20-3. A teacher who is proficient in art will provide many art activities; a teacher with interests in music will provide many musical experiences for the students.

While observing as a student teacher, you will find there are almost as many different teaching styles as there are teachers. Teachers tend to emphasize those areas of the curriculum which they feel are more important; they also tend to emphasize those areas in which they have greater expertise. The major characteristic of all truly great teachers, though, is their ability to empathize with their students. Look closely; does the teacher show evidence of really liking the students? Does that teacher CARE? CAREing is the secret to good teaching.

Fig. 20-3 This area was developed as a result of the teacher's and children's interests.

STEREOTYPING GOOD AND BAD In order to understand fully a teacher's style, one has to understand the teacher's philosophy and underlying attitude toward the students. Does this teacher accept the children? Does this teacher feel that children are inherently good? Some teachers believe that all children are essentially bad and have to be taught to be good. Their teaching style reflects this attitude. Usually autocratic, they have rigid classroom rules. Children are told that they will behave in a particular way; any infringement upon the rules usually will bring swift punishment.

Does the teacher feel that children can be trusted? The teacher's style will reflect this belief. Classroom rules will be solicited from the children, with the teacher reminding them of a rule they may have overlooked. Children who misbehave are not considered bad but as needing more socialization time in which to learn. Punishment often takes the form of physical removal from the situation and isolation until the child feels ready to rejoin the class.

Does Mr. Smith believe children are good or bad? Does Mrs. Jones? From the information presented so far, you only can guess that Mr. Smith believes children are inherently good and that Mrs. Jones does not.

A teacher may believe that most children are good and then have an experience with a psychologically damaged child who challenges this belief. At this point, the teacher may accept the fact that most, but not all, children are good. The danger is that the experience with the psychologically damaged child can lead the teacher to formulate a stereotype about all children who look like this child, who come from the same socioeconomic background, who belong to the same racial or ethnic group, or who are of the same sex. Of Mr. Smith and Mrs. Jones, which is most likely to use stereotypic thinking? Stereotypic thinking occurs more often in rigid people than in flexible people.

FLEXIBILITY Let us also look at another factor — curriculum planning. The amount of planning needed is often overlooked in a classroom like Mr. Smith's. The visitor does not realize how much work goes into the arrangement of the learning centers. The classroom looks open, free, and flexible. Indeed, it is all of these. None of it is possible, however, without a great deal of careful planning. Ask Mr. Smith how many years it has taken to develop his classroom and how much work he still does during free time to maintain the atmosphere. You will find that Mr. Smith is continually revising, updating, and trying out new things. Much careful planning goes into any successful open and free environment.

In contrast, observe Mrs. Jones. During questioning, you will discover that she is still using many of the materials she developed during her student teaching years and first years of teaching. If she makes a change, it is usually at the request of her principal or at the suggestion of the parent of a child she likes. She seldom makes changes on her own, and is quite comfortable with what she has always done. Some of her critics have suggested, "Mrs. Jones claims to have twelve years of experience; I maintain she has one year of experience which was repeated eleven times!" There is, unfortunately, much truth to the statement.

TWO NEGATIVE MODELS

For further contrast, let us take a look at a third teacher, Ms. Young. A visitor to Ms. Young's room is immediately impressed by the noise level. All the children seem to be talking at once. Confusion appears to reign, with children constantly moving from one area to another. Ms. Young prides herself on her love for preschool children. Her room is arranged so that table activities are possible on one side of a large, almost square, room. She usually has clay at one table, cut and paste activities at the second, changing activities at the third. One day the visitor might find materials for tissue paper collages; another day the activity might be fingerpainting; on another day, there might be macaroni of various colors to string. Along one wall are shelves with puzzle racks, books, boxes of crayons, and paper which the children may take to a carpeted area for play. Along another wall, there are blocks of different sizes and wheeled toys, such as trucks and cars, with a clear space for play. In the far corner opposite the door is a playhouse. The window wall has low shelves containing some articles that might be science-oriented — shells, a large magnifying glass, rocks, some wispy plants in a neglected terrarium (Ms. Young confesses that she really does not know much about plants). Along the last wall is a sink with a waterplay area. Two easels are found nearby. Cubbies for children's sweaters and share items are near the door. These cubbies serve to mark off the entrance area from the carpet area.

After becoming accustomed to the noise level and confusion, the observer notes that some children appear to be dominant. One large boy is ordering a group of boys at the block area to build a garage for his truck. A girl is ordering children around in the playhouse. One or two children seem to be confused by the noise; they are sitting rather unhappily on the sidelines. One boy catches your eye because he moves from one activity to another, staying only five seconds at each place. It seems there must be more than the twelve children in the room because of the mass confusion.

If asked about her philosophy of teaching, Ms. Young would answer, "Why, love, of course. I just love my children!" If asked about a schedule, she may answer, "Why, I don't need a schedule. I let the children decide for themselves what they want to do." If you were to point out that some of the children appear unhappy, Ms. Young is likely to reply, "Oh, they'll get used to it after a while."

How would one categorize Ms. Young's teaching style? Does she have one? The organized chaos of her classroom appears to fulfill the needs of some children, especially those from homes which have taught and encouraged self-sufficiency. But in looking at Ms. Young's classroom and her laissez-faire attitude toward the children, one will conclude that she does not have a teaching style. She does not have a philosophy of education; what she does in the room is haphazard.

The consequences of this aimless approach to curriculum is that some of the activities Ms. Young introduces are good, many are mediocre, and some are poor for the ability levels and interests of the children. Because of the lack of adequate supervision, there are occasional accidents and some of the more timid children's self-concepts are hurt. The more aggressive children are not helped either; they learn to be bullies and feel that "might makes right." They are not taught how to channel their aggressiveness into socially accepted actions. They are allowed to become leaders by default rather than learning how to lead and follow. To the trained observer, Ms. Young's classroom does not provide for the maximum growth of all the children.

Let us visit a private Christian preschool for our next example. Mr. Adams is the teacher of a class of three-year-olds. Upon entering his room, the visitor's first impression is how quiet it is. Every child seems busily engaged in one activity or another. Questions do not arise until one notices that few children are smiling. Mr. Adams rings a bell every twenty to thirty minutes, and children change activities as though they are automatons.

When asked about his philosophy of education, Mr. Adams responds that since children are born in sin, they must be taught to be good. He starts each day with a reading from the Bible, followed by a recitation of Bible verses by four or five children. He explains that each child is expected to memorize a Bible verse every day so that when they are called upon to recite, they can. He will tell a visitor that he calls upon the children in a random pattern, because "some children will always be prepared; others are seldom prepared." The children who are not prepared are called upon to recite more frequently and are punished.

Mr. Adams follows a rigid schedule; each child is assigned to a task and is expected to complete it before the bell rings. Every child rotates through each area of the room on schedule. Activities include clay, puzzles, housekeeping, blocks, easels, arts and crafts, and pegboards or some other manipulative task. Outside play is scheduled similarly: wheeled toys for ten minutes, swings, sandbox, climbing structure, etc. When Mr. Adams blows his whistle, children switch play equipment.

If asked about the harshness of the schedule, Mr. Adams would insist that they are learning discipline; that it is fair for everyone to have the same opportunity to play with materials. Questioned about the apparent joylessness of his charges, Mr. Adams might reply, "Children are born in sin and should obey their elders. While they are in my care, they will obey me just as they would obey their parents at home. It's what the parents expect of us."

Is Mr. Adams a congruent teacher? Given his fundamentalist Christian background, the answer would be yes. Is he acceptant? Obviously, the answer is no, unless the child is good. What are the characteristics of a good child? Mr. Adams will tell you that it is a child who obeys rules, who memorizes a Bible verse every day, and who completes all of the assigned work without complaint. Is Mr. Adams empathetic? Again, the answer is no. In fact, Mr. Adams is highly suspicious of terms like empathy and believes that humanistic education is the work of the devil. Is he acceptant of the children? He believes *they* need to accept *him*.

philosophy to show the relationship between stated beliefs and teaching style. We also suggested that there is a relationship between a teacher's ability to CARE and their philosophy of education, which leads them to establish clear curriculum goals for their students.

Of the four teachers described, Mr. Smith obviously CAREs; Ms. Young may CARE but makes the critical error of mistaking freedom in the classroom with lack of structure and limits. Mrs. Jones would protest that she does CARE, but in reality she lacks empathy for the slow learners in her room; Mr. Adams does not even see the need to be acceptant or empathetic. A rigid set of rules and expectations are all that is necessary. He would most certainly see himself as a congruent person as well as a reliable one.

What should you, as a student teacher, do? Perhaps of greatest importance is to discover your own teaching style. What areas of the curriculum are you most comfortable with? Why? Do you see yourself as a CAREing person? Do you have a philosophy of education? In our four examples, do you see the relationship between each teacher's beliefs and curriculum practices? Think about your curriculum goals; consider how your feelings about working with young children influence these goals. Remember, especially, the positive model of Mr. Smith. Think of how he looks upon himself as a learner, how he looks at each child, how he listens to them, how flexible his curriculum is, how student centered his curriculum style, and how democratic his leadership style.

Summary

We observed Mr. Smith, a model master teacher with a clearly stated (and written) curriculum philosophy and goal of education. We have also looked at what is perhaps a typical teacher, Mrs. Jones. Although more authoritarian than Mr. Smith and less acceptant of all children, Mrs. Jones' teaching style with its emphasis on the basics is admired by many parents. We presented Ms. Young, a teacher with no real philosophy of education or stated curriculum goals other than to let the children play. Finally, we described Mr. Adams' classroom, and explained his

Suggested Activities

A. Read Chapters 1 and 2 of *In Search of Teaching Style* by Abraham Shumsky. How do the descriptions of Teachers A and B compare to those of Mr. Smith, Mrs. Jones, Ms. Young, and Mr. Adams? Discuss the similarities and differences with your peers and college supervisor.

B. Write your philosophy of education. Describe it in relation to your curriculum style. Discuss this with your peers and supervisor.

Review

A. List two basic extremes of teaching styles and curriculums.

B. Read each question. Of the choices given, select the most appropriate answer.
1. Of Mr. Smith, Mrs. Jones, Ms. Young, and Mr. Adams, who is most likely to use stereotypic thinking?
   a. Mr. Smith
   b. Mrs. Jones
   c. Ms. Young
   d. Mr. Adams
2. Of the four, who is the most CAREing?
   a. Mr. Smith
   b. Mrs. Jones
   c. Ms. Young
   d. Mr. Adams
3. Who exhibits congruence?
   a. Mr. Smith
   b. Mrs. Jones
   c. Ms. Young
   d. Mr. Adams
   e. Both a and b
4. Of the four, who exhibits unconditional acceptance of their students?
   a. Mr. Smith
   b. Mrs. Jones
   c. Ms. Young
   d. Mr. Adams
   e. Both a and c
5. Of the four, who is consistent in his or her actions?
   a. Mr. Smith
   b. Mrs. Jones
   c. Ms. Young
   d. Mr. Adams
   e. Both b and d

C. Read the following descriptions of classroom interaction. Identify each teaching behavior as student centered or teacher centered. If a behavior is neither, identify it as such.
1. Teacher A is standing to one side of the playground during outdoor free play. She is busy talking to her aide. One child approaches another who is riding a tricycle. The first child wants to ride the tricycle and attempts to push the second child off. "How many times do I have to tell you you have to wait until I blow the whistle? You won't get your turn until you learn to wait!"
2. Teacher B is busy assisting four children on a cooking project. The bilingual aide is working with six children on a reading ditto. A parent volunteer is working with five others on an art project, and the student teacher is overseeing the remaining children on their unfinished reading assignments. A child with the student teacher complains in a loud voice, "This is a dumb assignment! I want to cook! Why can't I?" Teacher B looks at and signals the student teacher to try and resolve the problem alone.
3. Two boys are arguing loudly as they enter the preschool. Teacher C, who is standing by the door greeting each child, quickly takes a boy in each hand. She quietly asks, "What's the matter with you two today?" After listening to each boy and insisting that each listen to the other, she suggests a separate active play, based upon the knowledge of what each enjoys doing. They comply, and minutes later they and another child are spotted playing cooperatively with the large blocks.
4. Teacher D is standing in front of her class. The children are watching as she explains the activity: making pumpkins out of orange and black paper. After the children go to their assigned tables, it is apparent that at least two children do not know what to do. They sit glumly with their hands in their laps. Teacher D comes over and says, "Don't you two ever listen to directions?"
5. During roll, one of the boys in Teacher E's room begins to cry. Another child yells, "Crybaby." Teacher E quietly speaks, "Johnnie, remember that we agreed we wouldn't call each other by names that can hurt. Stevie, come up here by me so we can talk. The rest of you can choose what activities you want to do. Mrs. Rogers, will you take over so I can talk to Stevie?"
6. Several children are busy playing in the sandbox. Susie begins to throw sand at Ellie. Ellie retaliates

in the same manner. Soon others join in. Jimmie gets some sand in his eyes and cries. Susie stops throwing sand and is hit in the face by Ellie. Teacher F watches and wonders when the children will restore order.

7. Sammie runs excitedly into his room at preschool only to have Teacher G say, "Sammie, you know we don't run in school. Now, go back out and come in again like a gentleman."

8. The children are all sitting on the floor in a semicircle facing Teacher H. Teacher H asks, "Who has something they want to share today?" Several hands go up. "Let's have George, Anna, Mike, and Jan share today." Noting a look of disappointment on Mary's face, he says, "Mary, I know you're disappointed but remember, you shared something with us yesterday. Don't you think we ought to give someone else a chance today?" Mary nods in agreement, and George begins to speak.

9. Amy is standing at the front of the class reading a story from the basic reader. The other children are following along, reading silently. It is obvious that Amy is a good reader, and tries to vary her tone of voice. The child fluently reads the paragraph, but something is wrong. Teacher I interrupts her. "You are reading carelessly. It's not 'the coat,' it's 'a coat.' Now, start over again, and read every word correctly."

10. Ron is a new child in preschool. After greeting him and walking with him to the table with crayons and paper, Teacher J goes back to the door to greet more children. When Teacher J thinks to look back at Ron, he notices Ron is busy drawing all over the top of the table. He goes quickly over to Ron, hands him another piece of paper, and says quietly, "Ron, use paper for drawing." He later comes back with a wet sponge and shows him how to clean up the marks.

D. Identify whether the following statements are stereotypic or factual.
1. Women are more emotional than men.
2. Women are more nurturing than men.
3. Men think more logically than women.
4. Men are usually taller than women.
5. Asian children are better students than nonAsians.
6. Children from poor families do not do as well in school as children from middle-class families.
7. Boys from minority families fight more than other boys.
8. Attractive children are spoiled.
9. Children who are highly verbal are often gifted.
10. Homely children are not as bright as attractive ones.
11. Children who have no siblings are spoiled.
12. Oldest children are not as social as youngest ones.

Resources

Rogers, Carl R. *Freedom to Learn.* Columbus, OH: Charles E. Merrill Publishing Co., 1969.

Unit 21
The Whole Teacher —
Knowing Your Competencies

OBJECTIVES

After studying this unit, the student will be able to:

- Describe the major areas of teacher competency.
- Complete a self-assessment process.
- List desirable personal characteristics and abilities of teachers.
- Develop a plan which arranges, in order of priority, the student's future competency development.

Student teaching is both rewarding and demanding. The nature of the work requires a wide range of job skills and competencies. Gaining a clearer picture of teaching competencies will help you plan for your own professional growth. This unit pinpoints personal skills, abilities, and characteristics you may already possess which serve as the basis for teaching competency.

COMPETENCY-BASED TRAINING

Teacher education has experienced a movement toward competency-based training (sometimes called performance-based) as an outgrowth of the application of behavioristic psychology, economic conditions, and major teacher education evaluation studies (Tittle, 1974). Federal funds promoted the identification of the Child Development Associate (C.D.A.) competencies. A C.D.A. is a person who is able to meet the physical, social, emotional, and intellectual growth needs of a group of children in a child development setting. These needs are met by establishing and maintaining a proper child care environment and by promoting good relations between parents and the center. An assessment process designed by the C.D.A. Consortium awarded thousands of C.D.A. credentials to successful candidates by October 1978. Head Start teachers are the primary group of early childhood professionals who have applied for and completed the C.D.A. assessment. C.D.A. competencies are the most widely distributed and accepted listing of early childhood teacher competencies, figure 21-1.

Loretta Byers and Elizabeth Iristi have identified the following six areas of student teacher competencies:

- directing child learning
- counseling and guiding
- aiding children to understand and appreciate cultural heritage
- functioning effectively as a member of a staff
- assisting in maintaining good relations between the school and the rest of the community
- working as a member of the profession (1961)

A teaching competency listed by Levin and Long which seems to provide high levels of child performance is teacher acknowledgement or praise for correct responses and further probing (questioning)

A comprehensive, developmental program for preschool children is one in which the total design helps children acquire the basic competencies and skills for full development and social participation, while at the same time ensuring the quality of the child's experience. It must be emotionally satisfying and personally meaningful, and provide a basis for future learning.

Within such a child development program, the Child Development Associate will be expected to have the knowledge and skills in the following six competency areas.

A. *Establishing and Maintaining a Safe and Healthy Learning Environment*
   1. Organize space into functional areas recognizable by the children, e.g., block building, library, dramatic play, etc.
   2. Maintain a planned arrangement for furniture, equipment and materials, large and small motor skills learning, and play materials that is understandable to the children.
   3. Organize the classroom so the children can be responsible, as appropriate, for care of belongings and materials.
   4. Arrange the setting to allow for active movement as well as quiet engagement.
   5. Take preventive measures against hazards to physical safety.
   6. Keep light, air, and heat conditions at best possible levels.
   7. Establish a planned sequence of active and quiet periods, of balanced indoor and outdoor activities.
   8. Provide flexibility of space and schedule to adjust to special circumstances and needs of a particular group of children or make use of special educational opportunities.
   9. Recognize unusual behavior or symptoms which may indicate a need for health care.

B. *Advancing Physical and Intellectual Competence*
   1. Use materials, activities, and experiences that encourage exploring, experimenting, and questioning, and which fulfill children's curiosity, help them gain mastery, and help them progress to higher levels of achievement.
   2. Recognize and provide for the young child's basic impulses to explore the physical environment; master the problems that require skillful body coordination.
   3. Increase knowledge of things in their world by stimulating observation and providing for manipulative-constructive activities.
   4. Use a variety of techniques for advancing language comprehension and usage in an atmosphere that encourages free verbal communication among children and between children and adults.
   5. Work gradually toward recognition of the symbols for designating words and numbers.
   6. Promote cognitive power by stimulating children to organize their experience (as it occurs incidentally or preplanned) in terms of relationships and conceptual dimensions: classes of objects; similarities and differences; comparative size, amount, degree; orientation in time and space; growth and decay; origins; family kinship; causality.
   7. Provide varied opportunities for children's active participation, independent choices, experimentation, and problem solving within the context of a structured, organized setting and program.
   8. Balance unstructured materials such as paint, clay, and blocks with structured materials that require specific procedures and skills; balance the use of techniques that invite exploration and dependent discovery with techniques that demonstrate and instruct.
   9. Stimulate focused activities: observing, attending, initiating, carrying through, raising questions, finding answers and solutions for the real problems that are encountered, and reviewing the outcomes of experience.
   10. Support expressive activities by providing a variety of creative art-media, and allowing children freedom to symbolize in their own terms without imposition of standards of realistic representation.

Fig. 21-1 C.D.A. basic competency areas

11. Utilize, support, and develop the play impulse, in its various symbolic and dramatic forms, as an essential component of the program; giving time, space, necessary materials, and guidance in accord with its importance for deepening and clarifying thought and feeling in early childhood.
12. Extend children's knowledge, through direct and vicarious experience, of how things work, of what animals and plants need to live, of basic work processes necessary for everyday living.
13. Acquaint children with the people who keep things functioning in their immediate environment.

C.   *Building Positive Self-Concepts and Individual Strengths*
   1. Provide an environment of acceptance in which the child can grow toward a sense of positive identity as a family member and member of an ethnic group, as a competent individual with a place in the child community.
   2. Give direct, realistic affirmation to the child's advancing skills, growing initiative and responsibility, increasing capacity for adaptation, and emerging interest in cooperation, in terms of the child's actual behavior.
   3. Demonstrate acceptance to the child by including the home language functionally in the group setting and helping the child use it as a bridge to another language for the sake of extended communication.
   4. Deal with individual differences in children's style and pace of learning and in the social-emotional aspects of their life situations by adjusting the teacher-child relationship to individual needs, by using a variety of teaching methods, and by maintaining flexible, progressive expectations.
   5. Recognize when behavior reflects emotional conflicts around trust, possession, separation, rivalry, etc., and adapt the program of experiences and teacher-child and child-child relationships to give support and enlarge the capacity to face these problems realistically.
   6. Be able to assess special needs of individual children and call in specialist help when necessary.
   7. Keep a balance between tasks and experiences from which the child can enjoy feelings of mastery and success and those other tasks and experiences which are a suitable and stimulating challenge, yet not likely to lead to discouraging failure.
   8. Assess levels of accomplishment against the norms of attainment for a developmental stage, taking into careful consideration the child's strengths, weaknesses, and learning and development opportunities.

D.   *Organizing and Sustaining the Positive Functioning of Children and Adults in a Learning Environment*
   1. Plan the activities program to include opportunities for playing and working together and sharing experiences and responsibilities with adults in a spirit of enjoyment for the sake of social development.
   2. Create an atmosphere, through example and attitude, where it is natural and acceptable to express feelings, both positive and negative — love, sympathy, enthusiasm, pain, frustration, loneliness, or anger.
   3. Establish a reasonable system of limits, rules, and regulations to be understood, honored, and protected by both children and adults, appropriate to the stage of development.
   4. Foster acceptance and appreciation of cultural variety by children and adults as an enrichment of personal experience; develop projects that use cultural variation in the family population as resource for the educational program.

E.   *Bringing About Optimal Coordination of Home and Center Child-Rearing Practices and Expectations*
   1. Incorporate important elements of the cultural backgrounds of the families being served, e.g., food, language, music, holidays, etc., into the children's program in order to provide continuity between home and center settings at this early stage of development.

Fig. 21-1 (continued)

2. Establish relationships with parents that facilitate the free flow of information about their children's lives inside and outside the center.

3. Communicate and interact with parents toward the goal of understanding and considering the priorities of their values for their children.

4. Perceive each child as a member of his or her particular family, and work with the family to resolve disagreements between the family's lifestyle with children and the center's handling of child behavior and images of good education.

5. Recognize and use the strengths and talents of parents as they contribute to the development of their own children, and give parents every possible opportunity to participate and enrich the group program.

F. *Carrying Out Supplementary Responsibilities Related to the Children's Programs*
   1. Make observations on the growth and development of individual children and changes in group behavior, formally or informally, verbally or in writing; share this information with other staff involved in the program.
   2. Engage with other staff in cooperative planning activities such as schedule or program changes indicated as necessary to meet the particular needs of a group of children or incorporation of new knowledge or techniques as they become available in the general field of early childhood education.
   3. Be aware of management functions, such as ordering supplies and equipment, scheduling staff time (helpers, volunteers, parent participants), monitoring food and transportation services; protect health and safety requirements; and transmit needs for efficient functioning to the responsible staff member or consultant.
   4. Affirm the value of education by being ready to take advantage of classroom and in-service opportunities for educational advancement when available.

Fig. 21-1 (continued)

Fig. 21-2 Praising correct responses and probing inappropriate answers will promote high levels of teaching performance. This is a teaching competency.

when responses are inappropriate, figure 21-2. Children need to know why they are praised, and/or how they should modify their behavior (Levin and Long, 1981, p. 21).

THE WHOLE TEACHER

Teaching competency growth can be compared to child growth. Teachers develop intellectually, social-emotionally, physically, and creatively as do children. Skills often omitted on competency listings yet which are becoming more and more important to early childhood teachers in our society are stress reduction and stress management techniques, holistic health awareness and practice, moral and ethical strength, researching skill, parenting education and family guidance counseling, public relations, and political "know-how." Job situations can create the need for skills not covered in your teacher training. As society changes, the early childhood teacher's role as a partner to parents in child education changes.

PERSONAL ABILITIES AND CHARACTERISTICS

What personal characteristics, traits, abilities, or "gifts" are desired in early childhood teachers? N.L. Gage describes teacher behaviors on the basis of experimental evidence of their relationship with desirable outcomes or aspects of teaching:

Warmth — By warmth we mean the tendency of the teacher to be approving, to provide emotional support, to express a sympathetic attitude, and accept the feelings of pupils.

Teaching behaviors include:
- non-threatening acceptance of child feelings.
- praises or encourages.
- jokes in ways that release tension.
- possess an inveterate incapacity to think poorly of other persons, especially children.
- relatively nonauthoritarian.
- low or non-existent jealousy of others.
- causes pupils to feel their goals, sensibilities, abilities, and interests are taken into account.

Cognitive Organization — He carries with him a set of "organizers" for his subject matter that provides him, and so his pupils, with "relevant ideational scaffolding" that discriminates new material from the previously learned and integrates it "at a level of abstraction, generality, and inclusiveness which is much higher than that of the learning material itself."

Teaching behaviors include:
- presents information so that clear, stable, and unambiguous meanings emerge and are retained.

Orderliness — By "orderliness" we mean the teacher's tendency to be systematic and methodical in his self-management.

Teaching behaviors include:
- responsible and businesslike rather than evading, unplanned, slipshod.

Indirectness — A tendency toward indirect methods of teaching consists in giving pupils opportunities to engage in overt behavior, such as talking and problem solving, relevant to the learning objectives rather than merely listening to their teacher and to discover ideas and solutions to problems rather than merely receiving them from the teacher.

Teaching behaviors include:
- accepts or uses student ideas.
- asks questions.
- stimulating, imaginative conversationalist.
- encourages pupil participation and initiative.
- permits pupils to discover.
- willingness to forbear furnishing every answer the pupil needs to know in an activity but not abandoning the pupil.
- providing guidance rather than the explicit to the learner in the form of verbal explanation.

Ability to Solve Instructional Problems — By ability to solve instructional problems we mean the teacher's ability to solve problems unique to his work in a particular subdivision of the profession.

Teacher behaviors include:
- pinpointing significant problem aspects.
- ease in finding successful solutions. (Gage, 1971, p. 11)

According to Don Hamachek (1969), effective teachers who have few discipline problems possess a sense of humor, are fair, empathetic, more democratic than autocratic, and are able to relate easily and naturally to pupils on any basis — group or one-to-one, figure 21-3. Teacher behaviors which exemplify the "effective teacher" include:
- Willingness to be *flexible*, to be direct or indirect as the situation demands.
- *Ability to perceive* the world from the student's point of view.
- Ability to *personalize* their teaching.
- Willingness to *experiment*, to try new things.
- Skill in *asking questions* (as opposed to seeing self as a kind of answering service).
- *Knowledge* of subject matter and related areas.
- Provision of *well-established* assessment procedures.
- Provision of definite study helps.
- Reflection of an *appreciative* attitude (evidenced by nods, comments, smiles, etc.).
- Use of *conversational manner* in teaching — informal, easy styles.

Fig. 21-3 Effective teachers can relate easily to the children on a one-to-one basis or as a group.

C.D.A. training materials specify the following personal capacities as essential for Child Development Associates:

- To be sensitive to children's feelings and the qualities of their thinking.
- To be ready to listen to children in order to understand them.
- To use nonverbal forms and adapt adult verbal language and style to maximize communication with the children.
- To be able to protect orderliness without sacrificing spontaneity and child-like exuberance.
- To be perceptive to individuality and make positive use of individual differences within the group.
- To be able to exercise control without being threatening.
- To be emotionally responsive, taking pleasure in children's successes and being supportive in their troubles and failures.
- To bring humor and imagination into the group situation.
- To feel committed to maximizing the child's and family's strengths and potentials.

SELF-PERCEPTION

Researchers have attempted to probe how "effective" or "good" teachers view their abilities and the abilities of others. If a teacher likes and trusts him or herself, that teacher is more likely to perceive others the same way. According to Hamachek,

> They seem to have generally more positive views of others — students, colleagues, and administrators. They do not seem to be as prone to view others as critical, attacking people with ulterior motives: rather they are seen as potentially friendly and worthy in their own right. They have a more favorable view of democratic classroom procedures. They seem to have the ability to see things as they seem to others — from the other's point of view. They do not seem to see students as children "you do things to" but rather as individuals capable of doing for themselves once they feel trusted, respected, and valued. (1969)

A. W. Combs cites the results of several studies dealing with the way "good" teachers typically see themselves:

- Good teachers see themselves as identified with people rather than withdrawn, removed, apart from, or alienated from others.
- Good teachers feel basically adequate rather than inadequate. They do not see themselves as generally unable to cope with problems.
- Good teachers feel trustworthy rather than untrustworthy. They see themselves as reliable, dependable individuals with the potential for coping with events as they happen.
- Good teachers see themselves as wanted rather than unwanted. They see themselves as likable and attractive (in a personal, not a physical sense) as opposed to feeling ignored and rejected.
- Good teachers see themselves as worthy rather than unworthy. They see themselves as people of consequence, dignity, and integrity as opposed to feeling they matter little, can be overlooked and discounted. (1965)

Students entering the field of teaching have their own ideas regarding qualities which are important for success. They include being able to communicate ideas; having interest in people; having a thorough knowledge of teaching skills; having a pleasing manner and creative ability; being able to get along well with colleagues (*New Patterns of Teacher Education and Tasks*, 1974).

You have received feedback from your cooperating teacher, your supervisor, and perhaps others. This input is the basis of your understanding of how your competencies are viewed by others. Your perception of your teaching competencies is formed based on your own self-analysis and others' feedback.

SELF-ANALYSIS

Self-analysis will increase your awareness of discrepancies and inconsistencies between your competency goals and your present teaching behavior. As you become more accurate in self-perception, your professional identity and confidence will grow. You may even be able to predict how others will react to your teaching behaviors. You will resolve the tendency to center on yourself (a common tendency of beginning teachers), and develop the ability to focus more on children's learning and teacher/child interactions.

Numerous self-rating scales exist; figure 21-4 is one example. Other examples can be found in the Appendix.

After assessment, you can decide what additional skills you would like to acquire, figure 21-5. Put these in order of their importance to you. You are the director of your learning and your plan for future accomplishment.

---

1. Do I work within policies and procedures established by the placement site?
2. Do I make use of knowledge and understanding of child development and curriculum in early childhood education?
3. What are my relationships with each child?
4. How do I manage small and large groups?
5. Do I use good judgment in situations?
6. Do I plan for appropriate blocks of time indoors and outdoors?
7. Do I make good use of indoor and outdoor space?
8. Do I provide for transitions and routines?
9. Do I add to the attractiveness of the playroom?
10. Do I take care of equipment?
11. Do I consider health and safety factors in planning my activities?
12. Do I offer a wide range of experiences so that children can make choices according to their interests and needs?
13. Do I allow for various levels of ability among children?
14. Do I know how and when to ask questions?
15. Do I talk too much?
16. Do I make adequate provisions for variety in planned activities?
17. Do I see myself as a member of a team?
18. Do I coordinate my efforts with those of my co-workers?
19. Am I able to assume full responsibility in the absence of co-workers?
20. Do I participate in staff meetings?
21. Am I able to transfer concepts from theoretical discussions at staff meetings and workshops to action in my own programs?
22. Do I find ways to help children understand the roles of other adults at school?
23. Do I maintain good professional relationships with parents?
24. Do I recognize the importance of seeing the child as a member of the family?
25. Do I share a child's experiences with the parents?
26. Do I know when to refer parents' or a child's problems to an appropriate person?
27. Do I experiment with note-taking systems to assist in planning, to evaluate growth, and to form the basis for written records?
28. Do I use the information in records appropriately?
29. Am I a member of at least one professional organization in the field?
30. Do I attend meetings conducted by professional groups?

Fig. 21-4 Student teachers' self-evaluation guide

Summary

"The whole teacher" is made of a vast array of possible teaching skills and abilities. Teaching competencies (performance objectives) have been identified by individuals and groups based on value judgments concerning appropriate or desirable teaching behaviors. There are many teaching competency lists in circulation; the C.D.A. list is the most widely accepted.

Fig. 21-5 Working with other adults may be a skill you feel is important.

Each student teacher gathers feedback on teaching skills from others and from self-analysis. Examples of self-rating scales were presented to aid the student's development of a plan of priorities for future competency growth.

Suggested Activities

A. Write a self-analysis.

B. Develop a plan which lists, in order of priority, competencies you would like to acquire.

C. Invite a C.D.A. representative to discuss the C.D.A. assessment process.

D. Work in groups of three or four to draw a "perfect teacher" comic on a large poster or blackboard. Translate your drawing to the rest of the class.

E. Read the following and briefly describe your reactions and comments. Share your ideas with the class.

> There is no perfect early childhood teacher. Only individual teachers with varying degrees of competence exist. Teacher training should magnify strengths, and produce teachers who differ greatly.

F. Complete the following statements.
 1. My present strengths (teaching competencies) include. . .
 2. My plan for developing more competencies includes working on. . .

G. Make a copy of the following exercise. Where do you belong on the line between each extreme? Draw a stick person somewhere on the line to indicate where you belong.

Talkative_____Quiet
Eager to please_____Self-assured
Outgoing _____ Shy

Punctual _____ Late
Accepting _____ Rejecting
Leader _____ Follower
Flexible_____ Rigid
Sense of humor _____ Serious
Organized_____ Disorganized
Academic_____ Nonstudious
Patient_____ Impatient
Warm_____Cool
Enthusiastic_____ Apathetic
Active _____ Passive
Open_____ Secretive
Direct   Indirect
communicator_____communicator
Autonomous_____Conformist
Creative_____Noncreative
Animated _____ Reserved
Talented _____ Average
Sexist _____ Nonsexist
Specialist _____ Generalist

Review

A. Choose the answer that best completes each statement.
 1. A student teacher
   a. needs to develop all the competencies which experts recognize.
   b. should strive to display all competencies.
   c. should develop an individualized plan for competency development.
   d. should rely completely on feedback gained through the comments of others when developing a professional growth plan.
   e. can ignore competencies which others consider important.
 2. Lists of teacher competencies are based on
   a. research studies which correlate teacher behaviors and child accomplishment.
   b. value judgments of individuals and/or groups.
   c. recognized teacher abilities and skills.
   d. the qualities parents feel are desirable in teachers.
   e. what teacher training programs produce in student teachers.

3. The most widely accepted list of teacher competencies for teachers of children under age five is
   a. Head Start teacher competencies.
   b. graduating level competencies.
   c. NAEYC competencies.
   d. ECE competencies.
   e. C.D.A. competencies.
4. A student teacher's view of competency best forms when
   a. others comment on student teaching episodes.
   b. children are watched for growth through the student teacher's planned activities or behavior.
   c. self-evaluation and feedback are combined.
   d. parents assess the student teacher's effectiveness.
   e. feedback includes comments from the entire staff.
5. The main purpose of developing plans to acquire other teaching skills is to
   a. facilitate growth.
   b. have student teachers learn all listed competencies.
   c. make student teachers realize their limitations.
   d. make student teachers realize their strengths.
   e. make sure the profession maintains quality performance.

C. Are there C.D.A. competencies which you feel are not important or applicable in your present placement classroom? What are they and why?

Resources

Byers, Loretta, and Iristi, Elizabeth. *Success in Student Teaching.* Lexington, MA: D.C. Heath and Company, 1961.

Combs, A.W. *The Professional Education of Teachers.* Boston: Allyn and Bacon, Inc., 1965.

Gage, N.L. "Desirable Behaviors of Teachers," from *Studying Teaching,* 2nd ed., ed. J. Raths, J. Poncella, and J. Van Ness. Englewood Cliffs, NJ: Prentice-Hall, Inc., 1971.

Hamachek, Don. "Characteristics of Good Teachers and Implications for Teacher Education." *Phi Delta Kappan* (Feb. 1969).

Levin, Tamar, and Long, Ruth. *Effective Instruction.* Alexandria, VA: The Association for Supervision and Curriculum Development, 1981.

New Patterns of Teacher Education and Tasks. Paris: Organization for Economic Cooperation and Development, 1974.

Tittle, Carol K. *Student Teaching.* Metuchen, NJ: The Scarecrow Press, Inc., 1974.

Section 8
Professional Concerns

Unit 22
Quality Programs

OBJECTIVES

After studying this unit, the student will be able to:

- List ten factors of a quality program.
- Describe the different types of quality programs.
- Discuss the relationship between a program's philosophy and quality.
- Discuss the importance of the teacher and director in a quality program.

MEETING CHILDREN'S NEEDS

Among the factors to consider regarding the quality of an early childhood program is whether the program meets each child's developmental needs. There must be an awareness of and attention to the needs of the children.

What are the needs of children during their early years? Accepting the validity of theories discussed in previous units, their needs are to self-actualize, to know and understand, and to develop aesthetically. Children need to trust the significant people in their environment, resolve the questions of autonomy and initiative, and learn to become industrious.

IMPLICATIONS ACCORDING TO MASLOW'S AND ERIKSON'S THEORIES Let us briefly return to the theories of Maslow and Erikson. What are the implications for a quality program in

regard to these theories? The first factor would be an environment in which the child's physical safety was considered. Quality programs have the physical environment arranged so that the children can explore without encountering physical dangers such as electric cords, tables with sharp edges, unprotected electric outlets that children could poke at, etc. In a quality program, the physical environment has been childproofed, figure 22-1.

The second factor is attention to the child's need for psychological safety. Essentially, a quality program should provide for predictability, decision opportunities, and reasonable limits. Predictability teaches the rudiments to learning about time and safety. With predictability comes the safety of knowing that certain activities will happen at certain times, such as snacktime, group time, indoor and outdoor play, etc.

Fig. 22-1 Preschool classrooms are busy; therefore, all possible hazards should be carefully considered.

Children have little control over their lives, and, in our modern industrial society, they have little opportunity to contribute to the family welfare. If, however, they have freedom of choice within the limits set, they can and do exert control over this part of their lives and thus learn how to make decisions. They also learn to accept the consequences of their decisions. Limits allow the child the safety of knowing what behavior is acceptable and not acceptable. Limits teach the child the concept of right versus wrong and help the child develop inner control over behavior, figure 22-2.

Fig. 22-2 Waiting patiently for turns is a classroom rule in this quality program.

A third factor is attention to belongingness and love needs. A quality program will provide for these. All children need to feel that they are a part of a social group; a preschool, day care center, and family can provide the sense of group identity that is so important for the young child's positive growth.

Esteem needs are met in a quality program. Care is taken by all staff members to ensure that the children's self-concepts are enhanced. Look to see how the workers in a program relate to the children. Do they CARE? Do they take time to listen to the children? Do they compliment children when they have accomplished some goal? Do they make a conscious effort to bolster the children's self-esteem?

Are self-actualization needs met? Quality programs have enough equipment and materials with which the children can interact. Are there enough art materials, books, and cut and paste opportunities? Is there a climbing apparatus? Are there tricycles and swings, enough so that no child has to wait too long? Are there enough puzzles? Are they challenging? Is the playhouse corner well-furnished? Are there enough props to stimulate sociodramatic play? Are there both large and small blocks? Is there a water table, a sand area, a terrarium, an aquarium, a magnifying glass? Are there enough small manipulatives? Are the play areas and yard clean and well-kept? Do the children look happy?

BALANCED PROGRAM   A quality program will have a balanced curriculum: language, motor activities, arts and crafts, storytime, music, creative movement, counting opportunities, matching pictures, colors, shapes, science opportunities; none of these is neglected in a quality program. Because of its importance, language will be emphasized in all curricular areas in a quality program. Look at and listen how language is used and encouraged. It is during the preschool years of two and one-half to five that the child makes the most progress in language. Having a vocabulary of maybe only 300 words at two and one-half years, the preschool child will expand this to perhaps 3,000 by age five. In receptive vocabulary, the 800 known by the two and one-half-year-old will grow to nearly 10,000 by age five. At the same time, the child is learning the syntactic rules of the language: present, past, and future tenses; the use of the negative form, the interrogatory form, and the conditional. All of this language ability is, for the most part, acquired without formal teaching. A quality program, however, recognizes this growth of language in the young child and provides opportunities for the child to hear language being used in proper context, to listen to models of language, and to practice growing language competencies. In addition, a quality program affords many opportunities for language enrichment, figure 22-3.

A quality program will have a quiet corner or private space for the children so that any child can be alone when necessary or desired. Children, especially those who spend long hours in a center every day, need time and space to be alone. Some children live in homes which afford them little or no privacy.

PERSONNEL AND PHILOSOPHIES Perhaps the most important factor in quality programs is the personality of the teacher and director, essentially the physical, mental, emotional, and social characteristics. Is this a person who really *likes* children? Does this person appear to be upbeat? Are there "laugh lines" in the corners of the eyes? Does this person smile when talking? Does there appear to be a mutual respect among this person

and the children? When talking to the children, does this person stoop in order to be at their level? Is this person *with* the children or *over* the children? Is this a person trained in child development? A warm, loving, knowledgeable teacher and director can make almost any program — public or private — a quality one, given the space and materials with which to work.

The second most important factor is the underlying philosophy of the program, the basic principles by which the program is guided. Are there stated objectives? Is there a written statement of philosophy? Is the curriculum based upon a knowledge of child development principles? Are there printed materials describing the program in terms of what the teacher and director want for the children? Or is this a program with no statement of purpose, no written goals, no clear curriculum? Worse yet, is this a program which assumes that you know all you need to know about the program on the basis of its label, e.g., Montessori, Christian?

Beware of any program which uses a name and has no written philosophy or goals. Beware, also, of a program whose stated goals are not congruent with child development principles. Watch out for the program whose philosophy does not stress respect and love for each child. Beware of any program in which helping children acquire strong self-concepts is not listed as a goal. Be wary of a program in which one part of the curriculum is overemphasized at the expense of the others. A cognitive curriculum is fine *if* attention is also given to the child's social, emotional, and physical growth needs as well.

Fig. 22-3 A quality program provides many opportunities to explore literature.

STANDARDS OF QUALITY PROGRAMS

To assist you as a student teacher, there are many published source materials available. The National Association for the Education of Young Children (NAEYC), for example, publishes a leaflet "Some Ways of Distinguishing a Good Early Childhood Program." The factors discussed are:

1. There is ample indoor and outdoor space: about 35 square feet of free space per child indoors and 100 square feet of space per child outdoors.
2. Safe, sanitary, and healthy conditions must be maintained.
3. The child's health is protected and promoted.
4. A good center helps children to develop wholesome attitudes toward their own bodies and bodily functions.
5. The importance of continuity in the lives of young children is recognized without overstressing routines or rigid programming.
6. A good center provides appropriate and sufficient equipment and play materials and makes them readily available for each child's enjoyment and development (figure 22-4).
7. Children are encouraged to use materials to gradually increase their skills for constructive and creative processes.
8. Children are helped to increase their use of language and to expand their concepts.
9. Opportunities for the child's social and emotional development are provided.
10. Because young children are so closely linked to their fathers and mothers, a good center considers the needs of both parents and children.
11. Consideration is given to the entire family's varying needs, along with special recognition for the growth and protection of the child enrolled.
12. There are enough adults both to work with the group and to care for the needs of individual children.
13. A good center does more than meet the minimum standards set for licensing by the state and/or federal regulating agency.
14. Staff members have a positive outlook on life. They realize that human feelings are most important.
15. The adults in a good center enjoy and understand children and the process by which they learn.
16. Because the entire staff has a direct or indirect influence on each child, all members try to work with one another.
17. In a good center, staff are alert to observing and recording each child's progress and development.
18. The good center uses all available community resources and participates in joint community efforts (figure 22-5).

(Reprinted by permission from NAEYC. Copyright © 1981, National Association for the Education of Young Children, 1834 Connecticut Avenue N.W., Washington, D.C. 20009.)

Fig. 22-4 Quality programs have innovative and inviting outdoor climbing structures.

Fig. 22-5 Quality programs often encourage parent participation.

In studying this list, it is easy to see that, although not specifically stated, Maslow's hierarchy of needs is considered. Erikson's developmental tasks have been considered as well. NAEYC's list, however, goes beyond simply relating conditions to developmental theory. It also introduces the importance of looking at minimum standards as set by governmental authorities, suggesting that a good program exceeds such minimal standards. For example, federal or state standards may suggest that a ratio of twelve children (two- and three-year-olds) to one adult is sufficient. A quality program may have eight to ten children for every adult.

Although a school cannot become licensed without meeting minimum standards regarding indoor and outdoor space, there are programs which *average* the number of children throughout the day and exceed the minimum recommended number during hours of prime use. For example, a day care center may be licensed for twenty-eight children and have as few as ten present at 8:00 a.m. and eight at 5:45 p.m.; yet, they may have as many as thirty-four present between 10:00 a.m. and 3:00 p.m. The total number of children present throughout the day may be averaged so that a parent may never be aware of the overcrowding at midday. Some centers will employ a nutrition aide at lunchtime to assist in meal preparation. Although this person may never work with the children, he or she may be counted as an adult when figuring the ratio of children to adults. Many parents are unaware of these types of practices, none of which would be present in a quality program.

TYPES OF QUALITY PROGRAMS

It is important to recognize that there are many different types of early childhood programs; each one may be of quality. There are, for example, day care centers; state preschool programs; Head Start and Montessori programs; parent-cooperatives; and private, nonprofit and profit-making preschools and primary schools. In each of these, a student teacher or parent can find good programs, mediocre programs, and, unfortunately, poor programs.

Programs reflect the underlying philosophy of their director, head teacher, or proprietor. It takes time to interview and observe carefully in order to determine quality. One may discover, upon close observation, that children have no freedom of choice as to what toys they will play with, that they are, instead, assigned toys. It is also easy to be deceived by a glib promotional director, head teacher, or proprietor. Smooth talk and right answers do not make a quality program. Look carefully when presented with a persuasive director. Is this person putting into action policies which are in the interest of the children?

We are reminded of a private day care center in which there are many toys and materials for the children to play with. There is also a lot of space both indoors and outdoors. Yet, it is not a quality center and does not run a quality program. Why? Unfortunately, the owner has little or no background in early childhood education and, in an effort to keep down costs, employs two teachers who only *meet* minimum state standards for licensing. These teachers are underpaid; consequently, there is a high rate of turnover. The owner also brings her own child to the center and has difficulty relating to any child who does not play well with hers.

There is no easy answer to "policing" poor or mediocre programs. The day care center in the preceding example is the only one in a lower-middle-class neighborhood. There are many single parents in this neighborhood. In families with two parents, usually both parents work. Due to transportation difficulties and a lack of room in and eligibility for the community's well-known quality centers, this center is the only one available.

WHO DECIDES THE QUALITY OF A PROGRAM?

As we suggested, the director has a responsibility regarding the quality of a program. Indirectly, parents also have a say in a program's quality. Obviously, there would be no program without clients (parents). Thus, if a client buys an inferior service (education), he or she has the choice to stop using it. The solution is, however, not always so simple. Parents may not have many options in terms of the immediate neighborhood. This may be compounded by the parents' lack of knowledge; they may judge a program by its external appearance, e.g., its cleanliness, personal perceptions of the director's competence.

Quality is also dependent upon the type of program. For example, in a program sponsored by a public school district, quality is determined not only by a director or teacher but also by government regulations, by the principal in whose school the program is located, and, ultimately, by the local board of education and its policies.

A public program must adhere to prescribed standards. However, in most public schools, ultimate quality depends upon the teacher and the supervising principal. In a private program, quality may depend upon several people. In a proprietary preschool, quality is related to the personality and training of the proprietor. Is this person a loving, caring human being? Does this person have formal training in early childhood education, or does he or she hire people who are loving and caring and have formal training? In any proprietary school, you will find the same range of quality as in a public program.

Who determines quality in a Montessori program, for example? Does the name, Montessori, promise that all its programs will have the same standards, the same quality? In the United States, there are two main approaches to Montessori education, both of which are called Montessori schools. One branch is the schools which are under the sponsorship of the Associatione Montessori Internationale (AMI), with headquarters in Switzerland and headed by Maria Montessori's son. AMI schools adhere very closely to Maria Montessori's original curriculum. Its teachers are trained in the philosophy, with the didactic (teaching) materials designed by Dr. Montessori herself. In AMI schools, you will generally find the same materials being used regardless of where the school is located. You will also find that the teachers have basically the same training in philosophy and methodology. Still, there will be differences in quality. Just as in the public schools or in the proprietary centers, quality will depend, to a large extent, upon the teacher's personality. Does the teacher really *like* children? Does that person CARE? Are the children happy? Look carefully.

The other type of Montessori program is sponsored by the American Montessori Society (AMS), whose headquarters are in New York State. AMS schools are less like the original Montessori schools in that, although they use the didactic materials developed by Dr. Montessori, they make use of modern trends toward a greater emphasis on gross motor and social development. AMS programs vary widely; the personalities of the directors and teachers are the important factors.

Another determining factor is who or what organization sponsors the school. Many churches sponsor schools and day care programs. In this case, quality depends not only on the personality of the director and teachers but upon the philosophy of the sponsoring church. Church-sponsored schools can also be excellent, mediocre, and poor. The teachers or day care workers can make the difference.

Summary

In this unit, we attempted to provide guidelines by which you can evaluate the quality of an early childhood education program. We have suggested that a quality program is one which takes into consideration the developmental needs of the children and which exceeds, rather than meets, minimum standards for state licensing. We have also suggested that quality programs may be found in many different settings ranging from federally funded programs to parent-cooperatives and proprietary profit-making centers. Any of these programs can be good or bad.

We also presented the eighteen factors listed by the NAEYC, and noted how they met the developmental needs of the children and their families.

Quality programs depend upon you, as student teachers. You need to strive to preserve and improve upon these programs when you enter the field. Quality programs can exist only if quality people fight for them.

Suggested Activities

A. Visit at least three different types of early childhood programs: a Montessori school, a Head Start program, and a proprietary day care center. Evaluate them based on the eighteen factors of a good program from NAEYC. Are the programs equally good? Why?

B. Summarize your evaluations of the programs you choose to observe. Discuss your ideas with your peers and supervisor.

C. Read Maria Montessori's *The Montessori Method.* Discuss your comments with your peers and supervisor. Compare the program you visited with the ideas found in the book.

Review

A. List ten features of a quality early childhood program.

B. Read each of the following descriptions of different early childhood programs. Decide whether each paragraph is describing a quality program, a mediocre program, or a poor program. If you do not have sufficient data to make a decision, indicate this. Discuss your answers and opinions with peers and college supervisor.

1. This private preschool/day care center is located in a former public school. Each morning the director greets every child as they enter. Each child has a wide choice of activities to play with. Clay containers are placed on one table; crayon boxes and paper on another; scissors, old magazines, and scraps of construction paper are on a third, with sheets of blank paper and paste pots. Some children prefer to go to the block area, the book corner, or housekeeping corner. The outside play area beckons those who wish to climb, ride, swing, or play at the water table or in the sand box.

   The director as a degree in early childhood education as does the only paid aide. Parents are seen often, both fathers and mothers stay with their children for a few minutes. The director speaks to each parent and sends home a monthly newsletter to inform parents of special activities and to solicit help for special projects. (For example, both the indoor and outdoor climbing structures were built by parents.)

   The director carefully interviews every prospective family who wishes to place their children in the center. The director insists upon at least one visit by both parents and the child before final acceptance. Prospective parents receive a written statement of philosophy and curriculum. During these meetings, the director has been known to state, "I expect parents to interview me as carefully as I interview them."

2. This after-school program is sponsored by a franchised nonprofit organization. The director of the program has an AA degree in early childhood education. Certified teachers or C.D.A. holders work with the children (ages five to nine). In addition, there are many volunteers recruited from a local community college and high school. The program is located in empty classrooms in four elementary schools and in the nonprofit organization's main facility.

   Because the latter facility does not meet state standards, children are asked to join the organization. As a result, the organization is exempt from having to meet standards. For example, although there is ample outside play area at the school sites, there is none at the main facility site. This after-school program has a written statement of purpose and goals, a conceptual outline covering such items as safety, self-image, adult role models, a stimulating environment, etc.; a parent advisory group; and a daily schedule listing curriculum factors. The adult to child ratio is listed as 15:1 but has been known to exceed 25:1 when volunteers have been absent.

   The program schedules free time for the first thirty minutes so that the children can unwind from their school day. This is followed by snack time, activity time (arts and crafts, gymnastics, swimming, field trips, etc.), clean-up time, and free time during which quiet activities such as games, reading, homework, and drawing can be done.

3. This Montessori program (AMS) is located in the parish hall of a church. The director is a breezy, enthusiastic woman whose wealthy father sponsored her investment in the school. She received some training at the American Montessori Schools Center in New York, but she does not hold any degree. Her school has the usual Montessori

equipment, and children can be seen quietly engaged in a variety of the typical self-directed activities — fitting shapes into a board, placing cylinders of various sizes into the appropriate holes, washing dolls' clothes on the washboard, sweeping the walk, etc. One boy intrigues the observer; he is busy peeling carrots with a peeler and is very intent.

The director spends much time talking on the phone with friends; most of the instruction is left to the aides. She recently attended an EST seminar, and is anxious for her employees to do the same. She is not willing, however, to pay their way. The turnover among her employees is high; she pays an aide only minimum wage.

The children in the program appear subdued and do not display much spontaneity. At least one parent has removed a child from the program because the director ridiculed the child's obesity.

Unit 23
Professional Commitment and Growth

OBJECTIVES

After studying this unit, the student will be able to:

- Define professionalism.
- Explain the importance of acquiring a sense of professional commitment.
- List four alternative activities which promote individual professional growth.
- Name one early childhood professional association and describe the benefits of membership.

As a student teacher, you are already considered a professional. Professionals are those individuals whose work is predominantly nonroutine and intellectual in character. They make constant decisions which call for a substantial degree of discretion and judgment. Professional status is gained through a display and application of professionally recognized teaching skills and techniques. Admittedly, some of your skills are new, emerging, and wobbly, while others are definitely observable. You are currently being measured against standards established by those in the same profession.

PRIDE IN PROFESSION

Your teaching day includes tasks which, on the surface, appear custodial in nature such as helping at clean-up time, supervising the children as they wash their hands, serving snack, and encouraging them to rest. Each is a learning time for children, and your professional skill is at work. Helping a child who is struggling to slip on a sweater is done in a professional way and is an opportunity to help the child become more independent.

A teacher's pride in the profession is justified. Stevens and King describe the importance of a teacher's respect for the job.

The teacher of young children should see himself or herself as indispensable in the pivotal aspects of early childhood learning. Pride in one's profession and the attitude that it is one of the most vital jobs in our contemporary society cannot be over-stressed. (1976)

After student teaching, you will know that the job of an early childhood teacher is demanding, challenging, complex, necessitates constant decisions, and can be physically and emotionally taxing as well as being highly satisfying and rewarding.

The early childhood teaching profession should attract and hold the best candidates our society has to offer — "dedicated, conscientious, highly qualified, and highly trained men and women" — who work with our society's most prized resource and hope for the future — children and families (Stevens and King, 1976, p. 146).

PROFESSIONAL BEHAVIOR AND COMMITMENT

Professionalism, Betty Sawyers states, entails understanding both children and yourself plus "plain old hard work." She has identified some of the demands that "pros" make on themselves and their behavior:

1. Being a professional requires that you give full measure of devotion to the job.
2. Being a professional means you don't need rules to make you act like a professional.
3. A professional accepts responsibilities assigned to her with as much grace as she can muster up and then works in a positive way to change those duties that deter her teaching.
4. A professional joins with others in professional organizations which exchange research and ideas on how children learn and institute action which benefits all children.
5. A professional is aware of his prejudices and makes a concerted effort to get rid of them.
6. A professional treats children as people with feelings.
7. A real professional speaks up for the child when he needs somebody to speak out for him.
8. A professional is an educator who is informed about modern trends in education. (1971)

Each teacher's commitment to teaching could be placed on a continuum, figure 23-1. Where would you place yourself? Probably at the high end; student teachers spend long hours both in and out of their classrooms and may feel that they are barely hanging on. This feeling can continue through the first year on the job. Lillian Katz describes a new teacher's inner thoughts as being preoccupied with survival.

Can I get through the day in one piece? Without losing a child? Can I make it until the end of the week — the next vacation? Can I really do this kind of work day after day? Will I be accepted by my colleagues? (1972)

Anxieties stem from a desire to become a professional while at the same time questioning one's stamina, endurance, and capability to do so. Your commitment to the profession will be nourished by the supportive adults which surround you in your student teaching experience. According to Katz, student teachers vary greatly in the length of time spent in the survival stage. You may have already passed through "a mini survival stage" in student teaching and moved onto consolidation, Katz's Stage II. Figure 23-2 illustrates Katz's stages and possible teacher training needs.

Severe tests to a student teacher's professional commitment may happen if a placement site models attitudes which downgrade the value and worth of the profession. A good grasp on professional conduct and commitment helps the student teacher sort out less than professional behavior. Improved and continued high standards in the profession depend upon the newly trained professionals' enthusiasm, idealism, knowledge, and skills and the experienced professionals' leadership. Newly trained professionals can strengthen the field through their identification with practicing, committed professionals.

A code of ethics for the early childhood education profession offers a concise listing of standard professional behaviors, figure 23-3.

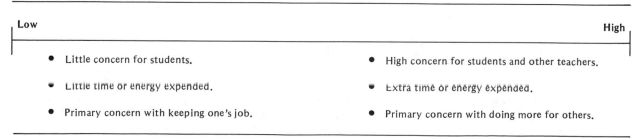

Fig. 23-1 Commitment continuum (Reprinted with permission of the Association for Supervision and Curriculum Development and Carl D. Glickman. Copyright © 1981 by the Association for Supervision and Curriculum Development. All rights reserved.)

Fig. 23-2 Stages of development and training needs of preschool teachers (From "Developmental Stages of Pre-school Teachers" by Lillian Katz. *The Elementary School Journal*, Feb. 1972.)

Commitment to Children and Parents

We work to increase the quality of each child's life, and establish and maintain a partnership with the child's family.

In fulfilling our duties and responsibilities, we:

1. Deal justly and considerately with each child.
2. Encourage individuality and promote uniqueness.
3. Offer an educational program and/or environment which helps each child in our care grow and develop.
4. Constantly seek to improve opportunities for learning.
5. Strive to preserve and increase each child's positive view of individual value, worth, and competence.
6. Promote child independence and self-help when appropriate.
7. Value child problem solving.
8. Design classrooms to satisfy individual and group needs.
9. Keep all information confidential unless we deem that its release serves a professional purpose or benefits a child or family.
10. Provide a caring, supportive environment, accepting and respecting each child and parent.
11. Believe in the integrity of each human being and respect differing values.
12. Oppose any form of discrimination based on race, sex, religion, ethnic origin, or handicapping conditions.
13. Resolve to ensure a developmental curriculum which maximizes each child's opportunities.

In fulfilling our obligations to the profession, we:

1. Recognize that a professional center must accept responsibility for the conduct of its members and understand that our own conduct is representative.
2. Strive to uphold and raise education standards and increase growth opportunities for young children.
3. Believe the quality of the services provided by early childhood educators directly influences the future of our nation and its citizens.
4. Exercise professional judgment.
5. Encourage conditions which attract and keep dedicated and competent individuals to careers in early childhood education.
6. Work for professional status and recognition of this stage of education.

Fig. 23-3 Proposed code of ethics for early childhood educators

PROFESSIONAL GROWTH

Early childhood teaching offers each professional a lifelong learning challenge. The goal of professional growth includes the unfolding of potentials and achieving greater self-actualization. True self-actualization leads to an increasing sense of responsibility and a deepening desire to serve humanity (Vargiu, 1978).

Maslow has described the conflict individuals face as they struggle toward increasing excellence.

> Every human being has both sets of forces within him. One set clings to safety and defensiveness out of fear, tending to regress backward, hanging on to the past. . .afraid to grow away from primitive communication with mother uterus and breast, afraid to take chances, afraid to jeopardize what he already has, afraid of independence, freedom and separateness. The other set of forces impels him forward toward wholeness of Self and uniqueness of Self, toward full functioning of all his capacities, toward confidence in the face of the external world at the same time he can accept his deepest, real, unconscious Self. (in Anderson and Shane's *As the Twig is Bent*, 1971)

Your management of professional growth planning is dependent upon you. When your future job includes promotional, material, or rewarding incentives, it may add impetus. Your attitude toward your professionalism will give a high priority to activities which contribute to your skill development.

As a professional, you will actively pursue growth. Maslow describes the struggle and possible outcomes of your pursuit.

> Therefore we can consider the process of healthy growth to be a never ending series of free choice situations, confronting each individual at every point throughout his life, in which he must choose between the delights of safety and growth, dependence and independence, regression and progression, immaturity and maturity. (in Anderson and Shane's *As the Twig is Bent*, 1971)

Your efforts to grow professionally will become part of your life's pattern. You will experience the "tugs and pulls" of finding the time and energy to follow your commitment.

INDIVIDUAL LEARNING CYCLES

Just as you have watched children take enormous steps in learning one day and just mark time another, your professional growth may not be constant and steady. Harrison observed the phenomenon of "risk and retreat" in self-directed learning.

> The learning cycle is our name for the natural process of advance and retreat in learning. We observed early in our experiments with self-directed learning that individuals would move out and take personal risks and then would move back to reflect and integrate the experience. (1978)

Reflection or standing still at times may give ideas time to hatch. Being aware of your own creative "idea hatching" can make you more aware of this creative process in children (Alexander, 1978).

Many other factors will influence the ebb and flow of your future growth as a teacher. The energy draining nature of preschool teaching's demanding work can sometimes dampen enthusiasm for future growth as can the attitudes of those with whom you work. You may periodically need contacts with other professionals to rekindle your commitment.

GROWTH OPPORTUNITIES

At times when the enthusiasm for teaching seems to dwindle, teachers need to pursue other courses of action to refreshen their excitement and eagerness to learn and grow. Early childhood teachers have a wide range of alternative routes to professional growth. For example:

- Additional credit coursework, advanced degrees
- Apprenticing and exchanging teachers
- Independent study
- Visitation and travel
- Professional group membership

Fig. 23-4 Study sessions promote teacher growth.

- Workshops, meetings, and skill and study sessions, figure 23-4
- In-service training
- Conferences

ADDITIONAL COURSEWORK Credit and noncredit college coursework leads to advanced skill and degrees. Coursework frequently results in on-the-job application of ideas, spreading enthusiasm throughout a preschool center. Get on the mailing list of all educational institutions in your area offering early childhood classes. Local college career placement centers and/or counseling centers provide a review of college catalogs and bulletins. Coursework descriptions and particulars can be examined for all colleges.

APPRENTICING AND DEMONSTRATING AND EXCHANGING TEACHING You may know a teacher with whom you would like to study and whose direction and tutelage could be growth producing. Volunteering in this teacher's classroom offers opportunities for closer examination of techniques. It may be possible to earn college credit through enrolling in a cooperative work experience program or independent study course; check your local college.

In a demonstration-teaching arrangement, you watch and discuss methods with practicing teachers. Hearing explanations and asking questions gives insight into different ways to accomplish teaching goals. Most professionals will provide this type of short-term arrangement.

Exchanging teachers within a school is sometimes considered growth producing. New partnerships stimulate new blends of techniques. Many schools permit a shifting of staff members, enabling gifted and talented teachers to share their ideas. Cross-matching and lively discussions act as healthy catalysts.

INDEPENDENT STUDY Self-planned study allows one to choose the subject, sequence, depth, and breadth of professional growth. Your home library will grow yearly, funds permitting! You will spend much time reading books and other material. These resources will be a tribute to your professional commitment. Professional journals and magazines provide research articles and practical suggestions. A brief list of periodicals follows:

- *Young Children* (bimonthly publication of NAEYC. See professional organization list.)
- *Day Care and Early Education*
- *Child Care Quarterly*
- *Early Years*
- *Teacher*
- *Child Study Journal*
- *Children Today*
- *American Education Research Journal*
- *First Teacher*

Organization and association newsletters, figure 23-5, carry timely information of interest.

A starting point for independent study may be the bibliographies and book titles you collected during your training.

VISITATION AND TRAVEL Other teachers' classrooms will always be a valuable resource and study possibility. Observing other classrooms offers good ideas, clever solutions, and provocative discoveries. Conferences often schedule tours of local outstanding programs.

Almost every country has group child care, and you probably developed a list of programs in your own community you would like to observe. The professional courtesy of allowing observers is widespread. Directors and staff members frequently

Building Blocks
Child Care Task Force
1400 East 53rd Street
Chicago, IL 60615

Bulletin of the Center for Children's Books
The University of Chicago Press
5801 Ellis Avenue
Chicago, IL 60637

The Calendar
Children's Book Council, Inc.
67 Irving Place
New York, NY 10003

Child Care Information Exchange
Child Care Information Exchange
Belmont, MA 02178

Day Care and Child Development Reports
Plus Publications
2626 Pennsylvania Avenue, NW
Washington, DC 20037

High Scope Resource
High/Scope Educational Resource Foundation
600 North River Street
Ypsilanti, MI 48197

*A Guide to Selected Newsletters and Journals
in Early Childhood*
ERIC Clearinghouse
805 W. Pennsylvania Ave.
Urbana, IL 61801

Educational Researcher
American Educational Research Association
1126 Sixteenth Street, NW
Washington, DC 20036

ERIC Clearinghouse on Elementary Childhood Education
University of Illinois
805 W. Pennsylvania Ave.
Urbana, IL 61801

Children
Division of Public Education
Office of Child Development
Department of Health, Education, and Welfare
PO Box 1182
Washington, DC 20013

Report on Educational Research
Capitol Publications, Inc.
2430 Pennsylvania Ave., NW, Suite G-12
Washington, DC 20037

Report on Preschool Education
Capitol Publications, Inc.
2430 Pennsylvania Ave., NW, Suite G-12
Washington, DC 20037

PEN — The Preschool Education Newsletter
Multimedia Education, Inc.
11 West 42nd Street
New York, NY 10036

E.C.E. Options
255 North Rd., #110
Chelmsford, MA 01824

The Training Center
PO Box 403
Palatine, IL 60067

Building Blocks — Child Care Edition
314 Liberty Street
Box 31
Dundee, IL 60118

Fig. 23-5 List of newsletters

provide guided tours which include explanation and discussions of goals, program components, and teaching philosophies.

PROFESSIONAL GROUP MEMBERSHIP
You will find professional early childhood group membership to be one of the best ways to locate skill development opportunities. A common goal of professional associations and organizations is to provide educational services and resources to members, figure 23-6.

Association publications are generally reasonably priced and current. Publication listings are available upon request from main office headquarters.

There are special student membership rates, and joining a local affiliate or branch group during student teaching is highly recommended. Association newsletters will keep you informed of activities and developments of interest to professionals.

The advantages of local professional membership are numerous. Workshops, study sessions, and conferences provide favorable circumstances for

AERA (American Educational Research Association, 1126 Sixteenth St., NW, Washington, DC 20036) An organization of educators and behavioral scientists interested in the development, application, and improvement of educational research. The association has a special interest group on early education and child development.

ACEI (Association for Childhood Education International, 3615 Wisconsin Ave., NW, Washington, DC 20016) Members include teachers, parents, and others interested in promoting good educational practices for children from infancy through early adolescence.

AMS (American Montessori Society, Inc., 175 Fifth Ave., New York, NY 10010) An organization which focuses on Maria Montessori's approach to early learning, which emphasizes providing children with purposeful work in an environment prepared with self-educative, manipulative learning devices for language, math, science, practical life, etc.

BCDI (Black Child Development Institute, Inc., 1463 Rhode Island Ave., NW, Washington, DC 20005) BCDI focuses on promoting black child development programs and providing technical assistance to day care centers whose children are predominantly black. Members serve as advocates of community development programs throughout the United States.

CDA (Child Development Associate Consortium, Inc., Suite 601-East, 7315 Wisconsin Ave., Washington, DC 20014) A private nonprofit organization (funded by the Office of Child Development) made up of approximately forty national associations. The consortium is concerned with the education and development of young children, the needs of children from minority populations, parents' concerns, and child care staff training and certification.

CEC (Council for Exceptional Children, 1920 Association Drive, Reston, VA 20091) An organization of teachers, school administrators, and teacher educators focusing on the concerns of children who are gifted; retarded; visually, auditorily, or physically handicapped; or who have behavioral disorders, learning disabilities, or speech defects.

CWLA (Child Welfare League of America, Inc., 67 Irving Place, New York, NY 10010) A federation of public and private child care agencies organized to raise the standards of child care, adoption, and foster family care.

DCCDCA (Day Care and Child Development Council of America, Inc. National Headquarters: The Children's Embassy, 622 14th St., NW, Washington, DC 20005) A nonprofit membership advocacy organization aimed at increasing the availability of children's services and raising the quality of child care programs through development of grass roots involvement and education. Services include the dissemination of information and publications and technical assistance to child care projects and community organizations.

Dissemination Center for Bilingual/Bicultural Education (6504 Tracor Lane, Austin, TX 78721) Staff members of this center collect and publish curriculum materials developed in bilingual programs and disseminate monthly annotated bibliographies of multicultural materials.

NAEYC (National Association for the Education of Young Children, 1834 Connecticut Ave., NW, Washington, DC 20009) An organization established to act on behalf of the needs and rights of children (birth to eight years), with primary focus on providing educational services and resources. Members are teachers, program directors, and others involved in nursery schools, day care centers, cooperatives, church groups, play groups, and similar groups with programs for young children.

Fig. 23-6 Resources, organizations, and associations

NCOCY (National Council of Organizations for Children and Youth, 1910 K St., NW, Suite 404, Washington, DC 20006) A coalition of organizations concerned with the needs of children and youth. The council serves as a clearinghouse of information and provides consultation, technical assistance, and other services to member organizations.

OCD (Office of Child Development, U.S. Department of Health and Human Services, PO Box 1182, Washington, DC 20013) Responsible for long-range planning and development of concepts in children's and parents' programs and legislation affecting children.

PCPI (Parent Cooperative Preschools International, 9111 Alton Parkway, Silver Spring, MD 20910) An organization of individuals and groups interested in promoting the exchange of resources and information among persons involved in cooperative nursery schools, kindergartens and other parent-sponsored preschool groups.

SACUS (Southern Association for Children Under Six, Box 5403 Brady Station, Little Rock, AR 72205) Serves the interests of Southerners concerned with child development, such as university researchers and teacher educators, kindergarten, nursery school, and day care teachers, school administrators, and proprietors of nursery schools and day care centers.

SRCD (Society for Research in Child Development, 5801 Ellis Ave., Chicago, IL 60637) A professional interdisciplinary society established to further research conducted in the area of child development. Members include anatomists, anthropologists, dentists, educators, nutritionists, pediatricians, physiologists, psychiatrists, psychologists, sociologists, and statisticians.

ERIC/ECE (Educational Resources Information Center, Early Childhood Education, 805 West Pennsylvania Ave., Urbana, IL 61801) Collects and catalogs material of interest to early childhood educators.

World Organization for Early Childhood Education (81 Irving Place, New York, NY 10003) Concerned with research and improving conditions affecting young children. Encourages workshops and study groups improving teacher education.

Fig. 23-6 (continued)

professional development. There are opportunities to meet other professionals, discuss views and concerns, and jointly solve problems. The talents of early childhood experts are tapped for the benefit of all the members.

A fascinating and exhilarating experience awaits the student teacher upon first attending a national conference. There will be so much to see and sample, so many inspiring ideas, materials, and equipment to examine a virtual overdose of stimuli that wholesomely feeds your attempt to grow.

WORKSHOPS, MEETINGS, SKILL AND STUDY SESSIONS Workshops, skill sessions, and meetings are smaller versions of state and national conferences. Diverse and varied, they cover topics related to early childhood. Practical "how-to's," theoretical presentations, and advocacy concern meetings are popular.

Identification with the spirit of professionalism, which can be defined as striving for excellence, motivates many of the attending participants. Most communities schedule many professional growth meetings each year and encourage student teacher attendance.

IN-SERVICE TRAINING In-service training sessions are designed to suit the training needs of a particular group of teachers and/or caregivers. They are arranged by sponsoring agencies or employers. Typically, consultants and specialists lead, guide, plan, and present skill development sessions and/or

assessments of program components. There is usually no fee, and attendance is mandatory. Often staffs decided the nature and scope of the in-service training, and paid substitutes free staff members from child supervision duties.

Summary

Student teachers strive for recognition of their professional skills and try to achieve standards established by those in the same profession. Pride in the early childhood profession grows as student teachers realize the dedication and skills of others already teaching. The important contribution the profession makes to children, families, and society cannot be overrated. The commitment to continually update, and gain additional skills begins in training and continues for a lifetime. Each professional teacher is responsible for his or her own unique growth planning schedule.

Many activity choices leading to advanced skills are available, and most professionals engage in a wide variety. Additional coursework and training, professional group membership, conference and workshop attendance, in-service training, visitation, and exchange teaching lead to the learning and discovering of new techniques. Social interactions in educative settings reinforce individual teachers' commitment to professionalism.

Suggested Activities

A. Name three books related to early childhood teaching that you plan to read.

B. Get on the mailing list for early childhood education publications.

C. In groups of four to six, develop a wallchart which lists factors that promote professionalism and those that impede professionalism in early childhood teachers.

D. Rate each statement based on the following scale. Discuss your results with the class.

strongly agree 1	mildly agree 2	cannot decide 3	mildly disagree 4	strongly disagree 5

1. Being professional includes proper make-up and clothing at work.
2. It is unprofessional to keep using the same techniques over and over.
3. Professional commitment is more important than professional growth.
4. Professional growth can involve coursework which does not pertain to children and/or families.
5. A teacher can grow professionally by studying children in the classroom.
6. Professional association fees are so expensive that student teachers can rarely afford to join.
7. One of the real causes for the lack of status of early childhood teachers is their own attitudes toward professional growth.
8. It is difficult to feel like a professional when salaries are so low.
9. Most teachers who pursue professional skills receive little recognition for their efforts.
10. You can learn all you need to know about handling children's behavior by watching a master teacher.

E. Invite a panel of practicing teachers to discuss the topic, "Best Ways to Grow Professionally."

F. Investigate groups in your community that schedule skill sessions, workshops, or meetings offering growth opportunities to early childhood teachers. Report your findings to the class.

Review

A. Name four benefits of professional group membership.

B. Match items in Column I with those in Column II.

I	II
1. rate of teacher growth	a. Katz's Stage II
2. commitment	b. code of ethics
3. standards	c. advances and retreats
4. consolidation	d. depends on individual's activities
5. learning cycle	e. ranges from low to high
6. professionals	f. constant intellectual decisions
7. apprenticing	g. expert advice
8. visitation	h. on-site training
9. workshops	i. studying with another
10. in-service training	j. professional courtesy

C. Select the answer that best completes each statement.

1. Based on Katz's "stages of development," student teachers are in the
   a. renewal stage.
   b. maturity stage.
   c. survival stage.
   d. consolidation stage.
   e. confusion stage.

2. Of the following entries, all are well-known early childhood professional associations except
   a. NAEYC (National Association for the Education of Young Children).
   b. ACEI (Association for Childhood Education International).
   c. AERA (American Educational Research Association).
   d. SACUS (Southern Association for Children Under Six).
   e. DLIHQC (Democratic League Interested in High Quality Care).

3. The person most responsible for a particular teacher's professional growth is
   a. the employer.
   b. the parent.
   c. the child.
   d. the teacher.
   e. None of these

4. Of the following entries, the one that is a well-known early childhood professional magazine is
   a. *The Whole Child.*
   b. *Child and Learning.*
   c. *Young Children.*
   d. *Helping the Child.*
   e. *The Professional Growth Journal.*

D. Describe attitudes toward the early childhood teaching profession which motivate teachers to spend time at weekend workshops.

E. Complete the following statement.
Lifelong learning is typical of the professional teacher who...

F. In the following paragraph, make note of all statements that indicate questionable professionalism.

I made an appointment to observe a class in a community school. As I arrived, the director nodded and indicated that I was to enter a classroom labeled "The Three's Room." The teacher and aide looked at me, then quickly looked away. I sat quietly near the wall. The teacher approached, demanding, "Who sent you in here?" "The director," I answered. She went back to the aide and whispered to him briefly. The teacher began a conversation with Mrs. Brown, who just arrived. She mentioned that her daughter, Molly, refused to eat lunch and kicked a hole in a cot at naptime. "I told you I'd tell your mother," the teacher said to Molly, who was standing at her mother's side.

Time for outside play was announced. The teacher and aide left the room for the play area. One or two children failed to follow the group outside. I wasn't sure if I could leave them inside so I stood in the doorway and looked out. The children must have headed out the other door to the director's office while I took note of the play equipment.

The aide approached. "Looking for a job?" he asked. "I could work afternoons," I answered. "Well, the person who teaches four-year-olds is quitting," he offered. "It's an easy job. You just watch them after naptime till their parents come." "Thanks for telling me about it," I said.

I left the yard to return to the director's office. She was on the phone with a parent and motioned me to sit in a chair opposite her desk. She was describing the school's academic program to the parent, and winked at me when she told the parent every child learned the alphabet, shapes, and colors besides reading a number of words. She hung up the phone and said to me, "Sometimes they're hard to sell." I thanked the director for allowing me to observe. She acknowledged this and asked, "Did you notice the teacher or aide leaving the children unsupervised? I've been too busy to watch them, but we've had a couple of complaints." "No," I lied, not wanting to become involved. Hoping to change the subject, I asked, "Do you have any openings for a teacher in the afternoon hours?" Since I needed money badly, a part-time job would be welcome. "We will have a position available starting the first week of October," she answered. The director then proceeded to describe the duties. They ranged from planning the program to mopping the floors at the end of the day. I told her I needed time to think over the offer. The director insisted she needed to know immediately, so I accepted.

Resources

Alexander, Robert. "Life, Death, and Creativity." *Human Growth Games.* Beverly Hills, CA: Sage Publications, 1978.

Harrison, Roger. "Self-Directed Learning." *Human Growth Games.* Beverly Hills, CA: Sage Publications, 1978.

Katz, Lillian. "Developmental Stages of Preschool Teachers." *The Elementary School Journal* (Feb. 1972).

Maslow, Abraham. "Defense and Growth," from Anderson, Robert H., and Shane, Harold G., *As the Twig is Bent.* Boston: Houghton Mifflin Co., 1971.

Sawyers, Betty J. "On Becoming a Pro." *For New Teachers* (1971).

Stevens, Joseph H., Jr., and King, Edith W. *Administering Early Childhood Education Programs.* Boston: Little, Brown and Co., 1976.

Vargiu, James G. "Education and Psychosynthesis." *Human Growth Games.* Beverly Hills, CA: Sage Publications, 1978.

Unit 24
Teacher Advocacy

OBJECTIVES

After studying this unit, the student will be able to:

- Define teacher advocacy.
- Describe present professional working conditions, status, salary, and benefits.
- List advocative activities.
- Name three pressures currently promoting teacher advocacy.

PROMOTING QUALITY

Members of the early childhood profession have joined the efforts of teacher organizations and associations, parent groups, private and public agency groups, community and neighborhood groups, and child interest groups to promote both the quality of day care and its availability. Campaigns, action plans, active involvement, legislative monitoring, and authorship continue to try to secure expansion of child services, upgrading of standards and teacher qualifications, reasonable child/teacher ratios, and other important issues.

Parents have become advocates of developmental care provided by trained professionals. Public media has sensitized many parents to the formative learning-packed years before elementary school. Most working parents seek child care that provides individually planned activities and opportunities that build foundations for further learning. During the 1970's, preschool child enrollment jumped from 30% to 50% of all America's children. Between 1980 and 1990, the number of working mothers with preschool children is expected to double.

Research indicates a correlation between child gains and their teachers' specific training in early childhood/child development, figure 24-1. Various groups and associations are urging professional training for young children's teachers, figure 24-2. The Executive Summary of the National Day Care Study prepared for the U.S. Department of Health, Education, and Welfare recommends that:

> Persons providing direct care for preschool children should have participated in a specialized program of child related education/training. (A.B.T. Associates, 1979)

Advocacy for children, quality, funds, specific teacher training are ongoing, ever-present activities. As a student teacher, your training experiences and coursework have made you aware of the field's need for a change and upgrading of its public image.

CAMPAIGN FOR PROFESSIONAL STATUS

Early childhood teachers have been slow to advocate on their own behalf. New teachers may or may not realize current professional status, salary, benefits, and working conditions, nor how past lack of teacher advocacy affects them. Teacher advocacy can be defined as speaking out or taking action on behalf of the early childhood teaching profession, its welfare, and well-being.

Fig. 24-1 Specific training for early childhood teaching promotes quality. (Courtesy of Nancy Martin)

Fig. 24-2 In order to become fully attuned to children's needs, teachers must be trained in every aspect of their learning process. (Courtesy of Nancy Martin)

Teacher advocacy can encompass a wide range of possible issues, including recognition, status, salary, benefits, working conditions, law and legislation, credentialing, standards, licensing of individuals, or any other aspect of professional interest and concern. Its objective is to change, or upgrade, existing conditions benefiting the profession itself, thereby benefiting the children, their families, and society as a whole.

PRESENT CONDITIONS

Until recently, factual data on working conditions has been scarce. Most professionals know from personal experience that a wide discrepancy exists in salaries and working conditions between programs. Hess and Croft have described salary and benefit differences.

Salary levels will differ in organizations of varying size and structure. Schools supported by public funds will probably be able to offer better salaries. In centers operating within public boards of education, the salary structure will be similar from center to center and may

be higher than a private school can afford to pay. In addition, fringe benefits — insurance, retirement, sick leave, and vacation with pay — will sometimes be better in a larger organization. Some schools, both public and private, may also pay tuition for teachers who want to take courses or workshops that give both inservice training and course credit. (1981)

Published surveys cite the following.

SALARIES AND WAGES (See Appendix for suggested readings.)

- (1978) The average hourly wage for teachers in publicly funded centers was $4.00; in privately funded programs it was $3.17.
- (1978–79) Staff members of proprietary centers earned less and had fewer benefits than workers in other centers. They were also less satisfied, and the centers had a higher turnover rate.
- (March, 1979) Teachers in public child care centers received an average hourly wage of $6.46 as compared to $4.91 in private centers. For head teachers, the average hourly rate was $7.43 in public centers as compared to $5.00 in private centers.

- (1978) Average annual wages for full-time head teachers and teacher's aides were $7,180 and $4,940, respectively.
- (1979) Of approximately 200,000 day care workers, 40% earned close to or less than minimum wage despite their training and education.
- (1978–79) The workers placed among the lower 10% of adult wage earners. Nearly 30% had gross monthly incomes of $500 or less, about 32% earned between $500 and $800 per month; only 14% had gross earnings of over $1,000 per month.
- (1981) On the average, a day care teacher's aide is paid a yearly salary of $6,575; a head teacher receives $9,557. In contrast, a starting letter carrier with the U.S. Postal Service receives $17,658.
- (1978–79) Of the staff surveyed, 63% worked several hours each week without pay in addition to full-time jobs. These hours included curriculum planning and preparation, meetings, parent contacts, and general center maintenance.
- (1982) Private sector teachers (twenty-one to thirty years of age) on monthly salaries averaged $100 more per month than monthly salaried thirty-one- to fifty-year-olds. Of public sector teachers on monthly salaries, the twenty-one- to thirty-year-olds averaged $986; thirty-one- to fifty-year-olds averaged $1,153; fifty-year-olds and older averaged $1,240.
- (1978–79) Staff wages were reduced due to workers purchasing supplies. Sixty percent made monthly contributions of as much as ten dollars for supplies due to inadequate budgets in the centers.

BENEFITS

- (1981) Staff members of publicly funded centers were more likely to receive medical coverage. They also received more paid holidays and sick days and longer paid vacations than those in private centers. About 50% received no medical coverage; 16% had no paid sick leave. Staff members who received the lowest wages also received the fewest benefits.

BREAKS

- (1981) More than one-third of the staff surveyed received a paid break. Of this number, 39% found breaks inadequate because there was no time and not enough staff to cover them.

This data (figure 24-3) leaves little doubt that teacher advocacy should be of concern to student teachers entering the profession.

RATE OF TURNOVER

Teacher turnover (change in a program's staff members due to termination or resignation) has become epidemic. Interwoven with job satisfaction, job security, and other factors, it has affected both the private and public sectors, figure 24-4.

Emotional and physical burnout has been described as a major cause of turnover; low pay, lack of benefits, and unpaid overtime are contributing factors. Burnout includes frustration, decreased interest in one's job, dissatisfaction, fatigue, low morale, and a desire to quit.

Burnout and its cause is the subject of popular debate. Some feel it is an advocacy issue; others see it as an administrative concern.

Causes of staff burnout in early childhood programs range from overwork and underpay to inadequate working conditions and poor staff relations, with a host of other causes in between.

Fortunately, staff burnout is neither inevitable nor incurable. As with most ailments, prevention is simpler than treatment. (*Keys to Early Education*, 1981)

PERSONNEL POLICIES

Early childhood workers sometimes have difficulty discovering their employers' personnel policies and practices. Whether large or small, each center can add to workers' security and satisfaction with written

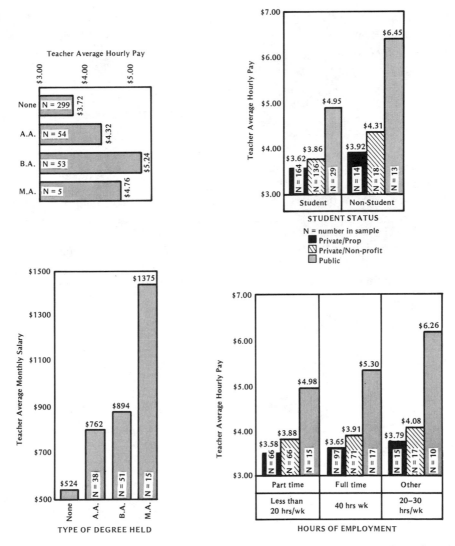

Fig. 24-3 Summary of data (From *The Letter Tree*, California Community College Early Childhood Educator's Newsletter, Vol. 5, No. 2, Feb. 1982.)

Group	Number	Number of Years at Current Job			
		1 year or less %	1–3 years %	3–5 years %	5 or more years %
Private proprietary staff	18	44	33	17	6
Private nonprofit staff	28	39	29	25	7
Public school staff	23	29	21	14	36
Other public staff	21	38	43	0	19
Total staff	90				
Average		37	31	14	17

Fig. 24-4 Comparisons of years on job in different programs (Adapted from Child Care Staff Education Project 1978–79, Berkeley, CA.)

policy statements. Stevens and King recommend the following as minimum policy areas:

1. The calendar for the current year, including dates the usual holidays will be observed and important dates for the program's staff.
2. Policies about sick leave and personal leave, including their accumulation and procedures to be followed in documenting their use.
3. Descriptions of the retirement, social security, and unemployment insurance, health benefits that the program provides for employees.
4. Procedures and policies about employment, covering items such as tenure, probationary periods, termination of employment by employer, and resignation.
5. Grievance procedures.
6. Salary information, including salary ranges, criteria for pay increases, and placement on the salary schedule.
7. Job descriptions and the organizational chart.
8. List of staff members by position.
9. The by-laws of the organization. (1976)

ADVOCACY AND THE STUDENT TEACHER

Advocacy takes time, energy, and knowledge. It involves everyday contact with people. Student teachers may have a desire to become involved, but lack both the knowledge of how to begin and the time. Dr. Bettye Lewis has given professionals advice on advocating.

Talk. Yes, talk! Only this time stop just talking to each other. Talk to parents — to the community — to decision makers. Take the concerns — the statistics — the relationship between the nation's health and its children's welfare — the cost effectiveness of day care. Talk at PTA meetings, civic groups and community organizations.

The second suggestion is Write! Write for the local paper. Write to Congressmen, to local legislators. Write to the college paper and the

children's school papers. Send home flyers describing the dangers of untrained caregivers and inadequate child care policies.

The third suggestion is stop squabbling about which kind of good child care is best. That is certainly important in itself, but it is irrelevant to the present need for good child care legislation. (1981)

Since advocacy means being aware of legislation, the legislative process, and individuals and groups who support child care issues, a first step is identifying groups or individuals who monitor and help author legislation. A list of helpful references can be found in the Appendix.

Carolyn Wilkerson Duncan, describing child advocacy efforts, has additional advocacy suggestions useful to teacher advocates, figure 24-5.

ESTABLISHING FRIENDSHIPS

1. Be a friend. Actively support the goals and objectives of other programs in your local community which you can endorse.
2. Become visible in your community. Take board jobs and do committee work.
3. Make everybody a "P.R." person. "Nothing makes a lasting impression like a good impression."
4. Open House — Open Door. "The program should always be at its best, and visitors welcome."
5. Have good rapport with parents.
6. Invite the opposition to your center.

INFLUENCING LEGISLATION

1. Register staff and parents to vote.
2. Communicate concerns.
3. Develop and maintain working relationships with legislative aides and offices.
4. Contact legislators.
5. Act!

Fig. 24-5 Guidelines to establishing friendships and influencing legislation (From "Winning Friends and Influencing Legislation for Child Care" by Carolyn Wilkerson Duncan. *Day Care and Early Education*, Vol. 7, No. 1, Fall 1979.)

FACTORS INHIBITING AND CONTRIBUTING TO ADVOCACY

The following factors minimize teachers' efforts to help themselves, increase salaries, and improve working conditions.

- Lack of job security due to funding shakiness.
- Lack of political awareness.
- Lack of teacher organizational strength and leadership.
- Fear of job loss.
- Inability to join groups because of costs.
- Turnover and burnout.
- Myths connected to teacher dedication and non-tangible reward superseding commensurate pay.
- Realization that parent fees may increase due to advocacy.
- Public sector teachers resisting supportive advocacy for private sector counterparts.

The following factors motivate teachers to react to adverse conditions, thereby improving their salaries and benefits.

- Economic pressures on teachers and teacher families.
- Lack of quality child care for the teacher's children.
- Formation of bargaining groups which have made gains.
- Realization that teachers' labor is actually subsidizing families.
- Annual exit of skilled co-workers.
- Reaction to media's image of the profession, figure 24-6.
- Reaction to public's view of the profession.
- Realization that quality for children and families depends on specifically trained personnel.
- Dedication to children and parents.

RIGHTS OF CHILD CARE WORKERS

Nancy Cannon has identified a prototype of rights, figure 24-7, for child care workers which she hopes will stimulate critical discussion rather than become a definitive statement.

It can be argued that for every right earned, an employee has a responsibility to the organization. In an optimal situation, employees would be guaranteed a set of rights which respond to both their occupational goals and the humanistic nature of their work. A model code of workers' rights would include job protection earned earlier this century by workers in industrial settings and human rights safeguards deriving from the concerns and experiences of contemporary labor force. (1979)

UNIONIZATION — A POSSIBLE CHANGE AGENT Preschool teacher unionization has occurred in a number of states. American Federation of Teachers, Public School Workers Unions, and Service Workers Unions are among the most prominent, figure 24-8. The field as a whole seems to be struggling with a decision concerning this vehicle as a possible solution to its problems. Figure 24-9 lists common union goals. Since schools grossing over $250,000 per year (and also some small schools with vast assets) fall under National Labor Relations Board control, smaller center staffs view union membership as viable only for others.

INDIVIDUAL NEGOTIATING   Negotiating on an individual basis has often been suggested. Specific step by step procedures are shown in figures 24-10 and 24-11.

Fig. 24-6 Is this the media's image of the teaching profession? (Courtesy of Wide World Photos, Inc.)

* The Right to Just Compensation
  * Rate of pay. Salary schedules which verify the importance of their work and provide a modicum of economic security.
  * Compensation for all hours worked.
  * Opportunities for salary increases.
* The Right to Adequate Benefits
  * Worker's benefits. Unemployment insurance and worker's compensation insurance.
  * Retirement benefits.
  * Health, dental and life insurance benefits.
  * Personal leave benefits.
* The Right to a Clear Work Commitment
  * Specific work assignment. A clear job description with specific job responsibilities and performance standards.
  * Job security. Annual renewable employment contracts.
* The Right to Decent Working Conditions
  * Hours. Regularity in hours and adequate break periods.
  * Range of responsibilities. Responsibilities commensurate with capabilities, and an adequate number of co-workers to insure proper attention to all children under their care.
  * Workspace. Workspace which acknowledges the nature of their work with young children.
* The Right to Personal Protection
  * Personal liability. Liability insurance and informed of their legal jurisdiction.
  * Freedom from discriminatory treatment.
  * Grievance procedure.
  * Organizing activity. For coffee, complaining, problem-solving or pre-union activity.
* The Right to Information
  * Future changes, current and future funding issues, internal organization, operational structure, role and jurisdiction of governing board if one exists.
* The Right to Participate in Decision Making

(*Note:* Original article can be obtained from CCIE, 70 Oakley Rd., Belmont, MA 02178.)

Fig. 24-7 Code of rights (Condensed from "Rights of Child Care Workers: A Prototype Code of Rights" by Nancy Cannon. *Child Care Information Exchange*, Nov. 1979.)

Fig. 24-8 Union membership is increasing.

* To *negotiate* contract salaries of professional employees.
* To *administer* health and welfare programs and pension plans negotiated at the collective bargaining table.
* To *provide* cost-of-living adjustments in contracts so that professionals are no longer strangled by the inflationary squeeze.
* To *monitor* legislation at local, state, and national levels to bring to bear union strength for advantageous laws and to stop repressive and regressive legislation.
* To *provide* continuing education programs through state and federal mechanisms.
* To *negotiate* federal grants to enhance the standards of the profession.
* To *increase* members' involvement in the profession.

Fig. 24-9 Union organization goals

A first step would be to analyze and list all of the ways one feels that he or she has been an asset to the center where employed. List items which show improvement in the quality of the children's instructional program, new duties assumed, and total duties performed. Rapport with parents, teaching materials made or provided, special talents developed are others. Of course, the more skills and abilities possessed, the greater are chances of convincing employers that one's services are valuable and worth keeping and paying for.

As a second step, arrange a time and place where you and your employer can discuss your salary without interruption. Try to structure the situation so that you are not outnumbered. If both a director and employer wish to attend, ask if you may bring a fellow teacher or professional organization representative.

If your director is not the school's owner and you are employed in a privately owned school, ask if the owner is available to listen to you. Most owners, not directors, make salary decisions. Start your conversation by asking if your work has been satisfactory or if there are areas which need improvement. If improvement is suggested: determine the specifics of the problem; explore plans for improvement by making suggestions; set a time limit for improvement to be shown; outline and identify criteria to be used to evaluate whether improvement has taken place. Arrange a definite date for your next meeting to discuss your improvement and raise.

In most salary negotiations, the employee makes a salary proposal. You cannot negotiate if you have not verbalized an increased wage or additional job benefits. Do not be afraid to ask for what you feel you deserve and is commensurate for your services. Do not just listen; this is the time to mention the assets you listed that make you valuable to your employer. Women, in general, tend to underestimate their abilities.

You may face a situation in which your employer tries to enlist your sympathy for his or her economic plight; food costs; and approved budget with a ceiling, set income, or parent fees, supply and equipment costs, etc. This is the time to mention that you too are facing rising costs on a "frozen" salary. Be sure you know past and present salary particulars; exactly how much is your hourly and monthly salary? When did you receive your last raise? Make a statement to the effect that you feel other teachers, directors, and assistants have been underpaid and that much needs to be done in the area of early childhood staff salaries.

If you work in a private school, you can estimate your employer's income and expenses. Usually the budget is such that resources can be found; there is always a profit margin. If you are employed in a publicly funded program, financial records should be available for your review.

Stick to your convictions, make your points, and then listen. Do not monopolize the conversation. Do not worry about silences; wait them out.

Involve a sense of justice, a fair wage for a fair day's work. Emotional appeals usually carry less weight than logical ones, but are sometimes added effectively.

Analyze exactly what would be acceptable as a wage or benefit increase. Ideally, your employer should make the first concession. Put all agreements in the form of a dated memo as soon as possible, ask for a signed copy for your records, and follow through in getting one. Leave on good terms, with the door open to further negotiating. Thank the employer for both time and sincerity, if possible.

Fig. 24-10 Negotiating as an individual

To: Mary Smith, Director
From: Bobbi Jones, Head Teacher
Date: June 1, 1984
Subject: Salary Negotiations

It is my understanding that during our meeting of _____ , we agreed on the following items:
1. My work is satisfactory, and you have no suggestions for improvement.
2. On July 1, 1984, my salary will be increased $50 to a total of $850 per month.
3. From this date, I will be paid at the hourly rate of $4.75 for attending evening parent meetings.

If you do not agree with my conclusions, please inform me in writing.

Fig. 24-11 Sample negotiation agreement

INDUSTRY-AFFILIATED CHILD CARE

The slow growth of industry-affiliated work site child care is seen by some as a ray of hope. Others question its impact on teacher status. Hopefully, child care professionals achieve parity with other professions employed by the sponsoring industry.

Voucher or contracted child care as an employee benefit offers a slimmer chance for professional improvement. This process involves the industry paying for employee child care in a community center. Contracting is similar. A company leases or donates space, and a contractor provides child care services. In both, the owner or contractor makes all personnel decisions.

A "wait and see" attitude prevails with most professionals. Legislation or industry tax credits could rapidly change existing practices. Child care consultants advising industry will play a crucial advocacy role.

While there is certainly reason to be enthusiastic about this new development, there is also some cause for caution. The problems facing the child care community are more than those of quality. Quality issues also impinge, particularly those relating to status and salaries of child care staff. Employer involvement in the field cannot be assumed to address these issues. Rather, early childhood advocates engaged in employment related child care must actively raise issues about status and salaries when consulting with industry. (Whitebook, in *Child Care Information Service*)

Summary

Early childhood professionals have joined the child advocacy movement but have been slow to fight for professional teacher concerns and rights. Student teachers' awareness of present conditions and lack of past teacher advocacy will affect their future professional actions.

Teacher advocacy involves a multitude of issues and concerns, primarily status, salary, benefits, and working conditions. A knowledge of current legislation and law, plus an understanding of politics and legislative process, is crucial to effective advocating. Change agents being examined by teachers to promote individual upgrading include union membership, industry-related sponsorship, and individual negotiating. Daily contact with others makes each student teacher a public relations person for the profession.

Suggested Activities

A. On the blackboard, list current myths and public views concerning preschool or early childhood teachers and teaching.

Example: All one has to do to work effectively with young children is to love them.

B. Read the following job satisfactions. Add your ideas.

Seventy-eight percent in our sample reported that direct work with children was what most engaged and pleased them about their jobs. Positive aspects of this work included immediate feedback, physical contact, facilitating and observing growth and change, and related opportunities for self-reflection.

Other sources of job satisfaction mentioned by staff included (in order of frequency): staff relations (learning how to communicate with and depend on each other through the many opportunities to problem solve within a context of shared purpose); flexibility and autonomy (the degree of control over day to day decision making and the fact that no two days are alike in child care); and opportunity to learn and grow on the job (relating to continually different issues). (Whitebook, 1981)

C. List consequences of the annual exodus of skilled, trained professionals.

D. Interview local teachers concerning status, salary, benefits, and working conditions. Report your results to fellow students.

E. Invite a union representative to speak. Make a list of questions you would like answered.

F. Compare individual and union negotiating differences with a small group of classmates. Report your ideas to the class.

G. Note all the advocacy activities which you have done this year, and resolve to double your activities next year. Discuss these activities in groups of three to five students.
    - Voted.
    - Read a candidate's position on children's issues.
    - Asked about a candidate's positions on children's issues.
    - Worked for a candidate.
    - Given money to a candidate.
    - Gone to a political fund raiser.
    - Written a letter to a policymaker about a children's issue.
    - Called a policymaker about a children's issue.
    - Actively lobbied a policymaker about a children's issue.
    - Checked a policymaker's voting record.
    - Thanked a policymaker for his or her vote or statement.
    - Looked at a legislative remap in terms of children's candidates.
    - Wrote a letter to the newspaper editor about children's issues.
    - Presented testimony to a hearing on children's issues.
    - Participated in a public forum on children's issues.
    - Helped organize advocates on children's issues.
    - Helped organize the public to respond to children's issues.
    - Used research data to discuss policies affecting children.
    - Spent some time with children and thought about why there is a need to advocate for them.

H. Read the following situations. Decide whether a worker's rights have been violated.
    1. The school where Maria works has called her daily and told her to stay home when only a few children are in attendance.
    2. Mark, a student teacher, has been asked by his cooperating teacher to clean windows in his classroom and in the adjacent classroom.
    3. Leetha, a teacher of four-year-olds, has just learned from a neighbor that the school where she works is for sale.
    4. At a job interview, Thien has been questioned about her marital status and about the type of care provided for her own children.
    5. The following work agreement form has been given to a new employee:

Date _____

WORK AGREEMENT

The Board of Directors agrees that _____ will be employed as a teacher assistant at _____ _____ for the school year 1980–81.

Duties will include all those as outlined on the job description and those decided collectively among center staff.

The rate of pay will be $5.75 per hour for no more than 20 hours per week. Included in those paid hours are weekly staff meetings, monthly parent meetings, and one-half hour preparation time per week.

**19th Street Day Care Center
Board of Directors**

_____
Signature of Employee

I. Rate each of the following items according to the scale of 1 to 5. In groups of four to five students, discuss your results. Report to the whole class.

1	2	3	4	5
strongly agree	mildly agree	cannot decide	mildly disagree	strongly disagree

Parents really will never care about teachers' salaries and/or working conditions.	Teaching young children is a relatively simple job if you have the aptitude.	Teachers probably will never organize because they sense added economic pressures on families.	The purpose of union membership is peaceful arbitration.
With enough public pressure, commensurate pay could happen.	An emotional appeal is probably the best way to influence legislators.	Public ECE teachers need to spearhead advocacy for private sector teachers.	The prime cause for teachers' leaving the field is low pay.
An increase in male teachers will bring better working conditions.	Some women are naturally skillful professionals needing little training.	Advocacy is self-seeking and puts teachers' needs before children's.	It is only a matter of time before the field will be unionized.
Teachers rarely publicly speak out about teacher exploitation.	Salary affects turnover, which in turn affects program quality, child progress and well-being.	If American males actually bore offspring, the country would have free, quality child care.	Most parents are unaware of early childhood teacher pay scales.
The nation's early childhood teachers are subsidizing American families.	Skillful, efficient budget management is the best possible solution at the present time for low pay and lack of benefits.	An individual (leader) who will fight for all teachers' rights will never be found.	Fear and ignorance are the root causes of the lack of societal recognition of the value of professional early childhood teachers.

J. Review figure 24-7. Discuss in small groups.

K. Collect press and media clippings or photos which show the public's image of the profession.

L. What type of situation comedy television program could help change the profession's public image? Write a brief description.

M. What are the names and addresses of four of your legislators?

Review

Select the *answers* that best complete each statement. (*Note:* There may be more than one answer for each.)

1. Advocacy for teachers includes
   a. law acceptance or change.
   b. everyday conversations with family and friends.
   c. conversations with strangers.
   d. objecting to wages of another vocation.
   e. raising money for a project.

2. American parents
   a. tend to know the level of professionals' salaries.
   b. prefer custodial care because it is less expensive.
   c. do not fully understand the meaning of developmental child care.
   d. plan to care for their own children during the 1980's.
   e. tend to be in a "Catch 22" position: being supportive of increased salaries for their child's teacher but unable to pay higher fees.

3. There is currently
   a. little evidence to support the idea that the quality of child care is related to the teacher's professional training.
   b. data indicating low salaries for early childhood teachers are the rule rather than the exception.
   c. data indicating teachers in publically funded child centers receive nearly twice the pay of teachers in the private sector.
   d. no effort to unionize preschool workers.
   e. a problem for workers who wish to bargain through unionization in small private centers.

4. The idea that satisfaction is the teachers' reward for working with young children is
   a. as valid today as it was fifty years ago.
   b. outdated.
   c. promotes workers subsidizing parents and private preschool business ventures.
   d. an idea that all professionals should accept.
   e. an idea that all entering the field should accept.

Resources

A.B.T. Associates. *Children of the Center: Final Report of the National Day Care Study.* Prepared for the Day Care Division, Administration for Children, Youth, and Families (March 1981).

Cannon, Nancy. "Rights of Child Care Workers: A Prototype Code of Rights." *Child Care Information Exchange* (Nov. 1979).

Hess, Robert D., and Croft, Doreen J. *Teachers of Young Children.* Boston: Houghton Mifflin Co., 1981.

Keys to Early Education, Vol. 2, No. 2 (Feb. 1981), Washington, DC: Capitol Publications, Inc.

Lewis, Bettye. *Options,* Vol. VI, No. 2 (March 1981).

Stevens, Joseph H., Jr., and King, Edith W. *Administering Early Childhood Education Programs.* Boston: Little, Brown and Co., 1976.

Whitebook, Marcy. "Employer Related Child Care and Early Childhood Staff Working Conditions." *Child Care Information Service,* Family Service of Santa Monica; Santa Monica, CA.

Whitebook, Marcy, et al. "Who's Minding the Child Care Workers?" *Children Today* (Jan.–Feb. 1981).

Unit 25
Current Issues, Trends, and Research

OBJECTIVES

After studying this unit, the student will be able to:

- Discuss one trend and its influence on planning young children's programs.

- Write a brief statement describing the nation's current public policy decisions and young children's care.

- Describe the relationship of research and ECE teaching.

- Identify four publications which review research or present full research study documents.

GENERAL PROBLEMS

Few specialists argue with facts indicating the ever-increasing need for child care for working parents.

- In 1981, 8.2 million preschool children had mothers who worked.
- Of the preschoolers in the United States, 45% have working moms.
- Preschool enrollment grew 15% over the past decade.
- Many school-aged children (and younger) are home alone.
- The birthrate is expected to rise during the 1980's, and preschool enrollment will approach seven million by 1989.

What is argued and debated, however, is the idea that every young child has a right to developmental rather than custodial care. Quality care on a sliding scale based on the parents' ability to pay is considered a nonattainable ideal. Some feel our national policy is responsible.

The United States has a national children's policy and it is that the family is the primary provider of care for children and that there should be no public intervention with the family's childcare and childrearing responsibilities, except in the event of calamity to the family or to the child, a universal health threat to children, or a national emergency. When such calamities do occur the government's usual intervention has been to help selective children in a selective area of need. (Beñas, 1978)

Inequities like the following promoted by the present national child care situation are gaining public attention:

- The lack of quality care for infants and toddlers within the financial reach of single parent workers.
- Middle-income (and higher) parents are supporting child care for low-income parents through taxes. Public programs have higher teacher qualifications and lower teacher-child ratios. Parents desire quality for their own children and find few private centers with ratios and teacher qualifications equal to publicly funded centers.
- Many parents want a center with a strong education component. Most state licensing laws for private centers only mandate child

custodial safety. Publicly funded centers have developmental child programs, but most tax-paying parents find their children ineligible for services.

These issues of national or family responsibility, child and family rights, and existing inequity will affect every early childhood educator.

STATE AND LOCAL FUNDING DECISIONS
As federal taxes are returned to states, decisions concerning amounts to be allocated to young children's programs and services will be made at state and local levels. Young children's needs will compete with other social and welfare needs. Professionals are fearful, and they worry about cutbacks in existing publicly funded operations. As taxpayers, they may support decreasing federal administrative costs while they also support increased federal funding for ensuring and expanding child program quality.

GROWING PRIVATE INVESTMENT AND PUBLIC SUPPORT
There appears to be a growing interest in federal support of child care. According to a 1980 Gallup Poll, Americans placed child care among the top five services the federal government should provide.

Private enterprise seems to be scrutinizing day care as a new, potentially lucrative industry. Chains of preschools grow with companies like Kinder Care, operating over 300 day care facilities and contemplating overseas expansion.

PARENTS AND CHILDREN WITH SPECIAL NEEDS
Early childhood teachers and directors are handling many "at risk" children and stressed families. Early childhood centers hopefully will be staffed by well-trained caregivers able to help special need, withdrawn, and/or disruptive children while offering supportive assistance to parents. Children who are systematically excluded from planned experiences because of special needs when teachers are unable to change behaviors may experience a form of subtle tracking. The need for center consultant assistance or special therapy provisions is growing as family economic pressures increase, teenage births continue, and the divorce rate increases.

NONSEXIST CURRICULUM   Early childhood nonsexist curriculum planning can be seen as another controversial issue. Many goals of a nonsexist program involve trying to reduce or eliminate the sexist roles of men and women. Developing the children's awareness of the *shared* responsibilities of men and women is also important, figure 25-1. The following suggestions are common in current early childhood teacher training literature:

1. The use of such neuter terms as "humankind" or "person" should be substituted for "man."
2. Females as well as males should be portrayed as problem solvers, creators, and executors of ideas.
3. Females should be portrayed as being successful in a variety of fields. They should be portrayed in more roles in which they are independent, competent, and athletic.
4. Females should, in some instances, be shown as taller, heavier, more intelligent, and/or more capable than males.
5. Males should be portrayed in a wide variety of homemaking activities.
6. Family relationships should not show individuals acting subservient to others because of sex.

Fig. 25-1 "I want to play the mother!"

Serbin and Connor have identified teaching skills that are useful in reducing the stereotyping of sex roles in preschool activities. They include teacher cuing and labeling; social reinforcement (attention and praise); teacher modeling; and teacher's physical presence.

By using these methods, it may be possible to double the amount of cooperative play between male and female preschoolers.

PARENT EDUCATION

Increasing the parents' awareness of the technical and skilled nature of raising children is an issue of great interest to early childhood educators. Parents seem to be searching for materials and techniques which will help them raise competent, capable, successful children. Most professionals support parent access to information and assistance, and see it as a component of a center's operation. With funding cutbacks, this service is usually the first to disappear. The goal of most parent education efforts is to strengthen and promote existing child-rearing practices rather than teach parenting. The issue involves early childhood professionals' abilities to pinpoint parenting skills accurately, teach them effectively, and give honest feedback to parents who do not see their teaching methods as affecting their child's progress. Another issue concerns hard-to-reach parents whose children have a need for change in their lives in order to cope with school life and society as a whole.

BACK TO BASICS   The "back to basics" pressure is very apparent to early childhood teachers, and the issue of creating a balance between child exploring, choosing, and doing, and structured teacher-guided academics seems to be a real problem. How do teachers promote a love of learning and preserve children's confidence in themselves as learners, while offering a "back to basics" preschool curriculum?

Teachers worry about preschool programs which concentrate on the rote memorization of the alphabet, phonics instruction, reading, and advanced number concepts. Parents may feel this type of program is desirable, and directors respond by pressuring teachers to provide it. This conflicts with what many teachers

feel to be best. When the bulk of instruction is based on uninteresting, highly symbolic, and abstract material, children's own interests, curiosity, and self-concepts are in jeopardy.

Lillian Katz (1981) attempts to clarify this issue; she defines a basic skill as:

- *transcurricular* in nature. It is useful in most curricular areas. (Example: Child being able to ask for clarification.)
- *having dynamic consequences.* This skill leads to acquiring greater skill. (Example: Highly verbal child interacts with adults, making skill grow.)
- *recursive*: it feeds on itself.
- a relatively *discreet unit of action*, observable in a short period of time, fairly visible. (Example: writing, counting.)
- something that can be learned in a lesson; *learned by direct instruction.*
- getting *better with practice.*
- something that can be learned in small steps.

She has also described a "disposition" for learning and compares this to a basic skill. A disposition is:

- a relatively enduring habit of mind.
- a tendency to respond characteristically across situations, e.g., curiosity, humor, inventiveness, quarrelsomeness.
- a habitual way of reacting.
- learned over a long period of time, largely from modeled behavior ("caught rather than taught").
- strengthened by being supported or shaped through reinforcement and appreciation.

One issue in Katz's discussion is that early childhood teachers are instructing basic skills at the expense of children's disposition to use them. Katz does not endorse a particular curricular model, but suggests programs should engage children's minds, encourage choices, promote child concentration, and have "return to" activities which sustain child interest over a period of time, figure 25-2.

Philosophies dealing with children's natural curiosity and programs that are intellectually focused seem to have positive "sleeper effects" (skills appear in later years) which outweigh basic-skill-oriented approaches during children's later school years. There are many related issues in the "back to basics" skills as opposed to self-guided instruction. These issues will be subject to much study and research in the future.

PUBLIC SCHOOL SPONSORSHIP   The issue of increased public school sponsorship of preschools continues. One side argues that increasing public school involvement is cost effective, ensures overall quality, fills empty classrooms, uses existing fiscal and operational management systems, and employs retrained elementary teachers. Others claim that private program sponsors and/or community sponsors are more responsive to parents, better located, and cheaper. Besides minimizing government involvement and control, they provide diversity, not mediocrity. Michael Usdan proposes increased public school sponsorship. According to Usdan, it is living side by side with other delivery systems and is becoming increasingly necessary in our changing society.

Educational institutions have an enormous stake in the possible growth of the early childhood enterprise. Public policy and services ultimately will have to respond to the dramatic changes in family life and social mores alluded to earlier, and the society will have to provide the necessary child care services as more and more women continue to work. Although the public schools may not become the exclusive

delivery system for early childhood services, it is certainly logical to assume that they should and will be active, major participants in providing preschool programs.

If the schools are to be successful with preschool children and their families, efforts must be made to develop closer ties with parents and their communities. This is particularly important with low-income and minority families which not infrequently are dubious about the depth of the commitment of public school personnel to the well-being of their children. (1981)

TRENDS

Most of the following trends in education are debatable issues. They are cited as trends because of their relatively recent appearance in early childhood theory and literature.

COMPUTERS AND YOUNG CHILDREN   In recent years, there has been much interest in computers and packaged software development. More and more, children are actually using computers rather than merely observing them. Companies are scrambling to create effects on color television screens with voice

Fig. 25-2 Interest in the alphabet varies widely in young children.

prompts, musical sounds, clever picture forms, and simple keyboards. As screen happenings are shared and discussed, child interest and motivation increase.

FAMILY DAY CARE LIAISON   As the desirability for day care homes increases, so do the fees. A merger of interests is evolving between in-home and in-center staffers. Networking has increased contacts. Professional early childhood conferences now offer sections specifically designed to attract day home operators and to probe mutual concerns. Another factor which has helped is the number of graduates with AA degrees who have opted to establish day homes of their own. Very often, economic rewards for day home operators surpass those of private proprietary in-center teachers.

RESEARCH

Research continually probes and searches for answers to diverse education concerns and problems. The whole field of education has been criticized for its slow response in putting new theories or research discoveries into practice. At the same time, educators have been chastised for being "fad followers," searching for simple answers to complex problems. These attitudes inhibit honest efforts toward excellence in education.

Student teachers desperately trying to incorporate training theory into their classroom teaching technique are viewed as being too shaky to handle additional research theory. Yet most student teachers sincerely want information on any current research that can help children even though it may require changing their teaching techniques and interactions.

This unit is selective in presenting a surface review of interesting research. It is offered to promote interest in current research and to help the student teacher realize that a vast collection of research is available for study purposes.

The validity of research is always a factor to consider. Conclusions are based on the researcher's skill and degree of expertise among other numerous factors.

PIAGET   The work of psychologist Jean Piaget, particularly his theory concerning distinct phases of

mental and emotional development, has kept researchers busy for the past twenty years. According to Robbie Case, many early childhood teachers and early childhood centers have reasoned that:

> If these are the stages of development through which a child passes, if the abilities he acquires are really the crucial ones from a cognitive viewpoint, and if one of our jobs as educators is to assist in intellectual development, then maybe we should start providing some assistance to the child in precisely the processes and achievements which Piaget has concentrated on. (1973)

Besides using Piagetian theory as a basis for a new early childhood curriculum, Case's research, in Case's view, has promoted the development of new intelligence scales. In addition, it has given "readiness activity" believers additional support. It has promoted interest in activity and self-discovery approaches which believe children should learn primarily from their own spontaneous activity.

Case concludes that early childhood educators may have gone too far in applying Piaget.

> However, what I have attempted to show is that most of the current "applications" of Piaget's work actually go a good deal beyond what he has established empirically, or even what he has theorized. At a deeper level, most of them depend for their justification on an additional set of assumptions, which are either untested as yet, or inherently untestable. (1973)

Thoughtful contemplation follows research study, and teachers continue to hope research will lead to improved quality in education.

LONG- AND SHORT-TERM EFFECTS OF PRESCHOOL ATTENDANCE   Past studies attempted to answer the question "Is preschool attendance good for children?" This emphasis has been curtailed, and current studies dealing with long-term (four or more years) effects are prevalent. Lillian Katz has described these studies as "sleeper studies" because positive characteristics seem to "awake" during years of late elementary school and adolescence (1981). Studies in this area provide additional information which substantiates the value of quality preschool education.

PRESCHOOL HUMOR   Researchers seem to be pinpointing a slapstick, teasing silliness as characteristic of young children's brand of humor. The value of humor in healing, eliminating stress, and preserving mental health is being widely researched and accepted, figure 25-3.

LANGUAGE   Researchers studying reading skills seem to be finding that the more children read and write, the better these skills become. Regarding speech patterns of different races, Dr. Alice Honig (1981) concludes that, with children, there are no significant differences in speaking abilities; however, social class differences exist; the higher the social class, the greater the language usage. Key factors are caretakers' responsiveness to child communication attempts, adult language specificity, and descriptiveness in conversational exchanges.

Summary

Most of society's economic, social, political, and technological trends affect families and young children.

Fig. 25-3   Researchers are beginning to study the development of children's senses of humor.

Knowledge of trends is crucial to effective teaching, program planning, and supportive relationships with parents. Changes occur which can enhance children's opportunities and potentials, have neutral effects, or create inequities or unfavorable development. Some of the issues discussed in this unit include quality, public policy, arising special needs, nonsexist program planning, parenting education, "back to basics" approach, public school preschool sponsorship, computer use, preschools as investments, and family day care liaisons.

Research, its study and application, will always be a part of teaching. Though education is criticized for its slowness in putting new theories into practice and criticized for faddism, the struggle toward excellence depends on careful, authentic, and valid research. Current research topics include Piagetian theory application, long- and short-term effects of preschool attendance, and language skills.

(*Note:* This unit was selective in its review of issues, trends, and research based on the authors' views on current happenings. There was no attempt to cover or prioritize *all* issues or trends affecting the profession.

Suggested Activities

A.   List what you feel are children's special needs categories.

B.   Read the following story to a small group of four-year-olds. Have a fellow student observe and record the children's reactions to the questions which appear throughout the story. Share the results with the class.

This is a guessing story. I'm going to ask you some questions. Any answer is okay, but I'd like you to guess.

Ricky and Annette are twins about your age. Let's talk about *twins.* Can someone tell me about twins? Right, they are two children in a family who are the same age. These twins are four years old. They go to a preschool just like ours. This is a story about them. One morning their mother calls them to get out of bed. One twin gets up right away and gets dressed. The other twin is called three times before getting out of bed.

1. Who got dressed right away? Ricky or Annette?
2. Who stayed in bed after being called three times?

One twin straightens out the bed covers and makes the bed.

3. Is it Ricky or Annette?

The twins are now in the kitchen. One gets out the cereal for breakfast.

4. Who do you think it is?

One twin leaves cereal in the bowl and doesn't eat it.

5. Is it Ricky or Annette?

One twin clears the table and puts the dishes in the sink.

6. Is it Annette or Ricky?

The twins are at preschool now. They are playing with the puzzles. A friend asks for a turn. One twin gives a puzzle to the friend.

7. Is it Annette or Ricky?

One twin is playing with trucks and cars.

8. Is it Ricky or Annette?

One twin is feeding the doll with a play baby bottle in the playhouse.

9. Is it Ricky or Annette?

The teacher tells one twin not to hit people.

10. Is it Annette or Ricky?

One twin puts the toys back on the shelf. This twin always returns toys.

11. Is it Ricky or Annette?

One twin bumps into the back of others' bikes.

12. Is it Annette or Ricky?

The twins are now home from school. One twin helps the mother cook dinner.

13. Is it Ricky or Annette?

You did a lot of guessing. Everyone's answers were different, and I don't know whether Ricky or Annette did the things you guessed. It could have been both children, couldn't it? Both boys and girls do many things the same way.

C. Read the following story to a group of adults, and record their answers. Do not discuss sexism prior to this. Share the answers with the class.

A man and his son were on vacation. While traveling, an auto accident occurred. The man was killed; the son was rushed to a local hospital in critical condition. Surgery was needed to save his life. The surgeon walked into the operating room, looked at the boy, and exclaimed, "I can't operate on him. That's my son!" How could that be?

D. Make a list of current issues in early childhood teaching. In groups of three to five, arrange them in order of their importance for young children's education and welfare in the United States. Share and compare results with the whole group.

E. Read an article on early childhood education (ECE), ECE teaching, or ECE programs. Use the *Reader's Guide to Periodical Literature* or some other resource to locate one. On a separate sheet, provide the following information to review the article.
- Title of article
- Author(s)
- Journal or publication's name
- Date of publication
- Pagination
- General findings of the study or article (number of subjects, ages, testing device or procedure, results); key ideas, points or conclusions
- Your reactions

F. In groups of five to six, identify research questions or hypotheses you feel should be studied in greater detail.

G. Read the information in figure 25-4. Identify libraries in your area which provide ERIC materials. Find and read material in your area of interest and report your findings to the group.

Review

A. List five current debatable issues of early childhood education.

B. Describe briefly what you feel is public policy on day care in the United States.

What is ERIC?

ERIC is a nationwide information system funded by the National Institute of Education. ERIC is designed to make information on all aspects of education readily available. ERIC covers such subjects as child development, classroom techniques, reading, science, social studies, counseling, career education, adult education, rural and urban education, teacher education, higher education, testing, educational administration, and special education.

Who can use ERIC?

You can — whether you are a teacher, researcher, librarian, student, legislator, parent, tinker or tailor. ERIC is for anyone who wants information related to education.

Where is ERIC?

More than 668 libraries and other institutions in the U.S. and other countries have the ERIC document collection on microfiche. Write to ERIC/EECE for a list of the ERIC collections in your state. Many more institutions subscribe to the printed indexes for the ERIC collection.

What is in ERIC?

When you use ERIC, you can find citations to:

> ERIC Documents — primarily unpublished or "fugitive" materials, including more than 160,000 research studies, program descriptions and evaluations, conference proceedings, curriculum materials, bibliographies, and other documents.
>
> ERIC Journals — articles in more than 700 education-related journals.

How do I use ERIC to find citations?

> ERIC Documents — Use ERIC's monthly abstract journal *Resources in Education* (RIE). *RIE* includes subject, author, and institution indexes and gives you an abstract of each cited document.
>
> ERIC Journals — Use ERIC's other monthly publication *Current Index to Journals in Education* (CIJE). *CIJE* lists about 1800 new journal citations each month and includes a short annotation for most articles cited.

What if I want to read a document or journal article cited in RIE or CIJE?

> ERIC Documents — The complete text of most ERIC documents is available on "microfiche" (a 4 x 6 inch card of microfilm) which must be read on a microfiche reader. Libraries and other institutions which have the ERIC collection have microfiche readers. Many institutions also have microfiche reader printers that can make paper copies from the microfiche.
>
> ERIC Journals — To read the article from a *CIJE* citation, you look up the journal in your library or ask your librarian to borrow it for you. (Articles cited in *CIJE* are not available on microfiche.)

How can ERIC materials be ordered?

> ERIC Documents — Most ERIC documents can be ordered from the ERIC Document Reproduction Service (EDRS) in Alexandria, Virginia. You can write ERIC/EECE for an order form or use the one in each *RIE* issue.
>
> ERIC Journals — About 75% of the journal articles cited in *CIJE* can be ordered from University Microfilm in Ann Arbor, Michigan. Write ERIC/EECE for an order form or use the order information in *CIJE*.

How can I search ERIC by computer?

One of the most efficient ways to use ERIC is to order a computer search of the ERIC data base on a particular topic. There are computer search services in many libraries and other institutions

Fig. 25-4 The ERIC system (Prepared by the ERIC Clearinghouse on Elementary and Early Childhood Education [ERIC/EECE].)

as well as at most ERIC Clearinghouses. To get a computer search, describe your topic to the person who will do the search; the search will then be designed and run through a computer. You will receive a printout with citations from *RIE* and from *CIJE*; a fee is usually charged for computer searches. Write any ERIC Clearinghouse for more information on search services in your state.

How does information get into ERIC?
Sixteen ERIC Clearinghouses, in various locations across the U.S., collect and process ERIC documents for *RIE* and prepare citations for *CIJE*. Each Clearinghouse is responsible for a different subject area, such as elementary and early childhood education or teacher education.

Do the Clearinghouses offer any other services?
The ERIC Clearinghouses offer various services including answering questions, searching ERIC by computer, and distributing mini-bibliographies, newsletters, and other publications. Check with individual Clearinghouses for details.

How do I find out more about ERIC?
Contact the ERIC Clearinghouse on Elementary and Early Childhood Education or any other ERIC Clearinghouse. We will be happy to send you additional information on ERIC, *RIE*, *CIJE*, other ERIC Clearinghouses, computer searches, or document ordering. We can also send you a list of ERIC collections and institutions offering computer searches of ERIC in your geographical area.

ERIC Clearinghouse on Elementary and Early Childhood Education
College of Education
University of Illinois
Urbana, Illinois 61801
(217) 333-1386

Fig. 25-4 (continued)

C. Elaborate on both sides of the nonsexist curriculum issue or the "back to basics" issue.

D. Choose the answer that best completes each statement.
1. The real issue in increasing public schools' sponsorship of preschool programs is
   a. the mediocrity of public education.
   b. our private enterprise system.
   c. lack of parent pressure for programs.
   d. quality care as a public priority.
   e. All of these
2. Based on studies of public attitudes toward a nonsexist preschool program for children, it is evident that
   a. all parents want this type of curriculum.
   b. some parents want this type of curriculum.
   c. most parents do not care.
   d. only parents with strong religious affiliations want this type of curriculum.
   e. only females think this type of curriculum is important.
3. Parent education components at early childhood centers are
   a. growing and viable.
   b. shrinking due to lack of parent interest.
   c. shrinking because of economics.
   d. growing within the public school system.
   e. remaining about the same in number.
4. Public monies for child care operations are now in jeopardy because
   a. the public wants to choose its own type of child care.
   b. volunteers are plentiful, and are flocking to empty church buildings to care for children.
   c. parents prefer family day care.

d. they compete with other kinds of welfare and social services for funding.

e. All of these

5. Parenting skills are

a. easy to teach.

b. seen as being technical in nature by a growing number of parents.

c. best taught in junior high school because of the growing number of teenage pregnancies.

d. so diverse they cannot be taught.

e. understood by most parents because of mass media's interest in them.

6. The "back to basics" movement has influenced early childhood programs by

a. ruining children's opinion of themselves as learners.

b. alerting teachers to solve the balance between "structure" and discovery.

c. increasing the number of abstract rote memorization activities in many schools.

d. Both a and b

e. Both b and c

E. List four subjects on which much research is currently focused.

Resources

Beñas, Evelyn. "Public Policy and Children." *The Bulletin*, Northern California Association for the Education of Young Children (Oct. 1978).

Case, Robbie. "Piaget's Theory of Child Development and Its Implications." *Phi Delta Kappan* (Sept. 1973).

Honig, Alice. Workshop presentation at NAEYC Conference, November 1981.

Katz, Lillian. "Salient Research on Learning in Early Childhood Education and Implications for Action." Alexandria, VA: Association for Supervision and Curriculum Development, 1981.

Serbin, Lisa A., and Conner, Jane M. "Environmental Control of Sex Related Behavior in the Preschool:" ERIC ED191 558.

Usdan, Michael D. "Realities of the 1980's: Implications for Teacher Educators." *Journal of Teacher Education*, Vol. XXXII, No. 4 (July–Aug. 1981).

Section 9
Infant/Toddler Placements

Unit 26
The Infant/Toddler Center

OBJECTIVES

After studying this unit, the student will be able to:

- List at least three characteristics of a quality infant/toddler center.
- Discuss some of the research on day care for infants and toddlers.

STANDARDS

Most infants and toddlers today are cared for by relatives or family day care homes. Many parents feel, rightly or wrongly, that the infant thrives better in an environment most like the home. This is why family day care homes are so popular. State licensing in California reflects the importance of a low adult:infant or adult:toddler ratio. The state of California will license a family day care home for six children to one adult. No more than two of the six children may be infants or toddlers. If the home is licensed to keep more infants, it must hire another adult to keep with the ratio. The licensing of infant/toddler day care centers reflects this same philosophy. The National Association for the Education of Young Children has been urging a ratio of 1:4 as a national standard. A quality center may deliberately choose to keep its ratio 1:3.

One of the reasons for the lack of national standards lies in the belief that all young children, especially infants and toddlers, belong at home with their mothers.

This attitude, however, does not reflect what is happening in the work place. The fastest rising group of new workers is women with children under six.

In 1960, fewer than 20% of women twenty-five years of age or younger with children under six chose to work; by 1976, this figure rose to nearly 40%. With women over thirty-five, the figures are dramatically higher. In 1960, approximately 20% of women in this age bracket with children under six either chose or had to work, a figure not much different from that of women under twenty-five. By 1976, this figure jumped to 54%. This reflects, perhaps, the rising divorce rate and the growing need for a two-parent income in order to fight inflation (Berger, 1981). In fact, according to the U.S. Census of 1980, the percentage of working women with children under six and with children in preschool was 84% (*Statistical Abstracts of the U.S., 1981*).

The number of women entering the work force with children younger than three has also been increasing. In 1960, this figure was less than 7%; by 1976, it was nearly 34% (Bureau of Labor Statistics Report, 1977).

The majority of mothers in one poll indicated they would use the services of their family or neighbors for day care of their infants and toddlers. Several mentioned that they would use an infant/toddler day care center, but either there was no center available or the center was full. Even when a center is available, many parents fail to budget enough for infant/toddler care. It is expensive, averaging from $50 to $90 per week. How is the difference between what is charged and what the program costs reconciled? Usually through subsidies, often through fees parents of three- to five-year-olds pay. In other words, although a parent of a three-year-old may pay $40 per week, it may cost only $30 each week to care for the child. Thus, the director has an extra $10 each week to apply to the deficit accumulated in the infant and toddler rooms.

CHARACTERISTICS OF A QUALITY INFANT/TODDLER CENTER

The eighteen characteristics of quality programs, as discussed earlier, are applicable to infant and toddler centers. However, perhaps physical and psychological safety should come first. Because of their helplessness, babies require a lot of warm, loving care. Erikson would say they need to know that the adults in their lives can be trusted. According to Maslow, they need to have the deficiency needs met — satisfying biological and physical safety needs, psychological safety needs, belongingness and love needs, and esteem needs. By meeting the deficiency needs, the center can help guide the infant and toddler toward self-actualization.

What is most important, perhaps, in the infant center is a genuine affection for the babies on the part of the caretakers. Parents looking for day care for their infants should look for this quality and choose very carefully. Watch for signs indicating the infant is unhappy. A child crying every morning when getting ready to leave, failing to gain weight as is appropriate for infants, or clinging to the parent when being left are all signs that something may not be right. We must always look at the infant's degree of discomfort. We can tell that something is wrong only through the infant's actions. We must, therefore, watch them closely

in order to discover whether things are all right with them.

VARIETY IN INFANT/TODDLER PROGRAMS There is probably as much variety in infant/toddler programs as there is in preschool programs. Each program will be, for the most part, a reflection of the person in charge. A loving director who truly CAREs will provide a warm, loving environment for the infants and toddlers, figure 26-1. The director will care enough to ensure that the rooms used by the infants and toddlers are safe. The director will care enough to have a safe, fenced-in outdoor area as well.

One of the more interesting programs is called Resources for Infant Educators (*RIE*). Its spokeswoman in the United States is Magda Gerber, and it is based upon the work of Dr. Emmi Pikler of Hungary. Pikler has stated, "I have to stress that by no means do we believe it is advantageous to rear infants away from their families. . . .Only if this is not possible should the infant spend time in group care." (Gerber, 1979, p. 1) She explains her philosophy as ". . .the infant needs an intimate, stable, adult relationship, and that is the leading principle of infant care and education as practiced..." (Gerber, 1979, p. 1)

Fig. 26-1 Encouraging motor activities is an essential part of a curriculum for toddlers. (Courtesy of Jody Boyd)

In particular Pikler believes that infants should receive *individualized care* in a group setting. Some infant centers have interpreted this to mean that the same caretaker should always, in as much as is possible, care for the same infant day after day. In this way, the infant can form a bond with the caretaker the same way a bond is formed with the infant's mother and/or father.

Some of the specific techniques endorsed by Pikler have become widely accepted in infant/toddler care centers in the United States. Some of the techniques are: assigning the same adult to the same infant; speaking softly and gently to the infant; and taking time to explain carefully the purpose of changing a diaper, figure 26-2. Due to the efforts of Gerber and university sponsorship, Pikler's philosophy and techniques are becoming well-known.

Other exemplary infant programs have been associated with major universities as a part of the training programs for students in child development. One such program is associated with the University of North Carolina at Greensboro. The infant/toddler program provides for what Keister calls "individual care in a group setting." (1977, p. 11) Because the center trains students, its caretakers are highly qualified, loving people. With the availability of student assistants, the adult:infant ratio is often as low as 1:2.

HOME VERSUS DAY CARE CENTER

Keister's original study compared infants who attended the center with infants reared at home. On a series of measures evaluating physical, social, emotional, and cognitive growth, the differences were not significant. In a follow-up study of the infants after their entry in school, no negative results were reported. Positive results pointed to the greater sociability of the infants who attended the center and their quicker assimilation into school routines, figure 26-3. The important point about infant/toddler centers is that group care is not detrimental as long as it is individualized, consistent, and nurturing.

Many researchers firmly believe that a mother should remain home with her baby. Burton White is among these, although he has modified his position somewhat. At the November 8, 1981 National Association for the Education of Young Children

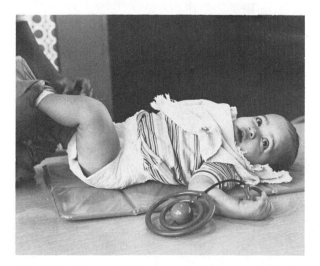

Fig. 26-2 The curriculum in an infant center includes changing diapers. (Courtesy of Jody Boyd)

Fig. 26-3 Self-help, when encouraged during the infant/toddler period, promotes further self-help in preschoolers.

Conference in Detroit, White mentioned that the attitude that a woman's place was to raise her baby should be changed; *both* parents should raise the baby. In the case of single parents, there should be support services to help the mother.

> Parents should consider sharing the child-rearing function. They might also consider using part-time (up to four hours a day) substitute care, if necessary, as an important resource in meeting their need for income or self-expression. High quality, part-time substitute care can make the difference between an oppressive child-rearing situation and a rewarding one. It can be the means by which a young woman can continue a career or other personal interest without penalty to her child. In general, high quality substitute care is available and afford-able. It should be used sparingly. (1980, p. 26)

Many professionals in the field of infant and toddler day care have decried White's position against substitute care for infants. However, he does raise some valid questions. Little research has been done in the area of the long-term effects of substitute care on infants and toddlers outside of the university setting.

One recent one (Stevens, 1982), however, summarized the follow-up data on 361 babies who had been cared for in eleven centers in New York City during the 1970's. In a carefully controlled study that compared the center-based infants and toddlers to those raised at home or in family day care homes, it was discovered that upon school entry the center-based children were significantly ahead of either the home-based or family day care-based children on cognitive and language measures. Perhaps of even greater significance was the fact that the center-based toddlers did not experience the drop in cognitive abilities at three years experienced by the home-based and family day care-based groups. The infants had entered the day care setting between eight weeks and fourteen months.

What we need now is additional research. Are there any long-term effects on infants and toddlers, especially those placed in what may not be quality programs? It is, as Burton White suggested, a question worth investigating.

A CURRICULUM FOR INFANTS AND TODDLERS

Another question often raised by people who are unfamiliar with infants and toddlers is "What do you mean when you say you 'teach' infants and toddlers?" Many people, including parents, misunderstand just how much their children learn during the first three years of life. Even those who do know may feel that all the child does is play.

A curriculum for infants and toddlers should be tailored to the developmental age of the child, figure 26-4. Noticing that an infant has just begun to reach and grasp, the curriculum should provide this infant with opportunities to do so, placing the child in an infant seat with attractive objects within sight and reach. Another infant may be starting to coo; speaking and cooing with the youngster can stimulate imitation. For the infant beginning to crawl, a safe area is essential.

Pikler advocates the use of an extra-large playpen, large enough for up to six babies in which they can crawl and manipulate objects without danger. She also advocates a fenced-in outside area where the children can safely crawl and manipulate. These

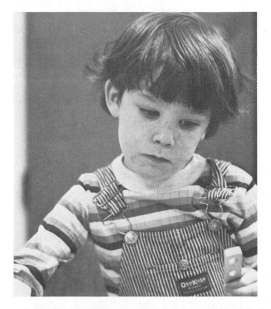

Fig. 26-4 This child's experiences are tailored to his developmental age.

playpens are not confining to the child; they provide a safe area and are large enough to stimulate motor activities.

Some good sources for activities to implement in an infant/toddler center can be found in Gonzalez-Meña's and Eyer's *Infancy and Caregiving* (1980), Bailey's and Burton's *The Dynamic Self* (1982), and Fowler's *Infant and Child Care* (1980). As infant/toddler day care becomes more common, we feel certain that more books focusing on curriculum for this age will emerge. Look for them.

Summary

In this unit, we discussed why there is a need for quality infant and toddler day care. We also mentioned some of the programs about which there is evidence indicating there are no long-term detrimental effects. In fact, some of the research tends to reveal more positive outcomes of early care, especially regarding later social adjustment, and cognitive and language development.

Suggested Activities

A. Read Burton L. White's *The First Three Years of Life*. Discuss the seven phases of development with your peers and college supervisor. Does the infant/toddler center where you are student teaching use some of the White's suggestions in its curriculum?

B. Read Magda Gerber's *Resources for Infant Educators*. Discuss Pikler's and *RIE*'s philosophies. Does the center at which you are student teaching employ any of Pikler's and *RIE*'s techniques?

C. Visit an infant center different from the one where you are student teaching. (If you are at a college center, visit a proprietary one. If you are at a publicly funded one, visit a privately funded one.) Discuss similarities and differences with your peers and college supervisor.

Review

A. List three characteristics of a quality infant/toddler center.

B. Complete the following statements.
1. The fastest rising group of new workers is women with children . . .
2. Most infants today are cared for by . . .
3. In her Resources for Infant Educators (*RIE*) program, Magda Gerber has popularized the philosophy of . . .
4. In the *RIE* program, each child is always assigned to . . .
5. In Keister's study, there were . . . between center infants and home-reared infants.
6. Burton White firmly believes that infants should be raised by . . .
7. White also believes that . . . should remain home with their infants.
8. The New York City study revealed that center-based infants were . . . of either home-based or family day care-based infants upon school entry.
9. A curriculum for infants and toddlers should be carefully tailored to . . . of the infant.
10. Pikler advocates the use of an . . . in which up to six infants can crawl in safety.

Resources

Berger, Eugenia Hepworth. *Parents as Partners in Education*. St. Louis: C.V. Mosby Co., 1981.

Gerber, Magda. *Resources for Infant Educators*. Los Angeles: Resources for Infant Educators, 1971.

Keister, Mary Elizabeth. *The Good Life for Infants and Toddlers*, 2nd ed. Washington, DC: NAEYC, 1977.

Statistical Abstracts of the U.S. Bureau of the Census. Washington, D.C.: U.S. Government Printing Office, 1981.

Stevens, Joseph H. Jr. "The New York City Infant Day Care Study." *Young Children*, Vol. 37, No. 2 (Jan. 1982), pp. 47–53.

White, Burton L. "Education During the First Three Years." Presentation at the NAEYC Conference, November 8, 1981.

White, Burton L. "Should You Stay Home with Your Baby?" (*Educational Horizons*, Vol. 59, No. 1 (Fall 1980), p. 26.

Unit 27
Student Teaching in an Infant/Toddler Center

OBJECTIVES

After studying this unit, the student teacher will be able to:

- Describe the general regulations of infant centers (including health concerns).
- Cite techniques for approaching and working with children.
- Describe caregiving as a teaching activity.
- Identify activities for infants and toddlers.

An infant/toddler center is an entirely new world, one that is completely different from the preschool environment. Every infant/toddler center is operated a little differently. However, most centers have similar regulations regarding children's health, caregivers' health, and diaper-changing procedures. A student teacher should request a staff handbook. Read it *before* you go to the center. Be prepared to ask questions about anything you do not understand. Babies need consistency, and it is important that you are able to fit into the center routines as quickly as possible. Most important — relax and enjoy the children!

GENERAL RULES AND REGULATIONS

The physical setting and philosophy of a center will determine how various routines are carried out, figure 27-1. Centers usually have specific routines regarding health and safety, medications, emergencies, feeding, diapering, and naps.

HEALTH AND SAFETY
- Smoking is not allowed in infant/toddler centers.
- Coffee, tea, etc. should be consumed in staff areas only.

- *Never* leave a child unattended on a changing table or in a high chair. Even very young children can wiggle around and have a serious fall.
- Do not leave children unattended inside or outside. They can easily injure themselves.

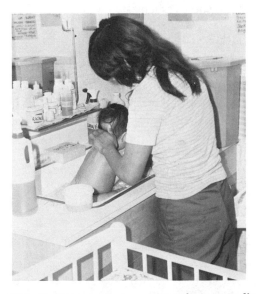

Fig. 27-1 Bathing routines require safe surroundings. (Courtesy of Irene Sterling)

This unit was contributed by Irene Sterling, Young Families Program.

- Ill infants should not be in the center. Infants who have bad colds, fevers, or contagious diseases are usually cared for at home.
- If you are ill, you should not be in the center. You will not be efficient if you are not feeling well. In addition, your illness may spread to the children. If you contract a contagious illness, notify the center immediately.
- *Wash your hands.* The most important health measure you can take is to wash your hands after diapering or cleaning noses and before feeding a child.
- Watch for signs that a child may not feel well. Some symptoms are digging at or pulling ears, listlessness, glassy eyes, diarrhea, limping, etc.

MEDICATION   Normally, only a staff person will be allowed to give medication. You should be aware of medication schedules for the children. You might need to remind the staff when medications are due.

You also need to be aware of the effects medications may have on the children. They may become sleepy, agitated, or show allergic symptoms. You must be alert to changes that occur when medicine is given and be able to communicate these to the staff.

EMERGENCIES
- *Stay calm.*
- Speak calmly and quietly to the child.
- Alert the staff that an emergency has occurred. They should be able to administer the appropriate first aid measures until the child can see a physician.
- Help calm the other children. They will respond to the situation the same way you do. If you are agitated and upset, they will respond to your feelings; likewise, if you remain calm, they will.

FEEDING
- Wash your hands.
- Read the child's chart to see what kind of food and/or formula to give and how much. (*Remember:* Do not feed a child from a baby food jar; use a dish, figure 27-2. Saliva, which contains bacteria, will get in the jar and spoil the remaining food.
- Gather all the things you need for feeding: bib, washcloth, spoons, sponges, etc. It may be helpful to bring one spoon for you to feed the child with and a spoon for the infant to "help."
- Tell the infant what you are going to do. Let the infant anticipate being fed.
- Settle the child comfortably. (You may want to make sure the child has a clean, dry diaper before feeding, so he or she will be more comfortable and attentive.)
- The child will let you know when more food is desired. When the child opens the mouth, respond by feeding. Do not just keep stuffing food in.
- Talk to the child. Eating is a time to enjoy pleasant conversation and socialization, and young children like being talked to. You can talk about the food, its texture, color, temperature, taste, etc. Eye contact is important.
- Encourage the child to help feed him or herself. It is a little messier, but it means more independence later.

Fig. 27-2   Children at this infant/toddler center are fed from dishes, not from jars; they are more sanitary. (Courtesy of Irene Sterling)

- Do not force a child to eat more than they want. If they refuse to take the last ounce of a bottle or the last little bit of solid food, do not push it. The child knows when he or she is not hungry.
- Be sure to burp bottle-fed children when they need it. You may want to check with the child's caregiver for any special instructions.
- When the baby is finished, wash the face and hands. Again, tell the baby you are going to do this. Encourage the child to take part in this activity. Be gentle with the wash cloth.
- Take off the bib, and put the baby down to play.
- Clean up. Be sure to wipe off the high chair, the tray, the table, and the floor. Put dishes and bottles in the sink.
- *Record* what and how the child ate. Parents like to know this information.

DIAPERING

- Gather everything you need to change the baby: diapers, pins, clean clothes, wash cloth, plastic pants, powder, medication, etc.
- Tell the child what you are going to do. Set the child on the diaper table.
- Take off the wet diaper, and clean the child thoroughly with a warm, wet cloth. Apply powder or ointment according to the parent's instructions.
- Keep one hand on the child at all times.
- Talk to the child about the process. Talk about being wet, dry, and clean. Describe the process of dressing and undressing; you can talk about the baby's clothes and body parts. Involve the baby in the process. Ask the child to lift the legs or give you an arm to put through the sleeve. (*Note:* How diapers are changed also gives children messages about their sexuality. If you are relaxed and casual about changing them and washing their genital area, children get the message that they are "okay.")
- Put the child in a safe place. Dispose of the diaper and soiled clothes according to the directions you are given.

- Clean the changing table. Use germicidal solution.
- Wash your hands. Clean changing tables and clean hands will help prevent the spread of disease.
- Record the diaper change. Be sure to note bowel movements. Make note of anything unusual: diarrhea, constipation, diaper rash, unusually strong urine odor, or anything else that seems out of the ordinary.

TOILET TRAINING If a child is being toilet trained, ask frequently if the child needs to go to the bathroom, figure 27-3. For a child who is just starting, you may need to say, "Let's try to use the toilet now." Do not force the issue and/or become upset if there is an accident. The child is not deliberately being naughty or incompetent; control has not been learned yet. If too much of an issue is made of accidents, the child may get overanxious and begin to believe he or she is not capable of being trained.

NAPTIME Young children may vary considerably in their naptimes. You must be alert to signs of

Fig. 27-3 Learning to use the toilet is a part of the curriculum. (Courtesy of Jody Boyd)

sleepiness in order to prevent a young child from becoming overtired. Toddlers usually learn very quickly to adjust to the nap schedule of the program. Watch for yawning, rubbing of eyes, pulling of hair, thumbsucking, and disinterest in toys or people.

All these are signs that a young child may be ready for a nap. Before putting the child down, quickly check his or her schedule. Make sure the child is dry and is not due to be fed soon. You may want to feed a child a little ahead of schedule if they are sleepy. Make sure you have a clean crib and blanket. Also, check to see if the child has any special toy to sleep with.

If you are helping a child who is new to the center, the child may be reluctant to take a nap. This is because the child is in a strange place, full of strangers.

Check to see if the child prefers to sleep on the back, side, or stomach; most children like to lie on their stomachs. If you do not know what the child likes, try the stomach first.

You may find it helpful to sing softly, rub the back gently, or rock in order to help the child settle down to sleep. Dimming the center's lights may help calm the child. Many times all the excitement of the center and the other children make it difficult for babies to sleep. Be patient, but firm.

Do not feel you failed if you do not get instant success. Ask the staff for suggestions. Infant center staffs are usually more than willing to answer questions, listen to concerns, or offer suggestions.

APPROACHING AND WORKING WITH CHILDREN

When working with infants and toddlers, remember that every child is an individual. Even tiny infants have preferences. They may like to sleep on their backs or sides rather than stomachs; they may like to be burped on the shoulder rather than on your knees. When you are caring for a child, take a minute to try and find out what some of their preferences may be.

When working with children of any age, act like a professional:

- Be aware that your size may be frightening to a child.

- Do not make negative remarks about children in their presence or in the presence of any other child. Even the youngest children will understand your tone and feeling.
- Keep confidential material to yourself. Medical, financial, personal, and family information is to help you understand the child more completely, not to share with parents or other students.

WORKING WITH INFANTS Children need to hear your voice, so *talk to them*. They need the social contact that only another person can provide. Hearing language is also the way children learn to talk. Be sure you use clear, simple language. *Speak softly*. Voice tone and volume greatly affect the children. If you speak in a loud, excited voice, the children are very likely to become loud and excited in response.

Encourage anticipation by telling the children what you are going to do. Say "Now we are going to change your diaper." Do not just grab the children off the floor and drop them on the changing table. They will respond and cooperate when you let them know what to expect.

Try to be at *eye level to the children*. Sitting or kneeling on the floor brings you closer to their line of vision. They need to see more than your feet in order to get to know you personally. *Make eye contact with the children*. When bottle feeding, playing, diapering, etc., look directly at the children. Meet and hold their gaze when talking to them. You like to have people look at you; babies undoubtedly feel the same way.

Move slowly around infants. Young children do everything in slow motion. They often get upset and overstimulated when adults run around them excitedly. Young infants need time to understand the changes that are happening. Be affectionate and warm but *do not hover*. Be ready to hug, hold, and comfort the children when they need it, but let them be free to explore. Young children need to be able to move around and experience their environment, figure 27-4. They need to find their own solutions to problems whenever they can. Let the children experiment with toys and invent uses. Intervene only when they are likely to get hurt, obviously in distress,

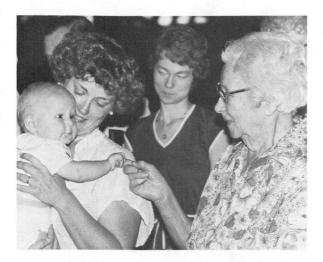

Fig. 27-4   Infants can meet new people as they experience their environment. (Courtesy of Nancy Martin)

or are too frustrated to cope. Becoming independent, competent, and self-sufficient is hard work; children need loving, secure adults and a safe place to begin the process.

Encourage the babies to help you in caregiving. They are people, not dolls. You need to dress them, change them, and feed them. However, they will help if you let them. Recognize their attempts to participate and encourage them. It does not take much longer, and the rewards are many times greater.

WORKING WITH TODDLERS
Toddlers are a very special group. They are just beginning to understand that they *are* people. They are seeing themselves as separate from their parents for the first time. They are compelled to explore and understand their environment. They must assert themselves as individuals. If you can recognize their need to be an individual without feeling personal insecurity, you will have made a giant step in dealing effectively with toddlers.

Toddlers, more so than infants, will challenge your authority. They will test you every chance they get, until they can feel secure in your response. You will need to call on all your reserves of strength, firmness, patience, and love to deal with the toddlers. They are loving, affectionate, giving, sharing, joyful, spontaneous people; take pleasure in them.

You may find some of the following ideas helpful when you are working with toddlers. Read the suggestions, and think about them. Try to put them into practice.

Make *positive statements.* Instead of saying "Don't put your feet on the table," say "Feet belong on the floor." When children hear the words "don't" and "no" constantly, they begin to ignore them.

Give choices only when you intend to honor them. If Johnny's mother said that her son must wear his jacket when playing outside, do not ask John, "Do you want your jacket?" Instead, say "Your Mom wants you to wear a jacket today." If you give a choice and the toddler says "no," you are already in a conflict you could have avoided.

Avoid problems by *being alert.* Watch for signs that a child may be getting too frustrated to handle a situation or that a fight over a toy is about to start.

Use distraction whenever possible. If you see two children insisting on the same toy, try to interest one of them in something else. You might point out a toy just like it or remind them of another enjoyable activity.

If an argument does erupt, *avoid taking sides.* If John takes away Kate's toy and she hits him, instead of punishing Kate for hitting or John for taking the toy, help both children understand how the other child feels. *Encourage the use of words* to handle situations. "Kate, use your words to tell John you are angry." "John, Kate gets angry when you take her toys." Encourage the children to name things, to express happiness, sorrow, excitement, etc. *Let the children talk.* Correct grammar and pronunciation will come later. Practicing verbal expression is the most important thing.

Act on your own suggestions. If you say, "Time to clean up. Start putting the toys away," the children are more likely to follow your suggestions if they are accompanied by actions.

Avoid making models or doing the children's work for them. Let the children make their own art. If the cars do not look too much like cars, so what? The important thing is that a child made something.

Make *alternative suggestions* if some children continually ignore safety rules or disturb others: suggest an alternate activity the child likes; suggest

Fig. 27-5 Interactions between children and adults enhance learning. (Courtesy of Irene Sterling)

taking turns; suggest cooperation; or remove the child from the activity. If you said "no," stick to it; be firm but calm. *Do not take the children's reaction* to discipline *personally*. You may hear "I don't like you!" Say, "I know you are angry. It's okay to be angry." Toddlers respect fairness and desperately want limits they can depend on.

Do not make promises you cannot keep. Just say you will have to ask if you do not know. Toddlers understand that.

CAREGIVING AS A TEACHING ACTIVITY

Caregiving activities are not just babysitting in a quality program. The interactions between adult and child enhance learning, figure 27-5. Developmental skills are encouraged. *RIE* uses the term *educarer* to describe adults who work with infants. They feel that these people not only care for the infants' physical needs but are an important part of the education process.

Consider the following curriculum areas, usually included in the preschool program: motor; cognitive; language; social; sensory; self-esteem; mathematics. All these areas are encountered during routine caregiving activities.

Think about the routines when you change a diaper:

- You talk to the child, telling what is going to happen. The child is developing a sense of sequential events. — LANGUAGE SOCIAL MATHEMATICS

- You take off the child's diaper and let the legs move freely. The child feels the air on the body. — MOTOR SENSORY

- You tell the child that the diaper is wet or has bowel movement. — COGNITIVE SENSORY

- You wash the child with a wash cloth. You apply powder or diaper rash medication to the behind. You talk about how this feels. — SENSORY LANGUAGE COGNITIVE

- You put a new diaper on the child and then, possibly, clothes. The new diaper is dry and feels more comfortable. — SENSORY LANGUAGE COGNITIVE

- You talk about what is happening, encouraging the infant to help you by lifting the legs, putting out an arm, etc. — LANGUAGE MOTOR SOCIAL

- The infant is now more comfortable and probably happier. You have had an opportunity for a special one-to-one experience with the child. For a few minutes of a busy morning, the infant has your complete attention. — SELF-ESTEEM SENSORY SOCIAL

What about feeding? After all, what could possibly be educational about baby food smeared all over an infant's face?

- You know it is time to give a bottle or feed a child. You tell the child you are going to prepare the food. You are again helping the child develop a sense of sequence of time. — MATHEMATICS LANGUAGE SOCIAL

- The young infant may be just starting to eat and learning to eat from a spoon; the older infant may be using fingers or learning to use a spoon. How special you feel when you succeed.

  MOTOR
  LANGUAGE
  SELF-ESTEEM

- You sit with the child or a small group of children while they eat lunch. You talk about what they are eating, about how it tastes, its texture, and color. A child who does not like peas may be encouraged to try three peas or two pieces of carrots.

  SOCIAL
  LANGUAGE
  COGNITIVE
  SENSORY
  MATHEMATICS

- The bottle-fed child or slightly older infant has your total attention. You talk to the child. You make eye contact while feeding the infant, holding the child close and safe. The milk is warm.

  SELF-ESTEEM
  LANGUAGE
  SENSORY

- After eating, you wash the face and hands with a warm, wet cloth. First, the right hand; then, left. The older child may be able to help you.

  SENSORY
  LANGUAGE
  COGNITIVE
  MOTOR

These are just two examples of the many routines that happen in an infant center. Think of how many things are happening to a child during these routines. Think about what else is happening. What other messages is the infant receiving? Think about bathing and dressing to go outside. What about naptime? What kinds of things could you do that would make naptime go more smoothly and be a more complete experience for each child?

ACTIVITIES IN THE INFANT/ TODDLER CENTER

Play can usually be divided into two types: social play, in which a child interacts with an adult or another child, or object play, in which the child interacts with an object or toy. Children of all ages engage in both types of play, and the following guidelines are true for any child.

EFFECTIVE SOCIAL PLAY

- Activities for infants are not preschool activities "geared down." Infants are a specific age group that need specific activities.
- Play *with* the children, not *to* them. Try to interact, not entertain. The adult can initiate the activity, but should wait for the child to respond.
- Involve different ways of communicating in your social interactions: looking, touching, holding, laughing, talking, rocking, singing, and laughing. Give infants a lot of different social responses to learn.
- Be sensitive to infants' signals. If they are interested, they will laugh, coo, look, smile, and reach. If tired or disinterested, they may fuss, turn away, or fall asleep.
- *Talk* to the infant. Children learn to talk from the moment they are born. The more language they hear, the more they will learn. Name actions, objects, and people.
- Offer new ways of doing things. Demonstrate how something works. Encourage persistence. Do not direct children as to the "right" way to use a toy, let them explore and experiment. (Obviously, if some danger is involved, use your judgment and intervene when necessary.)
- Be sensitive to variations initiated by the child and be ready to respond to them.

A child can use play materials either alone or with an adult. Adults should use judgment in the choice of materials presented to each age group. A toy that a two-month-old might enjoy might not be appropriate for a nine-month-old. When offering materials to the children, remember:

- Toys and materials should encourage action. Materials should not just entertain but elicit some action.
- Toys should respond to the child's action. When the child pushes or pulls a toy, the toy should react. The ability to control parts of one's world, to learn cause and effect, is an important part of learning at this early age.

- Materials should be versatile. The more ways a toy can be used, the better it is.
- Whenever possible, toys should provide more than one kind of sensory output. For example, a clear rattle lets the child see, as well as hear, the action.

Play and playthings are an important part of the environment. You should not be led to believe that constant stimulation is the aim. Even very young infants need time to be alone and to get away from it all. It is important to be sensitive to the infant's cues about feelings to help avoid overstimulation and distress.

The following are some activity ideas for infants (one to twelve months old). Remember that some activities are appropriate for many ages.

- Change the infant's position for a different view.
- Use bells, rattles, and spoons to make noise.
- Exercise the infant's arms and legs.
- Rub the infant's body with different textured materials.
- Put large, clear pictures at eye level for the infant to look at.
- Imitate the sounds the infant makes.
- Record the children's sounds, and play them back.
- Put toys slightly out of reach to encourage rolling over and reaching.
- Take the babies outside on warm days. Let them feel the grass, and see trees and plants.
- Call the children by name.
- Play "peek-a-boo" with the children.
- Hide toys and encourage the children to look for them.
- Attach a string to toys, and show the children how to pull them. (*Caution:* do not leave the child unattended with the string; they may get entangled.)
- Make puppets for the children to look at and hold.
- Let the children play with mirrors.
- Play games and sing, using parts of the body. Make up songs about feet, hands, noses, etc.
- Show children how to bang two toys together.
- Let the child feed him or herself. Give peas, dried cooked carrots, or small pieces of fruit to practice with.

- Play "pat-a-cake," "row-row-row your boat." Encourage the children to finish the songs for you.
- Listen for airplanes, trucks, cars, dogs, etc. outside, and call the children's attention to them.
- Roll a ball to the child and encourage the child to roll it back.
- Play "hide and seek."
- Play music for the children; encourage them to clap along.
- Have hats for the children to wear. Let them see themselves in the mirror.
- Read to the children. Point out the pictures; encourage the child to point to them.
- Let the children play with different textures.
- Put toys upside down and sideways. See how the children respond to the changes.
- Play pretending games.
- Show the children how to stack blocks.
- Make obstacle courses for the children to crawl over, around, and through.
- Let them play with measuring cups and spoons in water, sand, or cornmeal.
- Play "follow the leader."
- Make an incline for the children to roll objects down.
- Have the children set the table with plastic cups and dishes.
- Hide the clock or radio under a towel, and see if one of the children can find it.
- Have purses and bags for the children to carry things in.
- Give the children puppets to play with. Watch how they use them.
- Let the children fingerpaint with nontoxic paint.
- Bring junk mail for the children to read. They love the bright colors.
- Make a mailbox for them to put their mail in.
- Let them go barefoot in the sand and grass so they can feel the textures.
- Use old-fashioned clothespins for the children to put around the rim of a coffee can or plastic container. (Make sure that any sharp edges are filed down.)

- Encourage the children to help put their toys away.
- Let them practice opening containers, e.g., plastic margarine bowls. Put a toy in the container to encourage them to open it.
- Make toys for the children; be inventive! Let your imagination go. Remember that the toys should have no sharp edges and should be too large to fit in the mouth.

Infant activities grow gradually more and more complex as the children mature. Usually by twelve to fourteen months, the child is walking and beginning to talk. An infant of this age is quite accomplished mentally. The infant understands that objects are separate and detached. The infant rotates, reverses, and stacks things, places them in, and removes them from containers in order to further consider their separateness.

Projects for toddlers can be more complex in response to their increased mental and physical abilities. Small group activities can usually be tried with some success. When planning activities for and working with toddlers, remember that the activities should be kept as simple as possible. In addition, plan ahead. Anything that can go wrong will. Bring everything needed to start and finish the project. It is also important to remember that it is the process, not the product, that counts. Let the children experiment with different ways of using the materials.

Toddlers need much encouragement to be persistent and finish difficult tasks. *Give immediate praise* when a child succeeds or makes a good effort. Children learn to do things more quickly when they are praised promptly.

Give *positive, but realistic, evaluations* of the child's efforts. If the child tries to roll the ball and fails, say, "That was a good try; roll it again. I know you can do it!"

Praise the deed, not the doer. Saying "good girl" does not say anything about what the little girl has accomplished. She may even begin to feel that she is a good person when she succeeds and a bad person when she fails. Using a statement like "You did a nice job picking up the toys" tells the child about the accomplishment. Encourage the child to be proud of all accomplishments. Instead of saying "I'm proud of

you," say "You did a good job." Children learn about themselves from the adults around them. They tend to become what you tell them they are. Make it positive.

Below are some ideas you might want to try with the toddlers. Watch the children, and see what you can think of that they might enjoy.

- Easel painting (one-color paint, use soap to help it come out of clothes).
- Have waterplay. Use measuring cups for pouring.
- Coloring. Use a limited number of colors and a large sheet of paper. For a change, try covering the whole table with paper.
- Collage. Try using starch and tissue paper with paint brushes.
- Fingerpainting. For a change, try yogurt or pudding.
- Paint on cloth pinned to the easel. It makes a great gift for parents.
- Music. Use drums, rhythm sticks, clapping games, simple exercises to music.
- Flannelboard stories. Keep them short and graphic.
- Bubble blowing. This should be done sitting down. Emphasize blowing through a straw. Use a cup with water and soap. Collect *all* straws; they can be dangerous if a child falls on them.
- Gluing. Use torn paper, tissue, magazine pictures, etc. Avoid small beans, peas, etc. that could be swallowed or put up noses.
- Play dough, made with salt, flour, and nontoxic color.
- Hand and foot prints.
- Body tracings.
- Gadget prints. Limit the number of gadgets, and use only one or two colors.
- Paint a large cardboard box; cut shapes in the sides. Children can climb through the sides after they paint it.
- Go on a sock walk. Plant the seeds collected on a wet sponge. (More suitable for older toddlers.)
- Do simple shape rubbings. (More suitable for older toddlers.)
- Make simple roll-out cookies or use frozen dough for the children to roll out and cut with cookie cutters.

- Plant beans in small plastic containers.
- Put cornmeal or sand in the waterplay table for a change. (Supervise carefully. The floor gets slippery when it is spilled.)

Create! Invent! Enjoy! Try to let yourself see the world the way these very special little people see it. When the diapers are messy or you have soiled your new blouse, look for the humor in things. It really is there!

Summary

Infant and toddler center routines and procedures depend on the philosophy and physical setting. Every center has guidelines for the caregivers' behaviors. Knowing guidelines and fitting quickly into center practice is a prime student teacher goal.

Learning takes place during each child's encounter with a caregiver. Caregivers can develop many skills for the child's benefit. Many action activities and experiences planned for this age group incorporate reciprocal responses from adults and play objects. The roots of independence and verbal ability develop as do individual preferences.

Suggested Activities

A. Visit an infant/toddler center for one hour. List all staff behaviors which protect children's health or safety. Report your findings to the group.

B. Invite a panel of practicing preschool and infant/toddler teachers to discuss "Planning a Curriculum."

C. Research, through local licensing agencies, the number of infant/toddler programs that were licensed in the past year in your community.

D. In groups of three to four, discuss infant/toddler care for teenage parents. Decide what type of care would best suit the teenage parents in your community. Report your ideas to the whole class.

E. Obtain a job description for an infant/toddler teacher.

Review

A. Define "educarer."

B. Describe expected student teacher behavior during emergencies.

C. List ways a caregiver could promote learning when bathing a fifteen-month-old child.

D. List possible signals that indicate a child is tired.

E. Select the answer that best completes each statement.

1. The factor which may best limit the spread of infection is
   a. periodic caregiver screening.
   b. change of room temperature.
   c. handwashing.
   d. the use of clean sponges.
   e. the use of spray disinfectants.

2. When feeding a young child,
   a. watch for signals that indicate the child is full.
   b. make sure the child finishes a small serving.
   c. he or she is expected to try a little of everything.
   d. eat along with the child.
   e. All of these

3. Telling infants that it is time to change their diapers is
   a. ridiculous and silly.
   b. difficult.
   c. not important.
   d. important.
   e. important, but you should use baby talk.

4. An important part of student teachers' work in an infant and toddler center is
   a. recording care specifics and asking when in doubt.
   b. watching first, rather than pitching right in.
   c. to let the regular staff do most of the talking.
   d. to move quickly and efficiently.
   e. telling parents how their children are acting.

5. If an infant or toddler is using a toy incorrectly,
   a. show the proper usage.
   b. show *you* can do it correctly.
   c. leave the child alone if it is not dangerous.
   d. talk about the right way to use it.
   e. All of these

Section 10
Employment

Unit 28
The Search: Choices and Alternatives

OBJECTIVES

After studying this unit, the student will be able to:

- Identify several major decisions which precede employment.
- Develop long- and short-range career goals.
- Describe ladder and lateral career development.
- List five common ways to find job openings.

THE JOB MARKET

Planning ahead to land the right job for you can be an exciting and rewarding task. Your choice of different types of early childhood jobs is wide, figure 28-1, and will become wider and more diverse as the demand for trained teachers outweighs the supply during the 1980's as predicted.

Another headache for school officials will be the likelihood of a severe teacher shortage by the mid-1980's. Enrollments in teacher-training institutions have declined steadily, so as older teachers retire or quit, there will be fewer available to replace them. ("Challenge of the '80's," 1979)

Preschool enrollments are expected to rise in the years ahead, figure 28-2. Divorce rates and numbers of women entering the work force, figure 28-3, will increase pressure to expand day care provided by trained teachers.

Social forces will encroach on the classroom. Nursery schools — both public and private — will swell as more mothers take jobs. Enrollments already have tripled since 1968 and could include at least half the nation's 3-to-5-year-olds by the early '80's. In many places, such day care will go beyond baby-sitting and attempt to enrich and develop children's intellectual abilities. ("Challenges of the '80's," 1979, p. 5)

A job in the early childhood field will not be hard to find; however, a job that suits your talents and goals and offers satisfaction will. Many student teachers are employed on a part-time basis, awaiting the completion of training to upgrade themselves and find a better-paying or more rewarding position.

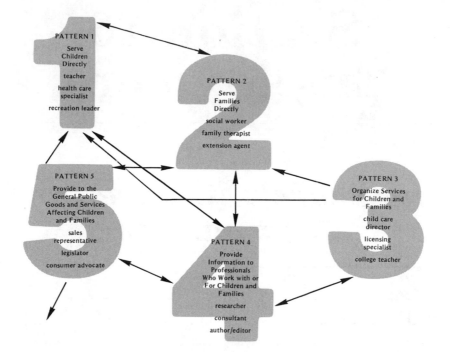

Fig. 28-1 Careers with young children (Reprinted by permission from *Careers with Young Children: Making Your Decision* by Judith W. Seaver, Carol A. Cartwright, Cecelie B. Ward, and C. Annette Heasley. Copyright © 1979, National Association for the Education of Young Children, 1834 Connecticut Avenue, NW, Washington, D.C. 20009.)

School Enrollments — A Look Ahead

Preschool (age 3–4)	1980	2,009,000	Up 28.1%
	1990	2,574,000	
Elementary (grades K–8)	1980	29,796,000	Up 13.7%
	1990	33,871,000	
High School	1980	14,329,000	Down 17.1%
	1990	11,876,000	
College	1980	12,376,000	Down 10.7%
	1988*	11,047,000	

*Latest projection.
USN & WR chart —
Basic data:
National Institute
of Education,
U.S. Dept. of Health,
Education, and Welfare

Fig. 28-2 School enrollment (From "Challenges of the 80's." *U.S. News & World Report*, Oct. 15, 1979.)

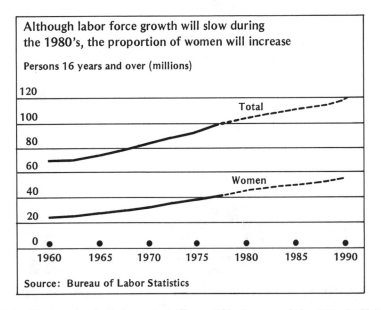

Although labor force growth will slow during the 1980's, the proportion of women will increase

Persons 16 years and over (millions)

Total

Women

1960 1965 1970 1975 1980 1985 1990

Source: Bureau of Labor Statistics

Fig. 28-3   Women in the job market (From "Challenges of the 80's." *U.S. News & World Report*, Oct. 15, 1979.)

LONG-RANGE AND SHORT-RANGE GOALS AND DECISIONS

One of the first decisions a graduating student teacher must make is whether to end training and find a job, pursue further coursework, or combine work and school. Although continual skill development updating is typical in teaching professions, heavy commitment to formal coursework is not recommended with full-time teaching responsibilities, particularly for beginning early childhood teachers. One has only so much stamina, time, and energy, and first-year employment is often described as a time-consuming, stress-producing "survival" year.

Examining closely the goals that immediate employment fulfills (besides wages, status, opportunities for upward mobility and skill development) is a necessary task. Writing long- and short-range professional goals clarifies the employment possibilities that best suit one's objectives. Long-range goals can be defined as an estimated, desired future professional attainment, figure 28-4. It involves dreaming, hoping, and "pie-in-the-sky" thinking. Usually, in long-range goal identification, one aims at the highest level of performance and potential. Goal setting helps realize

ambitions. ". . .never underestimate your dreams — your strength is in them." (Gordon-Novrok, 1979)

Short-range goals seem more forthright and practical. They pay the rent while one pursues upward job mobility and expanded skill development. Many short-range goals can be accomplished quickly and become sequential steps in long-range goal realization. Figure 28-5 displays levels of job titles and

Fig. 28-4   Training other teachers may be a long-range career goal. (Courtesy of Nancy Martin)

Baby-sitter
Mother's helper
Preschool, infant/
   toddler aide
Volunteer

No formal training or
high school child care
or child development
classes. Experience in
homes or at a supervised
center.

Private preschool assis-
tant teacher
Infant/toddler teacher/
   aide
Emergency children's
center instruct. permit
teacher, assistant
teacher, aide

18 years of age.
12 semester units of
college ECE/CD voca-
tional coursework com-
pleted or in progress;
      or
12 semester units of
coursework in ECE/CD
exclusive of fieldwork
and one of the follow-
ing:
(a) One year of experi-
    ence in an instruc-
    tional capacity in a
    child development
    program.
(b) A supervised field
    work course from
    an approved institu-
    tion.
(c) Enrollment in an
    ECE/CD training
    program at an
    approved institu-
    tion plus a written
    commission Form
    I-36 CCI from a pros-
    pective employer.

Private preschool
director

18 years of age.
15 semester units of
ECE/CD, including
3 units of administra-
tion
4 years experience; or
1 year of college
15 semester units
   ECE/CD
2 years experience; or
2 years college
15 semester units
   ECE/CD
1 year experience.

ECE teacher, assistant
teacher, aide

Completion of a voca-
tional certificate pro-
gram in ECE/CD
18–30 semester units,
varies between institu-
tions. Includes super-
vised student teaching.

Public children's center
   teacher
Head Start teacher
   (holds regular chil-
   dren's center instruc-
   tional permit)

60 semester units AA
degree ECE/CD. Includes
24 units ECE/CD, super-
vised student teaching,
16 units in general edu-
cation, including at
least one course in each
of the following areas:
   Humanities
   Social science
   Math and science
   English
Plus 1 year experience
in an instructional
capacity in a child
development program.

Fig. 28-5 Early childhood career ladder in California

(Holds life children's center instructional permit)

124 semester units BA or higher degree from an approved institution, 5 years experience in last 10 years while possessing or eligible for permit, at least 2 years of which have been continuous full-time employment.

Public ECE center director
Administrator (holds supervisory children's center permit)

Holds regular permit, BA, or higher degree
12 semester units ECE/CD
6 semester units administration and supervision coursework
2 years experience as teacher in ECE program.

Public school teacher (holds multiple subjects credential)
Teacher trainer
Director/administrator public program

25–30 semester units above BA in department of education leading to Multiple Subjects Credential (K-12);
or
MA degree ECE/CD or related field.

Early childhood ed. specialist (holds Early Childhood Ed. Specialist Credential)
Teacher trainer

Holds Multiple Subjects Credential
30 semester units of ECE coursework in college education department;
or
MA degree ECE/CD or related field.

Administrator, teacher trainer, theorist, researcher

Ph.D. — Doctor of Education or Early Education.

Fig. 28-5 (continued)

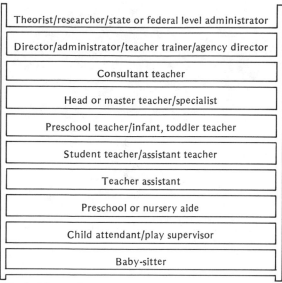

Fig. 28-6 Status and responsibility ladder scale

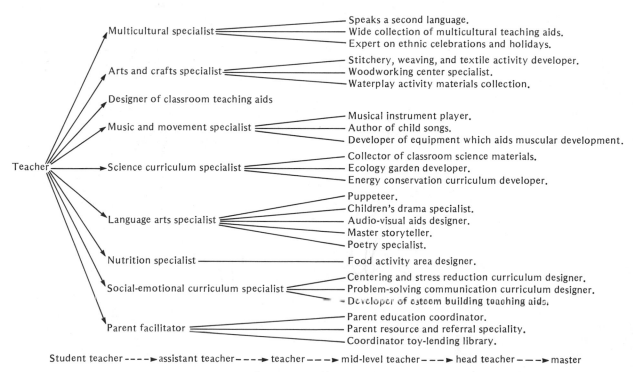

Fig. 28-7 Lateral development examples

certification in the state of California; these levels are similar to those of other states.

LADDER AND LATERAL MOBILITY

Job mobility can progress in two directions: upwards (ladder), figure 28-6, and laterally, figure 28-7. One can seek to move to higher levels of responsibility, or become increasingly adept and skillful at the same level. Aiming for a director's position while being a head teacher entails climbing a higher rung in a career ladder. Becoming an expert teacher puppeteer while working in the same position adds skills typifying lateral development, figure 28-8.

Individual goals may involve both ladder and lateral features. The revision of goal and action plans is a lifelong process.

GENERALIST VERSUS SPECIALIST

An early childhood teacher needs to be a generalist; it is the nature of the work. A multitude of teaching skills and competencies are necessary to promote children's development and interaction with parents, other staff, and community. Reaching a training program's graduating competency expectation level means you have acquired a number of general skills. As a student teacher, you may be painfully aware of your limitations and justly proud of teaching strengths. Specializing involves magnifying strengths. In job hunting, specialization is an important consideration. By developing strength areas, you may gain a competitive edge in attaining professional recognition, jobs, hence mobility and/or fulfillment.

PUBLIC OR PRIVATE

As a job hunter you will examine types of existing centers for job openings, figure 28-9. Public programs funded by federal, state, or local funds usually offer tenure, better job benefits, higher salaries, identifiable policies and philosophies, and lower child/adult ratios. These features may add to greater job security, satisfaction, and stability when compared with private school employment. Public programs primarily offer services to children and families of under-average economic means located near parent neighborhoods. Public agencies and organizations which regulate, license, or accredit programs are other job possibilities. Public agencies carry the following positions.

Fig. 28-8 Expert puppeteers are considered program area specialists. (Courtesy of Nancy Martin)

Fig. 28-9 You can choose the types of centers and children with whom you wish to work.

- Licensing
  representative
- Consultant
- Case worker
- Supervisor of
  programs

- Researcher
- Director
- Administrator
- Trainer
- Supervising specialist
- Resource consultant

Private sector programs are spread throughout communities, drawing families from a wider range of ethnic, social, and economic levels. Job security and salary differ greatly from program to program. Philosophies of operation are diverse and individual. Autonomy in decision making is typical regarding a school's operational and child program procedures. Licensing regulations give considerable decision leeway while protecting child health and safety. Private sector programs satisfy a vast array of American family child care needs, including serving parents at ski resorts, shopping centers, etc. or serving parents of one particular religious faith or philosophy preference. Both profit and nonprofit incorporated schools flourish in most communities. Many schools reward owners both financially and professionally. Other distinguishing features in private and public programs are detailed in figure 28-10.

DIRECT OR INDIRECT SERVICES   Direct services describe actual classroom child care and developmental work. An aide, assistant teacher, regular or substitute teacher, or volunteer handles daily program activities while interacting with young children, other staff, and parents.

Sponsor, owner/administrator	Characteristics
Public: Federal, state, or county agency such as Office of Economic Opportunity, Department of Health and Human Services, State Department of Education, State Social Services, school districts, college district. Other agencies such as a neighborhood council, community service organization, welfare agency, or community action groups.	Funds allocated by Congress, state legislatures, or county government or agencies. Program developers and supervisors may be quite remote from schools themselves, in off-site offices. Programs exceedingly varied. Primarily day care centers in low-income areas. May also include schools providing services to special groups such as retarded, handicapped, bilingual, after-school care, etc. Often a parent or community board serves an advisory function.
Private: Individual or group	A small or large school operated by a single owner or a large chain with absentee owners, run by a paid director and a staff.
Religious group	May use church personnel for staffing and have secular emphasis or may simply permit use of church facilities.
Parent cooperative	Parents hire a professional director and serve as assistants on a rotating basis, with regularly scheduled meetings for families, which usually include parenting education.
Private nonprofit	An incorporated entity which has been granted non-profit status through legal application to a federal, state, or local agency.

Fig. 28-10 Features of private and public programs

Indirect or support service work entails out-of-the-classroom tasks which enhance the quality of the program and realization of goals, figure 28-11. In some cases, jobs can combine both indirect and direct service duties.

Some student teachers realize indirect support service job responsibilities suit them better than direct service work. Careers exist in both sectors; combinations are another possibility.

Common support services involve administrative, child health and nutrition, parent or community liaison, and curriculum consultant specialities in furnishing, equipment, materials design, or supply areas. Figure 28-12 identifies both common and newly evolving support services to schools, teachers, children, families, and communities.

Your placement site, past school observations, or individual teaching philosophy gives clues to where you will seek employment. Additional observation and investigation offer other opportunities to gain data for decisions. Employees in the field or members of local early childhood teacher associations are additional sources of information.

SELF-EMPLOYMENT Innovative job creation and self-employment may offer considerable appeal. If you can find an unmet child care need, it can lead to a business venture. Using your special gifts or skills can be saleable and highly rewarding.

To do this, you will need to research the establishment of small businesses. A first step can be enrolling in courses in early childhood administration and supervision, and small business management. Partnerships, initial costs, resources for advice and capital, management styles, and law and accounting knowledge is indispensable. Interviewing competitors or others who have tried a similar venture is prudent.

In considering this type of business, remember that risks are plentiful; failure stories are abundant as are success stories.

Self-employment can involve direct or indirect services. Figure 28-13 describes a wide variety of early childhood related business ventures.

EDUCATIONAL SCREENING
and
PLACEMENT EVALUATION

Is your child in the right grade?

Testing Service for determining developmental age and appropriate school placement for children ages 2-8 years. Evaluators are credentialed teachers and Developmental Examiners qualified through the Gesell Institute of Human Development.

Darlene Clay (408)379-1234
Linda Garner (408)371-0000

Speakers available for workshops, training meetings and parent groups.

Fig. 28-11 Flyer describing indirect services

SERVICES TO CHILDREN OR SINGLE CLASSROOMS
Assessment specialist and consultant
Child psychologist or child psychiatrist
Therapist, social worker
Special education consultant
Volunteer, classroom activity preparer
Intergeneration grandparent

ADMINISTRATIVE SERVICES TO CENTERS AND PRESCHOOLS
Assistant director
In-service trainer
Secretary receptionist
Nurse, health aide, visiting doctor service
Nutritionist, cook, nutrition aide
Home/school liaison staff member/parent/home visitor
Auditor, billing, legal consultant
Insurance specialist
Advertising promotions specialist (brochures and campaigns)
Fund-raising specialist
Resource and referral services
Substitute service
Sick care provider family day home
School maintenance specialists
Handy person (small and large repair)
Grounds keeper, gardener
Placement services, job bureaus
Consultants
Photographer, videotape camera person
Industrial-sponsored program consultant developer
Extended day program consultant developer

MATERIALS AND SUPPLY SERVICES TO CENTERS AND PRESCHOOLS
Toy and outside yard equipment designer/supplier
Commercial product representative
Scrap (craft play) supplier
Supplier of emergency kits, first aid manual, local phone list, poison antidotes
Bus rentals for field trips
Audiovisual materials rental
Office materials supplier (forms, paper, etc.)
Food supplier
Maintenance (indoor, outdoor) machines and supplies
Interior and exterior advertising signs and/or figures
Publishers, child use and teacher reference materials, parent newspapers.

CHILD PROGRAM SERVICES AND TEACHER AIDS/SUPPLIES
Curriculum aids developer (planned daily and monthly activity aids)
Program area specialist: dance, foreign language, gymnastics, drama, puppeteer, storyteller,
    activity or skill demonstrator, etc.
Resource person scheduling service
Teacher aid developer and supplier (puppets, flannelboard activity sets, charts, recipe cards,
    dramatic play kits, waterplay kits, table game sets, etc.)
Rent-a-Santa or Easter bunny
Field trip service; locate, plan, and conduct (includes bus arrangements)

Fig. 28-12 Support services and specialities

Teacher or child clothing designer (personalized aprons, pins, tee shirts, etc.)
Rent-an-animal (includes informational presentation to children)
Union representative
Lobbyist

SERVICES TO PARENTS
Resource and referral agencies (find vacancies in local programs, match parent/child care need
    with local resources)
Family, crisis counseling
Weekend, night care
Single parent resource counseling
Weekend father workshop counseling
Trained baby-sitter registry
Sick care registry
Toy-lending libraries and services
Children's party specialists
In-home lesson speciality (dance, foreign language, music, etc.)
Publisher of parenting newspaper, child/parent activity aids
Infant/toddler care consultant

Fig. 28-12 (continued)

- Ski lodge child care
- Tennis or health club child care
- Weekend and overnight child care
- Weekend fathers child care group programming
- Parent newsletters (parenting aid sold to private schools
  and businesses)
- Professional identity item development and manufacture
  (apron, buttons, jewelry, etc.)
- Film and audiovisual rental service
- Photographic service
- Advertising/promotion service
- Resource and referral service
- Bulk food buyer
- Scrap item supplier
- Teaching aid manufacturer (puppets, toys, equipment, etc.)
- Curriculum idea books and magazine developer
- Field trip coordinator
- Resource visitor service
- Substitute service
- Consultants to industry child care
- Testing service
- Union or association organizer
- Lobbyist
- Family day home and foster parent service
- Workshop and in-service provider
- Speciality teacher (dance, foreign language, gymnastics, etc.)

Fig. 28-13 ECE-associated self-employment businesses and opportunities

OTHER DECISIONS   Additional decisions considered before devising an action plan in job hunting involve:

- Close analysis of skills, abilities, talents, values, and personal preferences.
- Age of children.
- Full- or part-time work.
- Size of school or business operation plan development.
- Availability for work in other locales.
- Position sought.
- Regular hours or flexible hourly workweek.
- Salary or wage requirements.
- Additional full-time training instead of employment.

THE SEARCH IS ON: LOCATING OPENINGS

Your search for a position may lead to a wide range of openings, a narrow range, or efforts to create a presently nonexistent job. There is need to review common job titles because terminology differs from employer to employer.

- Nursery school teacher
- Preschool teacher
- Child care specialist
- Child development teacher
- Day care staff member
- Child attendant
- Child caregiver
- Child caretaker
- Infant/toddler teacher
- Extended day teacher
- Early childhood teacher
- Prekindergarten teacher

Volunteering and substituting has been used as a viable strategy by many student teachers. Your placement site is already acquainted with your abilities. When the next opening occurs, you may have a chance for employment if the school is pleased with your talents. Extra efforts pay dividends. Speak to your cooperating teacher and the program's director if you wish to be hired. Other school volunteering and substituting will make you a known and appreciated person, increasing your odds for employment.

- Your instructor, college and department job board, college career center, or placement office.
- Local city or county office of education. Check listings for all departments including schools, recreation, welfare, social service, children's protective services, health, family services, and juvenile services for related job titles.
- Locate city, county, district, state, and federal personnel offices to check the previously mentioned departments or divisions.
- Locate city, state, or federal (unemployment, Human Resources Development) offices; check listings.
- Check local early childhood professional groups, organizations, associations. Many have employment chairpersons or job listings in newsletters; many post them at local meetings. Knowing members, being active in local groups is one of the *best* sources for meeting people who know about job openings. Volunteer to be the employment chairperson or to assist one. One can write the national headquarters of any ECE professional association and obtain names, phone numbers, and addresses for local chapters and contacts.
- Check newspaper help wanted ads.

Fig. 28-14   Job announcement sources

Figure 28-14 gives suggested job announcement sources. Before your search is in full swing, consider some less common approaches to finding job openings, figure 28-15.

Creating and building self-employment means heightened awareness of trends and careful examination of unmet services, needs, plus innovative thinking. It will be helpful to ask yourself the following questions:

- Is there a service you can perform that will enhance the quality of children's programs?
- What kinds of direct or support services do parents need in your community which do not now exist?

- Elicit help of family and friends.
- Call past graduates.
- Post notices in all ECE/CD college classes, especially night classes. Have tear-off slips with your name and phone number.
- Announce your availability at church and club meetings.
- Run an ad in the newspaper's situations wanted section.
- Send out an inquiry letter and resume to a large number of local programs. This takes a monetary investment but it may be money well spent.

Fig. 28-15   Innovative job search ideas

- What services to centers could be improved to satisfy needs, save time and effort, increase efficiency, or realize goals?
- Are teachers in need of materials or services which would make their jobs easier?
- How can your skills, talents, competencies, and training benefit your community and society?

Take the time to prioritize which existing jobs or self-efforts are the best employment match for you.

Summary

Taking a close look at decisions and possible early childhood employment opportunities clarifies job alternatives. Both short- and long-range goals are important factors in looking for employment. You may choose a job with upward and/or lateral mobility features, or decide to investigate self-employment. Volunteering and substitute teaching are ways to advertise talents. Reviewing job titles and identifying sources for job listings will alert a job hunter to existing openings and alternatives.

Suggested Activities

A. Interview three practicing teachers concerning career decisions and how they discovered their own job opening.

B. Make a resource list for job announcements, citing contact people, addresses, and phone numbers.

C. In small groups, identify your community's unmet child care needs.

D. List your strengths and special talents. Brainstorm to think of ways to use these for employment and/or fulfillment.

E. Identify your short- and long-range career goals. Estimate the time it will take to attain these goals, and list the necessary steps.

F. In groups of two, share ideas on the perfect job. Also discuss possible dead-end jobs which might inhibit goal realization.

G. Research "job sharing," and make a brief report of your findings to your class.

H. Make a report to the class on possible new early childhood job titles or specialities.

I. Discuss the list of job titles in figure 28-16 with another student teacher. Select the three most appealing titles.

- Summer camp counselors/teachers
- ECE teacher union organizer/representative
- Child party planner, supervisor
- Puppet designer, manufacturer
- Child center equipment designer, manufacturer, representative
- Children's bookstore owner, clerk, buyer, developer
- Children's toy store owner, clerk, buyer, developer
- Children's room designer
- Preschool architect specialist
- Publisher (teacher reference and curriculum aids)
- Children's book/magazine author, editor, publisher
- Foster and family day care parent
- Children's librarian
- Pediatrician
- Child nutritionist

Fig. 28-16   Job titles related to early childhood education

Review

A. Make a copy of the following exercise. Mark, on the following continuums, the spot that best suits your choice.

My short-range career goals are clearly identified. _____ No short-range goals as yet

I have clearly defined long-range career goals. _____ No long-range goals as yet

I plan to seek short-term employment. _____ Long-term employment

I want direct service work. _____	Support service work	Salary is of high importance. _____	Low priority
I prefer generalized employment. _____	Specialized employment	Fulfillment and intrinsic rewards are of high importance. _____	Low importance
I want a full-time position. _____	Part-time position		
Upward mobility is important. _____	Lateral development	Maximum autonomy in decision making is of high importance. _____	Joint or group decisions okay
I would like a job in an existing center. _____	Self-employment	I must work with others who have the same philosophy. _____	Can compromise my philosophy
I want employment in a public program. _____	Private program employment		
I have no mobility. _____	Highly mobile		

B. Draw a step graph which best depicts your long-range career plans. Indicate an estimated time at each level.

EXAMPLE:

1 year		2 years		1 year	3 years
Part-time job	Teacher in private school	Additional coursework	Developing musical speciality	Part-time work as music workshop leader and consultant	Opening own preschool with music, dance emphasis

C. Complete the following statements.
1. Volunteering and substituting may result in employment offers if. . .
2. Five common places to hunt for job announcements are. . .
3. Two unmet societal child care needs are. . .

D. Compare public sector versus private sector employment.

E. What early childhood-related work mentioned in this unit was new or intriguing?

Resources

"Challenges of the 80's." *U.S. News and World Report* (October 15, 1979).

Gordon-Novrok, Esther. *You're a Student Teacher.* Sierra Madre, CA: Southern California Association for the Education of Young Children, 1979.

Unit 29
Resumes, Applications, and Interviews

OBJECTIVES

After studying this unit, the student will be able to:

- Make the distinction between choosing and finding a job.
- Complete application forms appropriately.
- Prepare a resume.
- Describe preparational and follow-up activities.

FINDING AND CHOOSING A JOB

There is a psychological difference between finding a job and choosing one. Finding employment is a traditional point of view which emphasizes the employer's decision in hiring. A newer approach to employment is described as a "creative minority" or "self-directed" search (Bolles, 1980). This approach assumes that no one really knows the location of most vacancies. Richard Bolles believes many job hunters make two false assumptions. First, they think that most or all job openings are posted and advertised when actually four out of five openings are known only to employers who typically fill the opening through word of mouth. Second, job hunters seek vacancies before they pinpoint where and how they could best use their talents. The three keys to the "creative minority" approach to securing employment follow:

Key No. 1: You must decide just exactly what you want to do.

Key No. 2: You must decide just exactly where you want to do it, through your own research and personal survey.

Key No. 3: You must investigate the organizations that interest you at great length, and then approach the one individual in each organization who has the power to hire you for the job that you have decided you want to do. (Bolles, p. 66)

When seeking a job, keep in mind those qualities and abilities you have to offer and the type of work that suits your long- and short-range career planning goals. Since you have chosen a career that enriches the quality of children's lives, you will now choose a job which promotes personal and professional fulfillment and enriches your life.

Your mental attitude is of prime importance. Positive thoughts, written affirmations, and visualization techniques often aid job seekers. A written affirmation can bolster your spirit and maintain your motivation to choose the job that best suits your talents. An affirmation is a written statement which describes the kind of job you want, why you deserve it, and how you will get the job. In order for something to occur, it helps to *really believe* that it will occur. Couple this firm belief with a sense of humor, an ability to "roll with the punches," persistence, and an awareness of life's options; these are the characteristics of individuals who achieve their goals and obtain their desired employment (Cooke, 1981).

Name

Address

Phone

1. *Availability*

2. *Position Sought*

3. *Experience*
   Dates — Description

4. *Education*
   Dates — Description

5. *Personal* (optional)

6. *Special Skills* (optional)

7. *Professional Affiliations* (optional)

8. *References*

Fig. 29-1 Resumé outline

- Keep it *brief* and to the point.
- *Avoid* personal pronouns.
- Use descriptive *action* phrases.
- Clearly state your accomplishments, responsibilities, and variety of duties performed.
- Keep your resumé brief enough to fit on *one* page (two pages maximum).
- Arrange your *headings and dates* in a manner that *leads* the reader's attention.
- Make good *use of space*; work for the overall impression of neatness and orderliness.
- Write and rewrite until it is perfect.
- Resumés should be typed on quality bond paper by a professional typist.
- Investigate quick print and copy service costs for multiple copies.
- Take the time to do it right!

Fig. 29-2 General resumé guidelines

RESUMÉ PREPARATION

Preparation of your resumé entails skill, honesty, and attention to detail. Since your resumé represents you, proceed carefully in its development. Your resumé should reflect a strong, positive self-image and communicate that image to a chosen employer. A well-written resumé adds a professional touch and can quickly be attached to your application form.

Study figure 29-1, a resumé outline. (General guidelines are listed in figure 29-2.)

It is important to list both your home telephone number and a message telephone number in the *heading.* You will want to receive every employer call. *Availability* lets you identify exactly what date you can begin working.

Be clear about the *position sought.* You may be interested in more than one position; if so, apply separately for each. Resumé experts recommend just one job title per resumé. They suggest applying for one position at a time, even when others are posted by the same employer.

In listing your *experience,* begin with your most recent job and proceed backward to your earliest job. Make your experience summary interesting and exciting to read. Dates go in the left-hand margin, and are followed by your former employers' names and addresses, then your job title. Use narrative form to describe your job duties. In one paragraph, explain some of your important responsibilities and accomplishments. Show a broad range of duties when possible. Use phrases instead of full sentences. See figure 29-3 for words which focus on skills and figure 29-4 for function descriptions. Include volunteer work experience and student teaching assignments. List unrelated part-time and summer jobs if you feel they may enhance your image. It is not necessary to cite salaries, reasons for leaving, or supervisors' names at this point.

Education background is listed beginning with your highest formal degree, then informal training. Include each school's name and address, mentioning current enrollment. Dates can follow the school's or training program's name.

Professional conferences, workshops attended, or additional informal training can be listed separately

Accomplished	Controlled	Examined	Integrated	Produced
Acted	Cooperated	Exchanged	Interviewed	Promoted
Adapted	Coordinated	Expanded	Invented	Provided
Administered	Counseled	Facilitated	Investigated	Publicized
Advised	Created	Familiarized	Maintained	Published
Analyzed	Decided	Formulated	Managed	Recorded
Arranged	Defined	Fund raised	Monitored	Reported
Assembled	Delegated	Generated	Motivated	Represented
Assigned	Demonstrated	Guided	Negotiated	Researched
Assisted	Designed	Handled	Observed	Resolved
Authored	Detailed	Hired	Obtained	Revised
Budgeted	Determined	Identified	Operated	Scheduled
Built	Developed	Implemented	Ordered	Screened
Calculated	Devised	Improved	Organized	Selected
Catalogued	Directed	Increased	Originated	Served
Collaborated	Distributed	Individualized	Participated	Staffed
Communicated	Drafted	Influenced	Performed	Stimulated
Conceived	Edited	Informed	Persuaded	Supervised
Conceptualized	Educated	Initiated	Planned	Systemized
Conducted	Enlarged	Innovated	Prepared	Taught
Constructed	Established	Inspected	Presented	Teamed
Consulted	Evaluated	Installed	Presided	Trained
Contracted		Instituted	Problem solved	Wrote

Fig. 29-3 Words used to describe skills

under the heading *Other Training*. A statement like "numerous college training conferences, workshops, adult night school, including. . ." can lump all of this type of training together.

The *personal section* provides an opportunity to let the employer know more about you. Try to give a conceptual overview of how you see yourself in relation to the job. You do not have to include your age or marital status. This whole section can be omitted if you feel uncomfortable with it.

Special competencies and/or skills such as speaking an additional language, ability to play a musical instrument, clerical skills, child program planning specialities like yoga instruction, gardening, and puppetry should be mentioned.

Listing your membership in professional associations and organizations displays your interest and commitment. Graduating students who have been financially unable to join such groups give a high priority to doing so as soon as they secure a position. Student membership fees are usually below regular rates, so joining while still a student can be a good idea.

References are listed, giving each person's name, address, and updated telephone numbers (both work and home). Job titles and places of employment are included when references are professional rather than personal. An alternative statement, "Written references available upon request," is sometimes substituted.

Administrator	Group leader
Analyzer	Liaison
Communicator	Planner
Community organizer	Program designer
Community relations liaison	Program developer
Consultant	Public relations person
Coordinator	Researcher
Counselor	Specialist
Cross-cultural relations	Supervisor
Designer	Teacher
Director	Team leader
Editor	Team member
Educator	Trainer
Group facilitator	Writer

Fig. 29-4 Words used to describe functions

Toward the end of your student teaching placement, it is wise to ask your cooperating teacher for a letter of reference. It becomes difficult to trace past employers and/or supervisors for references as years go by.

RESUMÉ RESOURCES Most college career and placement centers provide assistance and reference materials valuable in resumé preparation. A list of helpful resources that deal with other resumé particulars can be found in the Appendix. A sample resumé is completed in figure 29-5.

FACT FINDING

Whether it is a self-chosen employment possibility or an advertised position, you will want to investigate the employer, the agency, and the operation. Specifics and details on job announcements, job descriptions, and/or specifications, figures 29-6 and 29-7, offer a better picture of the needs of the employer. Receptionists, personnel clerks, and other employees can add to your background knowledge. Brochures, public information statements, and/or employee or program manuals may be available for the asking. In doing so, you may gain enthusiasm for a position or realize that the position is not what you are seeking.

Phone calls to local programs can unearth job opportunities as can personal visits. Simply mailing out a prepared resumé with a cover letter is a strategy which has worked for others. This involves an investment in postage; it saves time and money in the long run by narrowing the prospects.

COVER LETTERS

It is an art to be able to write attention-getting cover letters. Three major objectives are usually kept in mind while composing a cover letter:
- Attract favorable interest
- Introduce the resumé
- Obtain an interview

The following introductions could create interest:

- Using the name of someone known to the employer.

  "Margaret Downing, your educational consultant, suggested I forward my resumé."

- Mentioning your present occupation.

  "My present position as an early childhood teacher qualifies me for a similar position with your agency."

- Citing your experience and education.

  "I believe my three years teaching experience and AA degree in Child Development may be the qualifications you are seeking."

- Knowledge of their operation.

  "Being well-acquainted with your innovative approach to cognitive learning through workshops presented by your staff, I am including my resumé and would like to discuss the possibility of my employment as a teacher at your school."

- Specific skill introduction.

  "I have developed a speciality in presenting drama to young children. The enclosed resumé..."

- Freshly graduated and available.

  "In June, I will graduate and would like to discuss the possibility of a position."

Linda L. Davis
17 Main Street
Newton, CA 94821
Tel. (408)255-5163
Message Tel. (408)313-6343

Availability   June 1, 1982

Position Sought   Early Childhood Teacher

Experience
1/82–5/82   CHILDREN'S SCHOOL, Claremont Community College. *Student Teacher* with four-year-olds. Conducted enriching morning circle times which increased children's sense of personal worth and language usage. Planned and arranged room environment to reflect weekly themes: butterflies, seashore, etc. Assumed responsibility for child completion of self-initiated learning projects. Presented new flannelboard stories, songs, fingerplays, and creative art and craft experiences. Promoted respect for friendship and individual differences.

10/80–2/82   PETER PAN PRESCHOOL. *Teacher Assistant* with three-year-olds. Prepared room for opening, supervised all room centers, programmed small-group activities. Added to room's challenge by designing and constructing additional table games. Enjoyed prompting children's problem-solving skills. Initiated a parent book-lending service.

Education
1980–82   CLAREMONT COMMUNITY COLLEGE
                 A.A. Degree in Early Childhood Education

Other Training
February 1981   Head Start Training Institute
November 1981   NAEYC Conference, San Francisco
May 1981   4 C's Workshop — Puppetry

Personal   Deeply interested in ecology and preservation of local wooded areas. Unmarried, age 22.

Special Skills Programming exploratory science activities which promote children's observation skills and positive attitudes toward the uniqueness of other living creatures. Autoharp proficiency

Professional   California Association for the Education of Young Children
Affiliations   Member, Lakeside Chapter
                  Metropolitan Wildlife Preservation
                     Committee — Member and docent
                  Claremont College Student Body — Women's Issues Representative

References   Molly Brown   Reverend Bob Hutching
                 Head Teacher   Methodist Youth Leader
                 Peter Pan Preschool   1443 Whiting Road
                 14 Lake Lane   Anthony, CA 91301
                 Campbell, CA 94301
                 408-362-1314

Fig. 29-5 Sample resume

DEFINITION
To develop and implement an educational program that provides for the full intellectual and social development of each child.

EXAMPLE OF DUTIES
1. Plans and prepares for the daily instructional program in cooperation with teacher aides.
2. Conducts the daily instructional program with the assistance of teacher aides.
3. Evaluates the instructional program as well as each child's progress and needs with the assistance of the teacher aides.
4. Supervises the education of children during noninstructional times of the day, e.g., outdoor activity periods, staggered arrival and departure times of children, nap period, etc.
5. Supervises the work of teacher aides and volunteers assigned to work with the team and during noninstructional times.
6. Reports pupil progress to parents and to the head teacher through periodic conferences.
7. Reports pupil progress to kindergartens receiving preschool pupils.
8. Participates in a viable parent involvement program.
9. Participates in the in-service training program provided by the center.
10. Makes home visits as required by the center's policies.
11. Maintains classroom safety.
12. Participates in staff meetings.

SUPERVISION RECEIVED
Reports directly to the head teacher.

DESIRABLE QUALIFICATIONS
Minimum
1. Children's center permit.

OR

2. Be currently enrolled in courses leading to a children's center permit. In addition, must have at least two years of employment in a position that involved work with young children *or* one year's experience in a program similar to children's centers, Head Start, state preschool, etc.

Fig. 29-6 Job description for preschool teacher

Some examples of statements included in cover letters, figures 29-8 and 29-9, that introduce resumés are as follows:

"The enclosed resumé describes. . ."
"I have attached a resumé so you may judge my . . ."
"As my resumé shows. . ."
"After reading my resumé, I hope you believe, as I do, that I will be an asset to your agency."
"I will be happy to send any further information which adds detail to my resumé."

Requests for an interview can take the following forms:

"I would like to talk with you about my interest in employment, and will telephone within the next few days."

"I would appreciate an interview at your earliest convenience."

"Let me discuss this with you. I will be available for an interview. . ."

"I will call for an appointment in the next few days unless I hear from you sooner."

"I feel an interview within the next few days would be mutually advantageous."

"I will be available for an interview. . ."

"When could we meet to discuss my qualifications?"

"An interview would allow you to probe what I have to offer, and give me a chance to display my sincere interest in a position."

DAY CARE CENTER TEACHER

NOTE: Applications must be in the County Government Center, Personnel Office by 5:00 p.m. on the final filing date. Applications postmarked after that date will not be accepted.

SALARY RANGE: $8,500–$12,000

FINAL FILING DATE: July 30, 1983

TIME & PLACE OF EXAMINATION: To be announced

THE POSITION:

Provides instruction and supervision of preschool children of parents who are working or in training; plans programs and activities providing appropriate learning experiences based upon needs, interest, and abilities of the children; determines supplies and equipment required; sees that necessary supplies and equipment are set up for use; reads stories, plays records, teaches and supervises games, and supervises and assists in art and crafts work; assists children in clean-up activities; sees that children rest at naptime; administers first aid in emergencies; supervises and directs the work of aides; holds conferences with parents; carries out emergency and safety procedures; and performs related work as required. Position *requires* working flexible hours during the week (Monday through Friday). Some holiday work is *required*; holiday work pays extra.

EMPLOYMENT STANDARDS:

Training and experience equivalent to completion of high school and two years of full-time experience in group child care *plus* completion of 24 semester units in courses related to early childhood education. Additional education with a major in one of the behavioral sciences may be substituted for the required experience on a year-for-year basis.

Knowledge of child development and psychology; early childhood education and infant education; teaching methods and techniques; first aid.

Ability to teach, supervise, and control children; organize and direct inside and outside activities; speak effectively; establish and maintain harmonious relationships with children and parents; supervise the work of others.

EXAMINATION:

Oral interview: 100%

Applicants scoring 80% or more will be placed on the promotion eligibility list.

As a condition of employment, each employee in this class must sign a payroll deduction authorization form providing for deduction of union membership dues or a service fee. A thirty-day cancellation period is provided.

It is important that your application show all the relevant education and experience. Applications may be rejected if incomplete. Copies of all materials submitted with application forms may not be returned to applicants. Original copies of Service Papers, DD 214's, etc. should not be attached.

Fig. 29-7 Job specifications

Your address
City, state, and zip

Date

Name of employer
Title of employer
Name of company, corporation, or government agency
Address
City, state, and zip

Dear _____,

Explain the type of employment you are seeking. Be as specific as possible. Give your availability dates.

Summarize your qualifications for the job for which you are applying, referring to any classes you have taken or experience you have obtained which would be relevant to the job. Sincerely state your interest in the position. Make reference to the application or resumé you are including.

Request the next step in the employment process. Ask for an interview date if the employer is local; indicate when you could meet. If the employer is not located in the immediate area, request an application form and further information about the company.

Sincerely,

Your name
Telephone number

Enclosure

Fig. 29-8 Sample cover letter

1635 Carter Lane
Campbell, CA 95017

March 30, 1982

Mrs. Thelma Harvey
Director
First Avenue Early Learning Center
125 First Avenue
Eastridge, CA 94121

Dear Mrs. Harvey:

In June of this year I will graduate from Central College with a degree
in Early Childhood Education. I would like to talk with you about the
possibility of becoming a teacher with your program.

As you can see from my enclosed resume, I have concentrated on music and
dance curricula for young children both in my studies and spare time. I
am able to offer children special depth in this area, as well as a well-
rounded learning program.

Would it be possible to arrange an interview for Monday, April 10, or
Tuesday, April 11? I will be free then, and would like to discuss the
possibility of joining your staff.

Sincerely,

Mary Smith
(408) 866-2881

Enclosure

Fig. 29-9 Sample cover letter

I.   PERSONAL DATA

(Mr.)
(Miss)

Name (Mrs.) _____   Position Desired _____

Present
Address _____   Until _____
        (Street)   (City)   (Date)

_____   Telephone _____
    (State)   (Zip)

Social Security No. _____

Permanent
Address _____   Telephone _____
        (Street)   (City)   (State)   (Zip)

Marital Status _____   Children _____   Maiden Name _____

Age _____   Height _____   Weight _____   Are you a U.S. citizen? _____

Health — physical defects, if any _____

General condition of health _____

II.   PREPARATION FOR TEACHING

	Schools Attended	Dates Attended	Diploma or Degree
A. Elementary	_____	_____	_____
Secondary, College or University	_____	_____	_____
	_____	_____	_____
	_____	_____	_____
B.A. Major	_____	Minor _____	
M.A. Major	_____	Minor _____	

B. College Work

Total number of semester hours you have in professional education courses _____

In which field of education are you majoring? Elementary? _____ Secondary? _____

Practice Teaching: Subject _____ or Grade _____

What is your college grade point average? _____

What foreign languages do you speak? _____

List five courses (including three education courses) you have taken which you think will be valuable to you as a preschool or primary teacher.

1. _____
2. _____
3. _____
4. _____
5. _____

What special training have you had in the following?

Music	_____	Children's literature	_____
Child growth/development	_____	Storytelling	_____
Physical education	_____	Arts and crafts	_____

Fig. 29-10 Sample job application

Guidance/counseling	_____	Nutrition	_____
Second language	_____	Language development	_____
Science and math	_____	Multicultural	_____

C. Extra-curricular Activities. List activities you have participated in and feel able to direct (parent counseling, first aid, etc.).

_____

_____

_____

D. Certificate or Credential
Name(s) of certificate/credential _____

_____ issued in the state of _____

III. *TEACHING EXPERIENCE*   Total years of teaching _____

Years (from–to)	Kind of school	Location	Grades or subject
_____	_____	_____	_____
_____	_____	_____	_____
_____	_____	_____	_____

IV. *WORK EXPERIENCE OTHER THAN TEACHING*

Years (from–to)	Employer and location	Type of work and/or position
_____	_____	_____
_____	_____	_____
_____	_____	_____

V. *REFERENCES* (administrators or supervisors with whom you have worked)

Name	Position	Address
_____	_____	_____
_____	_____	_____
_____	_____	_____

VI. *OTHER INFORMATION*
List participation within the last two years in any professional activity for the improvement of the school or schools where you have been employed, e.g., Curriculum Revision, Pupil Progress Reports. (If not employed in a school system within the last two years, write "not employed.")

_____

_____

_____

Do you have specially developed talents outside your teaching speciality? Do you play a musical instrument? _____

What is your salary range? _____

VII. *CANDIDATE'S SPACE* Write any information you feel may be helpful and pertinent to your possible employment which has not already been covered.

_____

_____

_____

_____

Signature of Applicant

Fig. 29-10 (continued)

In addressing your letter and envelope, try to identify the director or personnel manager by name with the correct job title. Your phone number should be placed directly under your signature.

JOB APPLICATION

Many job seekers underestimate the value of the appearance of the job application form. It can present an image, either good or bad, of the applicant to the employer. Resumés can often be attached, giving a professional aura to your application. Figure 29-10 shows a sample job application form with typical data requested. Dr. Bettye Lewis has three tips for filling out applications.

1. THE JOB APPLICATION IS A DEVICE FOR SELLING YOURSELF! In education in particular, with many people applying for every job opening, the application is *the* single most important item that determines whether the applicant gets past the screening committee to the interview.
2. TAKE TIME TO DO IT RIGHT! An application that is dashed off at the last minute is usually incomplete and often looks careless and does not represent the applicant well.
3. MAKE IT LOOK GOOD! The appearance, the ease of reading, clearly identified categories, short concise sentences, effective use of spacing, dots, capitalizing, underlining, italicizing and numbering are all important parts of an attractive application. (1980)

You may find your past fact finding will give your application a definite edge over the others. Knowing what the employer desires may help you to match and display your abilities more effectively.

INTERVIEWING

There are definite preparation steps for interviews. Some are just common sense; others are rather novel in their approach. Showing yourself off to your best advantage, while giving an honest picture of yourself, is your goal. Mona S. Johnson, discussing interviewing, states:

No one is more qualified to put such a portrait together than you since you are an authority on the subject — YOU. How accurate and dynamic the portrait is, makes considerable difference between getting into the job that *you want* and are *indispensable* for. (1980)

Those who conduct the interview need to be sensitive to an interviewee's opportunity to discuss the significance of early childhood education and the trained professional's ability to provide quality services to children and families.

There is a large population out there who know very little about our field and its significance. This ignorance is further distorted with cultural biases and stereotypes such as "anyone can take care of children", or "one doesn't need to have training to work with kids", "what does it take to play with kids." So the challenge is twofold:
1.) to demonstrate your training skill and competence with children and early childhood programs.
2.) to make the employer subtly aware of the significance of programs and training for young children and/or their parents. (Johnson, 1980, p. 2)

A first step can be returning to gather additional data about the center or organization. An on-site visit or tour prior to interviews may be possible. Literature describing the employer's or agency's philosophy or operational conduct and procedures needs close reading.

Concentrating on your interview appearance and dress is important. Feeling well-dressed, attractive, and well-groomed boosts your spirits and your confidence. Role playing, as in the following alternatives, may give critical insights concerning the image you project.

Alternatives include:
a. Mirror — talking while looking at yourself in the mirror. You become your own alter ego. You are able to watch and monitor body language quite closely to give insights. Some of the pointers to look for will be:

(i) Eye-contact — Do you look at yourself without staring or do you find yourself looking at the floor or somewhere other than the interviewer?

(ii) Posture — Are you fairly relaxed with hands in your lap or are you slouched or stiff and uncomfortable? Try to be at ease. Practice relaxing. Deep inhaling and exhaling should help you to relax.

(iii) Body language — Learn to read some of the simple cues. Are your arms folded, are you twisting that piece of paper to death? Relax and visualize yourself to be a warm, charming, positive and relaxed person. Experiment with positions and find your own combination.

(iv) Appearance — In my estimation it includes you from head to toe. Try to be "yourself," neither overdressed or too casual. Small pieces of jewelry will be more than adequate. You are well aware of first impressions as lasting impressions.

b. Audio tape recording — record your mock interview on tape and listen to it.

You may find a combined use of a and b to be even more effective as you see yourself and hear yourself. Visual images will recreate themselves in your mind and your assessment of self will be more complete.

c. Video recording — It is an expensive but a very realistic medium. You can not only hear yourself but also view the body language, gestures, posture, quality and tone of voice, eye contact or absence of it. (Johnson, 1980, p. 18)

Using visualization as a technique lets you shape your interview conduct mentally beforehand. You create your interview behavior in your mind. This exercise allows a type of mental rehearsal which envisions your entering an interview room, your confident fielding of questions after introductions, your asking your own questions, and tactfully concluding the interview and exiting.

A further preparation activity involves practicing answering the four most common interview questions. They are:
1. Why you want the position?
2. What you can do for the employer?
3. What kind of person you are?
4. How much you are going to cost? (Bolles, 1980)
Practicing the answers to other interview questions is another way to prepare. Figure 29-11 lists some possible interview questions for a teaching position.

A good technique to gain interview skill is to participate in mock interviews with other people who give you feedback, and to invite practicing teachers or directors to describe the interview process.

HINTS FOR INTERVIEWS During interviews, others will attempt to measure you. Your tact, maturity, courtesy, and professional knowledge will be indicators of how you will perform your duties and represent the organization or center (if hired) to the general public. Study and practice the following hints for interviews.

- Walk through the door smiling confidently. Scan all eyes in the room.
- Wait briefly to ascertain where you will sit.
- Do not volunteer something that can be construed as negative.
- Direct your conversation toward the interviewers' special enthusiasms and job needs if you know them.
- Demonstrate a knowledge of the organization or center.
- Be memorable.
- Maintain a sense of humor.
- Listen attentively.
- Ask questions to clarify.
- Pause and think before you answer.
- Know the skills and interests you possess which best fit the job you are seeking.
- Give the appearance of energy and vitality.
- Be relaxed and maintain eye contact.
- Take special note of interviewers' names and job titles.
- View interviewing as a learning experience.
- Have extra copies of your resumé with you.
- Bring samples of your work.

GENERAL

- What can you tell me about yourself?
- Why are you interested in this position?
- Why do you feel qualified for the job?
- What caused you to enter this field?
- What would you like to be doing five years from now?
- Why did you leave your last job?
- What is the minimum pay you will accept?
- What are your three greatest strengths and limitations for this job?
- Why should I hire you?
- How would you improve our operation?
- What is your greatest accomplishment to date?
- Of your past duties, which have you liked the best and least? Why?
- What is the ideal job for you?
- What attracts you to this center?
- What can you tell me about your experience?
- Do you have special training for this job?
- What kind of people appeal most and least to you as work associates?
- Could I see some samples of your work?
- How would you describe your health?
- Whom can we check as references?
- Do you prefer to work with two-, three-, four-, or five-year-olds? Why?
- What are your talents or skills?
- Can you describe how children (parents) best learn?
- What are important services which centers can provide for parents and a community?
- Can you describe a quality morning program for preschoolers?
- What is a typical morning schedule in your classroom?
- How could you provide young children with multicultural, nonsexist, developmental, creative, and physical development activities?
- What teaching strategies would you use during one of your planned activities?
- What do you feel promotes a spirit of teamwork between teachers working in the same classroom?
- What experiences have you had in working with parents?
- What guidance techniques work best for you?
- Briefly describe your philosophy concerning appropriate goals for an ideal preschool enrolling four-year-olds.
- How do you handle constructive criticism?
- Describe yourself as other teachers and supervisors have described you.
- What type of activities do you offer children with great enthusiasm and reluctance?
- Why did you choose a career working with young children and their families?
- Pick a theme and describe how you would offer that topic to young children.
- What well-known early childhood educator has made a lasting impression on you?
- Do you belong to any organizations or associations?

SITUATIONAL

- What would you do if a three-year-old child wet his or her pants?
- How would you react to a parent who angrily said, "This school is much too rigid!"?
- If your co-teacher never did his or her share of the activity planning, what would you do?
- A child just said, "You're an ugly witch!" How would you deal with it?
- A child's just kicked you; how would you handle it?
- A fellow teacher said, "The director is so unfair!" What would you do?
- You spotted an abused child in your class; what would you do?

Fig. 29-11 Possible interview questions

- Double-check time. Be there five to ten minutes in advance.
- Shake hands firmly.
- Answer situational questions with "One of the things I might consider would be. . ."
- Avoid overeager discussions of what is in store for you in the next three to five years.
- Avoid answers which reflect badly on your former employer.
- Avoid voice tension.
- Try clarifying direct salary questions by asking for salary ranges.
- When asked about weaknesses, mention those that are possible strengths, e.g., "I'm hard on myself when. . ."
- Go to an interview alone.
- Leave your troubles at home.
- End on a cordial note.
- Send a brief thank-you note if the situation calls for it.
- Do not ramble; stick to the question.
- Avoid vagueness; make your point and move on.
- Be assertive rather than pushy.
- Get a good sleep the night before.
- A fast heartbeat is natural; ignore it.
- Be alert.
- Do not interrupt.
- Answer weakness statements briefly.
- Avoid becoming defensive.
- Avoid being a name dropper.
- Prepare questions you would like to ask the interviewers.

QUESTIONS INTERVIEWEES ASK
It is expected that you will want to ask questions too. Time is usually provided near the end of the interview. Read over your notes; they will help jog your memory. It is best to keep your list of questions short. Some questions interviewees should ask are:

- Is there anything else I can tell you about my qualifications?
- Would you mind telling me the pay range?
- How soon will I know the outcome of this interview?

POST-INTERVIEW ANALYSIS
After an interview, assess your conduct and performance. Take note of your strengths and possible growth areas. One learns immeasurably from the interview experience and becomes a little more polished and relaxed during succeeding interviews. See figure 29-12 for negative interview factors. An after-interview questionnaire is given in figure 29-13. Some personnel departments will share interview ratings with applicants; this can be a valuable self-evaluation aid.

---

1. Poor personal appearance.
2. Overbearing, overaggressive, conceited, superiority complex and "know-it-all" personality.
3. Inability to express opinions clearly; poor voice, diction, grammar.
4. Lack of planning for career; no purpose and goal.
5. Lack of interest and enthusiasm; passive, indifferent.
6. Lack of confidence and poise; nervous, ill at ease.
7. Overemphasis on money; interest only in best salary offer.
8. Poor scholastic record; just barely passed.
9. Makes excuses, hedges on unfavorable factors in record.
10. Lack of tact.
11. Lack of maturity.
12. Lack of courtesy; poor manners.
13. Condemnation of past employers.
14. Lack of social understanding.
15. Lack of vitality.
16. Fails to look interviewer in the eye.
17. Limp handshake.
18. Indecision.
19. Sloppy application form.
20. Wants job only for short time.
21. Little sense of humor.
22. Lack of knowledge in field of specialization.
23. No interest in company or industry.
24. Name dropping.
25. Cynical.
26. Low moral standards.
27. Intolerant; strong prejudices.
28. Narrow interests.
29. No interest in community activities.
30. Lack of appreciation of the value of experience.
31. Radical ideas.
32. Late for interview.
33. Failure to express appreciation for interviewer's time.
34. Asks no questions about the job.
35. High-pressure type.
36. Indefinite response to questions.

Fig. 29-12 Negative factors which lead to rejection of an applicant

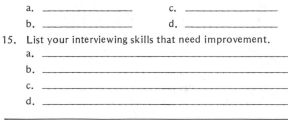

1. Were you relaxed, confident?
2. Did you control your part of the interview with good, solid answers?
3. Did you listen and pause thoughtfully before answering?
4. Was your knowledge of the center/agency adequate?
5. Was your personal appearance appropriate? Were you self-confident?
6. Were your remarks clear and concise?
7. Did you "jump" to answer questions quickly?
8. Were you convincing?
9. Did you relate the prospective job to past jobs or skills used in a previous job?
10. During the interview, did fear or tension immobilize you?
11. Were you able to justify your background in terms of the job requirements?
12. Did you demonstrate that you really wanted the job?
13. Did you do well overall?
14. List the areas in which you did well.
    a. _____ c. _____
    b. _____ d. _____
15. List your interviewing skills that need improvement.
    a. _____
    b. _____
    c. _____
    d. _____

Fig. 29-13 Post-interview questionnaire

1. Too much irrelevant information.
2. Not enough relevant information.
3. Vagueness.
4. General statements.
5. Incomplete data.
6. Inaccurate data.
7. Hard-to-read copies.
8. Lack of salary information.
9. Exaggeration of responsibility.
10. Conceit.
11. Distortion of background and earnings.
12. Lack of cover letter.
13. Wordiness.
14. Poor organization of information.
15. Resume not dated.
16. No location preference shown.
17. Position desired not mentioned.
18. Use of gimmicks.
19. Messy.
20. Misleading statements.

Fig. 29-14 Common resume problems (From *Personal Resume Preparation* by Michael P. Jaquish. London: John Wiley and Sons, Inc., 1968.)

Summary

Landing a job which is important to you is a challenging opportunity. Preparation, attention to details, fact finding, application, and interviews can be conducted in a professional fashion, giving you a definite edge in competing. Creating a resume which projects an honest and advantageous portrayal of your skills and abilities is well worth the time and effort. A resume cover letter is designed when one wishes to mail a resume to prospective employers. Many techniques and hints aid interviewees, and there are many novel approaches to interview preparation which afford insight and image-building strategies.

Suggested Activities

A. Prepare your resume.

B. Using figure 29-14, analyze your and another student's resumes.

C. Write a sample cover letter to accompany a resume in a search for possible unadvertised positions. Compare your cover letters with others.

D. Collect job application forms. Compare questions and blanks. Are there any questions which do not relate to the ability to perform the work? Discuss with a group of four to five classmates.

E. Make your own list of five items which you feel are important interview tips. Add your five items to a wallchart. If any items closely resemble those already on the list, place a tally mark after them instead.

F. Think of seven interview questions (or choose from figure 29-11). In groups of three to four, role play situations and give constructive criticism.

G. Design an interview rating sheet. Share it with others in class.

H. Invite a personnel director to speak to the class on the topic of "What I Look for in Job Applicants."

I. Using figure 29-15 as a guide, gather data on a center where you feel you may want to work.

If you plan to visit, be sure to call in advance. Before you place your call:
1. Double-check the phone number.
2. Read the ad in the yellow pages if there is one.

When you phone:
1. Be polite and courteous.
2. Introduce yourself, and state the reason for your call.
3. Ask for the director or person in charge.
4. Ask if they are willing to answer a few questions. If so, continue on. If not, call later when it is more convenient for them. If they do not want to answer questions, do not push for any.

You need to find out the following information from your visit, a phone call, or the yellow pages.
1. The center's hours.
2. Ages of the children.
3. Number of children.
4. Number of teachers.
5. Whether there is a cook and/or janitor.
6. Teachers' duties.
7. Salary.
8. Required level of education.
9. Teachers' working hours or shifts.
10. Schedules (all day, one-half day, etc.).
11. Program/activities for the children.

Fig. 29-15 Fact-finding guide

J. In groups of two to four, briefly discuss the topic: "Select Truths Carefully During Interviews." Report highlights of your discussion with the whole group.

Review

A. List possible ways to research and fact find prior to interviewing for a desirable position in a local children's center.

B. Briefly discuss the major differences in attitude between selecting and seeking employment.

C. List five important factors to remember when filing job application forms.

D. Rate the following resumé items on a scale of 1 to 3 based on their importance, 1 being the most important and 3 being the least important.
- Hobbies
- Availability
- Age
- Photograph
- Training
- Awards
- References
- Job-related interests
- Position sought
- Degrees
- Church affiliation
- Family background
- Grades
- Specific skills
- Height, weight
- Marital status
- Number of children
- Experience
- Affiliations
- Former employers
- Former job titles
- Former job duties

E. Select the answer that best completes each statement.
1. The "creative minority" approach involves
   a. finding existing vacancies.
   b. seeking the highest job level available.
   c. identifying employers with similar philosophies.
   d. creating positions for oneself.
   e. selecting and researching job options.
2. A statement such as "I've finished my training, and developed and magnified my communication skill"
   a. is a good resumé statement.
   b. is a visualization technique.
   c. is an affirmation.
   d. turns off people during interviews.
   e. is a good statement to include on job applications.
3. Resumés are
   a. requested during interviews.
   b. easy to prepare.
   c. reflections of your professionalism.
   d. attempts to present complete information about your personal worth.
   e. None of these
4. The best length of a resumé is
   a. one page.
   b. two pages.
   c. Either a or b
   d. two to three pages.
   e. None of these

5. In describing your job duties and responsibilities on a resumé, you should
   a. stretch the truth a little.
   b. include short, snappy phrases.
   c. concentrate on memorable achievements.
   d. make it interesting to read.
   e. All of these except a.
6. It is a good idea to
   a. gather a lot of personal references.
   b. gather ten professional references.
   c. gather references before employment terminates.
   d. give reference writers a sample reference letter form.
   e. All of these
7. Hints for interviews include
   a. wearing the latest style.
   b. acting casual.
   c. calling interviewers "madam" and "sir."
   d. suggesting you are the superior candidate in view of all who will be interviewed.
   e. None of these

8. Practicing entering an interview room and seating oneself appropriately was
   a. ignored by this text.
   b. a part of a suggested visualization technique.
   c. recommended.
   d. possibly a part of videotaping practice.
   e. Both b and d

F. List characteristics which typify and describe successful job hunters and goal achievers.

Resources

Bolles, Richard, as interviewed by Margaret Simmons, in *Quest/80*, Vol. 4, No. 9 (Nov. 1980).

Cindy Cooke. Presentation at New Life Options Conference, May 13, 1981.

Johnson, Mona S. *Job Interviews: Strategies for Success.* Macomb, IL: Association for the Education of Young Children, 1980.

Lewis, Bettye. *ECE Options*, Vol. 5, No. 3 (February 1980).

Unit 30
Law and the Student Teacher

OBJECTIVES

After studying this unit, the student will be able to:

- Understand teachers' and student teachers' liabilities.
- List laws which affect teacher qualifications and working conditions.
- Describe two types of mandatory employee insurance.
- Identify possible federal income tax deductions for teachers and student teachers.

Being knowledgeable about laws which affect early childhood teachers and their working conditions requires investigation and study. Since laws vary from state to state, this unit serves as a springboard for your own research. It describes and presents the most common laws related to early childhood teaching. You may discover other laws unique to your locality.

LICENSING LAW

Your placement classroom received permission to operate as a service to children and families from some legally authorized authority (granted by law through legislation). Licensing regulations protect the health, safety, and general welfare of children in group care. Licensing responsibility and regulatory functions are often performed by state welfare, state public health, or state education departments. Federally funded programs must abide by federal guidelines, usually Federal Interagency Day Care Requirements. Most programs come under the auspices of a number of regulatory laws.

Teacher qualifications can differ greatly, particularly when comparing publicly and privately funded programs. Often teacher qualifications are more stringent when public money is involved.

Law affects the program of child activities and experiences offered. Public support usually requires a planned developmental offering for each child rather than the custodial care minimums found in the proprietary (privately funded) sector. Schools can choose to present activity programs which are much more than minimum program requirements.

CHILD SPACE REGULATIONS

The law either specifically spells out facility square footage requirements (exteriors, rooms, and playgrounds) or states "sufficient or adequate" when describing space and its use. The former insures enforceable compliance; the latter can be a disputable value judgment. The following facility particulars are commonly regulated by law and usually require clearances, inspections, and/or permits.

- Zoning areas.
- Building and construction features.
- Fire safety.
- Health maintenance furnishings and equipment.

Space (square footage) determines the number of children enrolled at any given time. Law provides for a mandatory number of adults with any group of young children (child/adult ratios).

LIABILITY

Knowledge of the law is a form of teacher, as well as child, protection. When administrators (directors, owners, principals) become licensed, they establish a legal relationship recognized by the courts. They assume responsibility for their school's total operation. When teachers are hired, they also assume responsibilities which make them liable for lawsuits. If a teacher is legally challenged, a suitable explanation must be provided concerning how each job responsibility was met.

In most states, the law clearly stipulates that children must be supervised at all times, figure 30-1. Job descriptions for teachers include specific references to supervising and/or management of child learning and play. Written child center policies often include statements about replacing oneself with another adult before leaving a group of assigned children.

In student teaching assignments, cooperating or practicing teachers retain the liability of the student teaching placement. Student teachers are under their control and direction. The practicing teacher usually has a good grasp on the law governing the center's operation and the rules and/or guidelines which must be followed. Directors or teachers can carry insurance

Fig. 30-1 Swings are sometimes prohibited because schools feel they are risky. Children must always be supervised.

to protect them from suits involving their work. A clause, or rider, is added to either their homeowner, renter, or car insurance policies. Premiums can vary from seven to fifty dollars per year. Negligence and/or failure to perform duties has to be proved in court before an insurance company pays damages.

LABOR LAWS

Many states' industrial relations and industrial welfare laws have been drawn from the Federal Fair Labor Standards Act which stipulates worker rights. The following areas are usually described, and posters with specific items are, by law, available for reading by employed workers at their worksite (or central office): hours and days, workweek; minimum wage; overtime; age of workers, minors; split shifts; employee records; payment of wages; cash shortage and breakage; uniforms and equipment; meals and lodging; meal periods; rest periods (breaks); room temperature; and inspection and penalties.

A sampling of items found in California's Industrial Welfare Commissions Order No. 4-80 (regulating wages, hours, and working conditions in professional, technical, clerical, mechanical, and similar occupations) and Industrial Welfare Commissions Public Housekeeping Industry Order 5-80 (includes employees in private preschools) is found in the Appendix.

Items of great interest to early childhood staff members include rest periods, duty-free meal periods, overtime and compensatory time, workweek agreements, and resting areas. Programs which lack adequate numbers of staff members sometimes unlawfully omit break periods. Workweek assignments at other centers depend on day-to-day child attendance figures and may overlook law stipulations.

STATE EMPLOYMENT SECURITY

State law often requires unemployment insurance for workers. This provides benefits during periods when an employee is laid off for the summer, quits with a good cause, or is terminated without a just cause. Employers pay the insurance premiums. Often premiums rise when a number of successful claims are filed. This can encourage some employers to remain silent concerning this benefit or discourage employees from filing claims. Directors and owners are legally responsible for displaying informational posters at the work site.

Disability insurance premiums may be required for all employers in your state. If so, benefits are paid to eligible workers who are unemployed because of illness or injury which is not work related. Wage taxes are often paid to a state fund by an employee after they are collected (withheld) by the employer who by law forwards the taxes to the proper state agency. Persons employed by churches, church organizations, or certain nonprofit organizations are sometimes "special exclusions" and not covered by either unemployment or disability insurance benefits.

The following explains how one proceeds in the event of a disability and what decides how much is paid:

To receive benefits, an employee must be unable to perform regular work because of an illness or injury, have earned a minimum amount during the previous year base period, file a timely claim, and sometimes serve a waiting period. Payments are based on the wages received during the base period.

In some states a woman may be eligible for disability insurance benefits because of pregnancy if her doctor certifies that she is unable to do her regular or customary work. (Stevenson, 1981)

FEDERAL UNEMPLOYMENT TAX   Federal unemployment tax is paid only by the employer. An employer may receive credits for amounts paid to a state unemployment fund. Contributions depend on a fixed rate (3.4%) on the first $6000 of wages paid to each employee. It is wise for each employed worker to investigate whether she or he is covered by federal unemployment benefits. Some organizations are exempted from this federal law.

WORKERS' COMPENSATION INSURANCE
Injuries or death arising from job-related circumstances are covered by Workers' Compensation Insurance. All employers are legally required to pay premiums for two reasons: to make sure that an injured worker receives prompt and complete medical treatment and specific benefits for work-related injuries; and to enable the employer to assume a known and limited liability rather than risk the hazards of an unknown and possibly disastrous liability.

The employer pays the total cost of this insurance, which is computed by the size of the school's payroll and workers' job categories. Benefits include medical treatment; vocational rehabilitation; temporary disability payments; permanent disability payments; and death benefits for dependents.

State law requires employers to notify all new employees in writing, by the end of their first pay period, of their right to Workers' Compensation benefits in case of an industrial injury. Employers must also notify injured employees of Workers' Compensation benefits. They must post their insurance carrier's name and information about Workers' Compensation benefits.

Some compensation fund insurance companies return dividends to policy holders (employers) on a merit basis dependent upon the employer's success in preventing employee injury. This economic incentive may promote employers' attempts to discourage employee claim-filing. They may pay all of an injured employee's medical bills, hoping the employee will not file a claim.

SOCIAL SECURITY

By law, both the employee and employer contribute 6.7% of that employee's total wages to the federal Social Security (FICA) program. Tax-exempt organizations can elect to join this program and secure its benefits for employees. FICA contributions are deducted until wages surpass $32,400. The employee's and employer's matching contributions are forwarded to the Internal Revenue Service.

Benefits begin at retirement age or before if a worker is seriously disabled. Payment amounts vary depending on "quarters of coverage" and employees' average earnings over a period of years. The Social Security Administration maintains local offices throughout the country where further information can be obtained. Since private preschool program retirement plans are a rarity, older workers entering the early childhood field may wish to initiate early deductions into plans which supplement Social Security benefits.

INTERNAL REVENUE SERVICE

Your federal income taxes are withheld based on earnings and number of dependents. Early childhood workers contribute by law as do all other workers, figure 30-2. Since many early childhood professionals receive low pay, an awareness of legal income tax deductions is important. Deductible items can include certain education expenses; certain automobile and travel expenses; professional publications costs; professional membership fees; temporary absence from job expenses; job-hunting expenses; partial child care expenses; certain teaching tool and supply expenses; certain clothing expenses; required medical examination fees; home use for work preparation; union dues; tax counsel and assistance; employment agency fees; and certain protective clothing expenses.

Three small publications available at your local U.S. Department of the Treasury, Internal Revenue Service Office are informative and helpful. They are Publication 529 Miscellaneous Deductions; Publication 508 Educational Expenses; and Publication 503 Child and Disabled Dependent Care.

CIVIL RIGHTS LAW

Child programs using federal funds promise there will be no discrimination on the basis of color, race, national origin, or sex in employment of staff or admission of children. Since some state licensing is indirectly connected to federal funds, all licensed programs fall under this law's jurisdiction (Title VII of the Civil Rights Act of 1964).

The Equal Opportunity Act of 1972 also involves employers who receive federal funds. Age, race, creed, color, sex, and national origin discrimination in employer practices including recruiting, transfer, promotion, training, compensation, benefits, layoffs, and termination is prohibited. Job qualifications and job descriptions must be clearly specified in these programs under this body of law.

STATE INCOME TAX

In many states, an income tax is deducted from employee wages. Employers are usually required to obtain a state identification number. Withheld amounts are forwarded to a state office which holds the funds until the taxpayer files a tax return. It is then determined if enough has been withheld or whether a refund is necessary.

THE NATIONAL LABOR RELATIONS ACT

The National Labor Relations Act is designed to encourage and protect employees who want to form unions. Certain rights are guaranteed: You can form, or attempt to form, a union among employees where you work; you can join a union whether or not that union is recognized by the employer; and you can assist a union in organizing employees.

In forming a union, it is illegal for an employer to threaten you with firing, demotion, reprimands, or other punishments for engaging in union activity; threaten to take away benefits if the union wins the

Fig. 30-2 Knowing the law can help you prepare for filing tax returns.

election; or promise benefits in return for antiunion activity.

Particulars concerning employee elections, collective bargaining, and union contracts are part of this legislation.

CHILD ABUSE LAW

Many states require teachers to report suspected cases of child abuse. Abuse can be defined as cruelty and/or neglect. Teachers in early childhood centers often become children's confidants. Disclosing a wide range of feelings, fears, joys, and accomplishments during daily conversations, children cue teachers to important happenings in their lives.

Schools keeping growth and weight records, which monitor general health, are in a position to notice subtle changes and trends. Since outer clothing is sometimes removed during rest periods and soiled or wet clothing changed, injuries to the skin may be visible. Speaking to the cooperating teacher about questionable child behaviors, physical conditions, or verbalizations is recommended.

Summary

Licensing law, federal, and/or state guidelines regulate and specify a large number of particulars concerning facilities, equipment, staff qualifications, operational procedures, ratios, child guidance, child program, child ages, and other features of a center's operation. Law protects children and ensures at least minimum standards. A student teacher needs to be aware of liability under the law and teacher responsibilities mandated by law.

The law can provide employee assistance when necessary. Benefits are claimed for work injury or a break in employment. Working conditions stipulated in labor law provide worker protection. A review of federal income tax law may alert early childhood teachers and student teachers to a number of allowed deductions for work and education related items.

Suggested Activities

A. Ask your director for an appointment to review the law which licenses or regulates your placement classroom. Answer the following questions:
   1. Are the duties and responsibilities of teachers outlined? If so, list them.
   2. Are adult/child ratios stipulated?
   3. Is a morning health check required for each entering child?
   4. What does the law say about toys and/or equipment?
   5. How is the number of children per school or classroom determined?
   6. Are there any statements concerning child guidance?
   7. Can a teacher give children medicine?
   8. Are there any rules governing food service?
   9. Are there any rules governing emergencies?
   10. Are child rest periods mentioned?
   11. Did you find a statement which mentioned that children are to be supervised at all times?
   12. What was the name of the law you reviewed?

B. Find out what state or local agency licensed your placement site.

C. Investigate unemployment and disability insurance benefits. Report your findings to your classmates. Secure available written materials. Invite a guest speaker.

D. Interview three practicing teachers concerning break policy, overtime pay, and duty-free lunch periods.

E. Review highlights of the National Labor Relations Act at your local library. What is the status of very small centers whose yearly gross income is below $250,000?

F. Read the following situations. Discuss possible student teacher or teacher courses of action with a group of three or four others. What does your group feel is the best course of action? Then discuss your choice with the whole class.

1. A child has been injured severely while Katrina, a student teacher, was supervising a yard area. Katrina decides the child needs immediate attention so she...

2. Caleb, age four, calls another child an ethnic name. Bill, a student teacher, takes him firmly by the arm to the cooperating teacher. On the way Caleb jerks loose and picks up a hammer at the woodworking table. Bill rushes over to the cooperating teacher across the yard. When they return, Caleb has smashed and damaged Agatha's expensive new doll that she brought to school for sharing time. Later, the parents of Agatha sue the school for the loss of the doll. Bill should...

3. Randy, a student teacher, notices that the cooperating teacher often leaves the classroom for a much needed break period. This leaves Randy in full charge of the room. Randy should...

4. Eric, a student teacher, has been bitten by Mark, an angry and upset child. The bite punctured the skin and required a costly doctor's visit and tetanus shot. When Mark's mother drops him off the next day, Eric says...

5. Mrs. Plott, the practicing teacher, just left the building with a child who is experiencing a violent reaction to a bee sting. The father of another student, Marsha, has arrived to take Marsha home. Donna, a student teacher, checks school records quickly, remembering that Marsha's father is not authorized to pick her up. Donna then...

6. It is common practice in Judith's placement classroom to have two or three extra children over the legal limit. Judith should

7. Cantrell, a student teacher, has been assigned maintenance responsibilities which include cleaning the school kitchen's oven. Cantrell should...

8. Mark, a newly hired preschool teacher, is hit in the eye with a flying block thrown by a child. He is hospitalized briefly; it is determined that the eye is bleeding internally. Mark has no hospitalization plan. He should...

9. A child was injured when Theresa, a student teacher, opened the door to allow a child to get in the parent's car. The parent had pulled into the driveway by the school's front door and was honking the horn.

10. Monica is employed as a teacher at a school where it is policy to spank children. Knowing this is counter to licensing law, Monica approaches the director, who explains that each parent has given written approval for teachers to do so. Monica should...

11. A student teacher, Andy, has just received a court summons because a parent claims he caused a child to suffer serious trauma when disciplining. Andy should...

12. Michelle's employment as a teacher has been terminated because she discussed her union campaign with other employees at her preschool job site. She should...

13. Joe has been told that his services will not be needed during the summer. He has been employed for a year. He should...

14. When arriving on a scheduled workday Mona, the teacher of three-year-olds, is told she is not needed because six children are home ill. Mona notices she received no pay for the day so...

15. Miss Green, a newly employed teacher, is notified that she must attend parent meetings twice each month. She does not receive overtime pay for these three-hour meetings which are over her forty-hour workweek so...

16. Marty, a new teacher, has refused to wax the classroom floors and is fired. Marty should...

G. Obtain a copy of your state's licensing law and read it.

H. Obtain a current copy of Federal Interagency Day Care Requirements and read it. (U.S. Department of Health and Human Services, Washington, DC)

I. Invite a union representative to speak to the class on labor law.

J. Investigate insurance coverage costs to protect teachers from employment liability.

K. Invite a tax expert to class to speak on possible deductions for teachers.

L. Investigate law which requires teachers to report suspected child abuse.

Review

A. Match items in Column I to those in Column II.

I

1. teacher qualifications
2. licensed programs
3. unemployment insurance
4. Social Security
5. licensing agency
6. disability insurance
7. license
8. Federal Interagency Guidelines
9. value judgment
10. liability
11. Fair Labor Standards Act
12. Workers' Compensation Insurance
13. Internal Revenue Service
14. Equal Opportunity Act
15. National Labor Relations Act
16. Civil Rights Law

II

a. gives aid to employees injured on the job
b. legal authority
c. regulates Head Start
d. "sufficient and adequate"
e. can be sued
f. minimum wage identified
g. can choose to offer a development program not required by law
h. pays employee who is laid off for the summer
i. permission to operate
j. higher when program is supported by public tax dollars
k. covers nonwork-related illness or injury
l. offers retirement benefits
m. prevents an employer from firing an employee for union activity
n. ethnic discrimination prohibited
o. permits deductions for qualified job hunting expenses
p. prohibits age discrimination

B. Briefly explain the importance of a student teacher's knowledge of licensing law.

C. What employee rights are ensured in labor law? Identify which of the following statements are true.
1. Above-minimum hourly wages are specified in the Federal Labor Standards Act.
2. Early childhood employees have the right to join a union organization.
3. An employer must set a weekly workweek in advance.
4. An employer contributes an amount matching the employee's deduction for Workers' Compensation Insurance.
5. Social Security (FICA) might be paid to a permanently disabled employee.
6. An early childhood teacher can be forced to pay a large settlement sum if proven negligent.
7. All education expenses are deductible for student teachers on federal income tax forms.
8. Both sex and age discrimination in hiring practices are prohibited by law.
9. Employees who become ill from nonwork-related causes may collect benefits.
10. Employers must, by law, inform all new employees about their Workers' Compensation benefits.

D. Define the following terms.
1. liability
2. workweek
3. collective bargaining

E. Complete the following statements.
1. The body of law which licenses privately funded preschools in this state is called. . .
2. Publicly funded preschool programs must abide by rules and guidelines stipulated in. . .

Resources

Stevenson, Carol. "Insuring Your Program: Employee Taxes and Benefits." *Child Care Information Exchange* (Nov./Dec. 1981).

APPENDIX

UNIT 2
SAMPLE OF SCHOOL APPLICATION FORM

(From *Early Childhood Education: Planning and Administering Programs* by Annie L. Butler. Copyright © 1974 by Litton Educational Publishing, Inc. Reprinted by permission of Wadsworth Publishing Company, Belmont, California 94002.)

APPLICATION FOR _____ SCHOOL Date _____

Child's name _____
　　　　　　　　　　last　　　　　　first　　　　　　middle

Sex _____ Date of birth _____

Parent's name _____

Telephone number _____

Date when admission is desired _____

Comments _____

_____

_____

OPEN FAMILY INFORMATION CARD

Child's name _____
　　　　　　　last　　　　first　　　middle　　　name child is called

Home address _____ phone number _____

Father's name _____

Work address _____ phone number _____

Mother's name _____

Work address _____ phone number _____

Name(s) of persons who may call for the child

　　1. _____　　2. _____

　　3. _____　　4. _____

Emergency contact _____ phone number _____

Child's doctor _____ phone number _____

Allergies _____

_____

_____

_____

SAMPLE OF SCHOOL APPLICATION FORM

(From *Early Childhood Education: Planning and Administering Programs* by Annie L. Butler. Copyright © 1974 by Litton Educational Publishing, Inc. Reprinted by permission of Wadsworth Publishing Company, Belmont, California 94002.)

Child's name _____ Date _____

               Last   First   Middle

Name child is called _____ Birthdate _____

Address _____ Phone number _____

Other persons living in the household:

Name	Relationship	Birthdate
_____	_____	_____
_____	_____	_____
_____	_____	_____
_____	_____	_____
_____	_____	_____
_____	_____	_____
_____	_____	_____

Type of dwelling: House _____ Duplex _____ Apartment _____ Rooms _____

Previous school experience _____

Developmental History

Type of birth: Normal _____ Premature _____ Any complications _____

Age child began sitting _____ Crawling _____ Walking _____

Is child a good climber? _____ Does he fall easily? _____

Age child began talking _____ Current language abilities _____

Any difficulties in speaking? _____ Other languages spoken _____

Sleeping

What is child's bedtime? _____ What time does he get up? _____

Is he ready for sleep? _____ Does he have his own room? _____

His own bed? _____ Whom does he share with, if shared? _____

Does child have sleep disturbances? _____

What is child's mood on awakening? _____

Does child take naps? _____ From when _____ to _____

Does child tire easily? _____ Under what conditions? _____

Do you have any particular concerns about your child's sleeping habits? _____

Eating

Please describe the diet and pattern of eating of your child in the course of a day. _____

Does the child enjoy eating? _____

What are his favorite foods? _____

What foods are refused? _____

Does he feed himself? _____ With spoon? _____ With fork? _____ Hands? _____

Do you have particular concerns about your child's eating habits? _____

Toilet Habits

Is your child toilet trained for urine? _____ For bowels? _____

If so, at approximately what age did be become trained? _____

What word is used for urination? _____ For bowel movement? _____

How frequently do accidents occur? _____

How does the child react to them? _____

Does he need help with toileting? _____

Does the child wet the bed at night? _____ How often? _____

Do you have any particular concerns about your child's toilet habits? _____

_____

Social and Emotional Behavior

Nervous habits: Does the child have temper tantrums? _____ Frequent? _____

Upset stomachs? _____ Does he cry easily? _____ Does he suck his

thumb or fingers? _____ Bite his nails? _____ Handle his body?

_____ How would you describe his characteristic behavior? Calm _____

Excitable _____ Easily upset _____ Whining _____

Happy _____ Cheerful _____ Negative _____ Cooperative _____

With what age child does your child usually play? _____

_____

Into how many homes does he go frequently? _____

How many playmates come to his house frequently? _____

What kind of group contacts does the child have? _____

How does he get along with his brothers and sisters? _____

Does he enjoy playing alone? _____

How does he relate to strangers? _____

How does he relate to friendly adults? _____

What makes him mad or upset? _____

How does he show these feelings? _____

What do you find is the best way to handle him? _____

What kind of discipline is usually used and by whom? _____

_____

What are his favorite toys? _____

_____

Is he frightened of any of the following? animals _____ rough children _____

loud noises _____ sirens _____ dark _____ storms _____ water _____

Describe his special interests. _____

Has he had any travel experiences? _____

Are there particular ways you think we might be able to help your child? _____

_____

_____

_____

_____

_____

UNIT 5
STUDENT TEACHER-AUTHORED
EXAMPLE OF COMPLETED UNIT
(Courtesy of Harriet Althouse)

COMMON, CREEPY, CRAWLY CREATURES

Dear Father, hear and bless
Thy beasts and singing birds,
And guard with tenderness
Small things that have no words.

TABLE OF CONTENTS

GOALS

That, after exposure to this week-long unit, the children will be able to look at all specimens and pictures without expressions of disgust or loathing. That they will demonstrate behavior indicative of respect for life and appreciation of the strange beauty of insects, etc., by refraining from picking up, shaking, or otherwise disturbing creatures' homes.

SUGGESTED CLASSROOM MATERIALS

Sensory: Playdough and cornmeal trays with plastic bugs
Atmosphere: Pictures, etc. Ladybugs and crickets, praying mantises, etc. can be purchased. Buy some. Make "atmosphere" and science displays. Put crickets in a fancy "cricket cage" made of popsicle sticks, etc., to reinforce Chinese New Year, or just explain simply to children about the ancient Chinese custom of doing this. A spider can be caught and put in a jar with compost in the bottom and two twigs. A moth or fly can be fed to the spider daily and children will see the whole process. (I have done this; it works.) Snail races: snails in clear plastic shoe box with black construction paper on bottom. They will make visible trails. At Halloween, I put yarn spider webs in my window. This can be done, and paper or yarn spiders and flies set in there. Bug eggs, beehives, chrysalises, spittlebugs, etc.

SUGGESTED DAILY ACTIVITIES FOR WEEK

(Asterisk (*) indicates details are given at end of unit.)

MONDAY
BEGIN: with a music circle. Sing "Little Arabella Miller"* and do "Ladybug"* fingerplay. Read *The Very Hungry Caterpillar*. Chant "Burnie Bee"* and fly away!
Free Play, Arts & Crafts: String and glue spider webs on construction paper. Making headband antennae and large wings to wear for dramatic play. (Make some round, like beetles' wings for painting, and some like gauzy or glittery dragonfly wings.) Send home a note that each child shall bring cornmeal or oatmeal carton for Thursday's project.
Background Music for Free Play: "Flight of the Bumblebee"*
Motor & Music: Play "La Cucaracha"* and be dancing cockroaches. Quiet down by singing "Inchworm."*
Snack: Honeycomb from health food store. (Play "Honeycomb"* by Jimmie Rodgers.)
Repeat "Ladybug" fingerplay with flannelboard pieces.
Read book: *One Snail & Me.*

TUESDAY
CIRCLE: Sing "Arabella Miller" and "Eensy, Weensy Spider."* Do "Ladybug" fingerplay again. Do flannelboard story "Greenie and the Star."* Repeat "Burnie Bee" and fly away.
Craft Free Expression: Prepare Bug Juice* for snack and refrigerate. Food exp. (Have leaves such as lettuce, spinach to eat.) Collage on bug shapes.
Background Music: Play "The Butterfly Ball and the Grasshopper's Feast."*
Movement: Be waterbugs, striders, etc. Walk on top of imaginary water. If possible, have pond water with

waterbugs on display. "Flight of the Bumblebee" good for this. Can use crepe paper or ribbon streamers, if desired.

Review fingerplay again. Read: "Mrs. Brownish Beetle"* and do with flannelboard pieces.

WEDNESDAY

SING: "Arabella Miller" and "Eensy Weensy Spider" again. Read Rosetti's poem, "Hurt No Living Thing."* Do "Ladybug" fingerplay.

Read A Firefly Named Torchy.

Art/Free Expression: String painting combined with thumb & fingerprint bugs on construction paper. Marigold spider* or other bug with contact paper.

Music/Motor: Move to Burl Ives' "Ugly Bug Ball."* (If you find, please let me know; it's an older record. Thanks! Or you can use Jimmie Rodgers' "Honeycomb" — also old — but I have it.)

Snack: "crittables"* made from peanut butter modeling dough. Get moth & butterfly flannelboard pieces and talk about moths/night; butterflies/day. What do antennae do for insects? Give everyone butterfly stickers and dismiss.

THURSDAY

SING: "Arabella Miller" and "Inchworm". . .Do flannelboard "Life Cycle of the Butterfly."*

Go on bug walk. Lie on stomach and observe ants, etc. Watch snails in action.

Craft/Free Expression: Make bug catchers from oatmeal containers* brought in. Easel paint on big bug shapes (3 or 4 variations)

Snack: Ants on Log*

If available, do "Hucklebug" book and filmstrip.

Dance to "La Cucaracha" again.

Read The Grouchy Ladybug.

FRIDAY

DO "Arabella" and "Eensy, Weensy Spider" and review "Ladybug" fingerplay. Read The Way of an Ant.

Art/Crafts: Cut out simple beetle and bug shapes; paste on paper. (Children will make bug shapes from circles, triangles, etc.) Okay to have a few models for this. Then they paste on any way they wish. Can make flowers from shapes or whatever they want to,

even if they get off bugs completely.

Movement and Music: Put on bug wings and antennas. Some could be bees making a "honeycomb" putting square shapes on wall or bulletin board. Explain simply how bees give messages to one another about where to get honey. Show pictures of this. Play "Flight of the Bumblebee" as background mood music for this.

Snack: Pancake Art*

Do flannelboard: "My Daddy Gave Me A Present"*

CURRICULUM AREAS AND LEARNING OBJECTIVES

MATH

Make matching and sorting games from those beautiful butterfly stickers obtainable at Hallmark store. Make Caterpillar number game (felt circles and felt numbers pasted or sewn on).

Books: One Snail and Me, The Butterfly Ball, and The Hungry Caterpillar are all counting books. "Six Little Ladybugs"* from Rainbows & Dragons. Make a "bug parts" puzzle by pasting pictures on construction paper, contacting, and cutting up.

Objectives: That children, when exposed to these pre-math activities, will use them properly, demonstrating left-to-right progression (with caterpillar game), matching stickers and sorting properly, putting puzzles together correctly, holding up proper amounts of fingers for "Ladybug" poem, and filling in gaps when teacher pauses while reading the counting books.

*Please note that math and science curriculum areas overlap a lot in this unit.

SCIENCE

Mealworm, ant, or ladybug farm

Objective: That children, observing insects going about daily lives, will have conversations and refrain from disturbing insects.

*"Life Cycle of Butterfly" flannelboard.

Objective: That children will ask questions and will be able to tell in their own words how a butterfly develops. That this will move us onward, enabling them to further understand that moths are like butterflies, but nocturnal, and that they will also be able to explain this verbally.

"How Many Legs" game. (Make a simple game from tag or construction paper and cover with contact paper.) Make spider with eight legs and other various insects with six. This should be a matching game or devise some way that it will be self-correcting.

Objective: That children, when they have experienced this activity once or more, will be able to complete it successfully, and that by end of unit will be able to answer correctly when asked how many legs a spider has compared to the denizens of the insect world.

If possible, hatch a cocoon.

Objective: That children will see the flannelboard story come to life before their very eyes!

FOOD EXPERIENCES (Complete list in daily planning)
Honeycomb from health food store or beekeeper, and honey on oatmeal or some other food, such as bread.

Objectives: That children, when they've experienced these, will have physical knowledge of the product that bees make, and that, when asked, will verbally explain that the bees made these foods.

Pancake Art and Crittables
Objectives: That children, upon mixing batter and creating these snacks, will have their self-esteem enhanced by having cooked their own snack, will see and have conversation stimulated by the food's changing form, texture, etc., that they will be able to use their creative imaginations and fine-motor skills by performing this.

*PANCAKE ART — from *The Kids' Cookbook* by Barrett & Dalton, Nitty Gritty Productions.
Materials: Pancake mix, large spoon, bowl, griddle, and *imagination!* Children use the large spoon to pour pancake batter into griddle. They can try to make worms, bugs, etc.

*CRITTABLES — Peanut Butter Modeling Dough
    1 cup peanut butter
    1-1/4 cup nonfat powdered milk
    1 cup white corn syrup
    1-1/4 cup sifted powdered sugar
Mix and knead. Double for classroom. Provide

chocolate/carob chips, shredded coconut, nuts, seeds, etc. for decorations.

*ANTS ON LOG — Celery, peanut butter, raisins
Objectives: Imagination-stretcher, fine-motor spreading experience, and placing raisins on top.

*BUG JUICE from *The Kids' Cookbook*
Any kind of punch mix. Add anything you like: raisins, dried apricots, apple bits, strawberries, bananas, cherries. (Apple cider & raisins is nice!)
Objective: Children naturally pour their own, getting experience in self-esteem and lifting and handling; self-esteem also enhanced by their helping to create punch, suggesting how to make it and putting things in, etc. Talk about colors, taste combinations, etc. Inventive!

"CUT SANDWICHES LIKE A BUTTERFLY." My own children always wanted their peanut butter & jelly sandwiches cut in half diagonally, then quartered and the points of the triangle shapes put together on the napkin so it looked like a butterfly.
Objective: Fun, to tell the truth! Although they do get shape recognition and can even cut their own eventually, getting a little bit of parts and whole experience, pressure of knife, etc.

WASH LEAVES — SPINACH, etc., and eat.
Objective: Somebody very wise once said, "It's really hard to hate anyone you've *been*!" When we eat bug food, we *are* being BUGS. This is dramatic play, an imagination-stretcher, as well as being really nutritious.

MUSIC & MOTOR
Record:* "The Butterfly Ball and the Grasshopper's Feast," Alan Aldridge — William Plomer, narrated by Judi Dench and Michael Hordern
Decca Records, Argo Division
115 Fulham Rd., London, SW 3 6 RR
    This is British-made, and the words are hard to understand. Still, it's nice music to listen to for background during free play time.

*"The Ugly Bug Ball"....Burl Ives
Objectives: This has a strong beat to feel and move to. Enjoyment.

*"Inchworm"....Danny Kaye
This is from his Hans Christian Anderson interpretation. This is nice to use with Lionni's *Inch By Inch*.
Words:
Inchworm, Inchworm, measuring the marigolds
You and your arithmetic, you'll probably go far.
Inchworm, Inchworm, measuring the marigolds,
Seems to me, you'd stop and see
How beautiful they are!

Objectives: That children will recite the words and understand them in some future time, also math. Can even bring in rulers, etc.

*"Honeycomb"....Jimmie Rogers
Objectives: This is a fun song with a strong beat. Lively and just reinforces the word honeycomb and makes good upbeat background music.

*"La Cucaracha"....Percy Faith
Objectives: Multicultural. Means the cockroach. Good for interpretative dancing. Bouncy, irresistible beat, similar to "Mexican Hat Dance." Children will get large-motor exercise as they're led to this song through a routine including large- and small-motor activities.

*"Flight of the Bumblebee"....Rimsky-Korsakov
Objective: Children will be exposed to and move to classical music, in addition to all the other styles used with this unit. This stretches their imagination, as we close our eyes and imagine bees in flight and working among the flowers while we listen. When we put on our wings and our antennae and build our honeycomb, this learning is more exciting.

Circle Songs:
*"Little Arabella Miller" Little Arabella Miller found a wooly caterpillar
                           First she put it on her Mother
(tune of   Then upon her baby brother.
"Baa, Baa,   All said, "Arabella Miller,
Black Sheep")   Take away that caterpillar!"
(This is found in the "Eye Winker, Tom Tinker" songbook.)

*"Eensy, Weensy Spider" Eensy, weensy spider came up the water spout
                         Down came the rain and knocked the spider out

Up came the sun and dried up all the rain. . .and
The eensy, weensy spider came up the spout again.
(In case somebody doesn't know this!)

ARTS & CRAFTS
*Directions for marigold spider (listed under daily activities for Wednesday)

Marigold petals for head, body of fuzzy milkweed and red berries. Pine needles form the web parts (within a green twig outline). Legs and antennae could be twigs or yarn.
Objectives: This is a craft. It would need to be done with only one or two children at a time, and they should follow directions carefully and have the small-motor experience of handling all these little objects and placing them to make the spider in her web.

*Oatmeal Box Bug Cage (listed under daily activities for Thursday)
Materials:
    1 oatmeal box
    pencil
    yarn or cord
    poster paints
    piece screening, pref. plastic, old nylons
    scissors
    crayons or felt tips

Paint empty oatmeal or cornmeal box a light color with poster paints. Let dry. Draw flower shapes on box with pencil. Poke a hole in center of each flower with pencil. Put one blade of pair of scissors into each hole and cut out the flowers. (Teachers do this with sharp scissors.) Cut a piece of screening as tall as the box and long enough to fit around the inside. Roll it, fit into box. Poke a hole on both sides of box near top. Use a pencil. Thread a long piece of cord or yarn through both holes. Tie both ends together; pull cord so you can put cover on box. Keep lid on when bugs are inside!
Objectives: This is also a craft, and very ambitious for little kids. It would be one-on-one, or one-on-two at the most. A volunteer mom should come in and help with this one. Here they have the self-esteem of making their own, plus choosing colors to paint, making flowers, etc.

DRAMATIC PLAY — This is included under language mostly, but also under Food Experiences (when we pretend to be bugs eating leaves) and also under Music & Motor activities.

LANGUAGE EXPERIENCES (See book list for further language)
*"Ladybug" fingerplay:

I want you to meet Ladybug,
Her little sister, Sadiebug,
Her Mother, Mrs. Gradybug,
Her aunt, that nice Old Maidybug,
And baby — she's a fraidybug.
(David McCord)

Objectives: Dramatic play, finger dexterity, language development

*"Spider"
I saw a little spider with the smartest spider head.
She made, somewhere inside her, a little silken thread.
I saw her sliding down it. She dangled in the air.
I saw her climbing up it, and pulling up each stair.
She made it look so easy, I wished all day I knew
How I could spin a magic thread, so I could dangle too.
(Aileen Fisher)

Objectives: Science and language

*"Burnie Bee Chant":
Burnie bee, burnie bee, tell me when your wedding be
If it be tomorrow day, take your wings and fly away.

*"Mrs. Brownish Beetle" (I plan to make flannelboard pieces, but haven't yet.)
1. When it was October, and a hard frost came,
   Mrs. Brownish Beetle (I don't know her other name)
   said, "Dear me, it's chilly,"
   said, "My coat is thin"
   said, "Land sakes, I've got to find a place to cuddle in."
2. So Mrs. Brownish Beetle, after several tries,
   Found a hole beneath a tree that was a beetle's size,
   and said, "Oh my, how lucky!"
   said, "How very nice!"
   said, "I'll snuggle down, away from the wind and cold and ice."

3. "I'll set my clock at April," Mrs. Beetle said.
   "I'll wind it up and put it here beside my little bed."
   So Mrs. Brownish Beetle (I don't know her other name)
   Nestled down, and went to sleep.
   And slept 'til April came.
   (Aileen Fisher)

*"Hurt no living thing"
Hurt no living thing
Ladybird or butterfly
Or moth with dusty wing;
Nor cricket chirping cheerily
Nor grasshopper so light of leap
Nor dancing gnat, nor beetle fat,
Nor harmless worms that creep.
(Rosetti)

*"Six Little Ladybugs" (Language and Math activity)
Six little ladybugs, glad to be alive
One chased a little ant, then. . .
Five little ladybugs, walking on the floor,
One hid inside a crack, then. . .
Four little ladybugs, saw a tiny flea,
One tried to chase it, then. . .
Three little ladybugs, and what did they do?
One skipped far away, then. . .
Two little ladybugs, dancing in the sun
One hid behind a tree, then. . .
One little ladybug, left all alone,
Flew back to her house, then there were none.

*"My Daddy Gave Me a Present" flannelboard (See patterns at end of unit)

My Daddy gave me a present. I gave that present to Herm.
What was the present? (Let kids guess.) A WORM.
Slimy, slithery, slathery, squirmy worm.

My Mommy gave me a present. I gave that present to Matt.
What was the present? A CAT.
Feathery-furry, soft and tickly, whiskery prickly cat.

My sister gave me a present. I gave that present to Rhoda.
What was the present? SODA.
Stingly tingly, fizzly freezy, ice cold soda pop.

My brother gave me a present. I'll give that present
to you.
What was the present? GLUE.
A pocketful of icky, sticky, glicky glue.

*"Greenie and the Star" flannelboard story (See patterns at end of unit)

One day Greenie the Snail, who lived in the
bottom of the garden, went out to find a star. He
had never seen a star, because his eyes are very small,
and they are on the very end of his antennae.

He asked the first flower he met, "Have you seen a
star?" The white flower answered, "No I haven't. Ask
the turquoise blue flower over there."

Greenie slid over to the turquoise blue flower.
"Have you seen a star?" he asked.

"No, I've never seen a star," the flower said, "but
go down the path and ask the pink flower."

Down the path Greenie went until he came to the
pink flower. (Ask the children to participate with
Greenie.) "Have you seen a star?"

The pink flower said, "No, but ask the orange
flower next to me — he knows everything." "Thank
you," said Greenie.

"Have you seen a star?" he said to the orange
flower. "Why yes, I have," the flower said. "Go over
and talk to the yellow flower, and she will show you
a star."

"Oh, boy," Greenie said, as he slid on his one foot
toward the yellow flower.

When he saw the yellow flower, he asked, "Have
you seen a star?"

"Seen a star!" the yellow flower said. "I *am* a
star!" "I'm called the star flower."

Poetry for the flannelboard

Greenie the snail went out for a walk.
He found a garden where flowers could talk.
The white flower said, "Hey, who are you?"
The pink flower said, "Where is your shoe?"
Greenie said, "I've only one foot, and it slips."
The orange flower said, "Do you use it to go on trips?"
Greenie said, "That's how I came here."
The turquoise flower said, "You must live near."
Greenie said, "I don't live very far.
Just take a left turn when you see a star."

Order: Greenie, white, turquoise, pink, orange, and
yellow.

BOOK LIST

A Firefly Named Torchy (Bernard Waber)

About a firefly whose light is so bright he couldn't
twinkle as he yearned to. He met an owl who told
him to appreciate his own special gift. At the end, he
twinkles, but it no longer really matters to him.

The Way Of An Ant (Kazue Mizumura)

An ant climbs ever higher, until he comes to
realize he can never reach the sky, and he is satisfied with his accomplishments. (A very philosophical ant.)

Snail, Where Are You? (Tomi Ungerer)

This is a no-words (almost) book, with the spiral
shape of the snail subtly beckoning children to find it
on each page. Sophisticated, cartoon-like style.

Inch by Inch (Lionni)

Story of an inchworm

Dream Tree

The story of the butterfly's life cycle

Grouchy Ladybug (Carle)

A ladybug travels far, has many adventures. A
whale also featured here.

One Snail and Me (McLeod)

Child is joined in bathtub by snail and other
creatures in increasing numbers. This is a counting
book and is very humorous.

Spring Garden (In A) (Edited by Richard Lewis)

Lovely, dreamy illustrations with haiku-like verse
on every page.

Why Do Mosquitoes Buzz In People's Ears?

This is an African folk tale, but fits in here.

The Adventures of Christopher Cricket (Larry Shapiro)

Christopher has many exciting adventures in the
garden.

Squiggly Wiggly's Surprise (Arnold Shapiro)

This book has a finger-puppet caterpillar attached
as a very appealing visual aid. Of course, Squiggly's
surprise is the butterfly.

Flowing In the Dark (Strong)

Not really about bugs, but somehow seems to fit
in with unit, fireflies, etc.

RESOURCE BOOKS

Insects as Pets (Villiard)
Insect Zoo (Eubank)

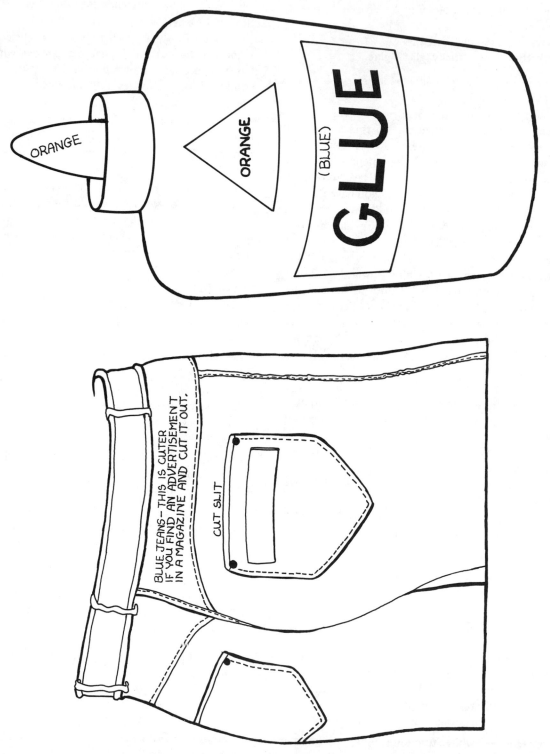

Patterns for "My Daddy Gave Me a Present"

WORM FOR HERM
CUT 1 FROM PINK FELT

CAT
FOR MATT

SODA
POP

SODA
FOR
RHODA

Patterns for "My Daddy Gave Me a Present"

Patterns for "Greenie and the Star"

UNIT 12

Emergency Shelter Program, Inc.
Parent-Child Education Center
Developmental Checklist

Name: _____   Birth date _____

I. Infants	Present	Date Observed
3 mo. Motor development		
Neck muscles support head steadily		
Moves arms/legs vigorously		
May move arm/leg on one side together		
On stomach, holds chest/head erect 10 seconds		
When picked up, brings body up compactly		
May bat at objects		
Reaches with both arms		
Perceptual development		
Follows slowly moving object w/ eyes and head from one side of body to other		
Looks at fingers individually		
Stops sucking to listen		
Visually seeks source of sound by turning head and neck		
Hands usually held open		
Social development		
Smiles easily and spontaneously		
Gurgles and coos in response to being spoken to		
Responds to familiar faces with smile		
Protests when left by mother		
Cries differentially when hungry, wet, cross, etc.		
Cognitive development		
Begins to show memory; waits for expected reward like feeding		
Begins to recognize family members and others close to him/her		
Explores own face, eyes, mouth with hand		
Responds to stimulation with whole body		
6 mo. Motor development		
Rolls from back to stomach		
Turns and twists in all directions		
Gets up on hands and knees, rocks		
Creeps on stomach; may go forward and backward		
Balances well when sitting, leans forward		
Sits in chair and bounces		
Grasps dangling object		
May sit unsupported 1/2 hour		
Rolls from back to stomach		

	Present	Date Observed
6 mo. Perceptual development		
Holds one block, reaches for 2nd, looks at a 3rd		
Reaches to grab dropped object		
Coos, hums, stops crying in response to music		
Likes to play with food		
Displays interest in finger-feeding self		
Has strong taste preferences		
Rotates wrist to turn and manipulate objects		
Often reaches with one arm instead of both		
Sleeps through the night		
Social development		
Prefers play with people		
Babbles and becomes excited during active play		
Babbles more in response to female voices		
Vocalizes pleasure/displeasure		
Gurgles when spoken to		
Tries to imitate facial expressions		
Turns in response to name		
Smiles at mirror image		
Disturbed by strangers		
Cognitive development		
Remains alert 2 hours at a time		
Inspects objects for a long time		
Eyes direct hand for reaching		
Likes to look at objects upside down and create change of perspective		
May compare 2 objects		
Has abrupt mood changes; primary emotions: pleasure, complaint, temper		
9 mo. Motor development		
Crawls with one hand full		
Turns while crawling		
May crawl upstairs		
Sits well		
Gets self into sitting position easily		
Pulls to standing		
May "cruise" along furniture		
Social development		
Eager for approval		
Begins to evaluate people's moods		
Imitates play		
Enjoys "peek-a-boo"		
Chooses toy for play		
Sensitive to other children; may cry if they cry		

	Present	Date Observed
9 mo. Social development (continued)		
May fight for disputed toy		
Imitates cough, tongue clicks		
Cognitive development		
Uncovers toy he has seen hidden		
Anticipates reward		
Follows simple directions		
Shows symbolic thinking/role play		
May say "dada" and/or "mama"		
Grows bored with same stimuli		
II. Toddlers		
12 mo. Motor development		
Can stand, cruise, may walk		
Pivots body 90 degrees when standing		
If walking, probably prefers crawling		
May add stopping, waving, backing, carrying toys to walking		
Climbs up and down stairs, holding hand		
May climb out of crib or playpen		
Gets to standing by flexing knees, pushing fr squat		
Lowers self to sitting position with ease		
Makes swimming motions in bath		
Wants to self feed		
May undress self		
Perceptual development		
Reaches accurately for object as (s)he looks away		
Puts things back together as well as takes them apart		
Builds tower of 2–3 blocks after demonstration		
Uses hammer and pegboard		
Likely to put 1–2 objects in mouth and grasp a 3rd		
Cares for doll, teddy bear — feeding, cuddling, bathing		
Enjoys water play in bath or sink		
Social development		
Expresses many emotions		
Recognizes emotions in others		
Gives affection to people		
Shows interest in what adults do		
May demand more help than needed because it's easier		
May refuse new foods		
Resists napping, may have tantrums		
Fears strange people, places		

	Present	Date Observed
12 mo. Social development (continued)		
Reacts sharply to separation from mother		
Distinguishes self from others		
Cognitive development		
Perceives objects as detached and separate to be used in play		
Unwraps toys		
Finds hidden object, remembers where it last was		
Remembers events		
Groups a few objects by shape and color		
Identifies animals in picture books		
Responds to directions		
Understands much of what is said to him		
Experiments with spatial relationships: heights, distances		
Stops when "no" is said		
Points to named body part		
18 mo. Motor development		
Walks well, seldom falls		
Sits self in small chair		
Walks up/down stairs one step at time holding hand of adult or rail		
Enjoys push toys		
Likes to push furniture		
Enjoys pull toys		
Enjoys riding toys to propel with feet on ground		
Strings large beads with shoelace		
Takes off shoes and socks		
Swings rhythmically in time to music		
Follows one/two step directions		
Perceptual development		
Demonstrates good eye-hand coordination with small manipulatives		
Will look at picture book briefly, turns pages but NOT one at a time		
Enjoys small objects (s)he can manipulate		
Social development		
Makes distinction between "mine" and "yours"		
Makes social contact with other children		
Smiles and looks at others		
May begin to indicate what (s)he wants by talking, pointing, grunting, body language		
Cognitive development		
Plays with blocks, can build tower of 2–3 blocks without model		
Can sort by colors, shapes (if exposed)		
Remembers where (s)he put a toy even if the next day		

	Present	Date Observed

III. Two-year-olds

Gross motor:

2.0 yrs. Runs well without falling

Kicks ball without overbalancing

Stairs: goes up/down alone 2 feet per step

Jumps from first step, one foot leading

Stops when running to change direction

Propels self on wheeled toy with feet on floor

Catches large ball by body trapping

Jumps 8" to 14"

2.6 yrs. Walks several steps tiptoe

Walks several steps backwards

Walks upstairs alternating feet

Stands on balance beam without assistance

Throws objects and tracks visually

Bounces ball, catches with both hands

Bends at waist to pick up object from floor

Jumps over string 2"–8" high

Fine Motor:

2.0 yrs. Turns knob on TV, toys, etc.

Turns door knobs, opens door

Builds 3–5 block tower

Holds pencil in fist

Scribbles, stays on paper

Puts ring on stick

Strings 1" beads

Puts small objects into container

Paints with whole arm movement

Folds paper in half

2.6 yrs. Removes jar lids

Builds 7–9 block tower

Completes simple inset puzzle

Traces circle

Paints with wrist action

Uses spoon without spilling

Holds glass, cup with one hand

Makes small cuts in paper with scissors

Places 6 pegs in pegboard

Language and speech:

Receptive:

Understands most commonly used nouns and verbs

Responds to 2-part command

Enjoys simple story books

	Present	Date Observed
Language and speech (continued)		
Receptive (continued)		
Points to common objects when they are named		
Understands functions of objects, e.g. cup-drink		
Understands 200–400 words		
Expressive:		
Verbalizes own actions		
Uses 2–3 word phrases		
Asks what and where questions		
Makes negative statements		
Labels action in pictures		
Approx. 50-word vocabulary (2 yrs.)		
Answers questions		
Speech sounds:		
Substitutes some consonant sounds, e.g., w for r, d for th		
Articulates all vowels with few deviations P, B, M, W, H, K, G, N, T, D		
Psychosocial skills:		
Sees self as separate person		
Conscious of possessions — "mine"		
Shy with strangers		
Knows gender identity		
Watches others, may join in play		
Begins to use dramatic play		
Helps put things away		
Participates in small-group activity (sings, claps, dances, etc.)		
Says "no" frequently, obeys when asked		
Understands and stays away from common dangers		
Cognitive skills:		
Responds to 3-part command		
Selects and looks at picture books		
Given 3 items, can associate which 2 go together		
Recognizes self in mirror		
Uses toys symbolically		
Imitates adult actions in dramatic play		
Self-help skills:		
Can undress self		
Can partially dress self		
Gains mastery over toilet needs		
Can drink from fountain		
Washes/dries hands with assistance		

	Present	Date Observed
IV. Three-year-olds		
Gross motor:		
3.0 yrs. Runs smoothly		
Stairs, walks down alternating feet		
Climbs ladder on play equipment		
Throws tennis ball 3 feet		
Pedals tricycle		
1 or 2 hops on dominant foot		
Can make sharp turns while running		
Balances briefly on dominant foot		
3.6 yrs. Stands on either foot briefly		
Hops on either foot		
Jumps over objects — 6 inches		
Pedals tricycle around corners		
Walks forward on balance beam several steps		
Fine motor:		
3.0 yrs. Uses one hand consistently in most activities		
Strings 1/2″ beads		
Traces horizontal/vertical lines		
Copies/imitates circles		
Cuts 6″ paper into 2 pieces		
Makes cakes/ropes of clay		
3.6 yrs. Winds up toy		
Completes 5–7 piece inset puzzle		
Sorts dissimilar objects		
Makes ball with clay		
Language and speech:		
Receptive:		
Understands size and time concepts		
Enjoys being read to		
Understands IF, THEN, and BECAUSE concepts		
Carries out 2–4 related directions		
Understands 800 words		
Responds to or questions		
Expressive:		
Gives full name		
Knows sex and can state girl or boy		
Uses 3–4 word phrases		
Uses /s/ on nouns to indicate plurals		
Uses /ed/ on verbs to indicate past tense		
Repeats simple songs, fingerplays, etc.		
Speech is 70%–80% intelligible		
Vocabulary of over 500 words		

	Present	Date Observed
Language and speech: (continued)		
Speech sounds:		
F, Y, Z, NG, WH		
Psychosocial skills:		
Joins in interactive games		
Shares toys		
Takes turns (with assistance)		
Enjoys sociodramatic play		
Cognitive skills:		
Matches six colors		
Names one color		
Counts two blocks		
Counts by rote to 10		
Matches pictures		
Classifies objects by physical attributes, one class at a time (e.g., color, shape, size, etc.)		
Stacks blocks or rings in order of size		
Knows age		
Asks questions for information (WHY and HOW)		
Can "picture read" a story book		
Draws somewhat recognizable picture and can explain what it is (*Note:* this is not always true)		
Self-help skills:		
Pours well from small pitcher		
Spreads soft butter with knife		
Buttons and unbuttons large buttons		
Blows nose when reminded		
Uses toilet independently		
V. Four-year-olds		
Gross motor:		
4.0 yrs. Stairs: walks down, alternating feet, holding rail		
Stands on dominant foot 5 seconds		
Gallops		
Jumps 10 consecutive times		
Walks sideways on balance beam		
Catches bean bag thrown from a distance of 3 ft.		
Throws 2 bean bags into wastebasket, underhand, from distance of 3 feet		
Hops on preferred foot distance of 1 yard		
4.6 yrs. Walks forward on line, heel-toe, 2 yards		
Stands on either foot for 5 seconds		
Walks upstairs holding object in one hand without holding the rail		
Walks to rhythm		

	Present	Date Observed
Gross motor: (continued)		
Attempts to keep time to simple music with hand instruments		
Turns somersault (forward roll)		
Fine motor:		
4.0 yrs. Builds 10–12 block tower		
Completes 3–5 piece puzzle, not inset		
Draws person with arms, legs, eyes, nose, mouth		
Copies a cross		
Imitates a square		
Cuts a triangle		
Creases paper with fingers		
Cuts on continuous line		
4.6 yrs. Completes 6–10 piece puzzle, not inset		
Grasps pencil correctly		
Copies a few capital letters		
Copies triangle		
May copy square		
Cuts curved lines and circles with 1/4 inch accuracy		
Language and speech:		
Receptive:		
Follows 3 unrelated commands		
Understands sequencing		
Understands comparatives: big, bigger, biggest		
Understands approximately 1,500 words		
Expressive:		
Has mastery of inflection (can change volume and rate)		
Uses 5+ word sentences		
Uses adjectives, adverbs, conjunctions in complex sentences		
Speech about 90%–95% intelligible		
Speech sounds:		
S, SH, R, CH		
Psychosocial skills:		
Plays and interacts with others		
Dramatic play is closer to reality with attention paid to time and space		
Plays dress-up		
Shows interest in sex differences		
Plays cooperatively		
May have imaginary playmates		
Shows humor by silly words and rhymes		
Tells stories, fabricates, rationalizes		
Goes on errands outside home		
Cognitive skills:		
Points to and names 4 colors		

	Present	Date Observed
Language and speech: (continued)		
Cognitive skills: (continued)		
Draws, names, and describes picture		
Counts 3 or 4 objects with correct pointing		
Distinguishes between day and night		
Can finish opposite analogies (Brother = boy; sister =)		
Names a penny in response to "What is this?"		
Tells which of 2 is bigger, slower, heavier etc.		
Increased concepts of time; can talk about yesterday, last week, today, and tomorrow		
Self-help skills:		
Cuts easy food with knife		
Laces shoes (does not tie)		
Buttons front buttons		
Washes and dries face without help		
Brushes teeth without help		
Toilets self, manages clothes by self		
VI. Five-year-olds		
Gross motor:		
5.0 yrs. Stands on dominant foot 10 seconds		
Walks backward toe to heel 6 steps		
Walks downstairs carrying object without holding rail		
Skips		
Jumps 3 feet		
Hops on dominant foot 2 yards		
Walks backward on balance beam		
Catches ball with 2 hands		
Rides small bike with training wheels		
5.6 yrs. Stands on either foot 10 seconds		
Walks backward 2 yards		
Jumps rope		
Gallops, jumps, runs in rhythm to music		
Roller skates		
Rides bicycle without training wheels		
Fine motor:		
5.0 yrs. Opens and closes large safety pin		
Sews through holes in sewing card		
Opens lock with key		
Completes 12–25 piece puzzle, not inset		
Draws person with head, trunk, legs, arms, hands, eyes, nose, mouth, hair, ears, fingers		
Colors within lines		
Cuts cardboard and cloth		

	Present	Date Observed
Fine motor: (continued)		
5.6 yrs. Builds tinker toy structure		
Copies first name		
Copies rectangle		
Copies triangle		
Prints numerals 1–5		
Handedness well-established		
Pastes and glues appropriately		
Cuts out paper dolls, pictures from magazine		
Language and speech skills:		
Receptive:		
Demonstrates preacademic skills such as following directions and listening		
Expressive:		
Few differences between child's use of language and adults'		
Can take turns in conversation		
May have some difficulty with noun-verb agreement and irregular past tenses		
Communicates well with family, friends, and strangers		
Speech sounds:		
Can correctly articulate most simple consonants and many digraphs		
Psychosocial skills:		
Chooses own friends		
Plays simple table games		
Plays competitive games		
Engages in sociodramatic play with peers, involving group decisions, role assignment, fair play		
Respects others' property		
Respects others' feelings		
Cognitive skills:		
Retells story from book with reasonable accuracy		
Names some letters and numbers		
Uses time concepts of yesterday and tomorrow accurately		
Begins to relate clock time to daily schedule		
Uses classroom tools, such as scissors and paints, meaningfully		
Draws recognizable pictures		
Orders a set of objects from smallest to largest		
Understands why things happen		
Classifies objects according to major characteristics, e.g., apples and bananas can both be eaten		
Self-help skills:		
Dresses self completely		
Ties bow		
Brushes teeth unassisted		
Crosses street safely		
Dries self after bathing		
Brushes hair		
Ties shoes without assistance		

	Present	Date Observed
VII. Six-year-olds		
Walks with ease		
Runs easily, turns corners smoothly		
Gallops		
Skips		
Jumps rope well		
Throws overhand, shifts weight from back to front foot		
Walks length of balance beam:		
forward		
backward		
sideways		
Rides bicycle		
Uses all playground equipment:		
swings self		
uses merry-go-round		
climbs dinosaur		
swings by arms across ladder		
Writes name, address, phone number		
Reads "I Can Read" books		
Can count to 100		
Can retell story after having read it		
Understands concept of numbers 1–10		
Understands concept of 1 more, 1 less		
Can complete simple arithmetic problems (addition and subtraction)		
Can write simple story		
Can illustrate story appropriately		
Plays cooperatively with others		
Stands up for self		
VIII. Seven-year-olds		
Performs all gross motor skills well except for mature overhand ball throwing		
Knows when to lead and follow		
Knows what (s)he does well		
Knows when to ask for help		
Can draw diamond		
Draws house with straight chimney		
Enjoys card games such as Rummy, Crazy 8's, Hearts, Old Maid, etc.		
Enjoys organized sports activities such as kickball, soccer, baseball, track, swimming, etc.		
Enjoys reading		
Enjoys games such as checkers, parcheesi, etc.		
Willing to tackle new problems		
Eats well-balanced diet		
Solid peer relations		
Is responsible		
Writes legibly		
Can articulate most speech sounds without distortion or substitution		

SUGGESTED READINGS

Standard Evaluation Measures

Boehm, A. E. *Boehm Test of Basic Concepts.* New York: Psychological Corp., 1971.

Brigance, Albert H. *Brigance Diagnostic Inventory of Basic Skills.* Woburn, MA: Curriculum Assoc., 1977.

Brigance, Albert H. *Brigance Diagnostic Inventory of Early Development.* Woburn, MA: Curriculum Assoc., 1978.

Caldwell, Betty. *Preschool Inventory*, rev. ed. Princeton, NJ: Educational Testing Service, 1970.

Dunn, Lloyd M., and Dunn, L. *Peabody Picture Vocabulary Test*, rev. Circle Pines, MN: AGS, 1981.

Dunn, Lloyd M., and Markwardt, Frederick C., Jr. *Peabody Individual Achievement Test.* Circle Pines, MN: AGS, 1970.

McCarthy, Dorothea. *McCarthy Screening Test.* New York: Psychological Corp., 1978.

Santa Clara Unified School District. "Inventory of Developmental Tasks," Santa Clara U.S.D., Santa Clara, CA.

Wabash Center for the Mentally Retarded, Inc. *Guide to Early Developmental Training.* Boston: Allyn and Bacon, Inc., 1977.

UNIT 13

INDIVIDUAL LEARNING PLAN FOR ALAN

1. Activity title: Watching a Live Bird
2. Curriculum area: Science and language arts (vocabulary)
3. Materials needed: Live bird in cage. Table or counter for cage.
4. Location and set-up of activity: Bird cage with parakeet will be set up in corner of room where two counters come together. This will keep cage safer than if placed on a table and counter is at eye level for children so they can see easily.
5. Number of children and adults: Alan and student teacher.
6. Preparation: Talk about pets with Alan. (Ask him what pet he has. I know he has a dog and two cats.) Ask him if he knows what a bird is. Tell him I am going to have a surprise for him.
7. Specific behavioral objective: Alan will watch the parakeet for at least three minutes. He will be able to call the bird a parakeet and say its name, Ernie. (Long-range objective could be to have Alan feed the bird and give him water.)
8. Developmental skills necessary for success: Willingness to watch and listen quietly.
9. Procedure: When Alan comes to school Tuesday, greet him at door; pin on his nametag; remind him that A-L-A-N spells his name; remind him about the surprise you promised. Take his hand; lead him to corner where bird cage is sitting. Ask Alan if he knows what is in the cage. Anticipate that he will know "bird." Tell him that this bird is called a parakeet and that the bird's name is Ernie. Ask him to repeat "parakeet" and "Ernie." Ask him what color Ernie is. Anticipate that he knows the color green. If he doesn't say green, remind him that Ernie is green. See what else is green and remind Alan that he knows what color green is — green like the grass, for example, or green like Tony's shirt, etc.
10. Discussion: Covered under procedure, I think.
11. Apply: Later in the day, ask Alan what kind of bird Ernie is. Ask him Ernie's name. (I anticipate that Alan will be intrigued with the bird and that he will want to come back over and over to watch Ernie, if only for a minute or two. Each time, I will name the type of bird and repeat Ernie's name. I think Alan will know both "parakeet" and "Ernie" before he goes home.)
12. Clean-up: Not necessary. I will keep the bird cage cleaned.
13. Terminating statement: Probably not necessary. Otherwise, I'll remind Alan that Ernie is a parakeet and suggest that he might want to see a book about birds (I've brought several in) or play the lotto game.
14. Transition: See #13.
15. Evaluation: Activity, Teacher, Child: I am hoping, of course, that this will be a great success for all the children but especially for Alan. I'll write the evaluation after Ernie is brought in.

UNIT 13
SUGGESTED READINGS

Charles, C. M., and Malian, Ida M. *The Special Student.* St. Louis: C.V. Mosby Co., 1980.

UNIT 14
SUGGESTED READINGS

Allen, K. Eileen. *Mainstreaming in Early Childhood Education.* Albany, NY: Delmar Publishers, 1980.

Annual Editions. *Educating Exceptional Children 82/83.* Guilford, CT: The Dushkin Publishing Group, 1982.

Charles, C.M. *Individualizing Instruction,* 2nd ed. St. Louis: C.V. Mosby Co., 1980.

Fallon, Nancy H. with McGovern, Jill E. *Young Children with Special Needs.* Columbus: Charles E. Merrill Publishing Co., 1978.

Gaddis, Edwin A. *Teaching the Slow Learner in the Regular Classroom.* Belmont, CA: Lear Siegler, Inc./Fearon Publishers, 1971.

Garwood, S. Gray. *Educating Young Handicapped Children.* Germantown, MD: Aspen Systems Corp., 1979.

Gearhart, Bill R. *Special Education for the 80's.* St. Louis: C.V. Mosby Co., 1980.

Guralnick, Michael, ed. *Early Intervention and the Integration of Handicapped and Nonhandicapped Children.* Baltimore: University Park Press, 1978.

Hardman, Michael L.; Egan, M. Winston; and Landau, Elliott D. *What Will We Do in the Morning?* Dubuque: W.C. Brown Co., 1981.

Lerner, Janet; Dawson, David; and Horvath, Lester. *Cases in Learning and Behavior Problems: A Guide to Individualized Education Programs.* Boston: Houghton Mifflin Co., 1980.

Neisworth, John T., et al. *Individualized Education for Preschool Exceptional Children.* Germantown, MD: Aspen Systems Corp., 1980.

Payne, James S., et al. *Exceptional Children in Focus.* Columbus: Charles E. Merrill Publishing Co., 1979.

Reynolds, Maynard C., and Birch, Jack W. *Teaching Exceptional Children in All America's Schools.* Reston, VA: The Council for Exceptional Children, 1977.

Ross, Alan O. *Psychological Disorders of Children.* New York: McGraw-Hill Book Co., 1974.

Safford, Philip L. *Teaching Young Children with Special Needs.* St. Louis: C.V. Mosby Co., 1978.

Shearer, M., and Shearer, D. "The Portage Project: A Model for Early Childhood Intervention," from T.D. Tjossem, ed., *Intervention Strategies for High Risk Infants and Young Children.* Baltimore: University Park Press, 1976.

Souweine, Judith; Crimmins, Sheila; and Mazel, Carolyn. *Mainstreaming: Ideas for Teaching Young Children.* Washington, DC: NAEYC, 1981.

UNIT 15
SUGGESTED READINGS

Berger, Eugenia H. *Parents as Partners in Education.* St. Louis: C.V. Mosby Co., 1981.

California State Department of Education. "Evaluating Report of E.C.E. ESEA, Title I, and EDY," 1974–75.

California State Department of Education. *Putting It Together with Parents: A Guide to Parent Involvement in Educational Programs.* 1973.

Ediger, Marlow. *Helping Your Child Achieve in School.* ERIC Document, ED 200 314, 1981.

Florida Learning Resources System. *Working with Parents.* Jacksonville: Crown Publishers, 1975.

Gazda, George M., et al. *Human Relations Development: A Manual for Educators.* Boston: Allyn and Bacon, Inc., 1977.

Jefferson County Public Schools. *Parent Involvement Handbook.* Colorado, 1975.

National School Public Relations Association. *School Volunteers: Districts Recruit Aides to Meet Rising Costs, Student Needs.* Arlington, VA 1973.

UNIT 16
SUGGESTED READINGS

Carkhuff, Robert R.; Berenson, David H.; and Pierce, Richard M. *The Skills of Teaching: Interpersonal Skills.* Amherst, MA: Human Resource Development Press, 1973.

Fast, Julius. *Body Language.* New York: Evans & Co., 1970.

Gazda, George M., et al. *Human Relations Development: A Manual for Educators.* Boston: Allyn and Bacon, Inc., 1977.

UNIT 17
SUGGESTED READINGS

Banks J. A. *Teaching Strategies for Ethnic Studies.* Boston, MA: Allyn and Bacon, Inc., 1979.

Byler, M. G. *American Indian Authors for Young Readers.* New York: Association on American Indian Affairs, 1973.

Chesser, B., DeFrain, J., and Stinnett, N. *Building Family Strengths.* Lincoln, NE: University of Nebraska Press, 1979.

Grossman, A. S. "Children of Working Mothers." *Monthly Labor Review* (January 1976), pp. 30–33.

Hayghe, H. "Families and the Rise of Working Wives — An Overview." *Monthly Labor Review* (May 1976), pp. 12–19.

Johnson, B. L. "Special Labor Force Reports Summaries: Changes in Marital and Family Characteristics of Workers, 1970–1978." *Monthly Labor Review* (April 1979), pp. 49–52.

Katz, W. L. *Teacher's Guide to American Negro History.* New York: Quadrangle, 1968.

Kenniston, K. "All Our Children: The American Family under Pressures." In *The Status of the American Family: Policies, Facts, Opinions, and Issues.* Washington, DC: National Education Association, 1979.

Kim, B. C. *The Korean American Child at School and at Home.* Urbana, IL: University of Illinois, School of Social Work, 1978.

Linskie, R., and Rosenburg, H. *A Handbook for Multicultural Studies in Elementary Schools: Chicano, Black, Asian, and Native American.* San Francisco: R & E Research Associates, 1976.

The Schooling of Native America. Washington, DC: American Association of Colleges for Teacher Education, 1978.

The State of Black America, 1979. New York: National Urban League, 1979.

Tachiki, A., Wong, E., Odo, F., and Wong, B. *Roots: An Asian American Reader.* Los Angeles: University of California, Asian American Studies Center, 1971.

Tiedt, P. L., and Tiedt, I. M. *Multicultural Teaching: A Handbook of Activities, Information, and Resources.* Boston: Allyn and Bacon, Inc., 1979.

U. S. Department of the Interior (Bureau of Indian Affairs). *Indian Bibliography.* Washington, DC: U.S. Government Printing Office.

Wigginton, Eliot, ed. The *Foxfire* Books. New York: Doubleday, 1972; Anchor, 1973, 1975, 1977, 1979.

Yankelovich, Skelly, and White, Inc. *Raising Children in a Changing Society. The General Mills American Family Report, 1976–77.* Minneapolis: General Mills, 1977.

Yankelovich, Skelly, and White, Inc. *Family Health in an Era of Stress. The General Mills American Family Report, 1978–79.* Minneapolis: General Mills, 1979.

UNIT 18
SAMPLE RATING SHEET

Student teacher's name _____   Rater's name _____

Date _____   School _____

STUDENT TEACHER EFFECTIVENESS SCALE

Excellent	Above Average	Average or Adequate	Needs Improvement	Unacceptable
1	2	3	4	5

A. Feeling Tone

Warm _____Cool
Friendly _____Withdrawn
Supportive _____Authoritarian
Interacts often _____Interacts rarely
Accepts dependency
  behavior_____Does not accept
                                                 dependency behavior
Physical contact   Rare physical
  often _____ contact

B. Quality of Presentation and/or Interactions

Organized _____ Seems disorganized
Enthusiastic _____ Neutral
Flexible _____ Rigid
Clear_____ Vague
Reasonable age   Unreasonable age
  level _____ level
Appropriate child   Inappropriate
  expectations _____ expectations
Promotes problem   Furnishes all
  solving _____ answers
Motivates _____ Turns off
                                                  Ignores or negatively
Rewards attention   reinforces attending
  to tasks _____ behaviors
                                                  Ignores expanding
Expands interests_____ opportunities
                                                  Activities limited by
Provides variety _____ lack of planning
                                                  Poor time
Manages time well _____ management
Lesson planning and   Poor or little lesson
  preparation _____ planning/preparation
Lesson smoothness_____ Poorly sequenced lesson
Lesson clean-up _____ Little or no clean-up

C.   Control Techniques

Positive _____
Firm _____
Supervises all _____ Supervises only a few
Uses modeling _____
Notices accomplishment _____
Restates rules _____
Uses redirection _____
Uses many methods to
     change behavior _____

D.   Verbal Interaction

Clear _____ Unclear
Receives children's non-
     verbal communication _____ Ignores
Specific directions _____ Vague directions
Questioning techniques _____
Develops concept formation _____
Volume _____
Eye contact _____

E.   Housekeeping

                                                    Ignores child's ability
Promotes child clean-up _____ to clean up
Replaces _____ Leaves out
Sees housekeeping tasks _____ Needs to be directed
                                                    Seems to spend more
Spends appropriate time _____ time than necessary

F.   General

Attendance _____
Well-groomed _____
Dependable _____
Total area supervision _____ Close focus
Excellent progress _____ Questionable progress
Attitude toward job _____
Performance on assignments _____
Communicative _____
Flexibility _____
Ability to take constructive
     suggestions _____
Could recommend as
     teacher aide _____
Could easily recommend as
     ECE teacher _____

Greatest Strengths:

Areas for Future Skills Growth:

Additional Comments:

SELF-EVALUATION QUESTIONS

(From "Let's Be Specific." ACEI Primary Education Committee, 3615 Wisconsin Avenue, Washington, DC 20016.)

Do you really believe —
- in the great worth and dignity of human beings?
- that each individual is unique?
- that there is a natural push for growth?
- that a strong, positive self-image is essential to learning?
- that nearly every child is above average in something, that each child has a strength or talent?
- that every human being can change, and change for the better, as long as he lives?
- that education should produce self-actualizing, independent thinkers?
- that no one of any age does anything with determination and verve without being involved in it?
- that any piece of information will have its effect upon behavior to the degree to which an individual discovers its personal meaning?
- that whatever derogates the self — whatever causes a person to feel that he is less liked, wanted, acceptable, able, dignified or worthy — that thing undermines both mental health and learning?
- that the purpose of the school system is to eliminate failure?
- that each child must experience success most of the time?

If a teacher gives only lip service to the above statements, there needs to be an honest self-assessment of values and behaviors.

What can I do in a specific way to help children develop adequate self-concepts?

Do I make it apparent that I really like children —
- by showing joy at being with them?
- by accepting their ideas as worthy of serious investigation?
- by using a positive way of asking, inviting, receiving and answering questions?

Do I talk so much that there is no time for children to express ideas?

Do I feel easy about taking time to capitalize upon children's ideas and knowledge —
- in open discussion?
- as recorded on experience charts (composite, individual plans, reports, evaluation of trips, science experiments, maps, graphs and charts)?
- in practical and imaginative writing?

Do I ascertain what children already know about a particular interest or subject?

Do I differentiate instruction to meet individual needs —
- by flexible and interchanging group patterns and as much individualization as is possible?
- by using various procedures and materials?

Do I make assignments for all children from the same book or duplicated sheet?

Do I stimulate individual thinking by asking —
- What do you think and why?
- How would you solve the problem?
- What is your opinion?
- What do you think is going to happen in this story as you look at the pictures? The title? The chapter headings?
- How do you feel about the story?
- How would you end the story?

Do I provide a healthy environment with a reasonable amount of guidance, direction and support so that there is intrinsic motivation to learn?

Do the children and I organize activities in which there is learning in cooperative endeavors?

Do I try to keep competitive activities to a minimum?

Do I help the child to be proud of any improvement, even if his work does not reach a standard?

Do I find ways to have a child indicate his own progress or improvement?

Do I show that I like or dislike a child by non-verbal communication (gestures, frowns, winks, reassuring pats)?

Do I show that I dislike a child by using sarcasm, negative criticism or labeling?

Do I set realistic goals for the age level of my group of children?

Do I help children set realistic goals for themselves?

Do I see that each child has a chance to display his work at some given time?

Do I arrange a parent-teacher conference for reporting progress and for finding out strengths and weaknesses of the child?

Do I write the parents notes or make telephone calls asking for information about the child, or expressing commendation?

Does a conference take place at times other than when the child has a problem or is in trouble?

Do I develop a child's diversified talents?

Do I make best uses of the child's resources?

Do I arrange an environment and activities so that each child can show where he can excel?

Do I ask parents to tell me about special aptitudes?

Do I let each pupil face up to his best and worst personal characteristics and come to accept his strengths and weaknesses?

Do I pigeonhole children as slow, bright, average, troublesome, show-off?

Do I evaluate skills and behaviors other than academic achievement?
- Creative talents, skills of communication, planning, decision making, leadership abilities, the making of wise choices, abilities having to do with mechanical and physical performance, giftedness in art, music and social relationships.

Do I help children recognize talents and abilities of others?

Do I invite custodians, cooks, clerks and other personnel of the school and community to tell about their work so that there can be appreciation of the value and dignity of all kinds of work?

Do we discuss occupations of fathers and mothers and how each person's work helps in the lives of others?

Do I encourage children to write thank-you notes to parents and school personnel expressing appreciation for taking time to talk or be with us?

Do I arrange for choice of activities and self-selection of materials and experiences?
- science corner
- library corner
- art at easels or murals
- modeling with clay, papier-mâché, dough
- listening post for music and poetry
- dramatic play — puppetry, role-playing, dress-up corners

Do I involve the children in planning and putting plans into effect? In evaluating programs?

Do I impose a teacher-planned list of activities to be neatly checked off one by one?

Do I keep those in at recess who have not finished the list of teacher-planned activities?

Do I take advantage of an individual's personal experiences and feelings with —
- a discussion of a current bit of news having to do with local, state or national events?
- a discussion of personal experiences of members of the class?
- questions sparked by looking at collections of rocks, plants, insects, animals, shells, nests?

Do I take time to relate children's personal experiences to book or story content?

Do I welcome to the classroom as resource persons parents and others in the community?

Do I relate all skill training to total learning so that a child recognizes his need for learning such skills?

Do I have a "show and tell" period, when some children may be placed at a disadvantage; a period that might encourage materialistic values?

Do I include time in the day's program during which children may have opportunity to tell of unique experiences, good books read, TV shows seen, records heard, of special incidents and trips, for showing prized possessions?

Do I teach understanding of cultural differences by showing strengths, talents, contribution of each culture represented?

Do I show favoritism in arrangement of groups in the classroom (ethnic, slow, fast, deprived)?

Do I like some of my pupils and only "tolerate" others?

Do I know that my observed behavior may determine attitudes of children toward each other?

Do I make rejecting comments to the children: "Isn't it nice that Bobby (troublemaker) isn't here today?"

Do I set up a situation in which a child is diminished before the group because of poor oral reading?

Do I display only the best work of the group?

Do I help children acquire general American English without making them ashamed because of dialects or grammar used in the home?

Do I embarrass a child by calling attention to mistakes of speech and writing before the group?

Do I make comparisons by giving gold stars and other rewards for accomplishments to the disparagement of some children?

Do I discourage children's efforts by changing their work myself?

Do I help each child attain success in his expected level of behavior and performance?

Do I show pleasure with a child's success because of what it does for him?

Does a child's success please me because it adds to my self-aggrandizement?

Do I help each child to become self-directing by looking at myself as a facilitator of learning rather than as a dispenser of information?

STUDENT TEACHER CHECKLIST

(Reprinted by permission of the publisher, from *Success in Student Teaching* by Loretta Byers and Elizabeth Irish [Lexington, Mass.: D.C. Heath and Company, 1961].)

To help you evaluate your progress in achieving the developmental tasks of a student teacher
(Rate yourself on each item)

	F	D	C	B	A

1. Gaining first-hand knowledge of child development and behavior. Observing children's needs.
   I know each child's first and last names
   I have observed the children in informal play situations
   I have conferred with the teacher about personal needs of children

2. Acquiring an understanding of the relation of the school curriculum to children's needs and the values of a democratic society.
   I have considered the appropriateness of the areas of study for the children of this age level
   I have discussed with the teacher and college supervisor the ways in which the curriculum meets the needs of the pupils in this room

3. Developing a professional conscience which impels him to organize the best possible learning experiences for his pupils, and to implement his own basic knowledges as necessary.
   I have demonstrated some initiative in my teaching
   I am punctual and dependable
   I take pride in careful workmanship — the materials I prepare for children are accurate and pleasing to the eye
   I analyze my teaching activities each day to note strengths and needs
   I am continually setting higher achievement goals for my teaching
   I am really putting forth my utmost effort to do a good job
   I allow adequate time to plan lessons and to prepare teaching materials
   When my content background is thin, I master sufficient information to enrich the children's learning
   My lessons are "ongoing." Each day's work grows out of needs demonstrated on the previous day

4. Applying psychological principles of motivation and learning in teaching techniques; adapting experiences to individual differences.
   I am able to motivate all of the children most of the time or most of the children all of the time. My skill in motivation is increasing every day
   I display sincere enthusiasm in the classroom
   I am able to identify the needs of individual children
   I am sympathetic and patient toward "slow growers"
   I plan ways to challenge fast-thinking children

	F	D	C	B	A

5. Learning to react objectively and with controlled emotions.

In my evaluative conferences with teacher or college supervisor I am able to accept suggestions objectively

When a child fails to obey a school or class standard, I do not become emotionally aroused

6. Developing an understanding of group structure: the kinds of interaction and the effect of the group upon individual children; factors which make for assimilation in or rejection by the group; the democratic control of groups of children.

I really like these children

I have identified the children who have won the most acceptance by the group

I know why these children are most acceptable

I have studied the isolates in the class and can see some reasons why they are not accepted

I can see some progress in their acceptance because of steps I have taken

I believe that these children are developing a better awareness of the tenets of democratic behavior

7. Acquiring familiarity with the best available learning aids.

I utilize my own skills and personal resources in enriching the school experience for the pupils

I take responsibility for providing effective learning materials and do not depend upon the teacher to find all of them

I am selective in using the materials which are available and try to use those which will meet the learning goal

8. Knowing the immediate community and utilizing its learning resources.

I have explored the community or at least the neighborhood sufficiently to become acquainted with its learning possibilities

I have used community facilities or people to vitalize my teaching

9. Developing skill in classroom management; in routinizing appropriate activities; and controlling physical aspects of the environment.

I get adequate rest so that I am at my best each day

I adjust the pitch and volume of my voice in the classroom

I begin my lessons promptly

I watch the timing of each lesson and endeavor to stay within the schedule

I pace the lessons so that interest is at a high pitch

My materials are prepared and in place before I begin

I take responsibility for the ventilation and adjustment of the physical environment without reminders from the teacher

	F	D	C	B	A

10. Securing pupil growth in purposing, planning, discussion, committee work, and evaluation.

I am successful in helping children to set appropriate goals

I help children to plan activities which will permit attainment of their goals

I encourage children to evaluate their activities in terms of their goals

My ability to conduct discussions is improving constantly

The supervising teacher says that I am showing real progress in formulating stimulating and effective questions

I feel that I am increasingly alert to children's ideas and suggestions

I help children to express themselves effectively

11. Utilizing effective evaluation procedures in assessing his own needs and in gauging children's growth.

The supervising teacher feels that the children are making satisfactory progress under my direction

I observe pupil reactions and development as a measure of my success

I recognize the importance of constant evaluation for my professional growth

I realize that I have a responsibility to make the evaluative conferences worthwhile

I invite appraisal and suggestions

I accept suggestions without alibiing

I make a sincere effort to try out the suggestions I receive

12. Meeting parents and planning with them for the guidance of their children.

I have assisted the supervising teacher in planning for a parent conference or meeting

If permitted I have participated in a conference

13. Getting acquainted with school services.

I am aware of all the special services which my teacher uses

14. Learning to work cooperatively and ethically as a member of the teaching profession.

I try to be courteous in all my relationships

I cooperate graciously with co-workers

I do not discuss classroom happenings with anyone except the supervising teacher and the college supervisor

Were most of your ratings in the A or B columns? Note especially the items which you rated as C or below. Try in the remaining weeks of teaching to improve in these items.

CRITERION-REFERENCED INSTRUMENT

Field-Based Assessment Competencies

The 10 areas include:
1. Child Development Principles
2. Program Planning and Curriculum Development
3. Program Implementation and Classroom Management
4. Program Administration
5. Family and Community Relations
6. Cultural Pluralism
7. Children of Exceptional Needs
8. Assessment of Children
9. Evaluation of Program Effectiveness
10. Professional Behavior

I. Child Development Principles
1) Demonstrates knowledge of various theories of development and current research that are responsive to the needs of the total child.
2) Demonstrates knowledge of children from conception through age 8; with the exception that the candidate will demonstrate more in-depth knowledge about the particular age of the children in the program.
3) Demonstrates knowledge of physical development and the forces which influence it.
4) Demonstrates knowledge of social-emotional development and the forces which influence it, including the effect of family, school, society, and culture.
5) Demonstrates knowledge of personal development and the forces which influence it.
6) Demonstrates knowledge of cognitive development, including language development and creativity and the forces which influence it.
7) Demonstrates knowledge of the significance and influence of play behavior on the child's growth and development.

II. Program Planning and Curriculum Development
Knowledge
1) Demonstrates knowledge of child development principles in planning programs.

2) Demonstrates knowledge of factors to consider in planning an appropriate environment, indoor and outdoor, which enhances the development of children.

Application
1) Implements a curriculum based on child development principles, including the areas of: a) Large/Small Motor Activities; b) Language Arts; c) Science and Math; d) Creative Arts; e) Social Sciences; and f) Personal Development.
2) Demonstrates the ability to work as an effective member of a team in program planning.
3) Helps provide an indoor/outdoor environment which meets the needs of young children.
4) Selects and utilizes alternate teaching techniques and curriculum materials in certain situations which would stimulate and encourage active child participation.
5) Demonstrates the ability to interpret and use collected data in planning curriculum to meet the individual needs of the child.

III. Program Implementation and Classroom Management
Knowledge
1) Demonstrates knowledge of appropriate teaching techniques in the learning environment.
2) Demonstrates knowledge of how to facilitate effective child/adult relationships.
3) Demonstrates knowledge of play as an appropriate teaching technique.
4) Recognizes the unique contributions of staff.

Application
1) Provides children opportunities for making choices in learning, problem solving and creative activities, whenever appropriate.
2) Utilizes play as an appropriate teaching technique.
3) Plans daily schedules which include a rhythm of physical and intellectual activities.

4) Utilizes positive suggestions in adult/child and staff relations.
5) Recognizes the importance of setting limits for children appropriate to their developmental level.
6) Models teacher behavior in accordance with expectations set for the children.

IV. Program Administration
Knowledge
1) Where applicable, discusses ways in which the candidate works with a governing board.
2) Can discuss philosophy of education for young children.
3) Has knowledge of licensing regulations and guidelines.
4) Has knowledge of revenue sources and conceptualization of budget priorities related to fiscal planning.

Application
1) Implements the regulations and guidelines regarding child development program operations, e.g., health, safety, and nutrition of the teacher and children; teacher/student ratios.
2) Maintains an effective record keeping system which includes information on required reports; child and family; and any other necessary information.
3) Utilizes an adequate handbook regarding personnel management.
4) Demonstrates ability to provide guidance and direction to co-worker.
5) Coordinates staff training and development programs.
6) Recommends and participates in selection and ordering of appropriate equipment and materials within the framework of the budget.
7) Develops a suggested budget for the program in one or all areas and assists the senior staff in establishing budget priorities.

V. Family and Community Relations
Knowledge
1) Demonstrates an understanding of the social, multicultural and linguistically relevant patterns and parenting styles of families.

Application
1) Provides for communication with parents and community and utilizes applicable community resources.
2) Encourages parent participation and provides opportunities for parent involvement.
3) Provides for assessment of parent needs and makes arrangements for appropriate parent education and/or utilization of available resources.
4) Provides for continuity between the child's home and school experience.
5) Utilizes a wide variety of community resources which could contribute to an effective program.
6) Provides guidance to parents regarding effective ways to meet the developmental needs of children.
7) Establishes and maintains effective channels of communication with parents, including conferencing and visitation.

VI. Cultural Pluralism
Knowledge
1) Has knowledge of cultural background and needs of target populations.
2) Discusses multicultural implications for the program with staff, parents, and community members.

Application
1) Demonstrates ability to relate to parents and children from a variety of social, cultural, ethnic, and racial backgrounds.
2) Demonstrates ability to develop in the classroom an atmosphere of interest and respect for each other's culture.
3) Provides opportunities in the classroom to help children value the similarities and differences in their cultural backgrounds.
4) Demonstrates ability to design classroom activities and materials that enable children to learn about each other's cultures.
5) Makes provisions for communicating with parents and children who have limited knowledge of English.

VII. Children with Exceptional Needs

Knowledge

1) Demonstrates knowledge of the unique needs of the exceptional child.
2) Has knowledge of various forms of handicapping conditions which have an impact on child behavior.
3) Has knowledge of the sources of information regarding the legal rights of parents of exceptional children.
4) Can discuss how to implement an Individualized Educational Plan (IEP) when the need arises. (This may be demonstrated if an exceptional child is enrolled in the program.)

Application

1) Demonstrates the ability to develop a classroom atmosphere of understanding, consideration, and respect for the handicapped children integrated into the program.
2) Provides effective and appropriate methods of mainstreaming handicapped children.
3) Demonstrates teaching techniques that reflect understanding of the handicapped child.
4) Provides facilities and curriculum materials appropriate to the handicapped child.
5) Demonstrates the ability to work with the support services available for handicapped children and their families in the program.

VIII. Assessment of Children

Knowledge

1) Demonstrates knowledge of appropriate instruments and assessment techniques for infants and children and the sources from where they may be obtained.
2) Recognizes the effect of the ethnic, linguistic, and cultural backgrounds of the children in test performance and the limitations of most currently available assessment instruments.

Application

1) Utilizes long-range and short-range assessment methods.
2) Utilizes appropriate instruments and assessment techniques for infants and children.

3) Demonstrates the ability to evaluate and report a child's progress in terms of stated objectives and philosophy.
4) Demonstrates the ability to observe objectively and record information accurately.
5) Makes an effort, whenever possible, to utilize assessment instruments and techniques that are not culturally biased.

IX. Evaluation of Program Effectiveness

Knowledge

1) Demonstrates knowledge of the purposes, principles, and practices of program evaluation with emphasis upon the importance of evaluating programs for young children.
2) Demonstrates knowledge of the significant areas to be considered in program evaluation, e.g., curriculum, child motivation, peer relationships, teacher/child relationships, etc.

Application

1) Demonstrates the ability to analyze and evaluate all program elements and the effectiveness in meeting the children's developmental needs.
2) Demonstrates the ability to evaluate the effectiveness of the program with the parents.
3) Utilizes effective program evaluation techniques for both long-range and short-range evaluation.
4) Utilizes evaluation results to continually improve the program if needed and to adapt to changing needs.

X. Professional Behavior

Knowledge

1) Has knowledge of the professional standards and behavior of an early childhood teacher.
2) Understands the significance and role of professional ethics in student/teacher interactions; teacher/teacher interactions; and parent/teacher/community interactions.
3) Maintains knowledge of current information in the field of early childhood/child development education relevant to one's own professional needs.

Application
1) Continues to grow and develop professionally through coursework and continued experience.
2) Understands and performs the teaching role with professional standards and demeanor.
3) Maintains professional ethics, including but not limited to keeping the confidentiality of the child and family.
4) Demonstrates ability to work as a member of a team.
5) Demonstrates personal qualities resulting in effective functioning as a teacher of young children.
6) Uses self-evaluation on a regular basis.

UNIT 20
SUGGESTED READINGS

"Advances in Teacher Research." *Journal of Classroom Interaction*, Vol. 15, No. 1 (Winter 1979), pp. 1–7.

Bennett, Neville, with Jordan, Joyce; Long, George; Wade, Barbara. *Teaching Styles and Pupil Progress.* Cambridge, MA: Harvard University Press, 1976.

Caban, L. "Durable Instruction: The Teacher-centered Classroom." *Education Digest*, Vol. 46 (Dec. 1980), pp. 33–35.

"Cognitive and Affective Orientations and Teaching Behaviors: A Study of Differentiation." *Scandinavian Journal of Educational Research*, Vol. 25, No. 1 (1981), pp. 1–7, EJ 244-513.

"Humanistic vs. Traditional Teaching Styles and Student Satisfaction." *Journal of Humanistic Psychology*, Vol. 20, no. 1 (Winter 1980), pp. 87–90, EJ 219-357.

"Instructional Design and Cognitive Styles of Teachers in Elementary Schools." *Perceptual and Motor Skills*, Vol. 52, No. 1 (Feb. 1981), pp. 335–338, EJ 243-395.

Mahlios, M. C. "Effects of Teacher-Student Cognitive Style on Patterns of Dyadic Classroom Interaction." *Journal of Experimental Education*, Vol. 49 (Spring 1981), pp. 147–157.

"Modality." *Instructor*, Vol. 89, No. 6 (Jan. 1980), pp. 44–47, EJ 218-994.

Newport, J. F. "Describing Teaching Styles in Operational Terms." *School Science and Math*, Vol. 80 (Oct. 1980), pp. 486–490.

Pendergrass, R. A., and McDonough, A. M. "Child-Centered Teacher: Rara Avis." *Phi Delta Kappan*, Vol. 62 (May 1981), pp. 674–675.

Rose, J. S., and Medway, F. J. "Teacher Locus of Control, Teacher Behavior, and Student Behavior as Determinants of Student Achievement." *J. Educational Research*, Vol. 74 (July/August 1981), pp. 375–378.

Seaburg, Dorothy I. *The Four Faces of Teaching: The Role of the Teacher in Humanizing Education.* Pacific Palisades, CA: Goodyear Publishing Co., Inc., 1974.

Shumsky, Abraham. *In Search of Teaching Style.* New York: Appleton-Century-Crofts, 1968.

Silvernail, David L. *Teaching Styles as Related to Student Achievement.* Washington, DC: NEA, 1979.

"Students' Ratings of Instruction." *Teacher Education*, Vol. 15, No. 2 (Fall 1979), pp. 2–5, EJ 226-582.

Thompson, B. "Teachers' Preferences for Various Teaching Methods (Elementary and Secondary Level)." *National Assn. of Secondary School Principals Bulletin*, Vol. 65 (Sept. 1981), pp. 96–100.

"Time on Task." *Instructor*, Vol. 91, No. 2 (Sept. 1981), pp. 55–59, 62; EJ 249-521.

Yamamoto, Kaoru. *Teaching: Essays and Readings.* Boston: Houghton Mifflin Co., 1969.

UNIT 22
SUGGESTED READING

Montessori, Maria. *The Montessori Method.* New York: Schocken Books, 1964.

UNIT 24
SUGGESTED READINGS

Teacher Advocacy and Child Care

A.B.T. Associates. *Children at the Center*, Executive Summary of the Final Report of the National Day Care Study. Cambridge, MA: 1979.

Annual Report on Publicly Subsidized Child Care Services, Part I, Child Development Programs, 1978-79, Executive Summary, California State Department of Education. Sacramento, CA.

CAEYC and California Community College Early Childhood Educators. *The Letter Tree, 1980 Survey*, Vol. 5, No. 2 (Feb. 1982).

Child Care Education Project, San Francisco 1978–79, as reported in "Who's Minding the Child Care Workers?: A Look at Staff Burn-Out," by Marcy Whitebook, et al., *Children Today* (Jan.–Feb. 1981), pp. 2–7.

Child Care Staff Education Project Interviews, 1978–79. Berkeley, CA.

Child Care Task Force of the Santa Cruz County Children's Commission. *March 1979 Child Care Wage and Benefit Survey*, as reported in CAEYC Newsletter, Vol. 9, No. 2.

Consortium for Longitudinal Studies. *Lasting Effects After Preschool*, Final Report of D.H.E.W. Grant No. 90C-1311. Washington, DC: U.S. Administration for Children, Youth, and Families.

Report on Preschool Education, Vol. 13, No. 6 (March 24, 1981). Arlington, VA: Capitol Publications, Inc.

Schweinhart, L.J., and Weikart, D.P. *Young Children Grow Up:* The Effects of the Perry Preschool Program on Youths Through Age 17. Monographs of the High/Scope Educational Research Foundation, No. 7 (1980).

Smith, Ralph. "The Subtle Revolution," from the Urban Institute as quoted in *The Gryphon House*, Vol. 1, No. 1 (1981).

Whitebook, Marcy, et al. "Who's Minding the Children?" *Children Today* (Jan.–Feb. 1981).

Teacher Advocacy References

Advocacy — Why Bother? On the Capitol Doorstep; 1107 Ninth St., Rm. 1034; Sacramento, CA 95814. Cost: $1.00.

A Handbook for Child Advocates at the State Capitol. P.O. Box 448; Sacramento, CA 95814. Cost: $1.00.

Where Do You Look? Whom Do You Ask? How Do You Know? Information Resources for Child Advocates; Children's Defense Fund; 1520 New Hampshire Ave., N.W.; Washington, DC 20036.

(These sources give step by step information on the legislative process and effective advocacy.)

UNIT 25
SUGGESTED READINGS

Studies on the Effects of Preschool Attendance

"Lasting Effects After Preschool"
Summary Report, HEW Grant 90C-1311 available from ERIC/ECE
University of Illinois
College of Education
805 W. Pennsylvania Avenue
Urbana, IL 61801

Cost Effectiveness

Quality preschool attendance pays for itself by reducing other social service costs, a number of studies conclude. Recommended readings are:

Freis, Ruth, and Miller, Miriam. *The Economic Impact of Subsidized Child Care.* Livermore, CA: Freis and Miller Associates. (1520 Catalina Crt., 94550)

Schweinhart, Lawrence J. *High Quality Early Childhood Programs For Low Income Families Pay For Themselves.* Ypsilanti, MI: High/Scope Educational Research Foundation, 1981.

UNIT 26
SUGGESTED READING

White, Burton L. *First Three Years of Life.* Englewood Cliffs, NJ: Prentice-Hall, Inc., 1975.

UNIT 28
SUGGESTED READINGS

Feldman, Beverly N. *Jobs, Careers Serving Children and Youth.* Los Angeles: Till Press, 1980.

Seaver, J. W., et al. *Careers with Young Children: Making Your Decision.* Washington, DC: NAEYC, 1979.

UNIT 29
SUGGESTED READINGS

Resume Resources

Jaquish, Michael, *Personal Resume Preparation.* New York: John Wiley & Sons, Inc., 1968.

Lathrop, Richard. *Who's Hiring Who.* Berkeley, CA: Ten Speed Press, 1977.

Stanat, Kirby W., and Reardon, Patrick. *Job Hunting Secrets/Tactics.* Milwaukee, WI: Raintree Pubs., Ltd., 1977.

UNIT 30
SUGGESTED READINGS

Guides

A Guide to Basic Law and Procedures Under the National Labor Relations Act. National Labor Relations Board, Washington, DC.

All About OSHA. U.S. Dept. of Labor, 1980.

Handy Reference Guide to the Fair Labor Standards Act. U.S. Dept. of Labor, Jan. 1981.

(All of the above materials are available from the U.S. Government Printing Office; Superintendent of Public Documents; Washington, DC 20402.)

Margonis, Stas. *Stand Up: A Guide to Workers' Rights.* San Francisco, CA: Public Media Center, 1982. (To order: P.O. Box 684, Santa Monica, CA 90406.)

Schandel, Terry K., and Schandel, Susan M. *Tax Tactics for Teachers,* rev. ed. New York: Atheneum Pubs., 1982.

Agencies

Labor-Management Services Administration — regional offices

National Labor Relations Board — regional offices (headquarters: Washington, DC)

Occupational Safety and Health Administration (OSHA) — regional offices

Directories

U.S. Offices of Workers' Compensation Programs Directory

U.S. Dept. of Labor — Regional Offices Directory

Newsletters

The AFL/CIO News. AFL/CIO, 815 16th St., N.W. Washington, DC 20006.

Child Care Employee News. Child Care Employee Project, P.O. Box 5603, Berkeley, CA 94705.

UNIT 30
EXCERPTS FROM CALIFORNIA'S INDUSTRIAL WELFARE CODE POSTED BY LAW AT THE WORK SITE

RECORDS

A. Every employer shall keep accurate information with respect to each employee including the following:

1. Full name, home address, occupation and social security number.

2. Birth date, if under 18 years, and designation as a minor.

3. Time records showing when the employee begins and ends each work period. Meal periods, split shift intervals and total daily hours worked shall also be recorded. Meal periods during which operations cease and authorized rest periods need not be recorded.

4. Total wages paid each payroll period, including value of board, lodging, or other compensation actually furnished to the employee.

5. Total hours worked in the payroll period and applicable rates of pay. This information

shall be made readily available to the employee upon reasonable request.

6. When a piece rate or incentive plan is in operation, piece rates or an explanation of the incentive plan formula shall be provided to employees. An accurate production record shall be maintained by the employer.

B. Every employer shall semimonthly or at the time of each payment of wages furnish each employee either as a detachable part of the check, draft or voucher paying the employee's wages, or separately, an itemized statement in writing showing: (1) all deductions; (2) the inclusive dates of the period for which the employee is paid; (3) the name of the employee or the employee's social security number; and (4) the name of the employer, provided all deductions made on written orders of the employee may be aggregated and shown as one item.

C. All required records shall be in the English language and in ink or other indelible form, properly dated, showing month, day and year, and shall be kept on file by the employer for at least three years at the place of employment or at a central location within the state of California. An employee's records shall be available for inspection by the employee upon reasonable request.

D. Clocks shall be provided in all major work areas or within reasonable distance thereto insofar as practicable.

REPORTING TIME PAY

A. Each workday an employee is required to report for work and does report, but is not put to work or is furnished less than half said employee's usual or scheduled day's work, the employee shall be paid for half the usual or scheduled day's work, but in no event for less than two (2) hours nor more than four (4) hours, at the employee's regular rate of pay, which shall not be less than the minimum wage.

B. If an employee is required to report for work a second time in any one workday and is furnished less than two hours of work on the second reporting, said employee shall be paid for two hours at the employee's regular rate of pay, which shall not be less than the minimum wage.

C. The foregoing reporting time pay provisions are not applicable when:

1. Operations cannot commence or continue due to threats to employees or property; or when recommended by civil authorities; or

2. Public utilities fail to supply electricity, water, or gas, or there is a failure in the public utilities or sewer system; or

3. The interruption of work is caused by an Act of God or other cause not within the employer's control.

D. This section shall not apply to an employee on paid standby status who is called to perform assigned work at a time other than the employee's scheduled reporting time.

CHANGE ROOMS AND RESTING FACILITIES

A. Employers shall provide suitable lockers, closets or equivalent for the safekeeping of employees' outer clothing during working hours and, when required, for their work clothing during nonworking hours. When the occupation requires a change of clothing, change rooms or equivalent space shall be provided in order that employees may change their clothing in reasonable privacy and comfort. These rooms or spaces may be adjacent to but shall be separate from toilet rooms and shall be kept clean.
NOTE: This section shall not apply to change rooms and storage facilities regulated by the Occupational Safety and Health Standards Board.

B. Suitable resting facilities shall be provided in an area separate from the toilet rooms and shall be available to employees during work hours.

HOURS AND DAYS OF WORK

A. An employee may be employed on seven (7) workdays in one workweek with no overtime pay required when the total hours of employment during such workweek do not exceed thirty (30) and the total hours of employment in any one workday thereof do not exceed six (6).

B. If a meal period occurs on a shift beginning or ending at or between the hours of 10 p.m. and 6 a.m., facilities shall be available for securing hot food or drink or for heating food or drink, and a suitable sheltered place shall be provided in which to consume such food or drink.

MINIMUM WAGES

A. Every employer shall pay to each employee wages not less than three dollars and ten cents ($3.10) per hour for all hours worked, effective January 1, 1980, and three dollars and thirty-five cents ($3.35) per hour for all hours worked, effective January 1, 1981, except:

1. LEARNERS. Employees 18 years of age or over, during their first one hundred and sixty (160) hours of employment in occupations in which they have no previous similar or related experience, may be paid not less than eighty-five percent (85%) of the minimum wage rounded to the nearest nickel.

2. MINORS may be paid not less than eighty-five percent (85%) of the minimum wage rounded to the nearest nickel provided that the number of minors employed at said lesser rate shall not exceed twenty-five percent (25%) of the persons regularly employed in the establishment. An employer of less than ten (10) persons may employ three (3) minors at said lesser rate. The twenty-five percent (25%) limitation on the employment of minors shall not apply during school vacations.

B. When an employee works a split shift, one hour's pay at the minimum wage shall be paid in addition to the minimum wage for that workday, except when the employee resides at the place of employment.

MEAL PERIODS

A. No employer shall employ any person for a work period of more than five (5) hours without a meal period of not less than thirty (30) minutes, except that when a work period of not more than six (6) hours will complete the day's work the meal period may be waived by mutual consent of employer and employee. Unless the employee is relieved of all duty during a thirty-minute meal period, the meal period shall be considered an "on duty" meal period and counted as time worked. An "on duty" meal period shall be permitted only when the nature of the work prevents an employee from being relieved of all duty and when by written agreement between the parties an on-the-job paid meal period is agreed to.

B. In all places of employment where employees are required to eat on the premises, a suitable place for that purpose shall be designated.

REST PERIODS

Every employer shall authorize and permit all employees to take rest periods which, insofar as practicable, shall be in the middle of each work period. The authorized rest period time shall be based on the total hours worked daily at the rate of ten (10) minutes net rest time per four (4) hours or major fraction thereof.

However, a rest period need not be authorized for employees whose total daily work time is less than three and one-half (3-1/2) hours. Authorized rest period time shall be counted as hours worked for which there shall be no deduction from wages.

INSPECTION

The Commission and duly authorized representatives of the Division shall be allowed free access to any office or establishment covered by this Order to investigate and gather data regarding wages, hours, working conditions, and employment practices, and shall be permitted to inspect and make excerpts from any and all relevant records and to question all employees for such purposes.

The investigations and data gathering shall be conducted in a reasonable manner calculated to provide the necessary surveillance of employment practices and the enforcement of the Commission's orders.

POSTING OF ORDER

Every employer shall keep a copy of this Order posted in an area frequented by employees where it may be easily read during the workday. Where the location of work or other conditions make this impractical, every employer shall keep a copy of this Order and make it available to every employee upon request.

EXCERPTS FROM LABOR CODE

SECTION 98.6 (a) No person shall discharge or in any manner discriminate against any employee because such employee has filed any bona fide complaint or claim or instituted or caused to be instituted any proceeding under or relating to his rights, which are under the jurisdiction of the Labor Commissioner, or has testified or is about to testify in any such proceeding or because of the exercise by such employee on behalf of himself or others of any rights afforded him.

Index